WOMEN AND THE FATIMIDS IN THE WORLD OF ISLAM

From Delia to Adelaide
From Simonetta to Anna Maria, Clementina and Violetta

WOMEN AND THE FATIMIDS IN THE WORLD OF ISLAM

DELIA CORTESE AND
SIMONETTA CALDERINI

EDINBURGH UNIVERSITY PRESS

Edinburgh University Press Ltd
22 George Square, Edinburgh

Typeset in Goudy
by Koinonia, Bury, and
printed and bound in Great Britain by
MPG Books Ltd, Bodmin, Cornwall

A CIP record for this book is available
from the British Library

ISBN 0 7486 1732 9 (hardback)
ISBN 0 7486 1733 7 (paperback)

Published with the support of the Edinburgh University
Scholarly Publishing Initiatives Fund.

CONTENTS

ANALYTICAL TABLE OF CONTENTS

FIGURES

PREFACE

On the sunny day of 23 January 1958 a large crowd gathered in a colourful assembly in the National Stadium of Karachi. To the sound of music played by the tuxedoed musicians of the Prince Aly Khan Orchestra, women in gleaming and flowing attire, men wearing elaborate headgear and playful children awaited in trepidation on the stands. At last a controlled commotion in the middle of the pitch signalled the beginning of the extraordinary ceremony that the joyful crowd had come to witness. High dignitaries in their fineries carrying the Holy Qur'an, the ceremonial sword of justice and other insignia flanked and followed a handsome young man as he made his way towards the centre of the pitch where a pulpit had been built for the occasion.

Walking by the young man's left side was a statuesque woman, with her head uncovered, wearing a stunning white sari, which further enhanced her mature beauty. The young man climbed alone to the top of the pulpit and, with great composure, reached its centre. A high dignitary presented him with the copy of the Holy Qur'an, thus marking the formal beginning of the ceremony. As the Holy Book was handed over, all those present lowered their heads and covered their faces at once: the women concealed their gaze under the most ornate veils, the men shadowed their faces with garlands made of flowers and coloured paper. Then, the young man on the pulpit stood up, donned the robe that had been worn by his grandfather and finally sat on a throne-like chair, basking in the admiration of those tens of thousands of people around him. The formal ceremony over, the stadium resounded again to the music of a Scottish bagpipe band while the young man, followed by the dignitaries, made his way out of the stadium escorted by the same woman who had accompanied him at the start of the event.

The young man was Prince Karim and the event formally celebrated his appointment as the fourth Aga Khan, the spiritual leader of some 15 million Shi'a Imami Isma'ili Muslims worldwide who believe him to be the 49th imam in a direct line of descent originating with 'Ali b. Abi Talib, cousin and son-in-law of the Prophet Muhammad. His Highness Shah Karim al-Husayni Aga Khan's succession to the imamate followed the death, on 11 July 1957, of his grandfather Muhammad Shah Aga Khan III. The Karachi event was but one of several accession ceremonies that, between the autumn of 1957 and the spring of 1958, Isma'ilis of East Africa and of the Indian Subcontinent staged in their regions to salute the new Isma'ili spiritual leader.

These events celebrated the transfer of spiritual leadership from one of the most influential Muslim men of our time to another; however, our interest here is on the stunning woman who so prominently figured throughout the ceremonial. She was known as Princess Taj al-Dawla and was the mother of H. H. Karim Aga Khan IV. A great beauty of her day, she was born Joan Barbara Yarde-Buller, eldest daughter of Lord and Lady Churston. After a first marriage to a member of the Guinness banking family, in 1936 she wedded Prince 'Ali, son of the third Aga Khan. Her knowledge of nursing practice inspired her father-in-law to appoint her, in 1944, health and education commissioner for the benefit of his followers in East Africa. After her divorce from Prince 'Ali, Joan based herself in London where she was to be a renowned hostess of socialites, intellectuals, politicians and diplomats. In the aftermath of her son's accession to the imamate, she played an important part in assisting him in the numerous demanding engagements that came with his new role. Late in life Joan married once more, thus becoming Joan Lady Camrose, and she dedicated herself to the patronage of the arts and of healthcare projects, engagements that she passionately cultivated until her death in 1997. The discreet, but nonetheless significant, mark that Princess Taj al-Dawla left in recent Isma'ili dynastic history was matched by that of a number of other glamorous women who joined the family, among them Begum Aga Khan III, known as Umm Habiba and honoured as Mata Salamat. Born Yvette Blanche Labrousse in 1906 in France, her background could not have been more different than Joan's. Daughter of a tram conductor and a seamstress, Yvette became a beauty queen in 1930, and in 1944, in Switzerland, became the fourth and last wife of the elderly Aga Khan III. The enduring love and devotion that Yvette showed to Muhammad Shah became the stuff of legend. Once widowed, she never re-married and, until her own death on 1 July 2000, she ensured that every day a fresh red rose would be placed on his immaculate white Carrara marble tomb, housed in a mausoleum overlooking the Nile in Aswan. Through her husband, Yvette had been introduced to Islam, a religion she came to genuinely and profoundly love and embrace and, like Joan, she also distinguished herself as an accomplished connoisseur of the arts, a generous patron of charities and a most exquisite hostess.

Joan's and Yvette's backgrounds, their eventful lives and the extraordinary lifestyle that both enjoyed, respectively as mother and wife of imams, mirror in many ways those of the many influential women in the history of the Isma'ilis who had preceded them almost a thousand years earlier. Those were the women who lived in the period which came to be known as the 'golden age' of Isma'ili history, the age of the Fatimids (297–567/909–1171). Those women belonged or were linked to the Fatimid dynasty and its courts and it is on their identities, roles, influence and achievements that the present work is focused. The first comprehensive study so far on women and the Fatimids, spanning areas as diverse as North Africa, Egypt and the Yemen, it addresses neglected aspects of the social and dynastic Fatimid history, thus enriching our knowledge of one of the most fascinating periods in the history of Islam as a whole.

ACKNOWLEDGEMENTS

We are very grateful to Professor Yaacov Lev (Bar Ilan University, Israel), Professor Michael Brett (Hemeritus Reader, SOAS, London) and Professor Heinz Halm (Tubingen University), who have over the years generously and patiently given us academic advice, encouragement and spent much time reading our numerous drafts. Their insightful and inspirational scholarly comments and feedback have always been greatly appreciated and have influenced in many ways the present work. Of course, we are solely responsible for any inaccuracies this book may contain.

In researching this book, we spent a great deal of the last eleven years at the Institute of Ismaili Studies, London, where we were privileged to meet many members of staff and students, who have always followed the progress of our research with great interest and warmth. In particular, we would like to give our special thanks to the Associate Director of the Institute and Head of the Department of Academic Research and Publications, Dr Farhad Daftary, for personally endorsing this project and for his constant support. Also we thank Hamid Haji for his precious advice on bibliographic and editorial matters.

Throughout our research work, we have greatly benefited from the efficiency and the help of all past and present staff in the Library of the Institute. In particular, we are grateful to the former Head Librarian, Dr Duncan Haldane, and the senior Librarian and Keeper of the Ismaili Collection, Alnoor Merchant, for facilitating our access to essential printed and manuscript material. An affectionate thank-you goes to Mrs Khadija Lalani-Pardhan, without whose presence the Library would not be the pleasant place that it is.

We also benefited from accessing the collections and using the facilities of several libraries in the UK and abroad, particularly the Library of the School of

Oriental and African Studies, University of London, where we are indebted to Peter Colvin, the Languages and Cultures Faculty Librarian, Islamic Middle East Section, for his assistance. We would also like to acknowledge Dr 'Abd Allah al-'Udhari in assisting us with the poetry featured in this text.

The staff of Edinburgh University Press deserve to be credited for their assistance in this project, and our gratitude goes in particular to Nicola Carr for her constant backing and the help she gave us.

Delia would like to express her gratitude to the Dipartimento di Studi e Ricerche sull'Africa ed i Paesi Arabi of the Istituto Universitario Orientale, Napoli (now Università degli Studi di Napoli "L'Orientale") for awarding her in 1996–97 a two-year post-doctoral fellowship to sponsor this research project in its initial phase. In particular, she would like to thank Professor Carmela Baffioni, whose academic endorsement of this project was instrumental in Delia obtaining the award. She would also like to acknowledge the overall support received from her colleagues in the School of Arts, Middlesex University, London. On a personal note … over the last decade Delia's life, with its many joys and a few sorrows, has been almost as adventurous – but not as financially rewarding – as that of the women featured in this book. Delia therefore wishes to pay tribute to family and friends for sharing the fun with her and for their unstinting love and support in less happy days. In particular, Delia's warmest thanks go to her partner, Chris Hill, for patiently reading and acutely commenting upon some chapters of this book but, above all, for all his love and for taking her to the most beautiful parts of the world.

Simonetta would like to show her appreciation to the Arts and Humanities Research Board for awarding her a Research Grant to cover research leave in 2004. This grant was matched by periods of research leave from Roehampton University, London, where a special thanks is due to the Head of the School of Arts, Dr Lyndie Brimstone, for her strong support for maintaining the practice of research sabbaticals. Simonetta would also like to thank colleagues and students at Roehampton. Her everlasting gratefulness goes to her husband Piers for his stoic patience. Not only did he accept his fate by proofreading all the drafts of this book and making intelligent remarks, he also survived a decade of evenings, weekends and months looking after the children while his spouse was occupied pursuing her projects. Finally, thank you Clementina and Violetta for bearing with a mamma busy writing about the 'Fatimids' instead of spending time playing with you or taking you to the park. You remain the most precious of princesses.

Finally, a big thank you, to all our friends in Italy, the UK, the Middle East and the rest of the world.

DC and SC

NOTE ON THE TEXT

To ease reading, the use of transliteration has been kept to a minimum in the main body of the text where names of persons, tribes and dynasties, geographical names and foreign terms of current use in the English language have not been transliterated.

For technical terms, in the notes and in the bibliography, the system of transliteration adopted is an adaptation of the version used in the second edition of the *Encyclopaedia of Islam*, with two main modifications: *j* is used here instead of *dj* and *q* instead of *ḳ*; also, no ligatures have been used.

The dates given in this book are according to both the Hijri and the Gregorian calendars. The Fatimids are known to have followed the so-called Misri calendar, which is a variant of the Hijri one, in that it includes a leap year every four years. The Misri dating is still in use among the Tayyibi Bohras in the Yemen. However, we have adopted the customary Hijri calendar because this is the one followed by the overwhelming majority of sources we have consulted in researching this book.

ABBREVIATIONS

AI	*Annales Islamologiques*
ArI	*Ars Islamica*
BIFAO	*Bulletin de l'Institut Français d'Archéologie Orientale du Caire*
EI2nd	*The Encyclopaedia of Islam*, edited by H. A. R. Gibb et al., Leiden: E. J. Brill, 1960–2004, 2nd edn
ESFAME	*Egypt and Syria in the Fatimid, Ayyubid and Mamluk Eras*, edited by U. Vermeulen et al., Leuven: Peeters, 1995, 1998, 2001
IFAO	*Institut Français d'Archéologie Orientale*
IFD	*Institut Français de Damas*
JBBRAS	*Journal of the Bombay Branch of the Royal Asiatic Society*
JRCAS	*Journal of the Royal Central Asian Society*
JESHO	*Journal of the Economic and Social History of the Orient*
JA	*Journal Asiatique*
JQR	*The Jewish Quarterly Review*
JSS	*Journal of Semitic Studies*
JSAI	*Jerusalem Studies in Arabic and Islam*
MH	*Medical History*
MHR	*Mediterranean Historical Review*
MIDEO	*Mélanges de l'Institut Domenicain des Études Orientales du Caire*
MS	*A Mediterranean Society*, S. D. Goitein, Berkeley: University of California Press, 1967–88, 5 vols
MW	*The Muslim World*
PSAS	*Proceedings of the Seminar for Arabian Studies*
Qur.	*The Qur'an*
REI	*Revue des Études Islamiques*

SI	*Studia Islamica*
SUNY	*State University of New York Press*
ZDMG	*Zeitschrift der Deutschen Morgenländischen Gesellschaft*

For personal names, b. is used to indicate 'son of' (*ibn*) or 'daughter of' (*bint*).

INTRODUCTION

1. Studying Women and the Fatimids: the Sources, the Methods and the State of Studies

The Fatimid period is one of the best-documented in medieval Islamic history. A considerable number of medieval non-Ismaʿili literary works, as well as documentary, epigraphic, artistic and archaeological sources, shed light on most aspects relating to the history of the Fatimid dynasty and of the societies in those areas under Fatimid rule or influence. Complementing this body of sources are the few historical works written by Ismaʿili authors and the historical references contained in the extensive Ismaʿili doctrinal literature. Ismaʿili and non-Ismaʿili primary sources represent the core material on which the contents of this book are based. Most of these sources have been discussed, explained and classified by Paul E. Walker in his *Exploring an Islamic Empire: Fatimid History and its Sources* (2001) and, more broadly, by F. Daftary, *Ismaili Literature: A Bibliography of Sources and Studies* (2004). In the present book the data drawn from a vast selection of primary sources are approached and interpreted through the methods of textual, socio-historical and contextual analyses.

As is the case with the overwhelming majority of medieval sources, none of the primary literature used here was written by women and, as a whole, none of the male writers dealt with women as their primary concern. Mediated, as they are, through the male voices, the references to women found in these sources may be said to a large extent to be more revealing about men's perceptions of women than the women themselves. In particular, they uncover the manner in which male writers, but also the male protagonists they wrote about, viewed women and what, on the basis of their world-outlook, backgrounds and aims, men thought it relevant to report. As a result, for a comprehensive and sound interpretation of the data on women in Isma'ili and non-Isma'ili sources, special attention has been devoted throughout this book, to the inference of the social, political and cultural contexts, which informed the writer's perspectives. Hence, the historical analysis of data is never too far removed from contemporary or subsequent social, political and doctrinal perceptions about women and their formulation through literary figures and topoi. In the course of the present book, the merits, limits and complexities arising from the use of these sources will be discussed when piecing together information about, and attitudes towards, the women of the Fatimid dynasty and the women living under Fatimid rule.

The relative abundance of primary sources, the increasing availability in print of Isma'ili literature and the greater accessibility to Isma'ili manuscripts have made the study of Fatimid history, and of Isma'ilism during that period, the most widely covered area of research in the field of Isma'ili studies. While contemporary aspects of Isma'ili women's participation in social, educational and ritual activities have been the subject of a number of recent studies, little attention has hitherto been devoted to the study of women in the Fatimid period. This lacuna is particularly noticeable when considering that the growth of interest in the academic study of the Isma'ilis in general, and the Fatimids in particular, coincided with the flourishing of studies on the position of women in Islam, past and present.

The aim of the present work is above all to unearth references to women so as to re-inscribe their role in the social history of the Fatimid era. This research is informed by an inclusive methodological stance, which results from the use of a variety of scholarly approaches to the study of women and Islam. We have resorted particularly to textual analysis and criticism, to the contextual and literary reading of historical records, as well as to the critical use of anecdotal material. In some, yet rare, cases we have been able to release from those narratives the voices of the women themselves. While seeking to pave the way to the development of additional perspectives and avenues of investigation in the study of medieval Islam and its women, this book also pays tribute to past and present landmark studies on women in the Islamic world and on gender and Islam.

The first studies on women in Islam by modern Muslim and non-Muslim scholars were to varying degrees informed by the debate on women's rights prevailing within not only European and American but also Egyptian and Turkish intellectual circles. Among these studies were, in the early 1940s, the groundbreaking articles and books by Nabia Abbott (1897–1981). Abbott's work was to inaugurate a type of research on the women of the early history of Islam which combined two approaches: the exegetical analysis of religious and legal statements about women in the sacred texts and the theological literature of Islam; and the contextual historical research of accounts about (in fact, references to) famous and influential women throughout Islamic history, such as the Prophet's wives and the 'queens of Baghdad'. Notwithstanding its limitations, Abbott's work was an eye-opener, especially with regard to source criticism, the use of which method was to be intensified and broadened from the 1980s onwards by a number of scholars. Among them, Fatima Mernissi focused her textual criticism upon misogynistic *ḥadīths*, Rifaat Hassan applied feminist reading to selected Qur'anic verses and Barbara Stowasser researched female figures in the Qur'an and non-Qur'anic literature. Through their works, these researchers, and those who follow in their footsteps, have raised awareness of the masculine bias of writers, historians and scholars in their readings and uses of sacred texts.

Within the field of social anthropology, since the late 1970s an increasing number of scholars devoted their studies to women in contemporary Islamic societies, with a focus on rural women. Although the contents of these studies are of limited applicability to research on women in medieval Islamic societies, the methods used to compile them are instrumental in further stimulating academic awareness of issues relating to the researcher's perspective. Scholars like Elizabeth Fernea and Nikki Keddie, by letting their 'informants' speak for themselves, aimed at overcoming the pitfalls of imposing Western or Western-inspired intellectual constructs on those women who were the subjects of their study.

The publication in 1992 of Leila Ahmed's *Women and Gender in Islam* constituted a major breakthrough in the history of gender studies in Islam, thanks to the author's aim to conceptualise women's history and issues of gender as discourse by identifying and exploring 'the way in which gender is articulated socially, institutionally, and verbally'[1] in Islamic societies past and present. Ahmed argued that it was in the early history of Islam that the principal terms of the core religious discourses were founded. One was the dominant 'voice' of hierarchical and 'establishment' Islam, which, Ahmed contends, elaborated a meaning of gender, an expression of which was the legal, social and economic subordination and marginalisation of women. The other was the 'ethical voice', stressing the moral and spiritual equality of all human beings, which, Ahmed continues, was emphasised by marginal groups that challenged the dominant political order and its interpretation of Islam, including its conception of gender. Among these anti-establishment groups she includes the Qarmatians, an early Isma'ili movement, which will be extensively dealt with in the course of the present book. Although based on a questionable selection of hostile primary sources, and a few, clearly outdated studies, Ahmed's reference to the Qarmatians nevertheless serves the purpose of illustrating a dissenting meaning of gender within a given medieval Islamic society.[2] When studying Isma'ili movements, the applicability of Ahmed's use of discourse stretches beyond the Qarmatians. To cite but one example, what Ahmed defines as the 'ethical' voice can be also 'heard' in the Fatimid sources covering the missionary activities of the early Isma'ili and Fatimid propagandists, where the inclusion of gender-related narratives served a politico-dynastic discourse.

The analysis of sources as literature, and of literature as a source, represents yet another method of research, which can help to provide a fuller picture of the perception held by a particular society of the status and expected roles of its women. Scholars such as Fadwa Malti-Douglas and Nadia El-Cheikh make use of *adab* literature as source to identify conventions in representing women, which reflect not only the writer's but also his society's understanding of gender roles. They contend that, unlike doctrinal and historical sources, literary texts are neither prescriptive nor professedly ideological and, even though repetitive and full of literary conventions, can still provide insights into shared social attitudes, which go beyond the 'official' records.[3] Most of the sources on which the present book is based, be they historical or doctrinal, do intersperse factual and interpretative accounts with anecdotal and clearly fictional ones. Rarely do the writers expressly introduce anecdotes as anecdotes, leaving it to the skills of the reader to distinguish between fact and fiction. The issue of literary conventions and how to interpret anecdotal stories come particularly to the fore in the chapters of this book that deal with court life and women's power.

The overwhelming majority of past and present monographs on women in classical and medieval Islam have focused on women in the Prophet's household and on women who belonged to Sunni dynasties, such as the 'Abbasids, the Saljuqs, the Mamluks and the Ottomans. As for women in Shi'ism, while there are a number of publications on contemporary issues relating to Twelvers, as well as to women in Isma'ili denominations such as the Druze, the Khoja and the Bohra, extensive studies on women in pre-modern Shi'ism in general, and in Fatimid Isma'ilism in particular, are indeed rare. In 1931 Husayn al-Hamdani published in the *Journal of the Royal Central Asian Society* an article on the life and times of the eleventh- and twelfth-century pro-Fatimid queen Arwa in the Yemen. Al-Hamdani's article was to be the first and, for long time, the only academic study specifically devoted to a female personality of the Fatimid period. With his publication in 1962 of *La Berbérie Orientale sous les Zīrīdes*, Hady Roger Idris provided the most comprehensive coverage to date on the women of the Zirids, the Fatimids' vassals in North Africa. However, a specific academic interest on prominent women of the Fatimid dynasty did not really start until the 1980s. In 1987, Yaacov Lev published in the *Journal of Semitic Studies* an article on the Fatimid princess Sitt al-Mulk that was to be the first publication exclusively devoted to a woman of the Fatimid dynasty. In the 1990s aspects of Sitt al-Mulk's life were further discussed by Heinz Halm in a handful of short articles while other scholars published a few more studies on queen Arwa. The single monograph to have ever appeared thus far on the subject of women in Fatimid Egypt is *al-Mar'a fī Miṣr fī 'l-'aṣr al-Fāṭimī* (*The Woman in Egypt in the Fatimid Period*), a book in Arabic by Nuriman 'Abd al-Karim Ahmad, published in Cairo in 1993. In contributing, through a study on women and the Fatimids, to bridging a gap in the field of Isma'ili studies, this book builds on the limited but nonetheless highly significant scholarly contributions just mentioned.

No study of this kind would be comprehensive without an overview of Isma'ili perspectives on some of the female figures from the early history of Islam, whose mention frequently recurs in Fatimid and Isma'ili post-Fatimid sources, where they are invested with numerous functions, the foremost being that of role model: the mother, the wife, the daughter, the supporter, the fighter for her own rights.

2. Medieval Ismāili Perspectives on the Women of the Prophet Muhammad's Household: Fatima and Khadija

Of the women of the Prophet Muhammad's family, Shi'i and especially Isma'ili writers focus on the figure of the Prophet's daughter Fatima, who is praised above all other women of his household, including his wives. The Qur'anic verses 33.32–3 on the privileged position of the 'women of the Prophet' (*nisā' al-nabī*), traditionally interpreted by all Sunni exegetes as referring to Muhammad's wives, are thus understood by Shi'is as indicating the female descendants of the Prophet, particularly Fatima, her daughters and granddaughters. Early Isma'ili writers claimed that blood ties, rather than ties acquired through marriage, were to be regarded as the strongest and most pure expression of the Prophet's family unit. Such an interpretative key clearly served the genealogical, political and religious claims of the Fatimids, thus named after Fatima. The dynasty did not utilise the term 'Fatimid' to refer to itself until the second half of the eleventh century, by which time its rule in Egypt had already been consolidated for almost a century while the doctrinal and philosophical system on which it based its right to rule had reached a high level of elaboration.[4]

The most prominent Fatimid authors re-interpreted narratives relating to female role models in Islam, such as Fatima and other important female figures, to reflect a religio-political discourse ultimately aimed at backing the Fatimids' dynastic claims. Indeed, throughout Islamic history, female role models have often been used as powerful advertisements to serve a range of aims: to state dynastic identity and legitimacy, to keep social stability by defining the ideal roles Muslim women ought to conform to, and even to stir up support and activism among Muslim women during particular periods of political ferment.

One of the most important female figures and role models for Muslims of yesterday and today, Fatima, known as *al-Zahrā'* (the Radiant) and *al-Batūl* (the Virgin), was the daughter of Muhammad and his first wife Khadija, presumably born around 604 CE. Besides epitomising the role of the devout and obedient daughter of the Prophet, the one who nurtured him during his illness and eventual death, and who died, distraught, only a few months after her father, Fatima also embodies the role of the suffering wife of ʿAli b. Abi Talib, who strives to make ends meet, and of the mother who has premonitions about the tragic fate of her two sons.

Our knowledge of Fatima's biography relies on an extensive body of narratives, legends and hagiographical reconstructions, where the prominent role she plays appears to rest more on her links to the men of her family than on her own merits. When aiming at supporting descent claims, the narrator emphasises Fatima's blood links to her father; when the purpose is to praise the virtues of her husband ʿAli in support for his succession rights, precedence is given to her role as wife; finally, when upholding the issue of the descent of the imamate, she is presented as the suffering mother of al-Hasan and al-Husayn. However, in a number of accounts included in popular and mystical works, Fatima does take centre stage and her personal virtues are praised when she is lauded for her roles as pious intercessor and ascetic believer.

Sunni as well as Shiʿi writers remark on her being the Prophet's most beloved and the most pious of his daughters. Nevertheless, it is her marriage to her paternal cousin ʿAli which brings her to the fore. Several Shiʿi and Ismaʿili narratives describe their marriage as being made in heaven. One of them is included in *Sharḥ al-akhbār*, a compendium of traditions on the virtues of the members of the *Ahl al-Bayt* ('the People of the Prophet's House', typically Muhammad, Fatima, ʿAli, and their sons al-Hasan and al-Husayn) by the most authoritative Fatimid jurist and chief missionary al-Qadi al-Nuʿman (d. 363/974). There al-Nuʿman reports a number of hagiographical stories that describe Fatima and ʿAli's marriage as being the result of a revelation to the Prophet Muhammad through the angel Gabriel. The marriage contract, witnessed by thousands of praising angels, was sealed in heaven before it could be signed on earth. Hence, their union was divinely ordained, and her excellence linked to the excellence of her husband, ʿAli, and reflected in their progeny.[5]

The marriage itself, though blessed by the birth of children, was reportedly not without difficulties. Some Sunni *ḥadīths* mention disagreements between the spouses and the recourse to the Prophet for counselling. Even in Shiʿi *ḥadīths* there is the occasional reference to ʿAli wanting to take another wife, whether or not this implied divorcing Fatima, but in the end all things are resolved either thanks to the direct intervention of Muhammad, or by resorting to the Prophet's statement that 'Fatima is a part of me, whoever harms her, harms me'.[6] What Shi'i, as well as Sunni, narrators agree upon is that Fatima and 'Ali lived a harsh, not comfortable life. With the aim of praising the generosity of both spouses, they state that the couple went for up to three days without food and that Fatima, embarrassed to receive her father at home without anything to offer him, prayed so intensely that, in answer to her prayers, a bowl of hot soup materialised and the whole family, including the two little children, could enjoy the meal.[7]

These hagiographical accounts are but an expression of a broader doctrinal and genealogical Shi'i discourse identifying Fatima as the initiator of the legitimate line of descendants from the Prophet. According to Shi'i thought, she is a member – the only female member – of the *Ahl al-Bayt*. When, during the ninth and tenth centuries, Shi'i and Sunni disputes over political and doctrinal issues intensified, Shi'i *ḥadīths* circulated about the members of the *Ahl al-Bayt* and their qualities, such as infallibility, purity and ability to intercede. In these *ḥadīths*, Fatima is hailed as infallible and as cleansed from the physical impurities of her gender: menstruation and post-partum bleeding. Like Mary, the mother of Jesus, she is called *batūl* and one tradition tells us that al-Hasan and al-Husayn were born out of her thigh. It is perhaps particularly in relation to her purity, and her other qualities, that one tradition identifies her as being the only woman to have been created equal to man. Further glorifying epithets are to be found in the work of the fifteenth-century Tayyibi Isma'ili scholar Idris 'Imad al-Din.[8]

Al-Qadi al-Nu'man reports a number of *ḥadīths* to illustrate Fatima's position of excellence among believers. In them, it is the Prophet himself who names Fatima as 'the foremost lady of the whole community of believers' or 'the first lady of the worlds', or even 'the first of the women of Paradise'.[9] She is indeed deemed superior to Mary, who in turn is described as the first lady *only* among the women of her own time. In Paradise, Fatima sits, a splendid image bearing a crown, on a throne and, on the Day of Resurrection, those who loved her and, through her, loved Muhammad, will be greeted by him in Paradise.[10] The ascription to Fatima of an eschatological role as intercessor was not the exclusive domain of speculations by medieval Shi'i and Fatimid scholars but extended to popular religious expressions. To this day her intermediation is sought by Twelver Shi'is, as shown at passion plays (*ta'ziya*) in praise of Fatima and her progeny.[11] An additional interpretative key to the roles ascribed to Fatima is presented in Shi'i and Isma'ili gnostic literature, where the Qur'anic verse of the Light is reinterpreted as referring to Fatima being the mother of imams, the lamp which contains the light of al-Husayn. She is thus further invested with a universal creative power by means of her shining light.[12] The affirmation of Fatima's primacy and the bestowal upon her of supernatural qualities were essential components of the doctrinal backdrop that Fatimid scholars elaborated to validate genealogical claims centred around her spouse and their progeny.

Early Fatimid scholars argued that, as daughter, Fatima held a position of precedence in relation to the Prophet's wives, because, unlike them, her link to the Prophet was direct, through blood. Her family ties were made even stronger when she married the Prophet's cousin, ʿAli. Their claim of Fatima's superior status served a clear purpose. By emphasising the superiority of blood ties over ties by marriage, these Fatimid scholars not only defended their support for ʿAli's succession over that of Abu Bakr, who was linked to Muhammad through the marriage of his daughter ʿA'isha, but also justified the legitimacy of any further succession claims by ʿAli and Fatima's progeny.

Two episodes in Fatima's life are particularly significant in the way they were reinterpreted to support succession claims based on the 'blood ties' argument as elaborated by the Shiʿis. Both are presented as exemplifying her role as fighter for her own and her family's rights. One is the so-called Saqifa affair. In the immediate aftermath of Muhammad's death, while, according to tradition, preparation was still underway for the Prophet's funeral, some notable members of the community gathered at Saqifat Bani Saʿida to discuss the issue of succession, the outcome of which would be the nomination of Abu Bakr as caliph. What ensued was a conflict between ʿAli and Abu Bakr. Even though in Sunni sources this episode is played down, one can still infer that, in the midst of this dispute, Fatima suffered threats in her own house. Shiʿi sources, instead, cover the incident in much greater detail and describe a direct physical confrontation in which Fatima defended ʿAli against Abu Bakr and his supporters.[13] Shiʿi commentators used Fatima's predicament to pass judgement on their opponents by denouncing their loss of respect towards the Prophet, his mourning daughter and the rest of his family, thus further highlighting the injustice perpetrated against ʿAli's rights, which they saw as legitimate.

The second of these episodes refers to the debate over Fatima's inheritance rights. In the Shiʿi accounts that cover it, she is portrayed as the main protagonist. The debate centred on whether the Prophet's property, that is, what he had acquired as a result of booty or treatises, was to be considered private or public, and, as a consequence, whether Fatima had the right to inherit her father's property, which consisted of an oasis, named Fadak, and its surroundings. Abu Bakr firmly dismissed Fatima's claims, arguing that a prophet cannot leave inheritance. The dispute on this matter between the first caliphs on the one side and ʿAli and his supporters on the other remained unresolved until 211/826, when the ʿAbbasid caliph al-Ma'mun at last granted Fadak to Fatima's descendants. Sunni and Shiʿi sources sharply differed on the interpretation of relevant Qur'anic passages and *ḥadīths*. The Sunnis held that a prophet's property was not personal and could be inherited only by the community through its leaders, who would administer it. For the Shi'is, who also adduced evidence from additional sources such as Fatima's *khuṭba* (Fatima's Speech), Fadak was the Prophet's own and therefore Fatima's claims to inheritance were legitimate.

Isma'ili and Fatimid writers extensively refer to this episode and lament Fatima being stripped of her rights. In varying degrees of pathos, Fatimid sources show Fatima as a woman with no protectors, who can only use her dialectic and oratory gift displayed in her well-known Speech, but to no avail. Al-Qadi al-Nu'man, for example, reports large extracts of the Speech in his *Sharḥ al-akhbār*, where he adds his allegorical interpretation of the passages. Overall, al-Qadi al-Nu'man argues that Fatima's Speech was not specifically about Fadak and its environs, but about 'the imamate from her and the progeny of the Prophet'.[14] This interpretative key is one which several medieval as well as contemporary Shi'i scholars endorse.[15]

The episode of Fatima's inheritance was widely used by the Isma'ilis for propagandist and other purposes. Claims of succession and the respect of Fatima's status became intertwined. In this vein, the tenth-century North African Isma'ili missionary Ibn al-Haytham could state that the two major sins of 'Ali's opponents were 'claiming the imamate and leadership ahead of God's friends [that is, the rightful imams] and taking away the veil of Fatima'.[16] Moreover, Fatima's right to inherit, and to inherit land, from her father had a considerable impact, as a legal precedent, on Fatimid inheritance law, as will be explained later on in the book. According to al-Qadi al-Nu'man, the denial of her inheritance left a bitterness from which Fatima was relieved only by her death. She organised her own funeral and asked to be buried at night, with only 'Ali in attendance, so that 'the enemies of the Prophet's family' would not be able to recite the funerary prayers over her.[17]

Fatima has remained a reference figure throughout the Fatimid period and beyond. Her name, or her titles, are found in coins and talismans and were reportedly mentioned in the blessings on the *Ahl al-Bayt* that were included in the *khuṭba* upon the Fatimid conquest of Egypt.[18] The Fatimids celebrated her birthday and made it into a holiday, when gifts were exchanged among the palace people. A rosary-like prayer known as *Tasbīḥ Fāṭima* (Fatima's glorification of God), is reported by Fatimid writers as consisting of three sections of thirty-three blessings or formulae, which, added to the *shahāda*, invoke the name of God one hundred times, for which Allah will grant benefits equivalent to 1,000 good deeds.[19] After the Fatimids, and particularly since the sixteenth century, with the establishment of the Safavid dynasty in Persia and the proclamation of Twelver Shi'ism as its official religion, popular accounts on Fatima have been revived among Shi'is and enacted in the passion plays, where she is portrayed as the suffering mother and the victim of injustice. Against the political background and ideological mobilisation that lead to the 1979 Iranian revolution, to her roles has been added that of the exemplary female activist. The social reformer and scholar ʿAli Shariʿati (d. 1977) presented Fatima as a role model for contemporary Shiʿi women who, while maintaining their traditional values of modesty, obedience and piety, are aware of social and political issues and fight for them.[20] It is outside the scope of the present work to investigate how far the praise of such female activism was in fact used by Iranian ideologues to encourage women's support for the Islamic revolution. In its aftermath, such praise was no longer forthcoming at a time when a call for the return to the traditional female domestic roles was implemented by the new regime in more ways than one.

Beside Fatima, the other woman in Muhammad's household who receives ample coverage in Ismaʿili and Fatimid literature is his wife Khadija. Among the Prophet's wives she is portrayed as being the most important and the most noble, not only because she was his first wife, the first woman the Prophet knew, the one who supported him emotionally and financially and who believed in the divine origin of his call, but also because she was the wife who was blessed with bearing his children. Motherhood is interpreted as a sign of her virtue and purity. It is indeed motherhood that ultimately distinguishes her because, by being Fatima's mother, 'she gave birth to the imams'.[21] She therefore cannot even remotely be compared to any of Muhammad's other wives, the only fitting comparison being with Mary.[22] Through al-Qadi al-Nuʿman's extolling of her virtues, Khadija comes across as the perfect Muslim woman: the devout wife, the quintessential mother, the first woman to have answered the call of Islam, whose daughter was to marry the first man to convert to Islam, the generous sponsor for the sake of Allah. Like Fatima, she is one of the women of Paradise, who, on earth, was endowed with foreknowledge: she knew that Muhammad was to be a prophet and was waiting for the signs to appear.[23] She is portrayed as pre-destined to be the consoling and supportive wife as evidenced by the supernatural knowledge she was granted as a divine gift.

Some Ismaʿili authors provide an allegorical interpretation of the roles and status of both Fatima and Khadija. In explaining the inner meaning of Fatima's Speech, al-Qadi al-Nuʿman had linked the inheritance issue to that of the succession of the imamate and concluded that Fatima had acted as a witness (*ḥujja*, lit. 'proof') to her contemporaries. This aspect of al-Nuʿman's argument was to be upheld and elaborated upon to a greater extent by the Yemeni Ismaʿili author Ibrahim b. al-Husayn al-Hamidi (d. 557/1162) in his *Kitāb Kanz al-walad*. Beyond Fatima, al-Hamidi reinterpreted allegorically the roles of other female figures within the context of his explanation of the spiritual cosmology that underpinned the Tayyibi formulation of Ismaʿili doctrine. Echoing Neoplatonic cosmology, he interpreted Eve's coming into being from Adam's rib as symbolic of the cosmic emanation of the Universal Soul from the First Intellect. Eve's esoteric role is that of being Adam's *ḥujja*, who embodies the esoteric interpretation of his prophet-hood.[24] Similarly, al-Hamidi identified Khadija as Muhammad's *ḥujja*. By marrying her both exoterically and esoterically, Muhammad received from her both the ranks of prophet and messenger (*nubuwwa* and *risāla*). As his *ḥujja*, Khadija is made responsible for his 'educational training' as imam or 'Master of the time', for elevating his status and explaining his rank. Echoing traditional Muslim accounts of her seniority to Muhammad, al-Hamidi invested her with an almost 'maternal' role, which could explain his statement that she was 'the high Mary'. Khadija is also presented as being the trustee of Muhammad's appointment of ʿAli as 'his *waṣī*, the heir of his knowledge and he who gathers in himself all the ranks'.[25] Al-Hamidi applied a similar interpretation to Fatima, whom he saw as the first of the most perfect figures (*atimmā'*) of the age of Muhammad, the one who inaugurated a spiritual line of descent which, through her sons al-Hasan and al-Husayn, reached its first perfection in Muhammad b. Ismaʿil.[26] This figure was the one the Ismaʿilis identified as their seventh imam, who inaugurated a period of concealment that, according to one group, was to come to an end with the establishment of the Fatimid caliphate.

The structure of this volume is topical and the roles and contribution of women are analysed first within the context of Ismaʿili dynastic and political propaganda in support of the spiritual leader: the imam. Having established the place of women in Ismaʿili and Fatimid genealogical history, their status and influence are assessed within the courts in their roles as mothers, courtesans, wives and daughters, as well as workers and servants. We examine the case studies of women whose political influence and power left a mark in the history of the Fatimid dynasty. Moreover, the finances of court women of substance are scrutinised against broader economic and legal contexts. Finally, an evaluation of aspects of the daily life of non-court women is offered. Throughout the book comparison is drawn with the status and roles of women in earlier, contemporary and subsequent Islamic as well as non-Islamic courts.

Notes

1 Ahmed, L., *Women and Gender in Islam*, New Haven and London: Yale University Press, 1992, p. 2.

2 Ahmed, L., *Women*, pp. 1–7; for the Qarmaṭians, see pp. 98–9, where she relies on ʿAbd al-Raḥmān al-Jawzī (d. 597/1200), a standard primary source on the Qarmaṭians, and as secondary sources the work by the late nineteenth-century Dutch scholar M. J. de Goeje and *The Arabs in History* by Bernard Lewis, published in 1958.

3 Malti-Douglas, F., *Woman's Body, Woman's Word: Gender and Discourse in Arabo-Islamic Writing*, Princeton: PUP, 1991; and El-Cheikh, N. M., 'Women's history: a study of al-Tanukhi', in Marin, M. and Deguilhem, R. (eds), *Writing the Feminine: Women in Arab Sources*, London: I. B. Tauris, 2002, pp. 129–48.

4 Even after this date the term *Fāṭimī* is by no means the only and most common term used by the dynasty to refer to itself: see Fierro, M. I., 'On *al-Fāṭimī* and *al-Fāṭimiyyūn*', *JSAI*, 20 (1996) pp. 130–61.

5 al-Qāḍī al-Nu'mān, *Sharḥ al-akhbār fī faḍā'il al-a'imma al-aṭhār*, ed. al-Jalālī, M. H., Qum: Mu'assasat al-nashr al-islāmī, vol. 3, 1412/1992, pp. 28, 66–7, 69.

6 al-Qāḍī al-Nu'mān, *Sharḥ*, pp. 30–1 and 60–1 (where divorce is indeed mentioned). In some *ḥadīths* there is even an indication of lack of consideration for women on 'Alī's part. For the suggestion of a link between 'Alī's attitude towards women and the attitudes towards them in contemporary Shī'ī Iran, see Azari, F., 'Sexuality and women's oppression in Iran' in Azari, F., (ed.), *Women of Iran: the Conflict with Fundamentalist Islam*, London: Ithaca, 1983, pp. 103–4.

7 al-Qāḍī al-Nu'mān, *Sharḥ*, pp. 25–7. On Fāṭima's frugality as a sign of asceticism, see also al-'Aqqād, 'A., *Fāṭima al-zahrā' wa-'l-Fāṭimiyyūn*, n.p.: Dār al-hilāl, n.d., pp. 52–3, where the author attempts an overall assessment of her 'personality'.

8 For a summary of varying interpretations as to the members of the *Ahl al-Bayt*, see Soufi, D. L., *The Image of Fatima in Classical Muslim Thought*, PhD thesis, Princeton: Princeton University, 1997, pp. 3–18, where the differing arguments by Moshe Sharon and W. Madelung are presented. For the purity of Fāṭima, see al-Kulaynī, Muḥammad b. Ya'qūb, *al-Uṣūl min al-kāfī*, ed. al-Ghaffārī, 'A. A., Tehran: Dār al-kutub al-islāmiya, 1973, vol. 1, p. 460 and for the birth of her sons from her thigh, see al-Khāsibī, al-Ḥusayn b. Hamdān, *al-Hidāya al-kubrā*, Beirut: Mu'assasat al-balāgh, 1986, p. 180. For the last remarks, see al-Astarabādī, in Soufi, D. L., *Image*, p. 158. See Idrīs 'Imād al-Dīn, *'Uyūn al-akhbār wa-funūn al-athār*, ed. Ghālib, M., Beirut: Dār al-Andalus, 1973, vol. 4. p. 13 and 1975, vol. 5, p. 11.

9 al-Qāḍī al-Nu'mān, *Sharḥ*, pp. 24–5 and 56.

10 al-Qāḍī al-Nu'mān, *Sharḥ*, p. 63. For Fāṭima in Paradise sitting on a throne, see *Umm al-kitāb* (an anonymous Central Asian proto-Ismā'īlī text) in Filippani-Ronconi, P. (Ital. trans.), *Ummu'l-Kitab*, Naples: Istituto Universitario Orientale, 1966, p. 94.

11 See passages from *ta'ziyas* and eulogies in Soufi, D. L., *Image*, pp. 132–49.

12 On Fāṭima as creative power, see numerous references in the *Umm al-kitāb*; see also al-Majlisī, Muḥammad, *Biḥār al-anwār*, Tehran: Sharikat-i ṭab'-i Biḥār al-anwār, 1956–72, vol. 57, pp. 192–3 and Ja'far b. Manṣūr al-Yaman, *Kitāb al-Kashf*, ed. Ghālib, M., Beirut: Dār al-Andalus, 1984, p. 35.

13 Sources quoted in Soufi, D. L., *Image*, pp. 84–5.

14 al-Qāḍī al-Nu'mān, *Sharḥ*, p. 40. For the text of the Speech, see pp. 34–40; for its interpretation, pp. 40–55.

15 For a summary of some scholars' interpretations, see Soufi, D. L., *Image*, pp. 104–6.

16 Ibn al-Haytham, Abū 'Abd Allāh, *Kitāb al-Munāẓarāt*, trans. Madelung, W. and Walker, P. E. in *The Advent of the Fatimids: A Contemporary Shi'i Witness*, London: I. B. Tauris, 2000, pp. 69–70. 'Tearing away Fatima's veil' is mentioned again on p. 131 and on p. 114, where it is listed as one of the violations against the religion of God, together with taking away her inheritance, murdering her and an unusual accusation of killing 'the infant of hers in her womb'.

17 al-Qāḍī al-Nu'mān, *Sharḥ*, p. 32. According to the sixteenth-century Shī'ī scholar Ḥusayn Kashifī, she even performed by herself the ritual funeral washing and dressing: see Soufi, D. L., *Image*, p. 130.

18 For her name on talismans, see Kalus, L., *Catalogue of Islamic Seals and Talismans*, Oxford: Clarendon Press, 1986, pp. 55–7, 99 (*wa-'l-batūl Fāṭima*); for her mention in the *khuṭba*, see

al-Safadī, Ṣalāḥ al-Dīn, *Kitāb al-Wafī bi-'l-wafāyāt*, Wiesbaden: F. Steiner, 1981–, vol. 11, n. 320, p. 225.

19 al-Qāḍī al-Nu'mān, *Sharḥ*, pp. 67–8.

20 Sharī'atī, 'A., *Fāṭimah Fāṭimah ast*, trans. Bakhtiar, L., *Fatima is Fatima*, Tehran: Sharī'atī Foundation, 1981, pp. 201–2.

21 al-Qāḍī al-Nu'mān, *Sharḥ*, p. 22; as to the virtues of her motherhood, see Ibn al-Haytham, *Munāẓarāt*, pp. 73–4. In the same passage Māriya the Copt is also mentioned as having mothered a child of the Prophet (who died as an infant) and this alone makes her superior to 'Ā'isha. As for Khadīja's superiority over Māriya, even though not directly spelt out in the text, one might infer that in addition to her status as a free wife rather than a slave given as a gift of honour, Khadīja's children survived to maturity and were able to have progeny of their own.

22 Ibn al-Haytham, *Munāẓarāt*, p. 73.

23 al-Qāḍī al-Nu'mān, *Sharḥ*, pp. 16 and 22.

24 al-Ḥāmidī, Ibrāhīm, *Kitāb Kanz al-walad*, ed. Ghālib, M., Wiesbaden: F. Steiner, 1391/1971, pp. 76, 216.

25 al-Ḥāmidī, *Kanz*, pp. 212, 216.

26 al-Ḥāmidī, *Kanz*, p. 257.

CHAPTER

1

WORKING THE PROPAGANDA SPINDLE

1. The *Da'wa*: A Historical Overview

In mid-eighth-century Baghdad, the Sunni ʿAbbasid caliphs had just undertaken the spiritual and secular leadership of the Muslim community when religious-political activists in Iraq and beyond began to challenge their right to rule. The ʿAbbasids rose to prominence by exploiting the sentiments of those who upheld the rights of the Prophet Muhammad's descendants to guide the Muslim community, only to ignore these ideals once in power and proceed to curb all dissenting groups. However, one of these groups – the Shiʿis – defied the ʿAbbasids' right to rule, with militant and spiritual action inspired by a conception of a divinely designed authority that led them to recognise Muhammad's descendants – via his cousin and son-in-law ʿAli – as their spiritual and secular leaders or imams. Shiʿis credit Jaʿfar al-Sadiq (d. 148/765), acknowledged as the fifth imam to descend from ʿAli, with having formulated a full-blown doctrine of imamate; a doctrine that was to be at the heart of all Shiʿi teachings to come.

The Shiʿi linking of the principle of authority to genealogy inevitably caused Shiʿi activists to split into groups, each aiming at affirming its own particular vision of spiritual and secular rule by defending the rights of its chosen candidate to the imamate. Among them, a group from Kufa, in southern Iraq, distiguished itself in supporting the imamate of Ismaʿil, who was Jaʿfar al-Sadiq's son, thus directly challenging the claims of their Shiʿi rivals who backed Ismaʿil's brother, Musa al-Kazim. It is to the activities of these supporters of Ismaʿil that the Ismaʿilis trace their ancestry.

As it transpires from the sources, early Ismaʿilism was far from being a homogeneous and unified movement. It consisted of a number of splinter groups entangled in debates and rivalries over religious-political leadership and messianic expectations. In time, one faction succeded in polarising ideas and energies towards the belief that Isma'il's son and successor, Muhammad, had not actually died but, rather, had gone into physical and spiritual occultation (*ghayba*) as a safety measure to escape from his opponents. Muhammad's followers awaited his return as a messianic figure (*al-mahdī*) who, one day, would usher an era of freedom and justice. While waiting, they developed the belief in the existence of a line of hidden imams who, though concealed, would exercise on his behalf both spiritual and secular authority.

According to the Isma'ili tradition, by the middle of the ninth century, the activities of this faction had evolved into a *da'wa* (missionary movement or propaganda) operating in areas as diverse as Central Asia, Persia, Yemen and Syria. Towards the end of that century, the Syrian town of Salamiyya came to be identified as the centre of a covert Isma'ili religious-political propaganda furthering the cause of the hidden imams, and poised at challenging the 'Abbasids and all other claimants to the leadership of the Muslim community. There is, however, disagreement among scholars about the extent to which this version of the development of the early *da'wa* is an accurate rendering of historical reality. What is argued is that, like the Isma'ili movement as a whole, its *da'wa* activities were, for the early centuries, far from being coherent and centralised. It would take two more centuries for a *da'wa* structure as such to be clearly identifiable.

Fluid as it might have been, this mission was initially carried out by *dā'īs* (missionaries, propagandists) who swore loyalty to the leadership of a certain 'Abd Allah the Elder, possibly a Persian from Ahwaz. The Isma'ili tradition regards him as the first of three hidden imams who escaped 'Abbasid persecution and settled in Salamiyya. By the last quarter of the ninth century, 'cells' were operating in western Persia and southern Iraq. The *dā'ī* Hamdan Qarmat and his brother-in-law, 'Abdan, were successful in attracting a significant number of supporters in Kufa, who were to become known as Qarmatians. Near this town, in 277/890, Hamdan Qarmat built the *dār al-hijra* (The Abode of Migration), an operational base for anti-'Abbasid activities and a welfare centre for Qarmatian men and women. From Kufa, Hamdan and 'Abdan eventually sent the *dā'ī* Abu Sa'id al-Jannabi (d. 301/913) to canvass in Bahrayn. Meanwhile, one of 'Abdan's Kufan supporters, Ibn Hawshab (d. 302/914), better known as Mansur al-Yaman (henceforth), arrived in Yemen. There, Mansur al-Yaman preached publicly and dispatched his relative, al-Haytham, to operate in north-west India. To the west, in 280/893, Mansur al-Yaman sent a fellow Kufan, Abu 'Abd Allah al-Shi'i (d. 298/910–11), to preach among the Kutama Berbers in North Africa. This was broadly the state of affairs until the end of the ninth century, when, having settled in Salamiyya, *another* 'Abd Allah took the leadership of the *da'wa* and forever changed it by openly claiming the imamate for himself.

'Abd Allah's claim caused a split between those *dā'īs* who continued to believe in the messianic return of Muhammad b. Isma'il and those who accepted 'Abd Allah as the imam of the time. By refusing to acknowledge 'Abd Allah, Hamdan Qarmat was 'spirited away' and 'Abdan was murdered by Zakarawayh, a former associate in Iraq. This Zakarawayh had initially pledged allegiance to 'Abd Allah but subsequently started a campaign of self-promotion among the Bedouins of the Syrian–Iraqi desert, lasting until his death in 294/907 at the hand of the 'Abbasids. In Bahrayn, Abu Sa'id al-Jannabi took over the Qarmatian leadership following the death of 'Abdan. In Yemen, on the other hand, Mansur al-Yaman endorsed 'Abd Allah's claim, thus provoking the opposition of his former ally, Ibn al-Fadl.

In 289/902, 'Abd Allah fled Salamiyya either to escape from Zakarawayh's supporters or the 'Abbasids, or indeed both. On fleeing Syria, 'Abd Allah had two options as to where to seek refuge and fulfil his messianic mission. He could have gone to Yemen. There, he had the support of Mansur al-Yaman, but dissent was creeping in among the *dā'īs* over 'Abd Allah's claims. Instead, 'Abd Allah headed for North Africa, which indeed proved to be the safest and – with hindsight – the best choice. There, the *dā'ī* Abu 'Abd Allah al-Shi'i had already successfully established over a period of ten years an ostensibly 'unified' Isma'ili propaganda network.

Allegedly Abu 'Abd Allah al-Shi'i had been converted in Kufa by the prominent *dā'ī* Abu 'Ali and sworn in by another *dā'ī*, Firuz, who then dispatched him to Yemen to join Mansur al-Yaman. In turn, Abu 'Ali and Abu 'Abd Allah's brother were sent to Egypt. On Mansur al-Yaman's instructions, Abu 'Abd Allah al-Shi'i reached Mila (eastern Algeria), having joined a caravan of Kutama Berbers returning home from their pilgrimage to Makka. Once settled in North Africa, Abu 'Abd Allah made Tazrut the *da'wa* base for at least a decade. There, he succeeded in converting the bulk of the Kutama tribesmen and built a *dār al-hijra* for the benefit of the converts, even though there is reason to believe that their understanding of Isma'ili doctrines remained superficial. On his part, Abu 'Abd Allah did his best to enforce the *sharī'a*, to give lectures to the Kutama converts and to instruct subordinate *dā'īs* to hold similar sessions in the areas under their sphere of activities. His endeavours brought long-lasting rewards in that the Isma'ili cause was to greatly benefit from the Kutama loyalty and amazing warfaring skills.

In 290/903, Abu 'Abd Allah al-Shi'i begun the military conquest of Ifriqiya, launching offensives on major towns. A year later, accompanied by Firuz, 'Abd Allah arrived in Egypt, in the city of Fustat, were he was welcomed by *dā'īs* who had been active there for some time. However, in the same year, Firuz deserted

ʿAbd Allah to join the dissident Ibn al-Fadl in Yemen. Feeling unsafe, in 292/905, ʿAbd Allah left Fustat typically disguised as a merchant and with Kutama support he eventually reached Sijilmasa, where he settled for four years. By 296/908, the ongoing victories of Abu ʿAbd Allah al-Shiʿi signalled the incipient fall of Qayrawan, near Raqqada, the royal city of the Aghlabids, who were the ruling dynasty in the region at the time. In the following year, the Aghlabid palace in the royal city fell, and by the summer of 296/909 Abu ʿAbd Allah and the Kutama took Sijilmasa. Initially, ʿAbd Allah was acclaimed as caliph and towards the end of the year, upon arriving in Raqqada, ʿAbd Allah's *mahdī*-ship was publicly announced and he was welcomed as ruler. ʿAbd Allah al-Mahdi (henceforth al-Mahdi) became the first of a dynasty of imam-caliphs, thus inaugurating the so-called 'golden age' of Ismaʿilism and a splendid period in Islamic history, art, intellectual and court life, which saw women as participants to an extent rarely found in other domains of the medieval Islamic world.

The public appearance of ʿAbd Allah in Sijilmasa and his proclamation as al-Mahdi in Raqqada mark the beginning of the North African phase of Fatimid history, to be distinguished from the pre-dynastic period of Ismaʿilism. The periodisation of Fatimid history into pre-dynastic, North African and Egyptian phases will be adopted throughout this book. The dynasty eventually became famous under the name of 'Fatimid' through Fatima, daughter of the Prophet Muhammad and wife of his cousin ʿAli, who is believed by all Shiʿis to have been the first imam, while his wife Fatima, as the bearer of the next generation of imams, has often been hailed as 'the mother of the imams'.

Within a year of his reign, al-Mahdi, fearing dissent at home, began a purge within his entourage. In 298/911, claiming the discovery of a conspiracy, al-Mahdi ordered the execution of its alledged instigators: Abu ʿAbd Allah al-Shiʿi, his brother and a number of Kutama chiefs. Like any other confident ruler, al-Mahdi set about building his capital, al-Mahdiyya, on the coast of what is today Tunisia, finally settling there in 308/920–1.

Elsewhere, a *mahdī* frenzy flared up within the broader 'Ismaʿili/Qarmatian' movement. In the Yemen, Ibn al-Fadl claimed the *mahdī*-ship for himself, as in Bahrayn apparently did Abu Saʿid al-Jannabi. But while Ibn al-Fadl's venture ended with his death in 303/915, the Qarmatians of Bahrayn continued to be a cause of concern for the Fatimids and the ʿAbbasids alike. In fact, their messianic aspirations escalated to the point that first, in 317/930, they snatched the Black Stone from the Kaʿba in Makka and, second, the following year, they announced the appearance of the 'god incarnate' in the figure of a certain Abu al-Fadl. The Bahrayni strand of the Qarmatian movement survived until 470/1077, despite frustration and hindered messianic expectations.

In 322/934, al-Mahdi died and was succeeded by his son, who took the dynastic name of al-Qa'im (d. 334/946). Al-Qa'im's intention to continue his father's political and religious programme was hindered by a prolonged anti-Fatimid revolt instigated by the Berber Zenata leader, Abu Yazid. According to a Fatimid, and therefore possibly biased source, Abu Yazid's plan to eliminate political-religious adversaries involved also the imprisonment, rape and killing of their women and children.[1] The revolt was eventually crushed in 336/947 by al-Qa'im's successor, al-Mansur.

This imam-caliph brought Sicily under Fatimid influence, founded a new capital, al-Mansuriyya, and reinforced the bond between the operations of *da'wa* and the judiciary as exemplified by the offices held by the Fatimid jurist and *dā'ī*, al-Qadi al-Nu'man. Al-Mansur was also involved in negotiations with the Qarmatians for the return of the Black Stone to Makka, which they finally gave back in 339/950. Under his reign, lectures on Isma'ili jurisprudence were delivered to the general public in the Great Mosque of Qayrawan and, later, in the main mosque of al-Mansuriyya. The so-called Sessions of Wisdom (*majālis al-ḥikma*), restricted to initiates, were held instead in a special room of the caliphal palace in al-Mansuriyya. Al-Mansur died prematurely in 341/953 and was succeeded by his son, al-Mu'izz (d. 365/975).

Al-Mu'izz is credited with transforming the Fatimid caliphate from a regional power into one of imperial proportions. Having inherited a region pacified by his father, al-Mu'izz favoured the intensification of the *da'wa* activities outside the Fatimid dominions, seeking a rapprochement with the Qarmatians as well as other Isma'ili communities in Persia and Central Asia. He was responsible for the promulgation and implementation of a distinctive Isma'ili law, mainly formulated by al-Qadi al-Nu'man, which aimed at imprinting with an Isma'ili character every aspect of life. Finally, al-Mu'izz could concentrate on territorial expansion to the detriment of the Fatimids' illustrious rivals, that is, the Umayyads of Spain, the Byzantines of Constantinople and above all the 'Abbasids of Baghdad. In 358/969, this expansion culminated in the conquest of Egypt masterminded by the general Jawhar and the foundation of a new Fatimid capital, al-Qahira (literally 'the Victorious', henceforth Cairo). Having left the vassal Zirid dynasty to act as Fatimid lieutenants in Ifriqiya, in 362/973 al-Mu'izz moved the headquarters of the caliphate to the new capital, with the intention of extending the Fatimid influence over the eastern Mediterranean region.

Under al-Mu'izz's son and successor, al-'Aziz (d. 386/996), court life flourished and the Fatimid dynasty (*dawla*) reached its political, territorial and economic zenith. As for the *da'wa* organisation, it evolved into a core institution of the Fatimid regime. By al-'Aziz's time, the *dā'īs* came to be formally organised into a complex hierarchical structure headed by a chief *dā'ī*. From Cairo, the imam-caliph seconded *dā'īs* to covertly set up new 'cells' in regions outside Fatimid control, as well as to overtly run the existing 'cells' scattered around Fatimid domains. From the provinces, the *dāʿīs* would return to Cairo for instructions but also to deliver to the imam-caliph the dues, no matter how small, collected in his name.[2] By the end of al-ʿAziz's caliphate, Fatimid sovereignty and Ismaʿili *daʿwa* activities extended from North Africa and Sicily to Palestine and parts of Syria, as well as parts of the Hijaz and the Yemen. In theory, it was the imam-caliph who would ultimately determine the rank each missionary would be allocated on the basis of the level of his esoteric spiritual attainment, scholarly credentials and seniority, as well as political and managerial skills. These were indeed the criteria drawn in the rare references in early Ismaʿili literature to the training and the ideal qualities of the *dāʿīs*. In practice, and especially in outposts away from the heart of the *dawla*, the management of the distribution of ranks was deputised to the local chief *dāʿī*, who was de facto in charge of particular areas of operation or 'islands' (*jazāʾir*).

Following al-ʿAziz's death, the reign of his son, al-Hakim (d. 411/1021), was marred by political, doctrinal and economic turmoil. The imam-caliph al-Hakim addressed these crises by resorting to a series of controversial measures, many of which affected the life of women (see Chapter 6). Al-Hakim's seemingly irrational behaviour came to be seen by many as a sign of questionable sanity and yet it would appear to others as a sign of his supernatural powers. In 408/1017, activists preached belief in al-Hakim's divinity, a move that mobilised the *daʿwa* leadership to counteract the spreading of such doctrines. Known as the Druzes, after their founder, al-Darzi, the movement experienced persecution at the hands of al-Hakim's son and successor, al-Zahir (d. 427/1036) and, once banished from Egypt, its members resettled in Syria and Lebanon, where small communities exist to this day.

The problems that affected al-Hakim's reign were inherited and temporarily resolved by al-Zahir. It was, however, during the long reign of al-Mustansir (r. 427–87/1036–1094) that major political, institutional and economic upheavals signalled the start of the dynasty's irretrievable decline. On the international front, the Fatimids lost control over important territories. In Ifriqiya, after over seventy years of loyalty, in 440/1048 the Zirids, under al-Muʿizz b. Badis, switched their allegiance to the ʿAbbasids; eventually, the Fatimids regained control of the area but did not secure it. Al-Mustansir witnessed with concern the rise in the east of a new powerful dynasty, the Saljuq Turks of Persia. It was, however, during his reign that, in 450/1058, the Fatimids' sovereignty was formally acknowledged, albeit briefly, in Baghdad. Nevertheless, after decades of tenuous hold, Syria and Palestine were finally lost to the ʿAbbasids and the Saljuqs. Finally, Sicily came under Norman rule in 463/1070–1.

On the domestic front, the reoccurence of devastating famines and epidemics, which intermittently hit Egypt during the eleventh century, highlighted a state of social, political and adminstrative collapse. We are told that women of the harem were forced to beg in the streets, that plump-legged women were eaten alive, and that women exchanged their finest jewellery for a handful of flour. Exaggerated as they may seem, these accounts show that chroniclers measured the index of efficacy of the dynasty by the scale of the predicaments affecting its subjects, including women. Politically speaking, the growing power of the viziers reduced that of the caliph to be merely nominal, with consequences also for the prestige of the *da'wa*. Moreover, signs of tension between powerful viziers and influential *dā'īs* are reflected in the uneasy relationship between the vizier al-Yazuri (d. 450/1058) and the most prominent *dā'ī* of the time, al-Mu'ayyad fi'l-Din al-Shirazi (d. 470/1078). It was, however, the arrival in Cairo in 466/1074 of the powerful Armenian vizier Badr al-Jamali that marked the defining moment in the transference of effective power to the vizier. Beyond the political sphere, this change would affect a broad range of domains including genealogical issues, dynastic marriage patterns, the influence of the harem, the female use of wealth and the landscaping of Cairo. In the Fatimid capital, the functions and activities of the *da'wa* became significantly reduced, so much so that, after al-Mu'ayyad, no major *dā'ī* figure can be found operating from the Cairo headquarters for the duration of the dynasty until its end in 567/1171.

On the other hand, at the periphery of the empire and in neighbouring regions, such as the Yemen, Syria and Persia, propaganda activites increasingly flourished in the aftermath of dynastic succession disputes that led to the emergence of varied branches within Isma'ilism. In the Yemen, the Sulayhid dynasty ruled on behalf of the Fatimids from 439/1047–8 to 532/1138. Its founder was 'Ali b. Muhammad al-Sulayhi (d. 459/1067), a Shafi'i convert to Isma'ilism who had brought the whole of the Yemen south of San'a' under his control after a series of successful military campaigns. Following 'Ali's murder, his son al-Mukarram (d. 477/1084) succeeded him; but, due to his illness, it was his wife, Arwa, who de facto held the reins of power till the end of the Sulayhid dynasty (see Chapter 4).

Following the death of al-Mustansir in 487/1094, a succession dispute brought about a major political and doctrinal split within Isma'ilism. Al-Mustansir had appointed his eldest son, Abu Mansur Nizar, to succeed him as imam-caliph. However, al-Afdal, who succeded his father Badr al-Jamali as vizier and commander of the army, sought to manipulate the issue of accession to the caliphate to secure his hold on power and his control over the palace. By backing the succession of Abu'l-Qasim Ahmad, who was Nizar's younger brother, al-Afdal overruled Nizar's designation on the ground that a subsequent appointment had been made in favour of Abu'l-Qasim. By doing so, al-Afdal succeeded in placing his protégé on the Fatimid throne, with the dynastic name of al-Musta'li (d. 495/1101). Nizar's attempts to challenge his brother by staging a resistance in Alexandria came to nothing and he finally died in 488/1095. In time, the Isma'ilis of Persia, Syria and Central Asia came to uphold Nizar's imamate and that of his successors. Under the leadership of the Persian Hasan-i Sabbah (d. 518/1124) and the Syrian Rashid al-Din Sinan, the Nizaris gave shape to a distinctive brand of Isma'ilism (*da'wa jadīda*) that was doctrinally, organisationally and politically independent from Cairo. From Crusaders' accounts, the Nizaris became known in the West as 'the Assassins' because of the practice attributed to them of murdering their enemies, allegedly under the effect of drugs. Despite suffering near-extinction at the hands of the Mongols by the mid thirteenth century, the Nizari tradition survived and has prospered to this day, as witnessed by the Shi'a Imami Isma'ili community, whose spiritual leader is H. H. Karim Aga Khan IV.

By contrast, the Isma'ilis of Egypt, the Yemen and western India acknowledged al-Musta'li's imamate. In 495/1101, al-Musta'li was succeeded by his five-year-old son al-Amir, with al-Afdal effectively acting as regent. Following the death of al-Afdal in 515/1121, al-Amir regained power and, under his rule, the *da'wa* activities focused on the refutation of the Nizari claims. His efforts, however, backfired as in 524/1130 the Nizaris assassinated him. The succession disputes that followed brought about yet another major spilt in the *da'wa*. One group – the *Ḥāfiẓiyya* – supported the succession of al-Amir's cousin, who eventually adopted the dynastic name of al-Hafiz (d. 544/1149). The other group – the *Ṭayyibiyya* – upheld the rights of al-Tayyib, a presumed infant son of al-Amir, as the rightful successor. The Tayyibi cause found its main supporters in the Isma'ili Sulayhid dynasty in the Yemen, under the leadership of queen Arwa, and the Tayyibis prospered both in the Yemen and India. Today, the mainly India-based Da'udi Bohras perpetuate their tradition. The Hafizis instead lost all impetus. With al-Hafiz's successors al-Zafir (d. 549/1154), al-Fa'iz (d. 555/1160) and al-'Adid (d. 567/1171) little more than puppets in the hands of powerful and scheming viziers, the Hafizi tradition effectively ended in 567/1171, with the demise of the Fatimid regime at the hands of the famous Saladdin.

2. Women and *Da'wa* in the Pre-Fatimid Period

There are still many conflicting arguments as to the organisation, the aims and extent of formalisation of the Isma'ili *da'wa*. While Isma'ili sources devote limited space to the practical working of the *da'wa* and of its ranks, there is abundant literature dealing with its metaphysical and philosophical dimensions. There is no doubt, however, that both the structure of the *da'wa* and the modus operandi of its *dā'īs* developed over time and varied according to historical, doctrinal and geographical context. An awareness of such a development provides us with the rationale for subdividing the coverage of the link between the *daʿwa* and women into three main sections. These correspond to the three main phases in the history of the Fatimid period already mentioned. By and large, the *daʿwa* was and remained a male domain, and it is only through a careful sifting of the sources that a thus-far-overlooked female contribution to its activities can at last be brought to light.

a. Trade and Family

Ismaʿili sources dealing with the activities of the early Ismaʿili propagandists highlight the secret and clandestine character of their mission, thus leading us to perceive the *dāʿīs* as private and reserved persons, who lived constantly on guard. According to these sources, the *dāʿīs* were instructed to carefully scrutinise prospective followers, to resort to religious dissimulation (*taqiyya*), reveal inner doctrines to none but a selected few and to disclose the identity of the imam only after securing a sincere and full commitment to the mission on the part of the initiate. A high degree of caution on their part was indeed justifiable, as persecution and repression of their cause came from many sides. The ʿAbbasids sought to curb any group that challenged their authority as spiritual and secular leaders of the Muslim community, while within the Ismaʿili movement itself, doctrinal disputes among groups raged with predictable consequences. Yet, against all the odds, the *dāʿīs* carried out their mission, often eluding their enemies by leading a conventional lifestyle and, ostensibly, observing the law of the land they lived in. To be successful, a missionary needed to have insider knowledge of the territory in which he operated, of its citizens and their likelihood to convert. This entailed not only long periods of residence, but also a continuous exposure to a wide spectrum of people. Under these circumstances, the leading of a 'normal' lifestyle provided the *dāʿī* with the best camouflage for his propaganda activities; it is as part of this unconspicuous lifestyle that women played an important, albeit mainly passive, role as companions, audience, helpers and role models in the service of the early *daʿwa*.

The modus vivendi and operandi of a *dāʿī*, not unlike that of other individuals, revolved around two poles: work and family. Sources point to the fact that, from the onset of the propaganda campaign, trading was the most common profession of those who operated underground in the name of the Ismaʿili cause. The Fatimid Ismaʿili tradition portrays ʿAbd Allah the Elder, reputedly the first of the 'hidden' imams, as being 'in appearance … an ordinary merchant' in Salamiyya.[3] Moreover, al-Husayn, identified by the Ismaʿili tradition as al-Mahdi's father, is mentioned as circulating (as a trader) among the women of Salamiyya.[4] In turn, al-Mahdi is reported to have worked as a cloth merchant in Syria and to have carried on this profession until his enthronement as the first

Fatimid imam-caliph in Ifriqiya. Similarly, in ninth-century Persia, the *dāʿī* Khalaf was reportedly an expert embroiderer who succeeded in converting a number of men and women.[5] Likewise, in Bahrayn, the *dāʿī* Abu Saʿid al-Jannabi earned a living as a merchant. Through trade, *dāʿīs* had an identifiable role within the community, they could easily mingle with people, attract converts and, while earning a living, were able to carry out intelligence work.

Trade represents a useful domain where one can seek to appraise women's involvement in the early *daʿwa* activities, for these merchant-*dāʿīs* women were the first point of contact as potential customers, as local informants and as audience for their propaganda. With reference to the beginning of the Ismaʿili *daʿwa*, the late tenth–early eleventh-century Persian Fatimid *dāʿī* al-Nisaburi retrospectively states: 'They [the *dāʿīs*] travelled ... carrying with them on their donkeys different wares, such as pepper, aromatic plants, spindles, mirrors, frankincense, and *different kinds of millinery that find demand among women*'.[6] Women (but also men) who frequented markets and attended typically female gathering places were also likely sources of local news and gossip, thus lending themselves – perhaps unwittingly – to be perceived as useful informants by the *dāʿīs*. Al-Nisaburi continues, 'Whenever children and women came around them [the *dāʿīs*], they would ask these whether there was in their locality a person answering such-and-such description.'[7] Indeed, according to Ismaʿili tradition, when, in Syria, the *dāʿīs* went searching for ʿAbd Allah the Elder, who was hiding from his enemies, it was a woman who informed them of his whereabouts.

Along with work, the other domain in the life of the *dāʿī*, which allowed him to carry out his mission while conducting a normal life, was the family. Early Ismaʿili books of guidance on the ideal qualities of the *dāʿī* recommend that his wives and daughters should act as models of virtue and piety for the community, thus leading us to infer that the women in his household played an important role with regard to the image the *dāʿī* projected of himself. Indeed, to educate his family and instil in its members moral values and good manners were two among the duties the Ismaʿili missionary was expected to comply with. Also, in order not to make himself and his family conspicuous, the *dāʿī* was advised to ensure that all family members were up-to-date with the payment of the prescribed alms-giving tax (*zakāt*). On their part, the women of the household were expected to be trustworthy and show loyalty to the Ismaʿili cause. Ideally, the *dāʿī*'s house was meant to be a safe haven, a port of call and a meeting place for his associates, their wives and their children. Accordingly, to complete this image of respectability and trustworthiness, Ismaʿili guidance books stress the importance for a *dāʿī* to be surrounded by honourable staff and house personnel, typically including a secretary, a chamberlain and a doorkeeper (*bawāb*). This was deemed necessary not only because in his house the *dāʿī* would discuss secret doctrinal matters that should not be divulged to the non-initiate, but also to ensure that women and children attending his house felt safe from harassment.[8] As for the women the *dāʿī* should employ in his house, beside his wives, they should either be relatives whom he would commit to marry according to *sharīʿa* rulings or be his slaves' wives.

b. Marrying into the Mission

In keeping with both past and present Muslim social conventions, an unmarried man was perceived as an oddity. In the specific case of a missionary, to be celibate would undoubtedly make him conspicuous, with negative consequences for an effective running of his *daʿwa* activities. For instance, the fact that Abu ʿAbd Allah al-Shiʿi had remained unmarried for a long time puzzled a great deal the Kutama tribesmen that he was trying to convert, so much so that he gave in to pressure and took as a companion a slave-girl who formerly belonged to the harem of the chief of the Mazata Berbers.[9]

Marriage served as a bonding agent between missionaries who were active in distant outposts and to build unity across the *daʿwa* 'cells', while also strengthening trade links. According to Idris ʿImad al-Din, ʿAbd Allah the Elder, before moving to Salamiyya, was an activist living in Chalus, on the southern shore of the Caspian Sea, where he had a consort.[10] The same source states that Mansur al-Yaman married the daughter of another *dāʿī*, Ahmad b. al-Khaliʿ.[11] He is also reported to have married in Sanʿa' the orphaned daughter of a Shiʿi rebel and to have won the entire family over to the *daʿwa*.[12] The *dāʿī* al-Haytham, whom Mansur al-Yaman sent to north-west India, is said to have been the cousin of one of Mansur's wives. The daughter of the prominent *dāʿī* Firuz, called Umm Abi'l-Husayn, married Muhammad, the son of the important *dāʿī* Abu ʿAli.[13]

Following a practice going back to the time of the prophet Muhammad, marriages served the purpose of forging tribal or family alliances and, therefore, gaining converts. Marriage alliances proved particularly effective among the Qarmatians. ʿAbdan himself was either married to Hamdan Qarmat's sister or Qarmat was married to the sister of ʿAbdan. The case is widely reported of Abu Saʿid al-Jannabi having become a Qarmatian as a result of his marriage in Kufa to a woman of a Qarmatian family, the Bani al-Qassar. Similarly, the marriage of al-Jannabi's daughter with a member of the Bani Zarqan helped to consolidate Qarmatian political and military alliances. In Bahrayn, al-Jannabi formed marriage alliances with the Ibn Sanbar brothers, who were among his first followers.[14]

Marrying into the *daʿwa* brought a *dāʿī*'s wife honours, financial benefits and recognition but it could also entail risks in that she shared her husband's misfortune. For instance, Mu'mina, the *dāʿī* Zakarawayh's wife, was publically humiliated by the victorious ʿAbbasids by being paraded in Madina, dressed in a silken attire and wrap, in front of her husband's corpse, in retaliation for the role that she had played in supporting her husband's missionary activities.[15]

c. Female Loyalty and Guile

Isma'ili literature apologetically praises the bravery of some women in the entourage of 'Abd Allah, the future al-Mahdi. Whilst hiding in Syria, because of persecution by the 'Abbasids and Zakarawayh, al-Mahdi was able to maintain contacts with the outside world thanks to the loyalty and efforts of a number of trustworthy persons at his service, some of them women. One such woman was Umm 'Ali al-Qahramana (lit. the housekeeper), who, loyal to her master, embarked, with another woman, on a potentially perilous journey from Salamiyya to Ramla to take care of al-Mahdi's child, Abu'l-Qasim (the future imam-caliphal-Qa'im). She was originally a Christian who had converted to Islam, and the wife of Abu Ya'qub, also a slave of al-Mahdi. She died in al-Mahdiyya and her grandson was to become head chef at the court of al-'Aziz. When al-Mahdi's enemies reached Ramla, they went looking for another woman at his service, La'b. As al-Mahdi's chief servant, La'b knew more than anybody else where her master was and, more importantly, where his fortunes were being kept. Having served al-Mahdi for some time as well as, before him, his uncle or guardian, Muhammad b. Ahmad, La'b refused to collaborate with the enemies and she paid for her loyalty with her life and those of her children.[16] Women also showed their loyalty to the Isma'ili mission in other ways. For example, Qarmatian women, like men, contributed to the financing of the *da'wa*. It is reported that, during 'Abdan's time, both men and women used to pay a tax called *quṭra*, amounting to one *dirham*. Eventually both men and women were required to give a fifth of their possessions and women, specifically, would contribute by giving a fifth of carded wool.[17]

Anecdotes reflecting women's dedication and loyalty to the *da'wa*, along with their guile, are occasionally found in anti-Isma'ili sources, included in narratives featuring factional disputes within early Isma'ilism. References to women served as a narrative device either to pass a comment on the male protagonist of the story or to fill a gap in the sequence of the events recounted. In his coverage of the origins of the Qarmatians, the famous tenth-century historian al-Tabari resorts, in one of his narratives, to the inclusion of a female character in order to explain the roots of certain beliefs ascribed to this group. Al-Tabari explains that some Qarmatians believed that their founder, Karmita, had miraculously been taken to heaven. The story goes that Karmita was inviting people to pray 50 times a day. Fearing that his preaching would disrupt the work of the farmers labouring in his estates, a certain al-Haysam locked Karmita in a room of his house with the intention of killing him. However, al-Haysam got drunk and fell asleep. At this point a maidservant, who was a sympathiser of the preacher, fooled her master by stealing the room's key, thus freeing the preacher and then replacing the key in its original place. When al-Haysam went to open the room the next day, he found it empty. As a result, the rumour spread that Karmita had been raised to heaven. Another instance of the 'woman's clever ploy' motif emerges from another story also reported by al-Tabari. Around 286/899, the *dāʿī* Zakarawayh was persecuted by the ʿAbbasids, as well as the Qarmatians, because of his initial support for al-Mahdi's cause. To abscond from his enemies, the *dāʿī* hid in the house of his brother-in-law, where a woman would cleverly place a movable furnace in front of the entrance to Zakarawayh's hiding place every time his persecutors came searching for him. The ruse was so successful that, according to the brother-in-law's testimony, Zakarawayh remained hidden in this way for as long as four years.[18]

In Bahrayn, following the death of the *dāʿī* al-Jannabi around 300/912–13, the Qarmatian leadership was taken over by his sons, the youngest of whom, Abu Tahir Sulayman (d. 332/944) declared a young Persian man, Abu'l-Fadl al-Isfahani, to be the 'god incarnate'. In the coverage of this curious episode in Qarmatian history, ample space is given to the role that women played in 'resolving' the controversy that followed Abu Tahir's declaration. In fact, whether factual or anecdotal, what transpires from the narrative covering the events surrounding the demise of Abu'l-Fadl, is that it was essentially down to a woman, Abu Tahir's mother, to expose the gullability of the Qarmatian leaders and to have the courage to do something about it. According to a number of accounts, this Abu'l-Fadl had disposed of several leading representatives of the Qarmatian *daʿwa*, including the husband of Zaynab, sister of Abu Tahir Sulayman. Having done that, Abu'l-Fadl took Zaynab as his wife and killed her son. At this point, the mother of Abu Tahir, Farha, with the backing of an old *dāʿī*, took the initiative to test Abu'l-Fadl's claim of divinity and to have him killed should he prove not to be the 'god incarnate'. Apparently, Farha faked her death and her son was dispatched to ask Abu'l-Fadl for a miracle to bring her back to life. As he refused or could not perform the miracle, Abu'l-Fadl was exposed as a conman and Abu Tahir was ordered to kill him. However, Abu Tahir refused, fearing that Abu'l-Fadl would use his powers to transform him into something else. In the end, it was Saʿid, Abu Tahir's brother, who killed the 'god incarnate'. Once the people were satisfied that Abu'l-Fadl was really dead, Zaynab is reported to have cut his body open, ripped out his liver and ate it.[19] The whole episode resulted in a massive embarassment for the Qarmatian leadership.

The overall scarcity of sources providing historical information on the inner workings of the various strands of the early, pre-Fatimid *daʿwa* prevents us from forming a more comprehensive picture of specific active roles that *dāʿīs*, let alone women, might have played. As shown above, most of the data on women available for this period are derived from later sources and refer primarily to the activities of the Qarmatians, thus giving the impression that Qarmatian women, more than others, were active participants within their group. However, their portrayal, coming as it did from hostile sources, was overall a negative one. Al-Tabari reports that Qarmatian women took part in raids against Makkan pilgrim caravans. After the attacks, accompanied by their children, they would deceptively offer water to the moribund pilgrims, only to finish them off if they showed any sign of life.[20]

These and other accounts fuelled the imagination of medieval anti-Isma'ili writers, who conjured up images of furious orgies, wife-swapping, incest and illicit births taking place among the Qarmatians. Suffice here to report the accusation that the Qarmatians of Bahrayn celebrated a night called *imāmiyya*, during which men exchanged wives and the children conceived as a result were called 'the brethren's children'.[21] In fact, contrary to this perceived licenciousness, the text of the Qarmatian oath of allegiance points to moral rectitude in marital affairs by including an injunction to the adept to remain with his spouse till death, thus discouraging the practice of divorce.[22] In keeping with the stereotypical portrayal of antinomian movements, hostile writers often accused Isma'ili activists of breaking away from the prescriptions of Islamic law. The fourteenth-century Yemeni Shafi'i jurist and historian al-Janadi colourfully reports that when al-Mahdi's former associate Ibn al-Fadl entered San'a' in 299/911, he blocked all the rain-flow channels and flooded the main mosque. He then ordered the captured women to be taken there 'unveiled and naked'. Looking down from the minaret, he chose the ones he liked and dishonoured them. According to al-Janadi, Ibn al-Fadl also captured a huge number of women in Zabid and eventually ordered his troops to kill them, fearing that the women would entice the soldiers and divert them from fighting their war. Al-Janadi sums Ibn al-Fadl up by saying that he legalised things prohibited and describes scenes of an orgy where, in the dark, men could take any woman, older or younger, irrespective of the Qur'anic prohibitions. Sardonically, al-Janadi hints that not all women resented the ordeal, and he refers to an old woman who would not let go of her younger man after their encounter![23] Once again, the inclusion of references to women's honour and sex functions as a narrative device to pass judgement on a male protagonist by enhancing his wickedness.

3. Women and the *Da'wa* in the Fatimid Period: The North African Phase

a. Dishing Out for the Propaganda

The jurist al-Qadi al-Nu'man states that his *Iftitāḥ al-da'wa* (*The Beginning of the Mission*) would be a much longer work had he included accounts on all the women who contributed to the *da'wa* at the time of Abu 'Abd Allah al-Shi'i. Instead, he only names one: Umm Musa, the daughter of al-Hulwani, whom he describes as one of the first missionaries in North Africa. According to the jurist, Umm Musa married Yahya b. Yusuf, known as Ibn al-Asamm al-Ajjani, a companion of al-Hulwani who had died long before Abu 'Abd Allah al-Shi'i's arrival in that region. As he was much older than her, Yahya groomed his young wife and taught her Shi'ism and its doctrine of spiritual and secular authority (*wilāya*). Upon his death, she inherited his property; his brother, Yasin b. Yusuf, also took care of her. Umm Musa lived until the time of Abu 'Abd Allah's arrival and responded to his *da'wa* by sponsoring militant activities and by preparing food for the activists and the sickly until, al-Nu'man states, her hands, worn out by so much grinding and cooking, bled! In accordance with her late husband's will, she bequeathed her inheritance to further the *da'wa* in the name of the *mahdī*. Al-Qadi al-Nu'man adds that her case was not unique. Old Kutama women were also engaged at *da'wa* level and attended the *majālis* to listen to the 'wisdom lectures'. They looked after the believers, healed the sick and showed discernment in learning to such an extent that they even corrected well-known men on literary and political topics.[24]

While al-Qadi al-Nu'man is generous in detailing the women's role in the early *da'wa*, he nevertheless overlooks the fact that Umm Musa and the others could not possibly have been supporters of al-Mahdi's cause, as, at that time, al-Mahdi's cause did not yet exist. Elsewhere in his *Iftitāḥ*, al-Qadi al-Nu'man tells the story of the *dā'īs* Abu Sufyan and al-Hulwani being sent to North Africa by the Shi'i imam Ja'far al-Sadiq, with the intent, as Michael Brett rightly states, of projecting al-Mahdi's mission back in time as an illustration of the gift of foreknowledge of the imams.[25] However, if ever Ja'far al-Sadiq did send *dā'īs* to North Africa, they would have been de facto Imami Shi'is and so would have been al-Hulwani's daughter. Even allowing that she might have lived a long life, encroaching on the earliest phase of Abu 'Abd Allah al-Shi'i's propaganda in North Africa, she might have become at best a supporter of the *mahdī*-ship of Muhammad b. Isma'il. Indeed, this belief was at the core of Abu 'Abd Allah al-Shi'i's propaganda for at least the first ten years of his activity among the Kutama. Therefore, at such an early stage, the 'cause' that Umm Musa and the other old women joined might have been an 'Isma'ili' one but certainly not al-Mahdi's.

An increased number of references – incidental or otherwise – to the participation of women in this phase of the *da'wa* activities may be a by-product of the growing availability of early Isma'ili and non-Isma'ili sources covering this period of Fatimid history as a whole. The participation of women in the North African mission, however, may also be explained on account of the reputed behaviour associated with Berber women at the time, as being culturally accustomed to a wide degree of social and cultural interaction.[26] Indeed, rather than attempting to impose unpopular gender-exclusive mores, as leader of a marginal anti-establishment group, Abu 'Abd Allah al-Shi'i turned women's participation to the advantage of his mission.

b. Early Legislation and Doctrinal Instruction

Following his enthronement in Raqqada, al-Mahdi instructed the local jurists to give legal opinions on the basis of Shi'i principles rooted in the teachings of Ja'far al-Sadiq.[27] The gradual reform of the mainly Maliki judicial system in Ifriqiya signalled a major shift in the purpose of the *da'wa*, from being essentially an ideological and revolutionary agency to one also responsible for the implementation and adminstration of Shi'i-inspired laws. Beside the domain of ritual, these new laws addressed family law, thus affecting – at least in theory – the legal status of women. For example, in keeping with Ja'farite inheritance law, women found themselves being granted extended inheritance rights on the basis of the legal precedent of Fatima's claim to the Fadak orchard.

In terms of *da'wa* techniques, the *dā'īs* continued to pursue the method of approaching women as merchants. The fourteenth-century historian Ibn 'Idhari tells us of Muhibb b. Sulayman al-Miknasi, one of al-Mahdi's propagandists, who followed to the letter his leader's instructions on how to carry out effectively the missionary task. The merchant-cum-propagandist's strategy consisted first of finding a convenient location, and then visiting a neighbour's wife ostensibly to sell goods in her husband's presence, but in reality to test the ground. Ibn 'Idhari adds that these missionary tactics were not appreciated by the locals and that some missionaries were killed, much to the dismay of their colleagues.[28] However, political motivations might have been a more likely cause of attacks against *dā'īs*.[29]

For the pre-Fatimid period, we can infer that women's involvement in *da'wa* activities was casual and mainly passive; for the North African period, their involvement was no longer casual, as the *dā'īs* formally addressed female audiences as part of their propaganda. Women, like men, being part of a society that was informed by new doctrines, needed to be instructed on how to conduct their lives, spiritually and ethically, according to the directives introduced by al-Mahdi. Women came to be seen not only as worthy of tailor-made doctrinal and legal instruction but also as individuals both legally accountable and accounted for.

One of the ways in which instruction to women is reported to have been delivered during this phase is reflected in the teaching method devised by the tenth-century Kutama *dāʿī* Aflah b. Harun al-Malusi (d. 310/922).[30] In his lectures he would address women by consistently referring to feminine articles like items of jewellery, ornaments and clothing. He would cite examples pertaining to spinning, weaving, costume, hair and so on, 'to suit their natural disposition'.[31] By the same account, he would also address craftsmen and shepherds using terms they could relate to. Simplistic and informed by stereotypes as it may seem, this method points, nevertheless, to a pedagogic awareness of female psychology. Praised in later Ismaʿili sources, al-Malusi, though placed in an identifiable historical context, impersonates the ideal *dāʿī*, whose preaching methods remain unsurpassed in gaining and instructing converts from all walks of life, *even women*! In his gender-inclusive approach, al-Malusi followed in the footsteps of his predecessor, Abu ʿAbd Allah al-Shiʿi, who was reputed to have preached to both the women and the Bani Saktan, who were to be the first North African converts to Ismaʿilism. Emblematic within the context of the impact the early Ismaʿili propaganda had upon women, is Idris ʿImad al-Din's anecdotal portrayal of the wise wife loyal to the Fatimids, whose intelligence is praised by the imam-caliph al-Mansur because, despite her ignorance, she succeeds in bringing her renegade husband back to the Fatimid cause.[32]

4. Women and the *Daʿwa* in the Fatimid Period: The Egyptian Phase

a. Women and the 'Shiʿitisation' of Egypt

At the time of the Fatimid take-over at the expense of the pro-ʿAbbasid Ikhshidids, the population of Egypt was predominantly Sunni and remained so till the end of the Fatimid rule, in spite of the fact that the Fatimids sought to imprint an Ismaʿili character to every aspect of public life, typically through the implementation of the law. For example, as early as 359/970 the general Jawhar ordered the Maliki *qāḍī* of the former Ikhshidid capital Fustat, Abu Tahir, to apply Fatimid law in cases of divorce and inheritance, an injunction which was further enforced following the arrival of al-Muʿizz in Egypt three years later.[33]

The successful advent of the Fatimids in Egypt was mainly due to the fact that they presented themselves as a dynasty able to bring stability and prosperity to a part of the world that had been witnessing hardship. The following anecdote reported by the famous fifteenth-century Mamluk Egyptian historian al-Maqrizi well illustrates how the Fatimids assessed the situation in Egypt prior to their conquest and how they depicted the decline of the Ikhshidid dynasty for their propaganda aims. A Maghribi *dāʿī*, sent to Egypt with the pretext of selling a female slave on behalf of al-Muʿizz's consort, reported that the slave was bought by a princess, the daughter of the founder of the Ikhshidid dynasty, Muhammad b. Tughj (d. 334/946), and that the princess in person had gone to the market to buy her. On hearing this, al-Mu'izz thus addressed the Kutama chiefs: 'O brothers, hurry up to march against Egypt: there is no obstacle there. When people arrive at the point of feebleness that a woman from the prince's family goes out by herself to buy a slave for her personal use, that indicates how slack her men are in terms of honour and how they lack jealousy.'[34] By measuring male honour by the meter of female dignity, al-Maqrizi colourfully reports, through al-Mu'izz's mouth, the view that no dynasty with honour left would subject a woman of high rank, such as a princess, to the humiliation of exposing herself by carrying out market transactions. Whether or not one can attribute any veracity to such anecdotes, al-Mu'izz's expansionistic vision towards Egypt proved correct, as the Fatimids' conquest of that region was rapid and went virtually unchallenged.

The *da'wa* activity played an important role in facilitating the Egyptians' response to the new dynasty. Shi'ism was not unknown in Egypt prior to the arrival of the Fatimids and, indeed, had a minority following. Burial records for the period between c. 295/907 to 395/1004 show a significant presence of Shi'i tombs in the Qarafa cemetery situated between Fustat and al-Qata'i', the urban centre around the Ibn Tulun mosque. This is not surprising, as a number of high-profile descendants of 'Ali had settled in Egypt since the eighth century and had gathered followers. In time, some of them acquired the status of 'saints', with devotees gathering at their shrines. Further Shi'i support might have been generated by Isma'ili propaganda activity dating to the time when al-Mahdi sojourned in Fustat while on his way to North Africa, considering that his *dā'īs* had been active in Egypt prior, during and after his arrival. Finally, to pave the way for the establishment of the new dynasty, covert Isma'ili propaganda in Egypt intensified during the ten years or so preceding the Fatimid take-over. In Egypt, like elsewhere, the *dā'īs* worked as merchants, and, as an eleventh-century Cordovan jurist observed, the Isma'ilis hid 'their true purpose under the pretext of legitimate activities such as commerce, or science, or itinerant Sufism'.[35] Because of the secretive and clandestine character of their mission, the *dā'īs* chose to canvass in semi-public, 'discreet' places such as cemeteries and to use the areas surrounding mausolea as convenient sites to spread their message[36] while, possibly, engaging in trade.

That cemeteries and mausolea were premier areas of gathering and religious ferment is signalled by the fact that already in 350/961 violent clashes erupted during the Shi'i festival of '*āshūrā*', between the Ikhshidids and pro-Shi'i activists near the tombs of two 'Alid saints, Umm Kulthum and Sayyida Nafisa.[37] Again, when on the '*āshūrā*' day of 363/973 Shi'i crowds completed the rituals of Muharram by visiting the tombs of these two 'saints', more clashes occurred as

Fatimid soldiers and Egyptian Shiʿis went from the above shrines to the markets to force merchants to close their shops.[38] In his extensive study of burial records in medieval Cairo, Gaston Wiet notes that many 'converts' to Shiʿism appeared to have been women. Women had indeed ample opportunities to familiarise themselves with the tenets of Shiʿism. The well-established devotion towards women of ʿAlid descent, and the fact that cemeteries were typical places for female gathering, all contributed to further successful propagandising among what was, supposedly, a predominantly female audience. Being already familiar with ʿAlid devotion, women would be more likely to respond to the ʿAlid claims of the Fatimids.

b. Getting the Message

Under al-Muʿizz and his successors, the programme of religious education for women – already initiated in North Africa by Abu ʿAbd Allah al-Shiʿi – was further developed and formalised. Doctrinal instruction for women might have been initially conceived to counteract the active female devotion directed towards the cult of saints in al-Qarafa or, more likely, to channel such devotion into the Ismaʿili doctrine. Since the early North African days of the dynasty a distinction was made between lectures intended for the general public and *majālis al-ḥikma* separately delivered to male and female Ismaʿili devotees (*awliyā'*, literally 'friends'). This implies that, on converting to Ismaʿilism, women, like men, underwent some formal initiation. Nowadays we find that the Da'udi Bohra branch of Ismaʿilism adopts separate oaths of allegiance for men and women.[39] In his study on Ismaʿili oaths of allegiance, Heinz Halm concludes that the close similarity between the text of the Bohra version for men and the extracts quoted by historians like al-Nuwayri and al-Maqrizi, points to continuity in the use of one version since Fatimid times.[40] This argument could in theory be extended to the extant Bohra text of the female oath of allegiance, notwithstanding the absence, to date, of comparable written evidence in medieval sources. An indication of the existence in the Fatimid period of an oath of allegiance especially devised for women is found in the *Rasā'il al-Ḥākim bi-Amr Allāh*. This is a collection of epistles belonging to the Druze literary tradition written by the eleventh-century Druze *dāʿī* Hamza b. ʿAli b. Ahmad, allegedly upon instruction by the imam-caliph al-Hakim. The oath (*mīthāq al-nisā'*) specifies the conditions for women's entry into the Druze community of believers: obedience, belief in *tawḥīd* (lit. unity and uniqueness of God) and restraint from immorality and pollution.[41]

During the reign of al-ʿAziz, grand-scale public lectures on Ismaʿili law were held in the capital's great mosques. Although this was at the initiative of the formidable Fatimid vizier Ibn Killis, it was the al-Nuʿman family who for generations were to retain the monopoly over the delivery of these sessions. According to the eleventh-century Persian *dāʿī* al-Mu'ayyad fi'l-Din al-Shirazi, the status of the al-Nuʿmans as chief *dāʿīs* was secured also thanks to the support of the Fatimid royal women. Al-Mu'ayyad had arrived in Cairo in 439/1047 with big ambitions, but only attained the post of chief *dāʿī* in 450/1058, due to the fact that the vizier of the time, al-Yazuri, had favoured the old Qasim b. al-Nuʿman. The vizier claimed to have been under pressure from 'the old women of the palace from the families of al-Hakim and al-ʿAziz, [who] considered al-Nuʿman as the founder of the *daʿwa* and therefore, in their view, his sons and descendants had the greatest legal claim to the post'.[42] Whether al-Yazuri had resorted here to a feeble excuse in response to a disappointed applicant to the post, or was indeed truly pressurised in his choice, the statement exposes a degree of complicity between the vizier and the harem or, at the very least, some influence that the harem might have exercised in determining the leadership of the *daʿwa* (see Chapter 4).

Under the imam-caliph al-Hakim, the *Dār al-ʿilm* (the Abode of Knowledge) was founded, serving as a meeting place for scholars, jurists and scientists. The smooth running of the educational sessions was, however, affected by al-Hakim's issuing of seemingly contradicting decrees, which at one time abolished and at other times reinstated the sessions. Nevertheless, by this time, *majālis* purposely designed for women were held on specific days at the palace of the imam for his female entourage, while those for ordinary women were delivered either at the chief *dāʿī*'s palace or at al-Azhar mosque.[43] The delivery of sessions for the instruction of women (as well as men) was indeed one of the duties that a *dāʿī* was required to commit himself to, when taking his oath of allegiance.[44] Even more significant in this context is the role played by women preachers in general. Around 415/1024, a woman called Umm al-Khayr al-Hijaziyya, famous for her probity and piety, was known to have acted as *wāʿiẓa* (preacher) for women at the ʿAmr b. al-ʿAs Mosque. Also known for her piety was Fatima bint al-Ashʿath.[45]

c. Female Participation in Religious Activities

At its core, the *daʿwa* teaching rested upon the doctrine of the imamate, according to which the imam was the fountainhead of the entirety of esoteric knowledge (*ta'wīl*), which had been handed down in full to him through generations of imams since the time of ʿAli b. Abi Talib. The exoteric expression of this inner knowledge was reflected in the *sharīʿa* rules and in rituals. Through instruction and gradual intellectual as well as spiritual progression, initiates could aspire to partake of such esoteric knowledge while remaining observant of the *sharīʿa*. Non-initiates were only expected to be commited to the outward, Shiʿi-inspired legal system in both *ʿibādāt* (religious obligations) and *muʿāmalāt* (social conduct). In fact, while the majority of people adjusted to Fatimid rule and adhered to its law, this very same majority did not turn to the Ismaʿili *madhhab* to make it their own faith. Nevertheless, through the implementation of the law, the Fatimids sought to remodel people's religious practices by adding an Ismaʿili/Shiʿi tinge to their rituals, by appealing to the authority of the early imams, blended with well-known prophetic traditions.

In his *Daʿāʾim al-Islām*, the most famous work on Fatimid law, al-Qadi al-Nuʿman lists a number of pronouncements, based on prophetic traditions and sayings by the imams, that regulated the behaviour of women in prayer, whether they were initiated or not. According to the *Daʿāʾim*, on the basis of Jaʿfarite tradition, a woman could utter the *adhān* (call to prayer) or pronounce the *iqāma* (second call to prayer) if she so wished: 'it is sufficient for her [to hear] the call for the *ʿaṣr* prayer; and if she has not heard it, it is enough for her to testify that there is no deity other than God and Muhammad is His Messenger'.[46] On the authority of ʿAli b. Abi Talib, however, she could not be coerced to do either. Although a woman was not allowed to lead men in prayer and should sit behind them, in the last row in mosques, she could lead other females by placing herself in the middle of the congregation.

As for the attire to adopt during the congregational prayer, Fatimid law sanctioned that free women, as well as pubescent girls, would have to cover their head and, according to ʿAli, the shoulders too. ʿAli b. Abi Talib 'enjoined women to pray in a head covering (*khimār*) and a shift (*dirʿ*), provided they are made of fairly coarse cloth. It is better, moreover, for them to wear a waist wrapping and a mantle too'.[47] Female slaves, however, should not dare to follow this practice – punishment by beating was legally allowed if they did – because a free woman should be distinguishable from a slave. Al-Qadi al-Nuʿman specifies that 'The Imam [Jaʿfar] disliked that the face be veiled during prayers unless there was a valid reason for it.'[48] By law a woman should always wear ornaments and jewels while praying. The more jewellery worn, the greater the merit; at the very least, she ought to wear a necklace or, according to ʿAli, a leather belt around the neck, so that men can be distinguished from women. If she did not possess any jewellery, she should instead perfume her fingers. In any event, women should always wear henna on their hands 'and never should [women] leave their palms like those of the men'.[49] As for etiquette during prayer, on the basis of a Jaʿfarite tradition, should a woman need something badly, she could attract attention by clapping her hands.[50]

Women's participation in religious activities was valued in more ways than one. Like men, those women who attended the *majālis* paid in cash, gold or silver, for the teaching they received. A record was kept of the names of these men and women, along with the amount of their donations. Those present at the sessions would then receive the imam's blessing (*baraka*) bestowed by the officiating *dāʿī*, who would wave or point over the head of each paying participant a piece of rolled-over parchment inscribed with the imam's signature.[51] One can assume that, for the sake of revenues and other purposes, the *dāʿīs* replicated, possibly on a smaller scale, such a ceremony throughout Egypt and in the domains of the Fatimid *dawla*.

d. The Feminine in the 'Language' of the Daʿwa

In addition to the delivery of various levels of instruction on the doctrinal principles on which the dynasty based its legitimacy, the *dāʿīs* held other responsibilities. In those areas where direct access to the imam was not possible, they were his spiritual, legal and political representatives. Some *dāʿīs* were scholars who, within a wide spectrum of genres, wrote extensive doctrinal and legal works, ostensibly under the imam's supervision and with his approval. Such literary activity led to the formulation of comprehensive systems of esoteric doctrines (*bāṭin*) complemented by an exoteric (*ẓāhir*) legal apparatus based on their premises.

As a way to convey the esoteric content of these doctrines, the 'language' of the *daʿwa* often resorted to the use of feminine symbolism and metaphors. In the *Kitāb al-Rusūm wa-'l-izdiwāj wa-'l-tartīb* (*The Book of Rules, Coupling and Arrangement*), attributed to the Qarmatian *dāʿī* ʿAbdan, the institution of marriage is exalted by allegorically comparing the relationship between wife and husband to the one between body and spirit, pupil and master, exoteric and esoteric knowledge.[52] In another early Ismaʿili work the function of the oath of allegiance is symbolically equated with that of the marriage contract as 'a key to religion ... which renders it either sacred or profane, like the difference between marriage and fornication'.[53] Bridal symbolism is used to great effect in the poetry of the prince Tamim b. Maʿadd, son of the imam-caliph al-Muʿizz, who compares the institution of the imamate to a young beautiful woman and a bride.[54]

References to various aspects of motherhood were used for didactic purposes. Breast-feeding is paralleled to the introduction of the initiate to wisdom: the disciple is like an infant who is initially breast-fed and only as he grows is given more nourishing food.[55] Infant development, that is, the suckling, the upbringing of the child and the development into adulthood, is compared to three stages of initiation. For a successful outcome of this process the disciple must be fed gradually like a mother would feed her child. Like a husband who, having impregnated his wife, no longer interferes in the development of the embryo, yet looks after the pregnant woman, the imam imparts knowledge to the *dāʿī* and continues to care for his well-being, without interfering with the ripening of his knowledge. In Yemeni Tayyibi Ismaʿili literature, symbolism attached to pregnancy, embryo development and birth-giving came to be used in conjunction with the Tayyibi elaboration of cosmological doctrines and, significantly, with the roles played by the *dāʿīs* in the provinces.[56]

Unlike during the North African phase of the dynasty, references, even if anecdotal, to women's missionary activism in the Egyptian period are conspicuous for their absence. This is a reflection of the fact that, once successfully established in Egypt, the Fatimids toned down 'door-to-door' canvassing and focused on power consolidation, territorial expansion and identity-shaping, hence the formal delivery of doctrinal and legal sessions. By contrast, in the provinces of the empire, proselytising and activism continued to be at the core of the *daʿwa* to ensure continued support for the Fatimid dynasty. For instance, in the Yemen, the *daʿwa* was given a new impetus to consolidate and extend to India the Ismaʿili religious message, as well as securing the commercial interests of the Fatimids in the region.

In the Yemen, it was a woman who was to embody this new-found impetus. Towards the end of the eleventh century, the Sulayhid queen Arwa (see Chapter 4) was formally entrusted with the management of the local *daʿwa*. In a *sijill* dated 481/1089, the imam-caliph al-Mustansir assigned to the queen the overseeing of the *daʿwa* affairs in India. In the document, al-Mustansir refers to a previous letter received from Arwa, in which she had informed him of the death of Marzuban, the *dāʿī* in India. Al-Mustansir regrets that one of Marzuban's sons, Ismaʿil, formerly a *dāʿī* in Oman, had left the *dāʿī*-ship to exclusively pursue his commercial interests and that, as a result, the community languished in his absence. Al-Mustansir enjoins Arwa to take care of the *daʿwa* affairs of the region, as well as to circulate embassies with messages of support in order to strengthen the spirit of the people and encourage the further spread of the *daʿwa*.[57] From the Yemen, Arwa obliged and the outcome of her activities in the service of the Fatimids eventually opened an entirely new chapter in the history of Ismaʿilism.

5. The Decline of the Dynasty: Late Eleventh Century to 567/1171

a. Feminine Disguise and Intelligence Work

In the aftermath of the Nizari–Mustaʿli split, *daʿwa* activities were by and large limited to militancy in both camps. The Nizaris were plotting to sabotage the Cairo establishment and, in response, the Mustaʿlians resorted to the circulation of anti-Nizari propaganda as well as the gathering of intelligence, in an attempt to curb and prevent what was, in their eyes, no less than Nizari 'terrorism'. As for the role that women played in this phase of the history of the *daʿwa*, it appears to have been limited and intentionally marginalised in Persia, where the Nizari *da'wa* organisation is reported to have pursued a male-only policy. According to the thirteenth-century Mongol historian 'Ata Malik Juvayni, from Alamut the *dā'ī* Hasan-i Sabbah dispatched his wife and two daughters to Girdkuh and wrote to his counterpart there, Ra'is Muzaffar: 'Since these women work the spindle on behalf of our propaganda, give them their needs as wages therefor.'[58] Juvayni adds that, from that time onwards, the officials in charge of areas under Nizari control would have no women with them while in office.

Instead, in the Musta'lian camp women played a significant role in the *da'wa* both as spies and as witnesses to genealogical claims. Among the Fatimids, the practice of choosing women to conduct intelligence work goes back at least to the time of the imam-caliph al-Hakim, when old women where instructed to spy on other women by visiting their houses and then reporting back to the caliph.[59] Al-Hakim's half-sister, Sitt al-Mulk, used to gather intelligence through her favourite female servant. Female espionage appears to have been used more systematically from 487/1094 onwards. During the fateful events that in 488/1095 led to the demise of Nizar, the vizier al-Afdal sent his mother to markets, mosques and cemeteries to solicit people's opinions about him and ascertain people's allegiances.[60] Cunningly, she would pose as the complaining mother of one of al-Afdal's soldiers so as to extract comments from her interlocutors. She would then denounce those who made negative remarks, thus sealing their fate at the command of al-Afdal. Such was the case of al-Far al-Sayrafi in Cairo, who was the father of a highly positioned prince in al-Afdal's entourage, whom she exposed as a Nizari partisan. The mosque of al-'Atfihi is the architectural testimony to her intelligence work. Al-Afdal's mother had approached incognito Wahata b. Sa'd al-'Atfihi and badmouthed al-Afdal to him. In response, Wahata reprimanded the woman for insulting no less than 'the Sultan of God on earth'. On hearing his mother's report, al-Afdal paid al-'Atfihi tribute by embellishing the oratory named after him.[61]

Ironically, al-Afdal himself was fooled by 'female' disguise. Keen on curbing any potential source of sedition and to limit the activites of the *da'wa*, al-Afdal had arrested Barakat (d. 513/1119), the leader of a group called al-Badi'iyya, and closed down the *Dār al-'ilm* where he and his followers held sessions. However, palace insiders secretly supported Barakat and his group, as proven by the report that, on escaping from prison, Barakat was smuggled, disguised as a slave-girl, into the palace where he continued to hold meetings with his followers. He used this camouflage until his death, when his accomplices among the eunuchs are reported to have told the *zimam al-quṣūr* (the palace head of personnel) that one of the old ladies of the palace had died.[62] Al-Afdal's purge of his opponents, however, failed and in 515/1121 he was assassinated by Nizari activists or, according to other sources, by order of al-Amir himself.

Al-Ma'mun al-Bata'ihi, who was al-Afdal's successor as the vizier of al-Amir, continued to develop and exploit the resorting to female espionage. On the occasion of the 518/1124 census of Egypt, he employed experienced and knowledgeable women to visit the houses of suspected Nizaris and gather information about their activities and opinions. According to al-Maqrizi, it was as a result of this intelligence work that al-Ma'mun outlawed Nizari activities altogether.[63] This measure, however, was to no avail, as both al-Amir and al-Ma'mun were to be assassinated by Nizari emissaries.

b. Female Testimony at the Service of the Da'wa

Musta'lian propaganda turned some elite court women into witnesses in the support of the legitimacy of al-Musta'li's appointment. It is reported that al-Mustansir's sister revealed that, on his deathbed, the imam whispered to her his appointment of Abu'l-Qasim Ahmad al-Musta'li as his successor, thus making her the repository of his intended designation. There is, however, reason to believe that she colluded with the vizier al-Afdal.[64] Al-Musta'li's mother too, al-Sayyida al-Malika, was witness to the controversy surrounding her son's accession. In the official correspondence to the Yemeni queen Arwa dated 489/1069, she asserted her son's claim to the succession by designation, as well as her version of events of al-Musta'li's handling of the dispute with Nizar. In the epistle she reminded Arwa of the high station she held in the *da'wa*, no doubt intending to strengthen al-Musta'li's case in a far-flung province.[65]

The Musta'lian author of *al-Hidāya al-Āmiriyya*, a twelfth-century anti-Nizari refutation, goes to extreme length to report the testimony of Nizar's sister. In the presence of witnesses, she is reported to have denounced her brother's claims to the imamate, to have condemned his attitude and cursed all those who supported him. The writer adds that, by offering such testimony, 'God desired to purify her from the pollution of disobedience before her death, and granted her the end of the faithful one'.[66] The subtext of this statement points first to the fact that, at some stage, the princess must have 'disobeyed', that is, she must have supported the imamate of Nizar. Second, the ominous reference to her 'purification' before her impending end makes us suspect that, with al-Musta'li in power – rather than Nizar, as she might have originally anticipated – she might have been under pressure to save herself and to produce her testimony as a last resort. The episode of this testimony is reported in greater detail by al-Maqrizi in his coverage of the events for the year 516/1122 and is linked to a possible court-led Nizari plot against al-Amir uncovered by his vizier al-Ma'mun al-Bata'ihi. The fact that al-Ma'mun 'prompted' this testimony almost 30 years after the Nizari–Musta'ili split had taken place, at a time of high political destabilisation in Egypt caused by Nizari activists, places the whole episode of the witness in the context of al-Ma'mun's propaganda to counteract the Nizaris. The testimony of Nizar's sister is reported as having been a carefully staged and relatively 'public' affair, witnessed by all the highest dignitaries, her children and her close relatives, and to have been given great publicity by being recorded on a *sijill* read at sermons across Egypt.[67]

It is somewhat problematic to assess the historical value of these accounts. Being mainly reported by partisan sources, which were written sometime later than the events they are referring to, they could have been constructed and projected back in time and placed in the mouths of women to validate one interpretation of past dynastic history. Even if accepted at face value as genuine statements made by women, the question still remains as to whether they reflect a sincere endorsment of genealogical claims or were obtained as a result of pressure. Beyond hermeneutical concerns, what is astonishing is that Musta'lian literature ultimately pinned the very legitimacy to rule of the Musta'lian dynasty on the testimonies of a number of old elite women.

The contribution of women to the Isma'ili *da'wa* in the early Fatimid period was initially confined to the practical working of the organisation. In time, however, women came to be seen as accountable and valued recipients of teachings, as a medium for their dissemination and as financial sponsors of the *da'wa*. With the decline of the Fatimid dynasty and the consequent debasing of the Cairo-endorsed Musta'li *da'wa*, the contribution of women is limited to that of a few elite court ladies who, willingly or otherwise, interfered in matters of dynastic legitimacy and palace power struggles.

The Musta'lian tradition continues to this day, with the Da'udi Bohras, who still exhibit a *da'wa* with a complex yet functional hierachical structure headed by a chief *dā'ī muṭlaq* (absolute *dā'ī*). By contrast, the Nizari tradition has simplified and changed its *da'wa* organisation to a substantial degree; no longer a proselitising agency, it has been focusing on care and education, for and within the Isma'ili community. In recent times, the value of women's participation in the Nizari *da'wa* was fully appraised and encouraged by the late Aga Khan III. His promotion of Muslim women's rights as a whole represents a cornerstone of his teachings and philanthropic activities. Today, under the guidance of H. H. Karim Aga Khan IV and the example set by prominent female members in his family, Isma'ili women follow in the footsteps of their forerunners. At various levels, worldwide, they are both representatives of their community and participants in its life, management and growth. Through active membership of institutions and welfare organisations, they contribute to the overall prosperity of their community by being engaged in academia, religious education, ritual, law, health, business, art and crafts.

Notes

1 al-Qāḍī al-Nuʿmān, *Kitāb al-Majālis wa-'l-musāyarāt*, ed. al-Faqī, Ḥ. et al., Tunis: al-Maṭbaʿa al-rasmiyya li-'l-jumhūriyya al-tūnisiyya, 1978, p. 322.

2 al-Qāḍī al-Nuʿmān, *al-Majālis*, p. 246, pp. 406–8, on a *dāʿī* from the east excusing himself with al-Muʿizz for the little amount he was able to collect; al-Muʿizz's response shows his awareness of corruption among some *dāʿīs*.

3 al-Nīsābūrī, Aḥmad, *Istitār al-imām wa-tafarruq al-duʿāt*, ed. and trans. Ivanow, W., *Ismaili Tradition Concerning the Rise of the Fatimids (Rise)*, London: OUP, 1942, p. 162.

4 al-Maqrīzī, Taqī al-Dīn, *Kitāb al-Muqaffā (tarājim maghribiyya wa-mashriqiyya min fatra al-ʿubaydiyya)*, ed. al-Yaʿlāwī, M., Beirut: Dār al-gharb al-islāmī, 1987 (abridged edn), p. 69.

5 Niẓām al-Mulk, Abū ʿAlī Ḥasan, *The Book of Government or Rules for Kings*, trans. Darke, H., London, Henley and Boston: Routledge & Kegan Paul, 1978, 2nd edn, p. 209.

6 al-Nīsābūrī, *Istitār*, p. 158.

7 al-Nīsābūrī, *Istitār*, pp. 158–9.

8 al-Nīsābūrī, Aḥmad, *al-Risāla al-Mūjiza al-kāfiya fī shurūṭ al-daʿwa al-hādiya*, facsimile edn in Klemm, V., *Die Mission des fāṭimidischen Agenten al-Mu'ayyad fī d-dīn in Šīrāz*, Frankfurt: P. Lang, 1989, p. 55–6; and Ivanow, W., 'The Organization of the Fatimid Propaganda', *JBBRAS*, NS, 15 (1939), pp. 34–5.

9 al-Qāḍī al-Nuʿmān, *Kitāb Iftitāḥ al-daʿwa*, ed. Dachraoui, F., Tunis: al-Sharika al-Tūnisiyya li-'l-tawzīʿ, 1975, p. 121 (Ar.)

10 al-Nīsābūrī, *Istitār*, p. 162 states that ʿAbd Allāh the Elder married in Salamiyya.

11 Idrīs ʿImād al-Dīn, *ʿUyūn al-akhbār wa-funūn al-athār*, ed. Ghālib, M., Beirut: Dār al-Andalus, 1975, vol. 5, p. 37.

12 Halm, H., *The Empire of the Mahdi. The Rise of the Fatimids*, trans. Bonner, M., Leiden: E. J. Brill, 1996, p. 38.

13 al-Yamānī, Muḥammad b. Muḥammad, *Sīrat al-ḥājib Jaʿfar*, ed. and trans. Ivanow, W., *Rise*, London: OUP, 1942, pp. 194–6.

14 al-Nuwayirī, Shihāb al-Dīn, *Nihāyat al-arab fī funūn al-adab*, ed. al-Ḥusaynī, M., Cairo: al-Maktaba al-ʿarabiyya, 1984, vol. 25, pp. 191, 233, 244.

15 al-Ṭabarī, Abū Jaʿfar, *The History of al-Ṭabarī (Ta'rīkh al-rusul wa-'l-muluk). Vol. 38: The Return of the Caliphate to Baghdad*, trans. Rosenthal, F., Albany: SUNY Press, 1985, p. 179.

16 al-Nīsābūrī, *Istitār*, pp. 172, 176–8.

17 Eventually the *quṭra* tax was renamed *hijra*, amounting to one *dīnār* per person, then subsequently renamed *bulgha*, equivalent to seven *dīnārs*. The payment in wool by women of a tax in the name of the imam is attested among the Nizārī Ismāʿīlīs of Persia as late as the fifteenth century; see Isfizarī, Mu'īn al-Dīn Muḥammad, *Rawḍat al-janna fī awṣāf madīnat Harāt*, ed. Sayyid Muḥammad Kāẓim Imām, Tehran: 1338 sh, vol. 1, p. 307.

18 al-Ṭabarī, Abū Jaʿfar, *The History of al-Ṭabarī, Vol. 37: The Abbasid Recovery*, trans. Fields, Ph.M., Albany: SUNY Press, 1987, pp. 171–2; and al-Ṭabarī, *History. Vol. 38*, p. 168.

19 See Halm, H., *Empire*, pp. 261–2.

20 al-Ṭabarī, *History, Vol. 38*, pp. 175–6.

21 See Ibn ʿIdhārī al-Marrākushī, Aḥmad, *Kitāb al-Bayān al-mughrib, Histoire de l'Afrique et de l'Espagne intitulée al-Bayano'l-Mogrib*, vol. 2, French trans. Fagnan, E., Algiers: Imprimerie Orientale P. Fontana, 1901, p. 421.

22 al-Nuwayirī, *Nihāyat*, p. 219.

23 al-Janadī, Bahā' al-Dīn, *Kitāb al-Sulūk fī ṭabaqāt al-ʿulamā' wa-'l-mulūk*, ed. and trans. Kay, H. C., in his *Yaman, its Early Medieval History*, London: E. Arnold, 1892, pp. 199–201, 203.

24 al-Qāḍī al-Nuʿmān, *Iftitāḥ*, pp. 131–2 (Ar.)

25 Brett, M., *The Rise of the Fatimids: the World of the Mediterranean & the Middle East in the Tenth Century* CE, Leiden: E. J. Brill, 2001, p. 88.

26 Idris, H. R., *La Berbérie orientale sous les Zīrīdes*, Paris: A. Maisonneuve, 1962, vol. 2, pp. 773–4; and Golovin, L., *Le Magrib central a l'époque des Zirides*, Paris: Arts et Metiers Graphiques, 1957, pp. 161, 179.

27 Ibn ʿIdhārī, *Bayān (Histoire)*, p. 221.

28 Ibn ʿIdhārī, *Bayān (Histoire)*, p. 263.

29 Ibn al-Haytham, Abū ʿAbd Allāh, *Kitāb al-Munāẓarāt*, trans. Madelung, W. and Walter, P. E. in *The Advent of the Fatimids: A Contemporary Shiʿi Witness*, London: I. B. Tauris, 2000, p. 64, n. 3. In 309/921, several missionaries were killed in the area under the control of al-Mahdī's Berber commander, Masala b. Ḥabūs al-Miknasī, whom scholars suspect of having been responsible, with his sister, for the killings.

30 Idrīs ʿImād al-Dīn, *ʿUyūn*, vol. 5, p. 137. For Aflāḥ's teaching methods, see also the passage by Ibn al-Haytham, *Munāẓarāt*, pp. 169–70.

31 Ibn al-Haytham, *Munāẓarāt*, p. 170.

32 On religious education, see Halm, H., *The Fatimids and their Traditions of Learning*, London: I. B. Tauris, 1997, pp. 24–5; on the anecdote, see Idrīs ʿImād al-Dīn, *ʿUyūn*, vol. 5, p. 305.

33 Lev, Y., 'The Fāṭimid Imposition of Ismāʿīlism on Egypt (358–386/969–996)', *ZDMG*, 138 (1988), 2, pp. 320–1.

34 al-Maqrīzī, Taqī al-Dīn, *Kitāb al-Mawāʿiẓ wa-'l-iʿtibār fī dhikr al-khiṭaṭ wa-'l-āthār*, Beirut: Dār al-ṣādir, n.d., offset of Būlāq 1324 edn, vol. 1, p. 353 (henceforth *Khiṭaṭ*).

35 Quoted in Remie Constable, O., 'Muslim merchants in Andalusi international trade' in Jayyusi, S. K. (ed.), *The Legacy of Muslim Spain*, Leiden: Brill, 1994, p. 764, based on Ibn Sahl, *Thalāth wathāʾiq*.

36 Bloom, J. M., 'The Mosque of the Qarāfa in Cairo', *Muqarnas*, vol. 4 (1987), pp. 13–16.

37 Sayyid, A. F., *La capitale de l'Égypte jusqu'à l'époque Fatimide*, Beirut/Stuttgart: F. Steiner, 1998, p. 109.

38 Ibn Muyassar, Tāj al-Dīn, *Akhbār Miṣr*, ed. Massé, H., as *Annales d'Égypte*, Cairo: IFAO, 1919, p. 45; Lane-Poole, S. A., *A History of Egypt in the Middle Ages*, London: Methuen, 1925, vol. 6, p. 115; and Lev, Y., 'The Fāṭimid Imposition', p. 318.

39 MS 140/881 *ʿAhd nāmah (Khuṭbat ʿahd al-nisāʾ* ff.17v–31r), in Cortese, D., *Ismaili and Other Arabic Manuscripts*, London: I. B. Tauris, 2000, p. 86.

40 Halm, H., 'The Ismaʿili Oath of Allegiance (*ʿahd*) and the "Sessions of Wisdom" (*Majālis al-ḥikma)* in Fatimid Times', in Daftary, F. (ed.), *Medieval Ismaʿili History and Thought*, Cambridge: CUP, 1996, p. 98.

41 Cf. ʿAbd al-Karīm Aḥmad, Nurīmān, *al-Marʾa fī Miṣr fī'l-ʿaṣr al-Fāṭimī*, Cairo: al-Hay'a al-miṣriyya al-ʿāmma li-'l-kitāb, 1993, pp. 13–14.

42 al-Mu'ayyad fī'l-Dīn al-Shīrāzī, *Sīrat al-Muʾayyad fī'l-Dīn dāʿī al-duʿāt*, ed. Kāmil Ḥusayn, M., Cairo: Dār al-kātib al-miṣrī, 1949, p. 91.

43 al-Maqrīzī, *Khiṭaṭ*, vol. 1, p. 391; on the *Majālis al-ḥikma* during al-Ḥākim's reign, see al-Musabbiḥī, Muḥammad b. ʿUbayd Allāh, *Nuṣūṣ min ḍāʿiʿa min akhbār Miṣr*, ed. Sayyid, A. F., Cairo: IFAO, n.d. [1981], p. 29.

44 al-Qalqashandī, Shihāb al-Dīn, *Subḥ al-aʿshā fī ṣināʿat al-inshāʾ*, ed. Ibrāhīm, Cairo: Dār al-Kutub al-Miṣriyya, 1331–8/1913–20, vol. 10, pp. 436–7.

45 See al-Maqrīzī, *Khiṭaṭ*, vol. 2, p. 450, under the heading '*masjid al-waẓīriyya*', for information on al-Ḥijāziyya in relation to a *ribāṭ* dedicated to her. See also ʿAbd al-Karīm Aḥmad, N., *al-Marʾa*, p. 86, n. 51.

46 al-Qāḍī al-Nuʿmān, *Daʿāʾim al-Islām fī dhikr al-ḥalāl*, trans. Fyzee, A. A. A., *The Pillars of Islam: Vol. 1, Acts of Devotion and Religious Observances*, revised and annotated by Poonawala, I. K.

H., New Delhi and Oxford: OUP, 2002 p. 184.

47 al-Qāḍī al-Nuʿmān, *Daʿāʾim*, trans. Fyzee, p. 221 and pp. 190, 193, 195.

48 al-Qāḍī al-Nuʿmān, *Daʿāʾim*, trans. Fyzee, pp. 218–19.

49 al-Qāḍī al-Nuʿmān, *Daʿāʾim*, trans. Fyzee, pp. 221–2.

50 al-Qāḍī al-Nuʿmān, *Daʿāʾim*, trans. Fyzee, p. 216.

51 For the *majālis* see, al-Maqrīzī, Taqī al-Dīn, *Ittiʿāẓ al-ḥunafāʾ bi-akhbār al-aʾimma al-fāṭimiyyīn al-khulafāʾ*, ed. al-Shayyāl, J. and Ḥilmī, M., Cairo: Lajnat iḥyāʾ al-turāth al-islāmī, 1973, vol. 3, p. 337; for the participants' contributions, see al-Maqrīzī, *Khiṭaṭ*, vol. 1, p. 391.

52 MS 1174 (ArI, ZA) in Cortese, D., *Arabic Ismaili Manuscripts, The Zāhid ʿAlī Collection in the Library of the Institute of Ismaili Studies*, London: I. B. Tauris, 2003, no. 65.

53 Jaʿfar b. Manṣūr al-Yaman, *Kitāb al-ʿĀlim wa-ʾl-ghulām*, ed. and trans. Morris, J. W., *The Master and the Disciple: An Early Islamic Spiritual Dialogue*, London: I. B. Tauris, 2001, p. 78.

54 Smoor, P., ' "The Master of the Century": Fāṭimid Poets in Cairo', in Vermeulen, U. and De Smet, D. (eds), *ESFAME*, Leuven: Peeters, 1995, pp. 153–5. In late Nizārī/Ginān literature, the relationship between the imam and the devotee finds in the image of the woman separated from her beloved its most common symbolic expression: the woman representing the pining human soul, while the beloved represents the imam as divine epiphany. Alternatively, the woman-soul is likened to a bride awaiting her marriage, thus sublimating the longing of the believer for the spiritual union with the imam/bridegroom. The Ismāʿīlī scholar Ali Asani observes here the importance of gender reversal, the 'feminisation' of the male believer, and suggests that gender itself is endowed with religious significance. Asani, A. S., 'Bridal Symbolism in Ismāʿīlī Mystical Literature of Indo-Pakistan', in Herrera, R. A. (ed.), *Mystics of the Book: Themes, Topics and Typologies*, New York: Peter Lang, 1993, pp. 389–404.

55 Reported by ʿAbd al-Jabbār b. Aḥmad, *Tathbīt dalāʾil nubuwwat Sayyid-nā Muḥammad*, ed. ʿUthmān, ʿA., Beirut: Dār al-ʿarabiyya, 1966, p. 595. According to al-Nīsābūrī, the infant should not be overfed.

56 Ibn al-Walīd, al-Ḥusayn b. ʿAlī, *Risālat al-Mabdaʾ wa-ʾl-maʿād*, ed. and French trans. Corbin, H., *Trilogie Ismaélienne*, Paris and Tehran: Paris University Press and Kayan, 1961, ch. 2, sections 28–30; 38–9 (pp. 111–12; 115 Ar.), where the earth and the rain are allegorically equalled to the uterus and the semen. For the use of such symbolism in relation to the work of the *dāʿī*, see ch. 2, section 36 (p. 114 Ar.).

57 Idrīs ʿImād al-Dīn, *ʿUyūn al-akhbār*, vol. 7, ed. and trans. Sayyid, A. F., *The Fatimids and their Successors in Yaman*, London: I. B. Tauris, 2002, pp. 69–70 (Eng.); 153–4 (Ar.).

58 Juvaynī, ʿAṭā Malik, *Taʾrīkh-i jahān-gushā*, trans. Boyle, J. A., *The History of the World-Conqueror*, Manchester: Manchester University Press, 1958, vol. 2, p. 680.

59 Juvaynī, *History*, vol. 2, p. 656; Lane-Poole, S. A., *A History of Egypt*, vol. 6, p. 121.

60 al-Maqrīzī, *Ittiʿāẓ* , vol. 3, pp. 15–16; and al-Maqrīzī, *Khiṭaṭ*, vol. 2, pp. 451–2.

61 Sayyid, A. F., *La capitale*, p. 472.

62 al-Maqrīzī, Taqī al-Dīn, *Kitāb al-Muqaffā al-kabīr*, ed. al-Yaʿlāwī, M., Beirut: Dār al-gharb al-islāmī, vol. 2, p. 571. According to Idrīs ʿImād al-Dīn, *ʿUyūn*, vol. 7, pp. 81–2 (Eng.), pp. 236–7 (Ar.), this Barakāt was a *dāʿī* and a protégé of al-Āmir, who was allegedly instrumental in his hiding at the palace unbeknown to al-Afḍal.

63 al-Maqrīzī, *Itti ʿāẓ*, vol. 3, p. 108.

64 al-Maqrīzī, *al-Muqaffā*, vol. 1, p. 666.

65 *al-Sijillāt al-Mustanṣiriyya*, ed., Mājid, ʿA., Cairo: Dār al-fikr al-ʿarabī, 1954, *sijills* 35 and 43 and Idrīs ʿImād al-Dīn, *ʿUyūn*, vol. 7, pp. 77 (Eng.), pp. 199 and ff (Ar.).

66 *al-Hidāya al-Āmiriyya fi abṭāl daʿwat al-Nizāriyya*, ed. Fyzee, A. A. A., London: OUP, 1938, p. 14 (Ar.).

67 al-Maqrīzī, *Ittiʿāẓ*, vol. 3, pp. 87–8.

CHAPTER

2

FAMILY TIES: WOMEN AND GENEALOGY IN FATIMID DYNASTIC HISTORY

'To our mothers we owe half of our lineage' (*li-ummati-nā niṣf ansābi-nā*). Thus the famous Fatimid court poet Ibn Hani' al-Andalusi (d. 362/973) sets to conclude an elegy for the death of the mother of one of his patrons. Obvious as it might seem, this statement is set within the context of acknowledging the virtues of mothers, who are to be praised in equal terms as the fathers.[1] This affectionate and respectful laude echoes the virtues and importance of the most noble of all mothers, Fatima, whom the poet repeteadly hails as the mother of the Fatimid imams.

Within the context of tenth-century Sunni–Shiʿi doctrinal debates, the Shiʿis argued for the superiority of Fatima over ʿA'isha, to be interpreted as mirroring the pre-eminence of ʿAli over Abu Bakr. When the tenth-century Ismaʿili *dāʿī* Ibn al-Haytham was asked why he supported ʿAli's imamate instead of Abu Bakr's leadership, considering that the latter had given his daughter ʿA'isha in marriage to Muhammad, the *dāʿī* replied by quoting the Qur'anic verse: 'He is the One who created humankind from water, then He has established for it relationships of lineage (*nasab*) and marriage tie (*ṣihr*)' (Qur. 25:54).

Ibn al-Haytham interpreted this verse as: 'A son-in-law's marriage tie with God's Apostle is better than being related through a wife of his ... Those who are tied to the Apostle of God by marriage with his daughter are his descendants, his offspring ...'.[2] The *dāʿī*'s argument in favour of the ʿAlid line of descent is therefore based on blood links because, as he clarifies further, relationship by marriage is discontinuous but relationship via members of the Prophet's household is continuous. In other words, blood links supersede all others. Who could then epitomise this close relationship better than Fatima, the Prophet's own daughter, 'a piece of my flesh',[3] as the Prophet called her?

Not only the Prophet's female descendants, but also his female ascendants were regarded as embodiments of purity to be passed on to their progeny. Purity of ascent is the prerequisite but also the sign of prophethood and of imamate. In a multi-layered passage by the same Ibn al-Haytham, purity of birth is traced back to Moses, as well as Jesus, down to Muhammad and ʿAli. The link between the last two is provided by the common grandmother, that is the mother of Muhammad's and ʿAli's respective fathers. The whole passage is an exaltation of ʿAli, his closeness to Muhammad, and his right to the imamate. The meanings of the terms indicating the special relationship between Muhammad and ʿAli, that is, 'brotherhood', 'friendship', 'closeness', are fused together when Muhammad and ʿAli are called 'brothers' (*shaqīqāni*) on account of sharing the same grandmother. Once the legitimacy of ʿAli as the rightful successor to Muhammad is established, Fatima's direct blood link to the Prophet is invoked to further legitimise the rights of hers and ʿAli's offspring against those who upheld the claims of a son born to ʿAli from another woman, al-Hanafiyya.[4]

The Ismaʿili argument in favour of the ʿAlid line of descent was therefore based on blood ties traced back to the 'holy family' of the Prophet through his grandmother and his daughter Fatima. This argument places paramount emphasis on the idea that the 'nobility' of the mother was a condition in establishing a legitimate line of descent. We can note such emphasis in those Ismaʿili narratives glorifying the ʿAlid antecedents of Ismaʿili sacred history and in those instances where the issue of a mother's pedigree was raised for anti-ʿAbbasid propaganda purposes. Rulers born of slave mothers would be depicted as being of inferior status when compared to those of 'noble' descent, in spite of the fact that, according to the *sharīʿa*, the child born of a slave was free. Ibn Hani' al-Andalusi does not refrain from scorning Nutayla, the mother of the founder of the ʿAbbasid dynasty, as having been a slave. The poet sets out to show how unequal the comparison would be between the humble Nutayla and the 'radiant' (*al-zahrā'*) Fatima. He asks the rhetorical question: 'Which legacy has God bestowed upon Nutayla and her descendants? How could a slave be on the same level as a free person?'[5]

By contrast, when it comes to the few accounts aiming at reconstructing the more immediate ancestry of the Fatimid dynasty, it will be shown that the family pedigree of the imam-caliphs' mothers plays no role in arguments aiming at authenticating their lineage. Although in the Arab world it was an established practice for a man to marry the daughter of his paternal uncle, male members of the ruling elites often by-passed this custom and chose wives and concubines with as diverse a background as one can possibly imagine. We will see that a number of Ismaʿili sources retrospectively identify the wives of some early Fatimid imam-caliphs as daughters of their paternal uncles. Although one cannot exclude that this might have been the case, one must nevertheless allow for the fact that writers might have resorted to an educated guess in the face of lack of detail about the identities of these women.

The liberal use in the sources of terms aimed at describing the relationship between the Fatimid imam-caliphs and their female consorts raises problems when one seeks to establish the exact nature of such a relationship. An accurate interpretation of terminology is hindered by the fact that, for example, authors were conditioned in their choice and understanding of terms by their ideological positioning, their geographical provenance, the historical context in which they lived and the extent of their access to the original Fatimid sources.

For instance, when sources refer to a Fatimid royal female consort as a 'wife' (*zawja*), this would not necessarily imply that a formally contracted marriage had occurred, or that the marriage was legally valid.[6] Also problematic is the relatively extensive use of words denoting a concubine, whether slave or free. The most commonly used terms are *jāriya* and *ḥaẓīya,* the latter typically indicating a free concubine or a favourite companion. Other words include the noun *sarā'ir* or *sarārī*, possibily pointing to rank among the harem concubines. Frequently used is the term *jiha* (lit. side), liberally applied to the wives and concubines of the imam-caliph, of his children and, in time, of high dignitaries (see Chapter 3).

Often also blurred is information relating to the status of the Fatimid royal women as free or slaves, as well as the circumstances that determined the transition from bondage to freedom. As for the royal concubine, one life-changing event would be to give birth to a child fathered by the imam-caliph, which would raise her status to that of *umm al-walad* (lit. the child's mother). If the woman was a slave, the event could even secure her manumission. The birth of sons in particular changed the status of a woman from that of one among many royal consorts to that of mother with dynastic investment. *Umm al-walad* is the common term used by the sources to refer to a concubine, whether free or slave, who would acquire rights upon giving birth to her master's child. Legally, the child born of a slave was free and the mother could not be sold or sent away from the household. Moreover, at her master's death, she would become a free woman.[7] Even though the Qur'an could be interpreted as allowing concubinage with a man's own slave, it does not define the position of the *umm al-walad.* According to a tradition attributed to 'Ali, if the master wished, he could set free his *umm al-walad* and consider her manumission as her bridal gift.

Many Fatimid imam-caliphs were indeed sons of *umm al-walads*; however, it is hard to establish the way in which the imam-caliphs complied to the laws regulating the relationship between a slave *umm al-walad* and her master. One example among many is that of Rasad, the imam-caliph al-Mustansir's mother. She was a slave who had been bought by the imam-caliph al-Zahir and became *umm al-walad* by her royal master. Despite the extensive coverage of the influence that Rasad was to exercise at court, it is still unknown whether or not she was manumitted during al-Zahir's lifetime.

The practice of choosing future rulers among children born of concubines was by no means exclusive to the Fatimid imam-caliphs. Other dynasties also followed this practice, alongside investiture of children born from legally sanctioned marriages.[8] However, it took five more centuries before a Muslim dynasty – the Ottomans – overwhelmingly endorsed royal reproduction and descent through concubinage at the expense of descendants from legal marriages.[9]

1. Female Figures in Isma'ili Pre-Fatimid Genealogical History

The Shi'i belief in the continuity of a physical and spiritual lineage of the imamate from 'Ali's time onwards places the issue of genealogy at the core of all Shi'i claims to spiritual and secular legitimacy. As a dynasty, the Fatimids 'never made a public proclamation and official announcement of the genealogy which they claimed, and which was so much disputed'.[10] Therefore, what we know about their ancestry comes from either polemists or supporters of the dynasty who endeavoured to reconstruct, a posteriori, a genealogy of the Fatimids either to refute or validate their legitimacy.

In the writings of the early Fatimid period, the occurrence of details that would enlighten us as to the genealogy of the dynasty was somewhat incidental. It is in post-Fatimid Tayyibi literature that we see a concerted effort to reconstruct the line of Fatimid ancestry by collating information from those earlier Fatimid works. In order to validate the legitimacy of the religious leadership they supported, Tayyibi writers first identified the lineage linking the Fatimid dynasty to 'Ali and Fatima through Isma'il b. Ja'far, and then established a genealogical link with those activists whom they perceived to be the 'founders' of the dynasty of imam-caliphs. The final outcome of such a genealogical reconstruction was to evidence the uninterrupted sequence from the Fatimid caliphs to their eponym, al-Tayyib.

The continuity of a spiritual lineage could be, and indeed was, argued on the basis of elaborate theological and cosmological theories. These served as explanatory devices to the doctrine of *naṣṣ*, or formal appointment, by an imam, of his successor. It is still unclear when *naṣṣ* developed from being a theoretical principle to being used as a decisive factor in an actual succession. In practice, the right of primogeniture – or father–son succession – was generally applied. However, as shown by the instances of some first-born such as Tamim son of al-Mu'izz, Nizar son of al-Mustansir, and the successor of al-Amir, the right of primogeniture could be by passed, while at the same time explicit evidence is lacking of *naṣṣ* favouring those who succeeded in their stead as imam-caliphs. As for the continuity of physical descent, Fatimid and post-Fatimid writers found it a much more problematic and potentially divisive issue to evidence. The physical descent of the imam-caliphs needed to be fully supported by a 'neat' sequence in the male line, as well as through the identification of the imams' biological mothers.

The identity of the mothers of the early imams is shrouded in myth. Among the most comprehensive genealogical narrative reconstructions naming mothers and wives of the early imams down to Fatimid times are those contained in the works of the Tayyibi *dāʿīs* Hatim b. Ibrahim al-Hamidi (d. 596/1199) and Idris ʿImad al-Din (d. 872/1468). In al-Hamidi's account, the Fatimid genealogy is disclosed in the form of a prediction ascribed to the Prophet Muhammad, through the witness of ʿAli b. Abi Talib. Thus begins the narrative of the imams' lineage: 'O, Abu'l-Hasan [ʿAli b. Abi Talib], when the daughter of the Kisra (i.e. the Persian king) Hurmuz shall be taken prisoner ... verily this girl shall become the mother of the Imams from my progeny.'[11] Hence, the royal princess at the centre of this story comes to embody both the glorious Muslim victory against the Persians and, by 'marrying' ʿAli's son al-Husayn, the contribution of her royal blood to the 'holy' line of imams descending from the Prophet himself through ʿAli. According to the same prediction, al-Husayn's son, Zayn al-ʿAbidin, would marry Umm Salim (lit. 'the mother of Salim'), daughter of Khalid, who would give him four sons.[12] One of them would become the fourth imam, Muhammad al-Baqir, who would marry Umm Jaʿfar. The fifth imam, Jaʿfar al-Sadiq, would marry Salma (or Fatima, according to other Ismaʿili and Shiʿi sources) and also have concubines. In turn Jaʿfar's son Ismaʿil, the sixth imam, would wed the daughter of his paternal uncle. With reference to Jaʿfar al-Sadiq, the early Ismaʿili author and *dāʿī* Jaʿfar b. Mansur al-Yaman states that he followed the example set by the Prophet Muhammad and ʿAli, in that he remained monogamous during the lifetime of his wife, the mother of his successor Ismaʿil.[13]

When dealing with the three imams of the phase of occultation (*satr*), al-Hamidi's narrative becomes blurred. Some information on female figures associated with the imams of this phase comes instead from the much later Idris ʿImad al-Din. He informs us that Muhammad b. Ismaʿil hid in Nishapur and married a woman from that town, by whom he had a son called ʿAbd Allah, surnamed al-Radi (in fact ʿAbd Allah the Elder).[14] In his *ʿUyūn al-akhbār*, Idris narrates: 'Then the imamate went to imam al-Radi ʿAbd Allah b. Muhammad b. Ismaʿil ... He returned to Nihavand, where he married (*tazawwaja*) the daughter of Hamdan, son of *ʿamm* [uncle?] Mansur b. Jawsh, who was from the Karzun family. She gave the imam [al-Radi] a son, ʿAli b. ʿAbd Allah ... and a daughter Fatima'. When 'Abd Allah the Elder went into hiding in a village called Ashnash (read Chalus) in Daylam, he married there an 'Alid woman who gave him a son, Ahmad, who was to become his successor.[15] Of this Ahmad, all that is said is that he married and had a son and successor, al-Husayn. This would be the same person as al-Husayn b. al-Shala'la', the alleged father (or stepfather) of the first Fatimid imam-caliph, al-Mahdi.

While the reference to the mothers of the early imams constituted a necessary narrative corollary within myths on the origins of the Fatimids, Isma'ili historiography tells us nothing about these women's identities other than their mere agnomen (*kunya*, that is 'the mother of ...'). When indicating that the woman in question was for example an 'Alid, as in the case of Ahmad's mother, the intention of the writer was not so much to establish the woman's religious affiliation per se, but rather to further reinforce the 'Alid lineage of the imam's family. All in all, these nameless women exist solely in these reports for the purpose of establishing the line of descent.

In the uncertainty surrounding the identity and ancestry of al-Mahdi, a variety of narratives are offered by both Isma'ili and non-Isma'ili sources about his mother and his wives. According to some, al-Mahdi's real name was Sa'id b. al-Husayn. The lack of an openly announced official genealogy, on the part of the early imam-caliphs, prompted medieval polemists to produce a number of genealogies, ranging from plausible to totally far-fetched.[16] One of the most popular and enduring anti-Fatimid genealogical accounts is the one that links al-Mahdi directly to a certain Maymun al-Qaddah by tracing the ancestry of his alleged father, al-Husayn, back to this figure often portrayed in hostile terms. To add more colour, the theory of a Qaddahid ancestry came, in some instances, to be infused with the myth of al-Mahdi's Jewish origins.[17]

All that most Isma'ili sources state about al-Mahdi's mother is that she had married al-Husayn b. al-Shala'la', the third of the hidden imams according to Isma'ili tradition. In one Isma'ili source, however, the so-called *Dustūr al-Munajjimīn*, it is stated that al-Mahdi's mother was a Maghribi midwife (*min muwallidāt al-Maghrib*) referred to as Wasan or Wisan (?), and that al-Mahdi had two sister-german called Rashida and Zubayda.[18] This is to date the only known reference to the name, the provenance and the profession of al-Mahdi's mother, as well as to the existence of two sisters of his.

The overall lack of information on al-Mahdi's mother in all other Isma'ili sources is surprising, considering the paramount importance of al-Mahdi as the first Fatimid imam, especially when contrasted with the mention, even if just by title, of the mothers of his own alleged ancestors. From an Isma'ili perspective, this reticence could be explained on the basis that, al-Mahdi's father being an imam of the occultation period, his circumstances were not known and, even if they were, they could not be revealed.

From an anti-Isma'ili stance, the silence around al-Mahdi's mother paved the way to the formulation of diverse stories about her Jewish identity, to further undermine al-Mahdi's 'Alid claims. She is variously described as being either the widow of a Jew called al-Haddad or as being his Jewish widow. A penniless great beauty, she is reported to have had a son by al-Haddad named Sa'id (al-Mahdi), who resembled her in looks. The sources state that her second husband, al-Husayn, totally doted on his stepson al-Mahdi and that, as al-Husayn had no children of his own, 'the sages of the *da'wa*' gave their allegiance to this stepson instead. Thus it is also explained why al-Mahdi came to be known as the 'orphan'.[19]

Up until al-Mahdi, references to female figures were set within 'the myth of the origins' of the Fatimids. But with al-Mahdi's arrival in North Africa and the ensuing establishment of the dynasty, a new era was dawning, and with it the need for more information on the 'women of the imam-caliphs'.

2. Women in the Fatimid Dynasty

a. The North African Phase

Isma'ili sources agree that al-Mahdi, in line with Muslim tradition, married a cousin, who was to become the mother of his successor, al-Qa'im. The marriage is described by Ja'far, al-Mahdi's chamberlain, in his biography. She is identified as the daughter of al-Mahdi's paternal uncle Abu 'l-Shala'la' (d. c. 286/899), a proto-Isma'ili activist also known as Abu 'Ali al-Hakim or Muhammad al-Sa'id b. Ahmad, who, having lost his male offspring, designated his nephew al-Mahdi as his successor. While Isma'ili sources provide accounts on the caring role of al-Qa'im's wetnurse, Umm 'Ali al-Qahramana, they make no reference to al-Mahdi's wife and mother of his heir. There is no mention of her even in the accounts describing the adventurous transfer of al-Mahdi's 'harem' from Syria to North Africa. This conspicuous lack of information on a woman who was, from a Fatimid perspective, no less than the mother of a progeny of imam-caliphs, could indicate that she might have died when al-Qa'im was still an infant. A more plausible interpretation of her absence from the narratives is that, like the pre-dynastic female figures mentioned above, the statement on her very existence served purely dynastic purposes. Introduced as al-Mahdi's paternal first cousin, she represented on the one hand a further link to consolidate his ancestry within a 'holy family', and on the other a means by which Isma'ili historiography could establish the line of descent.

If al-Mahdi's wife remains nameless, other women in his life are mentioned in slightly greater detail, thus contributing to a fuller picture of the Fatimid family tree. Al-Mahdi is reported to have had eight daughters: Amina, Zabib,

Fatima, Umm al-Hasan, Umm al-Husayn, Sakina, Umm ʿAli and Rashida. The last four died in North Africa while the remaining four died in Egypt.[20] According to the Ayyubid historian Ibn Zafir, instead, beside the sons, al-Mahdi had seven daughters and, of his concubines, six were *umm al-walad*.[21]

Al-Qa'im, the second Fatimid imam-caliph, married one Umm Habib, who, according to Ismaʿili sources, was a Byzantine/Greek slave who had belonged to his father. However, another source names as Karima the slave-mother of the succeeding imam-caliph, al-Mansur.[22] Altogether, al-Qa'im appears to have had at least seven concubines and four daughters: Umm ʿIsa, Umm ʿAbd Allah, Umm al-Husayn and Umm Sulayman. They all died in Egypt.[23]

From among al-Qa'im's sons, it was al-Mansur who, after a power struggle with his brothers, emerged as the third Fatimid imam-caliph. Beside his mother's name, we also know that he had a wetnurse called Salaf, who had great influence over him. Both women played a role in securing al-Mansur's accession to the throne.[24] The female involvement in al-Mansur's dynastic accession is echoed in a story narrated by al-Qadi al-Nuʿman in his *Kitāb al-Majālis wa-'l-musāyarāt*. In wishing to highlight the gift of foreknowledge of the imams, al-Nuʿman reports that one of al-Mahdi's concubines told him of a dream she had about holding the moon on her lap and breast-feeding it. On hearing this, al-Mahdi took the dream to be a presage on the genealogical sequence of the dynasty and placed the newly born al-Mansur on her lap, thus implying his destined role as imam-caliph.[25] With this narrative al-Qadi al-Nuʿman retrospectively validated the legitimacy of al-Mansur's imamate and, consequently, al-Muʿizz's equally disputed succession. The mother of al-Mansur's son and future imam-caliph, al-Muʿizz, was one of his three *umm al-walads*. Al-Maqrizi identifies her as *umm al-umarā'* (lit. mother of the princes) and places her date of death in 364/974, one year before that of her son.[26] A much later Ismaʿili source, which names al-Muʿizz's mother as Durrzadeh, narrates of her influence upon her son who, supposedly, postponed the conquest of Egypt to respect his mother's wish to spare the life of Kafur, the last effective ruler of Egypt prior to the advent of the Fatimids.[27] Besides one of his *umm al-walads*, a concubine called Qadib and his wetnurse, other identifiable women in al-Mansur's family entourage were his daughters. He had at least five: Habah, Arwa and Asma', who died in Egypt during al-Muʿizz's reign, Umm Salama, who died during al-ʿAziz's reign, and Mansura (or Sammura), who died in North Africa.[28]

The above details show that, with the establishment of the dynasty in North Africa, there is a shift in the amount and nature of information about the women of the dynasty. First of all, references to royal women can be found in both Ismaʿili and non-Ismaʿili sources, thus indicating a different relevance of details for different authors and audiences. Second, with a line of imam-caliphs becoming manifest and embodying political as well as spiritual authority, new agendas were set for those who chronicled Fatimid history. Isma'ili authors developed an interest in documenting the formative early history of the dynasty and responded to a dynastic need for biographical documentation, which was provided in retrospect and was inclusive of information on both male and female members of the dynasty.

The fact that the names of several of these women came to be chronicled by non-Isma'ili historians such as al-Maqrizi, who had access to and relied extensively on well-informed Fatimid insider sources, shows the incidence of information available about the Fatimid royal women. One of the reasons why non-Isma'ili historical sources would include the mention of women was not to prove dynastic or genealogical arguments, but to complement their narratives with data that would demonstrate their eye for detail in reporting historical events. Women would typically be placed in the historical context of their times, the indication of their date of death situating them in relation to particular historical events and a specific geographical context. What is relevant here is not only the interest of a particular author, but also his response to the expectations of a wider audience, which had evidently developed a taste for biographical details interspersed with factual accounts.

b. The Egyptian Phase

Like his father, the fourth Fatimid imam-caliph al-Mu'izz had to fight for his seat, probably with the help of his mother. New evidence on internal dissent at this particular time emerges from a statement in the anonymous work *Muqābalat al-adwār wa-mukāshafat al-asrār*, where reference is made to a hidden son of al-Mansur and the beginning of a period of concealment after him.[29] Be that as it may, with al-Mu'izz, we have at last a growing amount of data pointing not only to the identity but also to the activities of the women in the royal household. According to the already mentioned prediction reported by al-Hamidi, al-Mu'izz would marry the daughter of his paternal uncle and she would give him two sons, one of whom, al-'Aziz, was to become the fifth Fatimid imam-caliph. Al-Mu'izz would also have sons by his concubines. Alternatively, the mother of al-'Aziz is described as an Arab slave named Durzan (d. 385/995), known as *taghrīd* (lit. twittering) because of her beautiful voice.[30] While there is no factual evidence to doubt or sustain the Arabian provenance of this woman, or indeed her talent, one should also remember that it was a common stereotype of the time to assume that all good singers came from Arabia. Rather than as a singer, Durzan's legacy is primarily that of having been a prominent architectural patroness (see Chapter 5).

The imam-caliph al-Mu'izz is credited with having been opposed to marital promiscuity. In an address to a group of Kutama dignitaries, he is reported to have said: 'O venerable elders, in your privacy do like me, do not show off haughtiness or pride ... do good and spread justice. Then, devote yourselves to your women, and stick to the one who is yours; do not be greedy by having a number of them and feeling lust for them ... One man should only consider one woman. We need your assistance, in body and mind ...'.[31] Beyond being a reflection of the adoption of an actual practice, this statement might have served both genealogical and propaganda purposes. On the one hand, it could echo a reference to 'Ali's monogamous marriage to Fatima; on the other, it could project an image of the probity of the Fatimid imam-caliph in contrast to the perceived licentiousness of other rival dynasties.

Al-'Aziz had become the legitimate successor of al-Mu'izz, following the death of his elder brother 'Abd Allah, probably born of another of al-Mu'izz's consorts. Apart from 'Abd Allah, Tamim and al-'Aziz, as well as several other sons, the imam-caliph al-Mu'izz had seven daughters.[32] Only three of them are sufficiently known: Sitt al-Malik (possibly a daughter of Durzan), Rashida and 'Abda. The last two were born in North Africa, died in 442/1050 in their nineties and gained fame for their fabulous wealth (see Chapter 5). As for al-'Aziz, it appears that he had at least two consorts. One was an *umm al-walad* who became his wife (*zawja*) and who is only known through her title: al-Sayyida al-'Aziziyya or al-'Aziza (d. 385/995).[33] She was a Melchite Copt, whose two brothers were appointed by al-'Aziz as patriarchs of the Melchite Church. Also, her father, according to al-Maqrizi (or one of her brothers, according to other sources), was sent as ambassador to Sicily by al-'Aziz.[34] Most sources identify her as the mother of Sitt al-Mulk, one of the most famous women in the whole history of Islam. Sitt al-Mulk exemplifies, to a great extent, one of the types of women leaders who challenged the established female roles of their society. She never married and was powerful in her own right by virtue of her birth, not as a result of a marriage to a man in a position of authority. Her political influence and her stormy relationship with her half-brother, the imam-caliph al-Hakim, as well as her image as portrayed by the sources, will be analysed in Chapter 4.

It is a matter of academic controversy whether al-Sayyida al-'Aziziyya was also the mother of al-Hakim, or whether Sitt al-Mulk and al-Hakim were the children of two different women. Evidence points overwhelmingly in favour of the opinion that al-'Aziziyya was not al-Hakim's mother. This debate has in turn raised questions as to the religious affiliation of al-Hakim's mother: was she a Muslim or a Christian?[35] The Crusader chronicler William of Tyre links al-Hakim's destruction of the Church of the Holy Sepulchre in Jerusalem in 400/1009 to the imam-caliph's eagerness to deny all allegations of being a 'Christian', which had been mounted against him on the account of having being born to a Christian woman.[36] By contrast, an anecdote reported by al-Maqrizi, on the authority of al-Musabbihi, indicates that al-Hakim's mother was perceived as being a Muslim. Al-Musabbihi recounts that in 371/981 [sic!] Ibn al-Washa' (d. 397/1006), a legal scholar originally from al-Andalus, had been arrested by order of al-Hakim. As al-Hakim had fallen ill, his mother asked Ibn al-Washa', on account of his piety, to pray for her son to be healed. Not only did the scholar oblige, he also copied the entire Qur'an in the inner surface of a bowl using ink made of musk and saffron. He then asked his servant to take the bowl to al-Hakim's mother, to instruct her to wash it with water from Zamzam and to administer the mixture to her sick son. That she did and voilà! al-Hakim recovered. As a sign of gratitude, she demanded the release of Ibn al-Washa' and he was indeed freed, together with all his Andalusian associates.[37]

Druze sources identify al-Hakim's mother with the daughter of ʿAbd Allah, one of al-Muʿizz's sons and therefore a brother of al-ʿAziz. However, it is more likely that this woman was in fact a wife of al-Hakim, rather than his mother. It could be argued that the Druzes' emphasis on al-Hakim's descent from an endogamic union served their doctrinal purpose of reinforcing the charisma genealogically transmitted within the 'holy family', thereby enhancing the political and doctrinal status they bestow upon al-Hakim.

The sixth imam-caliph, al-Hakim, had as a consort the *umm al-walad* Amina, daughter of the late prince ʿAbd Allah, son of al-Muʿizz, who was surnamed Ruqayya and who became the mother of his son and successor al-Zahir. This woman could be the same as the one mentioned in the prediction reported by al-Hamidi, where it is stated that in 390/1000 al-Hakim would choose an orphan girl of good stock brought up by his father al-ʿAziz and that she would become the mother of his successor.[38] While al-Maqrizi claims that Sitt al-Mulk was hostile to this Amina, other sources instead state that Sitt al-Mulk offered refuge to al-Zahir and his mother as they were fleeing from al-Hakim's persecution. It is also reported that, in 390/1000, al-Hakim married the *jāriya* known as al-Sayyida,[39] but it is unclear whether this statement refers to al-Hakim's marriage to Amina or to another woman. Al-Hakim had at least one daughter, Sitt Misr (d. 455/1063), described as a generous patroness, and as noble and of good character.

The seventh imam-caliph, al-Zahir, also took a slave as his companion; she was an Abyssinian, Sudanese or Nubian woman whose name is given by al-Maqrizi as Rasad and who mothered the next imam-caliph, al-Mustansir. She had formerly been the slave of a Jewish merchant, Abu Saʿd al-Tustari, who eventually became vizier under al-Mustansir. While Rasad's son was a minor, she reportedly acted as regent for him and exercised considerable influence within the court. As for al-Zahir's female offspring, we have information about two daughters. One, according to the Mustaʿlian tradition, was very close to her german brother al-Mustansir and played a role as witness in the controversy

Fig. 1 A twelfth-century marble tombstone featuring the title of *Sitt al-nisā'* bestowed to a lady from the Fatimid elite. The tomb and its inscription have been studied by A. al-Zayla'i, *Tombstones in Dar al-Athar al-Islamiyyah, Kuwait*, Kuwait, 1989, pp. 17–18 and 39. The foliated Kufic inscription reads: "'Every soul shall have a taste of death in the end to us shall you be brought back" (Qur. 29:57). In the name of God the most gracious and merciful, this is the tomb of Sit-al-Nisā' (the best of women) bint al-'Abbās ibn Hasan ibn al-'Abbās. May God have mercy on her and grant her His forgiveness. She died in 501[1107].'
LNS16S. Copyright © Dar al-Athar al-Islamiyyah, Kuwait National Museum.

surrounding her brother's succession. The other daughter, reported to have been 'the last child left to him', died aged three during the night of the Epiphany of Dhu 'l-Qa'da 415/1024. The chief *qāḍī* in person, Qasim b. 'Abd al-'Aziz b. al-Nu'man, conducted the funeral service of this infant, who was buried in the palace 'Saffron mausoleum' (*turbat al-za'farān*).[40]

All in all, the historical reality of the imam-caliph's women during the Egyptian period is documented more broadly than was the case with their predecessors. Some of them, like Sitt al-Mulk and Rasad, played a significant role in Fatimid history as a whole. The imam's women of this period are mostly known by their honorific titles (*Sitt al-Mulk* 'the lady of sovereignty', *al-Sayyida* 'the lady', *Mawlātu-nā* 'our lady, mistress') in contrast with the use of agnomen ('mother of') in the previous periods. As the contemporary Egyptian scholar Nuriman 'Abd al-Karim Ahmad has observed, titles such as the generic *Sayyida* were given to the close relatives of the imam. When complemented with the imam's dynastic name, like *al-Sayyida al-Mu'izziyya* or *al-Sayyida al-'Aziziyya*, the title denoted the consort of the imam-caliph. A title like *Sitt al-Mulk* was, typically, reserved for the female offspring of the imam-caliphs, as in the case of the daughters of al-'Aziz, al-Zahir and al-Hafiz.[41] Significantly, when Badr al-Jamali made the position of vizier hereditary within his family, the title of *Sitt al-Mulk* was also bestowed upon his own daughter. The use of female titles in Fatimid Egypt mirrors the increased formalisation of palace and state protocol (see Fig.1). Court etiquette across dynasties demanded that the proper names of female relatives of the caliph should not be mentioned in public as a sign of respect.[42] For any dynasty, image and status were part of the politics of power; the Fatimids of Egypt were no exception. The use of female titles expressed a dynastic desire to impress and to further advertise the status of their holders' male relatives.

c. *Caliphs' Sons and Viziers' Daughters*

The long and eventful caliphate of al-Mustansir witnessed the shift of emphasis, during the vizierate of Badr al-Jamali, in the power balance between the caliph and his vizier. The effects of this major shift will be reflected in the circumstances surrounding the marriages of al-Mustansir's successors. Al-Mustansir had at least two main consorts: one who bore him his eldest son, Abu Mansur Nizar, and at least one daughter, and who was, according to an Isma'ili source, a Byzantine/Greek (*rūmiyya*). The other consort was the *jiha 'aẓīma* who became the mother of Abu'l-Qasim al-Musta'li.[43]

It is in conjunction with the disputes over al-Musta'li's accession to the caliphate that we have the clearest evidence of the interlinking between the vizier's and the imam-caliph's families matured through marriage. Al-Mustansir concluded the marriage contract (*ʿaqada*) between Sitt al-Mulk, the daughter of Badr al-Jamali, and his son al-Mustaʿli.[44] For the occasion Sitt al-Mulk was given by her father a splendid trusseau and jewels, which her brothers eventually came to possess.[45] The ceremony of this marriage is described in *al-Hidāya al-Āmiriyya:* 'when he [al-Mustansir] married him [al-Mustaʿli] off to the daughter of the *amīr al-juyūsh* (commander of the armies), and he contracted the marriage to her, al-Mustansir made him sit on his right hand side while the rest of his children he made sit on his left and, on that day, he gave him the title of *walī ʿahd al-mu'minīn*, which he did not use for his other two sons'.[46] The author of this treatise retrospectively interprets the bestowal of the title and the seating arrangement of the groom as evidence of al-Mustansir's appointment of his younger son, al-Mustaʿli, as his successor.

Whether it was al-Mustansir himself who arranged this marriage – as more than one source suggests – or the vizier Badr al-Jamali, the plan to merge dynastically the caliphal and vizier's families came to nothing since al-Mustaʿli, who had previously fathered children, died before having any with Sitt al-Mulk.[47] In the face of this setback, further attempts were made to tie the two families by the vizier al-Afdal, Badr al-Jamali's son. Under his vizierate, al-Mustaʿli's son, al-Amir, succeeded his father to the throne aged five. According to the Fatimid historian Ibn al-Tuwayr, al-Afdal had total control over the life of the young caliph, who was kept in seclusion under the care of eunuchs and the maternal grandmother. Al-Afdal's masterplan was to arrange a marriage between his daughter and the caliph al-Amir, regardless of expense. The famous historian Ibn Khaldun states that this was indeed a forced marriage and that al-Amir had married her 'under compulsion' (*ʿalā karhin min-hu*).[48] Al-Amir's reluctance is somewhat confirmed by the fact that, according to Ibn al-Tuwayr, al-Afdal took care of the marriage contract and closely supervised its redaction to avoid possible disputes over its legal validity. The contract read as follows: 'the *amīr al-mu'minīn* [al-Amir] chose her of his own accord from all the women … [and] the imamate would come from the progeny (*nasl*) of the viziers'.[49] Al-Afdal's intended outcome of such a union was the birth of a male heir, but his hopes were in vain, as the marriage was never consummated.

Al-Amir is known to have had several *jihas*, the most prominent of whom is named by the sources as ʿAlam, and she is known to have been a prolific architectural patroness. This caliph also married the Bedouin *jāriya* ʿAliya, to whom sources refer in juicy anecdotes concerning her coveting of beautiful objects and her love verses addressed to her male cousin (see Chapter 3). Circumstances are obscure regarding al-Amir's progeny. More than one source states that al-Amir died without male offspring. There is reference, however, to the existence of a daughter, known as Sitt al-Qusur, born to him by ʿAlam, and of another daughter who was born to him posthumously by a slave.[50] Against this view, documentary and historical evidence points to the birth of a son of al-Amir, identified with the name of al-Tayyib. The fate of al-Tayyib is obscure. Those Isma'ilis who upheld his succession rights became known as the Tayyibis. Other narratives report of a son, nicknamed Qufayfa, also born of a 'slave-girl' after his father's death. His mother is said to have concealed him to protect him from al-Hafiz, the cousin of al-Amir, who had meanwhile risen to the Fatimid leadership. However, al-Hafiz eventually found out about the existence of the boy and had him killed.[51]

The caliph al-Hafiz had at least two consorts: Jiha Bayyan, a singer *jāriya* who also played the lute, and Jiha Rayhan; both are renowned as patronesses of mosques. He also had a daughter, known as al-Sayyida al-Sharifa or Sitt al-Qusur, who was instrumental in avenging the murder of her brother, the caliph al-Zafir b. al-Hafiz (see Chapter 4). Al-Zafir's mother was an *umm al-walad* known with the title of Sitt al-Wafa' or Sitt al-Mana.[52] As for the penultimate Fatimid caliph, al-Fa'iz, sources provide scanty details about him: he was born in 544/1149 and died at the age of 11; his mother was an *umm al-walad* called Ihsan, who was referred to as Zayn al-Kamal or Sitt al-Kamal.[53] As for his successor, al-'Adid, Ibn Taghribirdi notes that he was not al-Fa'iz's son (not surprising, given his young age at death) and that his mother was also an *umm al-walad* known as Sitt al-Mana.[54]

Al-'Adid's power was by now merely formal but the splendour of his court was still awesomely impressive. William of Tyre reports the account of the Frank envoy Hugh of Cesarea, who was received in Cairo by al-'Adid, whom he described as a handsome 16-year-old youth of generous disposition and impeccable manners. To the detailed accounts of the elaborate court ceremonial and the meticulous protocol that, incidentally, Hugh subverted by making al-'Adid shake his hand, the envoy adds in passing that al-'Adid had a large number of wives.[55]

One of these women must have been the daughter of the Fatimid vizier Tala'i' b. Ruzzik. Al-Maqrizi specifies that Tala'i' coerced the young caliph into marrying his daughter by having him imprisoned until he agreed to it.[56] This course of action triggered the harem revolt against the vizier, who was murdered allegedly at the instigation of one of al-'Adid's aunts in 556/1161(see Chapter 4).

With this marriage of a Fatimid caliph to the vizier's daughter, we witness once more, and for what was to be the last time, an attempt to implement the plan (to bring about blood union between a dynasty of viziers and the caliphal family) devised almost a century earlier under the vizierates of Badr al-Jamali and his successor. By now, however, the caliphate had become an institution void of any effective power. Whatever future the vizier Tala'i' had envisaged with regards to the dynastic outcome of this union, his plan had failed. The Frankish invasions of Egypt and the arrival of Saladdin, ironically to become the last of the Fatimid viziers, brought to an end the Fatimid rule. The Fatimid dynasty, however, continued albeit briefly. Al-ʿAdid died at 21, leaving at least two sons. Despite the almost total disintegration of the Fatimid power in Egypt, succession claims continued sporadically for almost a century. A supposed great-grandson of al-ʿAdid was a Yusuf al-Hadi, whose identity was kept hidden for fear of persecution. The story goes that Yusuf's mother had left al-ʿAdid's palace pregnant and that she gave birth in North Africa to a boy who was raised among the Berbers, learnt their language and later studied in Marrakesh.[57] The narrative seems to go full circle, from the Berber support for the Ismaʿilis of the pre-Fatimid phase to the refuge sought among the Berbers by the progeny of the last Fatimid caliph. However, this time genealogical pretensions were of no consequence to the remaining supporters of the Hafizi line based in Egypt and in Syria.

3. Women in the Dynasties in the Regions Outside the *Dawla*: The Zirids, the Nizaris and the Sulayhids

In his *La Berbérie orientale sous les Zīrīdes*, Hadi Idris Rogers provides a wealth of information regarding the women of the North African Zirid dynasty.[58] The dynasty was founded by Buluggin (d. 373/983–4) and its members ruled Ifriqiya on behalf of the Fatimids until 440/1048, when al-Muʿizz b. Badis changed the Zirid allegiance, for some ten years, in favour of the ʿAbbasids. One of Buluggin's wives was Yaʿlan, who became the mother of Buluggin's son and successor Mansur (d. 386/996). Mansur had a daughter he gave in marriage to a Zenata chieftain, whom he made governor of the strategically important centre of Tubna. But it was another daughter of his who was to become one of the famous women of this dynasty. She was known as Umm Mallal (d. 414/1023) and her mother was ʿUdat al-ʿAziz bi-'llah. Her prominence at the Zirid court is shown by the visibility she is given in the sources and by the public recognition they describe. She is reported to have sent presents in 405/1014–15 to Sitt al-Mulk, the imam-caliph al-ʿAziz's daughter. More importantly, when Badis died in 407/1016, it was to her that in al-Mahdiyya the Berber dignitaries formally offered their condolences. Their condolences were soon followed by congratulations as she paraded her nephew al-Muʿizz in the cortège with drums and insignia that she had staged to publically announce his succession. Idris infers that she acted as al-Muʿizz's regent. Finally, her funeral was described as featuring flags, tambourines and palanquins of a pomp that had not been seen before for either kings or their subjects.

Other prominent women of the dynasty were the widow of Badis, who died in 412/1021–2 and was also honoured with a famously lavish funeral; the mother of al-Muʿizz; and his sister Umm al-ʿUlu, who died probably in Sousse in

445/1053–4. Very little is known about al-Mu'izz's mother, who was presumably not the same person as the main wife of Badis, except that she must have been influential at court given the power gained through her by the dignitary in charge of her affairs. As for al-Mu'izz's sister, Umm al-'Ulu, her sumptuous marriage in 415/1024 to her cousin, the son of the sovereign of Qal'a, further consolidated a peace agreement that her brother had signed with his father some seven years ealier. Umm al-'Ulu too is reported as having exercised some influence at court; in one instance she convinced her brother to reinstate a disgraced chancellor.[59]

In 413/1022–3, at the age of 15, al-Mu'izz b. Badis married Umm Yusuf Zulaykha, whom he is reported to have loved greatly. In keeping with the policy of marriage alliances he had already promoted through his sister, al-Mu'izz gave his own daughters in marriage to rival Hilalian Arab princes as a part of a wider diplomatic and military policy. Among more distant descendants of al-Mu'izz b. Badis, two women feature in the sources, both called Ballara. One was the daughter of al-Mu'izz's son Tamim, who, for alliance purposes, was given in marriage in 470/1077–8 to al-Nasir, a member of the rival Hammadid dynasty. Their union is described as both prolific and happy.[60] The other woman was Ballara bint al-Qasim b. Tamim, who married a Zirid prince. In 503/1109, the prince was exiled to Alexandria and Ballara accompanied him together with their young son 'Abbas. Upon arriving at the Fatimid court in Cairo, they were well received by the caliph al-Amir. Once widowed, Ballara married al-'Adil 'Ali b. al-Salar (d. 548/1153), who became the vizier of the Fatimid caliph al-Zafir.[61] This marriage impacted significantly upon Fatimid dynastic history. Ballara's son 'Abbas – a *maghribī* – conspired to kill his stepfather, a *mashriqī* of Kurdish origin, seized the vizierate, and in 549/1154 was instrumental in the murder of the caliph al-Zafir and in placing on the throne al-Fa'iz, the five-year-old son of the murdered caliph. These events that followed Ballara's arrival in Egypt acquire further significance when placed within the wider context of the ongoing ethnic-based power rivalry between the *mashāriqa* (the Eastern faction) and the *maghāriba* (the North African faction) within the Fatimid *dawla*.

Many more details are available on the influence, wealth and lifestyle of the Zirid court women and they will be discussed elsewhere in this book. This abundance of systematic information is remarkable in comparison with the sparse incidence of references to contemporary Fatimid court women, as found in a much broader spectrum of sources. Being Berber, or at least raised in a Berber environment, the Zirid princesses epitomise the somewhat liberal participation in many aspects of life typically associated with Berber women up until the advent of the Almohades towards the end of the twelfth century. Their visibility made it possible for North African chroniclers to acknowledge them in their works, as shown by Ibn 'Idhari, who went as far as devoting a whole section of his *al-Bayān* to the North African court women.

In the East, in the aftermath of the Nizari–Musta'li split, the claims of Nizar to the imamate were upheld by the Isma'ilis of Persia, Syria and, later, Central Asia. In Persia, as a result of the missionary activity of Hasan-i Sabbah, the Nizaris established their headquarters in the fortress of Alamut, affirmed themselves as a politically and doctrinally independent group from Cairo, and took hold of a number of fortresses in north-west Persia. From there, the Nizaris endeavoured to challenge the Sunni Saljuqs, who were the dominant power in the region at the time. Following Nizar's death in Alexandria, the Nizaris believed that the genealogical lineage from his progeny had continued in Persia. About Hasan's female kin we are informed that, besides having had at least a wife and daughters, he had a sister whose son was put in charge of the fortress of Ardahan.[62]

Both Isma'ili and non-Isma'ili sources sought to reconstruct the circumstances surrounding Nizar's offspring.[63] Many of them featured stories centred upon the role played by the figure of a pregnant slave-girl. Al-Maqrizi, for example, reports that when Nizar escaped to Alexandria, his *jāriya* left the caliphal palace while pregnant with his son.[64] To illustrate this Persian connection, the same historian relates an anecdote where Hasan-i Sabbah, having shown a pregnant *jāriya* to his followers, declared: 'The imam hides in this.' His followers believed him, a boy was born and he was named Hasan.[65] In a similar vein, the Persian Juzjani narrates that Hasan-i Sabbah brought a pregnant slave of his to Alamut, paraded her to the people and declared that she was pregnant by the imam-caliph al-Mustansir, and that he had taken her to the fortress because she was fleeing from the enemies who knew she would give birth to the imam-to-be.[66] Different accounts establish a much stronger link between Nizar and Hasan-i Sabbah. Some state that Nizar entrusted Hasan with one of his children, whom the *dā'ī* took to Alamut, others that Nizar had married Hasan's daughter, whom he had met in Alexandria; their union bore a son, whom they called Muhammad.[67] Regarding Nizar's female offspring, the Nizari Isma'ili tradition mentions that one of his daughters married a certain Ibn Akhi b. al-Mudabbir, who was to be killed, at the time of al-Mustansir, during the revolt of the Turks.

Following Hasan-i Sabbah's death, the leadership of the Nizari *da'wa* first passed on to the Daylami *dā'ī* and commander Buzurg Ummid (d. 532/1137–8) and later to his son, Muhammad (d. 557/1162). Buzurg Ummid appears to have belonged to a good family, as his sister is recorded as having been the wife of Hazarasp I, a Buwayhid prince of the Badusepan dynasty in Rustamdar. Buzurg's wife was the daughter of Shah Ghazi Rustam.[68] None of the three Nizari leaders are known to have named any imams after Nizar. However, at Alamut in 560/

1164, the fourth leader Hasan II, *ʿalā dhikri-hi al-salām*, introduced a major doctrinal revolution that also had implications for genealogical matters. In the middle of the month of Ramadan of that year, Hasan announced the proclamation of the *qiyāma* (resurrection) on earth. This event was interpreted by many as marking the end of the outward observance of the *sharīʿa* among his followers. Initially, Hasan claimed that the *qiyāma* had been brought about by the hidden *imām-qāʾim* (lit. imam-resurrector), of whom he presented himself as the sole representative. Subsequently, Hasan hinted that he was the actual *imām-qāʾim*, but it was his son and successor, Muhammad II, who clearly claimed for his father (and, logically, for himself) such a status.

From a genealogical point of view, Muhammad II's claim implied a leap from a line of leaders and *dāʿīs* to a line of imams. According to the Nizari tradition, there had been no interruption in the line of imams since Nizar but, rather, a concealment of their existence. The third of these hidden imams was believed to be the real father of Hasan II, who therefore would only apparently be the son of Muhammad b. Buzurg Ummid. The strongly anti-Nizari historian ʿAta Malik Juvayni provides us with his own version of the ways in which the Nizaris sought to solve this apparent contradiction. In his narrative, once again, female figures are called upon to resolve a genealogical riddle. In one account it is claimed that Muhammad b. Buzurg Ummid's wife had committed adultery with Nizar's grandson, or great-grandson, and that she consequently bore a son, Hasan, who was effectively the direct descendant of an imam. In another story a mysterious woman is at the centre of a case of child-swapping. She surreptitiously entered the fortress of Alamut and substituted the son of Muhammad b. Buzurg Ummid with the son born to the imam on the same day.[69] Beside these anecdotal women, the only woman in Hasan II's life for whom we have some indirect information is his wife, who was the daughter of the Twelver Shiʿi Buwayhid lord Namwar and whose brother Husayn eventually stabbed Hasan II to death in Lammasar.

Anecdotes concerning the Nizari imams of the period preceding the Mongol onslaught of the Nizaris contain some references to the women in their lives. As is the case with most of the information relating to this period, caution should be applied, given the strong anti-Nizari stance of the sources; the narratives ought therefore to be appreciated more for their colorfulness than for their historical accuracy. Concerning Jalal al-Din Hasan III (d. 618/1221), the third Nizari imam of the post-*qiyāma* period, much is made in anti-Ismaʿili sources of his mother being a Sunni. She is reported to have gone on pilgrimage to Makka in 609/1212–13, been treated with honour in Baghdad and, along the pilgrimage route, had her cortège placed in front of those of other rulers. Juvayni informs us that Jalal al-Din asked in marriage the women of the princes of Gilan. The princes held back and refused to agree without sanction from Baghdad, until permission was eventually granted to them to ally themselves in marriage with the Nizari lord. By virtue of this, Jalal al-Din took four wives from the daughters of the princes of Gilan, the first of whom was the sister of Kayka'us, the ruler of Kutum (today Kuhdum). She is identified as the mother of Jalal al-Din's son, 'Ala' al-Din Muhammad. Those same wives, though, were later suspected of having poisoned Jalal al-Din in collusion with his sister and some kinsmen. They were eventually put to death by the vizier of Jalal al-Din's successor, 'Ala' al-Din. Juvayni states that this 'Ala' al-Din had a child from a Kurdish servant of his and that, as soon as she was found out to be pregnant, she was sent back to her father's house. Nobody dared to say who the father of this child was. However, Rukn al-Din, 'Ala' al-Din's legitimate son and successor, tried to use this half-brother as a decoy when he found himself in danger from the Mongols, but to no avail. Also, 'Ala' al-Din was reputed to have had as a mistress the wife of Hasan of Mazandaran, who was the closest of his associates and favourites but nonetheless indicated as responsible for the murder of 'Ala'.

Accounts about the last of the Nizari imams of Alamut, Rukn al-Din (d. 655/1257), acquire romantic overtones. Having succumbed to the Mongols, he was deported with his court to Qazvin, in north-west Persia. He fell in love with one of the daughters of 'the vilest of the Turks' (in fact, the Mongols) and offered his kingdom in return for her love. In the end, by Hülegü's command, she was given to Rukn al-Din. Once the marriage had been consummated, Rukn al-Din asked Hülegü to be sent to the court of the great Khan of Mongolia, Mengu Qa'an. Hülegü agreed, and in 655/1257 sent him there, but Rukn al-Din was murdered along the way by his Mongol guards.[70] The tragic fate of Rukn al-Din did not mark the end of the line of Nizari imams, which, according to the Nizari tradition, has continued uninterrupted to this day down to the present 49th imam, H. H. Karim Aga Khan IV.

In anti-Isma'ili works female figures associated with the Nizaris are often featured as part of the myths and legends surrounding this branch of Isma'ilism. In the few extant Nizari sources there is altogether an absence of data on women. This could be explained by the overwhelmingly doctrinal – rather than historiographical – nature of the few Nizari works that survived the destruction of the famed Nizari libraries by the Mongols. Moreover, the intensive militancy that characterised the activities of the early Nizaris – living as they did, entrenched in remote mountain fortresses – did not favour the development of a palace life comparable to the one enjoyed in urban courts, making any visible form of female participation impossible to record.

In the Yemen, two women came to play a prominent role in the history of the Sulayhid dynasty. One was Asma' b. Shihab (d. 467/1074), who was the wife of the founder of the dynasty, 'Ali b. Muhammad al-Sulayhi. Their daughter Maymuna died of grief in 458/1066, following the death of her brother the prince al-Aʿazz. Another son of ʿAli and Asma' was Muwaffaq, who married a cousin, Fatima bint Ahmad b. al-Muzaffar al-Sulayhi, who might have originally been the widow of his brother al-Aʿazz. This Fatima was to die when her house was set alight following the attack by the rival Najahids, and came to be considered a martyr by her own people.[71] Asma''s influence became visible after the murder of her husband, as the mother of his heir and successor, al-Mukarram. The Fatimid imam-caliph al-Mustansir granted her the honorific title of 'mother of the chosen princes' (*umm al-umarā' al-muntajibīn*).[72] Asma' also bore ʿAli two more daughters, who, as customary, married within the Sulayhid clan: Mu'mina wed ʿAli b. Hisa b. al-Muzaffar al-Sulayhi, while Fatima married ʿAli b. Malik b. Shihab al-Sulayhi. According to Yemeni popular lore, Asma''s greatest accomplishment is to have groomed at her palace the other Sulayhid woman to rise to promience so much as to become one of the most famous queens of the medieval Islamic world. She was the orphaned niece of Asma''s husband, and became her daughter-in-law when she married al-Mukarram in 458/1066. Her name was Arwa b. Ahmad b. Muhammad al-Sulayhi, her mother was Bint ʿAmir al-Zawayhi and, besides sons, she is known to have had two daughters, Fatima (d. 534/1139) and Umm Hamdan (d. 510/1116). Umm Hamdan married Ahmad b. Sulayman al-Zawayhi, son of her maternal uncle, while Fatima married Shams al-Maʿali ʿAli, son of the *dāʿī* Saba' b. Ahmad. Arwa had also a sister who married Saba''s other son, Muhammad.[73] Arwa came to be primarily known with the titles of al-Sayyida al-Hurra and al-Sayyida al-Malika, and reigned, first jointly with her husband and later by herself, from 460/1067 until her death in 532/1137–8, which also marked the end of the Sulayhid dynasty. The eventful life of this queen and her overall contribution to Fatimid and post-Fatimid Ismaʿili history will be fully discussed in Chapter 4.

4. Women in the High-Ranking Families at the Service of the Fatimid Dynasty

There is some evidence that, following the establishment of the Fatimid courts, alliances were consolidated between the families of dignitaries working in the various palace departments, by way of marriage. An early, yet never fully pursued, attempt to facilitate political alliances with the Fatimids through marriage was made by Muhammad b. Tughj, the Ikhshidid governor of Egypt on behalf of the ʿAbbasids. When the powerful Fatimid neighbours in Ifriqiya first attempted to expand their domains to Egypt, Muhammad b. Tughj, unsure of the ʿAbbasid support, proposed marriage alliances with the caliph al-Qa'im by offering to marry one of his own daughters to one of al-Qa'im's sons.

However – perhaps a shortsighted decision on the Ikhshidids' part given what was to come – the matrimonial plans were called off. The governor received confirmation of his position from Baghdad and, at the same time, the revolt of

Abu Yazid in North Africa prevented, among other factors, any further Fatimid military intervention in Egypt for the next twenty years. However, when eventually the Fatimids took over Egypt at the Ikhshidids' expense, matrimonial plans were restored at another level. Ja'far b. al-Furat (d. 392/1001) known as Abu'l-Fadl, was the Ikhshidid vizier who saw – and politically survived – the transition of power in Egypt from one dynasty to another. The marriage of his son Abu 'l-'Abbas to the daughter of the ultra-potent Fatimid vizier Ibn Killis might have been instrumental in the continuation of Abu'l-Fadl's successful career under the new rule.[74]

In 375/985 Muhammad b. al-Nu'man, himself a *qāḍī* and the son of the more famous al-Qadi al-Nu'man, married his son Abu'l-Qasim to the daughter of the renowned general Jawhar, who had led the Fatimid conquest of Egypt. The marriage contract was signed at the levee of al-'Aziz, in the exclusive presence of the officers of the court. The dowry settled by the bridegroom was 3,000 pieces of gold and the trousseau consisted of a single robe of one uniform colour. Eventually Abu'l-Qasim served as a judge. Links between the two families were further strengthened by the marriage of the general Jawhar's sister to Muhammad's brother, 'Abd al-'Aziz b. al-Nu'man.[75]

Within the context of civil unrest and military ethnic-based in-fighting, which plagued al-Mustansir's long reign, it is possible that a marriage helped to seal a brief alliance between the leaders of two rival factions. Ildeguz, 'one of the greatest princes', who was the commander of the Turks in Cairo, married his daughter to the general Ibn Hamdan (d. 465/1073).[76] Families of powerful viziers also became, in time, inter-linked through marriage. A son of the vizier al-Afdal, who worked in the administration of the vizier Tala'i' b. Ruzzik, was also closely related to the Bani Ruzzik through marriage with Tala'i''s granddaughter.[77]

In Syria, military chiefs also fell victim to marriage in the line of duty and beyond. The Turk Yarukh, known as 'Alam al-Dawla, whom the imam-caliph al-Hakim had appointed as Fatimid governor of Syria, married a daughter of the vizier Ibn Killis.[78] Under the imam-caliph al-Zahir, Anushtigin al-Duzbari, who in 429/1037–8 brought the Fatimid power in Syria to its zenith, held the post of military chief commander of Syria. His own marriage to Shawwaqa, the daughter of the Buwahyid ruler in Iraq, Samsam al-Dawla,[79] which pointed to a possible shift of alliance with another dynasty, could be appraised within the context of al-Duzbari's quarrel with the Fatimid vizier al-Jarjara'i, who for some time had dismissed him from his post.

The Fatimid hold on Syria was tenuous and constantly threatened by local hostile tribes, which, through coalitions, managed at times to seize control of the region. The Fatimids took advantage of the shifting nature of these tribal alliances by sealing counter-alliances, also through marriage. A vivid example of these intricate family ties, and their relevance to local politics, is provided by the case of al-Duzbari's family. He had a son from the daughter of a Wahb b. Hisan and four daughters from different mothers. These mothers belonged to the local nobility, such as the family of the prince Husam al-Dawla al-Bajnaki and 'Aziz al-Dawla Rafi' b. Abi'l-Layl. In turn, one of al-Duzbari's daughters eventually married another prince, Sarim al-Dawla Dhu 'l-Fadilatayini. He also had other daughters from two courtly concubines.[80]

When historians recorded the names and filiation of the women involved in the consolidation through marriage of such tribal and political alliances, they were not attaching relevance to these women per se. Rather, they documented and detailed the use of marriage alliances for the political and military value that was primarily attached to these unions. Nevertheless, by reporting the circumstances surrounding the forging of these marriages, writers provide us, by default, with valuable information on the identities and the lifestyles, for example the wealth, of the women in the families of high dignitaries.

With the exception of the perceived – or suggested – mythical origins of the dynasty from Fatima, women feature overall as incidental characters in the narratives relevant to Fatimid genealogy, as the line of descent remained strictly male-based. Incidental as their role might have been portrayed, it is nevertheless important to establish how these women fitted within the framework of Fatimid genealogical history. This is because the lifestyle they enjoyed at the courts, the power and influence they were able to exercise, and the wealth and patronage they became famous for, were ultimately due to the kinship relationships that they, as mothers, daughters, sisters, wives, *umm al-walad* and aunts, had with the Fatimid imam-caliphs and important men of the palace.

Notes

1 For the *dīwān* of Ibn Hāni', see Zāhid, 'Alī, *Tabyīn al-ma'ānī fī sharḥ dīwān Ibn Hānī'*, Cairo: Maṭba'at al-ma'ārif, 1352/1933, *qaṣīda* n. 59, pp. 785–96, the verse quoted is on p. 795; see also al-Ya'lāwī, M., *Ibn Hānī' al-Maghribī al-Andalusī: shā'ir al-dawla al-Fāṭimiyya*, Beirut: Dār al-gharb al-islāmī, 1985, pp. 234–5.

2 Ibn al-Haytham, Abū 'Abd Allāh, *Kitāb al-Munāẓarāt*, trans. Madelung, W. and Walker. P. E. in *The Advent of the Fatimids: A Contemporary Shi'i Witness*, London: I. B. Tauris, 2000, p. 73. For a tenth-century Mālikī–Shī'ī debate in Ifrīqiyā on this subject, see Idris, H. R., *La Berbérie orientale sous les Zīrīdes*, Paris: A. Maisonneuve, 1962, vol. 2, p. 699.

3 Ibn al-Haytham, *Munāẓarāt*, p. 131.

4 Ibn al-Haytham, *Munāẓarāt*, p. 87: 'Muḥammad b. al-Ḥanafiyya was distant from the Apostle of God, whereas 'Alī b. al-Ḥusayn was a descendant of Fāṭima …'; see also p. 80.

5 Quoted from the Arabic verse in Yalaoui, M., *Un poète chiite d'occident au IVème/Xème siècle: Ibn Hānī' al-Andalusī*, Tunis: Publications de l'Université de Tunis, 1976, p. 312.

6 See Ibn al-Ṭuwayr, al-Murtaḍā, *Nuzhat al-muqlatayn fī akhbār al-dawlatayn*, ed. Sayyid, A. F., Stuttgart and Beirut: F. Steiner, 1992, p. 5, where reference is made to an ancestor of al-Āmir who had not fully completed a marriage contract.

7 For a general Fāṭimid legal theory concerning the *umm al-walad* and the status of her child, see al-Qāḍī al-Nu'mān, *Da'ā'im al-Islām fi dhikr al-ḥalāl*, ed. Fyzee, A. A. A., Cairo: Dār al-Ma'ārif, 1961, vol. 2, pp. 314–15.

8 On some famous *umm al-walads* under the 'Abbāsids, see Tucker, J., 'Gender and Islamic history', in Adas, M. (ed.), *Islamic and European Expansion*, Philadelphia: Temple University Press, 1993, pp. 47–8.

9 See Peirce, L. P., *The Imperial Harem: Women and Sovereignty in the Ottoman Empire*, New York and Oxford: OUP, 1993, pp. 29–31.

10 Ivanow, W., *Ismaili Tradition Concerning the Rise of the Fatimids*, London: OUP, 1942, p. 27.

11 *Majlis* 117 from the *Majālis* by al-Ḥāmidī in Ivanow, W., *Rise*, p. 305.

12 Note that al-Qāḍī al-Nu'mān identifies the mother of Muḥammad al-Bāqir as Umm 'Abd Allāh [Fāṭima], daughter of al-Ḥasan 'Alī b. Abī Ṭālib, in *Sharḥ al-akhbār fi faḍā'il al-a'imma al-aṭhār*, ed. al-Jalālī, M. H., Qum: Mu'assasat al-nashr al-islāmī, n.d., 1412/1992, vol. 3, p. 276. In the proto-Ismā'īlī text *Umm al-Kitāb* she is called Amīna; see Filippani-Ronconi, P., *Ummu'l-Kitab*, Naples: Istituto Universitario Orientale, 1996, p. 5.

13 See Ja'far b. Manṣūr al-Yaman's *Asrār al-nuṭaqā'*, trans. in Ivanow, W., *Rise*, p. 295.

14 Idrīs 'Imād al-Dīn, *Zahr al-ma'ānī*, trans. in Ivanow, W., *Rise*, p. 241.

15 Idrīs 'Imād al-Dīn, *'Uyūn al-akhbār wa-funūn al-athār*, ed Ghālib, M., vol. 4, Beirut: Dār al-Andalus, 1973, pp. 357–8.

16 For the identification of and a discussion on at least three different genealogies, see Halm, H., *The Empire of the Mahdi: The Rise of the Fatimids*, trans. Bonner, M., Leiden: E. J. Brill, 1996, pp. 154–9.

17 Modern scholarship has proved that the Qaddāḥid ancestry was not sustainable because Maymūn al-Qaddāḥ, who indeed had a son called 'Abd Allāh, lived in the eighth century, some hundred years before al-Mahdī. For the blending of the Qaddāḥid and Jewish 'myths', see al-Safadī, Ṣalāḥ al-Dīn, *Kitāb al-Wafi bi-'l-wafāyāt*, Wiesbaden: F. Steiner, 1981–, vol. 19, pp. 364–7.

18 *Dustūr al-munajjimīn*, Arabic extract from Goeje, M. J. de, *Mémoire sur les Carmathes du Bahraïn et les Fatimides*, Leiden: E. J. Brill, 1886, 2nd edn, p. 205.

19 This version of events is reported by al-Maqrīzī, based on the authority of Ibn Shaddād, Ibn al-Athīr and 'Abd al-Jabbār in al-Maqrīzī, Taqī al-Dīn, *Kitāb al-Muqaffā (tarājim maghribiyya wa-mashriqiyya min fatra al-'ubaydiyya)*, ed. al-Ya'lāwī, M., Beirut: Dār al-gharb al-islāmī, 1987, (abridged edn), pp. 55; 69–70; 73.

20 For the first four, see al-Maqrīzī, *al-Muqaffā*, (abridged edn), p. 94, and also Ibn Ḥammād, Abū 'Abd Allāh, *Akhbār mulūk banī 'Ubayd*, ed. and French trans. Vonderheyden, M., in *Histoire des Rois 'Obaïdites (Les Califes Fatimides)*, Algiers: J. Carbonel; Paris: P. Geuthner, 1927, p. 31 (Fr.), p. 17 (Ar.). For the others, see Idrīs 'Imād al-Dīn, *'Uyūn*, vol. 6, p. 185.

21 Ibn Ẓāfir, Jamāl al-Dīn, *Akhbār al-duwal al-munqaṭi'a*, ed. Ferré, A., Cairo: IFAO, 1972, p. 12.

22 al-Yamānī, *Sīra*, and *Majlis* 117 by al-Ḥāmidī, Ḥātim b. Ibrahīm in Ivanow, W., *Rise*, pp. 189–90 and p. 308; for Karīma, see Ibn Ḥammād, *Histoire*, p. 37 (Fr.), p. 21 (Ar.).

23 al-Maqrīzī, *al-Muqaffā* (abridged edn), p. 123; see also Idrīs 'Imād al-Dīn, *'Uyūn*, vol. 6, p. 185, and Ibn Ẓāfir, *Akhbār*, p. 16.

24 Halm, H., *Empire*, p. 311.

25 al-Qāḍī al-Nu'mān, *Kitāb al-Majālis wa-'l-musāyarāt*, ed. al-Faqī, Ḥ., et al., Tunis: al-Maṭba'a al-rasmiyya li-'l-jumhūriyya al-tūnisiyya, 1978, pp. 542–3.

26 al-Maqrīzī, Taqī al-Dīn, *Itti'āẓ al-hunafā' bi-akhbār al-a'imma al-Fāṭimiyyīn al-khulafā'*, ed. al-Shayyāl, J. and Ḥilmī, M., Cairo: Lajnat iḥyā' al-turāth al-islāmī, 1387–93/1967–1973, vol. 1, p. 216; see also al-Maqrīzī, *al-Mawā'iẓ wa-'l-i'tibār bi-dhikr al-khiṭaṭ wa-'l-āthār*, Beirut: Dār al-ṣādir, n.d., offset of Būlāq 1324 edn, vol. 1, p. 352 and al-Maqrīzī, *al-Muqaffā*, vol. 2, p. 178.

Ibn al-Qalānisī, Ḥamza b. Asad, *Ta'rīkh Dimashq*, ed. Zakār, S., Damascus: Dār Ḥassān, 1983, p. 23, also calls her an *umm al-walad*.

27 Based on 'Idrīs 'Imād al-Dīn, quoted in Smoor, P., 'Fatimid poets and the "*takhallus*" that bridges the nights of time to the imam of time', *Der Islam*, 68 (1991), p. 238, n. 17.

28 al-Maqrīzī, *Itti'āẓ*, vol. 1, p. 91; al-Maqrīzī, *al-Muqaffā*, vol. 2, p. 178; and Ibn Ẓāfir, *Akhbār*, p. 20. Idrīs 'Imād al-Dīn, *'Uyūn*, vol. 6, p. 185 states that they all died in Egypt.

29 MS 1315 (Ar I, ZA), *Muqābalat al-adwār wa-mukāshafat al-asrār*, in Cortese, D., *Arabic Ismaili Manuscripts, the Zāhid 'Alī Collection*, London: I. B. Tauris, 2003, no. 108.

30 According to al-Ḥāmidī, Durzān was not a slave but a cousin: see *majlis* 117 in Ivanow, W., *Rise*, p. 309.

31 Ibn Sa'īd, 'Alī b. Mūsā, *al-Nujūm al-zāhira fī ḥulā ḥadhrat al-Qāhira*, ed. Ḥusayn Naṣṣār, Cairo: Dār al-Kutub, 1970, pp. 39–40; cf. al-Maqrīzī, *Itti'āẓ*, vol. 1, p. 95; and al-Maqrīzī, *Khiṭaṭ*, vol. 1, p. 352.

32 Ibn Ḥammād, *Histoire*, p. 71 (Fr.), p. 47 (Ar.); and Ibn Ẓāfir, *Akhbār*, p. 28.

33 al-Musabbiḥī, Muḥammad b. 'Ubayd Allāh, *Nuṣūṣ ḍā'i'a min akhbār Miṣr*, ed. Sayyid, A. F., Cairo: IFAO, n.d. [1981], p. 15.

34 al-Maqrīzī, *al-Muqaffā*, vol. 3, p. 62.

35 This controversy is summarised in Bariani, L., 'Parentela e potere: uso ed abuso. Indagine sulle "madri" del califfo al-Ḥākim bi-Amr Allāh al-Fāṭimī", *Al-Qanṭara: revista de estudios Árabes*, 16 (1995), 2, pp. 361–2, who concludes that al-Ḥākim and Sitt al-Mulk were children of different mothers. To support this view, see evidence found in *majlis* 117 by al-Ḥāmidī, where it is clearly stated that al-'Azīz married a woman, near the end of his reign, who gave birth to al-Ḥākim, after having 'married' a slave-girl of good stock (Ivanow, W., *Rise*, p. 309). On this controversy, see also Assaad, S. A., *The Reign of al-Hakim bi Amr Allah (386/996–411/1021): A Political Study*, Beirut: The Arab Institute for Research and Publishing, 1974. Heinz Halm argues that al-Ḥākim's mother was either an Egyptian Christian or a Greek concubine: see his 'Le destin de la princesse Sitt al-Mulk', in Barrucand, M. (ed.), *L'Égypt Fatimide: son art et son histoire*, Paris: Presses de l'Université de Paris-Sorbonne, 1999, p. 69; and his *Die Kalifen von Kairo*, Munich: C. H. Beck, 2003, p. 313.

36 William of Tyre, *A History of Deeds Done Beyond the Sea*, ed. and trans. Babcock, E. A. and Krey, A. C., New York: Octagon Books, 1976, vol. 1, pp. 66–7.

37 al-Maqrīzī, *al-Muqaffā*, vol. 5, pp. 212–13.

38 *Majlis* 117 from the *Majālis* by al-Ḥāmidī, in Ivanow, W., *Rise*, p. 310.

39 al-Maqrīzī, *Itti'āẓ*, vol. 2, p. 124; and Ibn al-Dawādārī, Abū Bakr b. 'Abd Allāh, *Kanz al-durar wa-jāmi' al-ghurar: al-durra al-muḍīya fī akhbār al-dawla al-Fāṭimiyya*, al-juz' al-sādis, ed. al-Munajjid, Ṣ., Cairo: O. Harrassowitz, 1961, p. 265. H. Halm identifies this wife with a freed slave of his sister, Sitt al-Mulk: see Halm, H., *Kalifen*, p. 312.

40 al-Musabbiḥī, Muḥammad b. 'Ubayd Allāh, *Akhbār Miṣr*, ed. Sayyid, A. F. and Bianquis, T., Cairo: IFAO, 1978, vol. 1, p. 71.

41 'Abd al-Karīm Aḥmad, Nurīmān, *al-Mar'a fī Miṣr fī'l-'aṣr al-Fāṭimī*, Cairo: al-Hay'a al-miṣriyya al-'āmma li-'l-kitāb, 1993, pp. 50–4.

42 For an instance of a respectful and polite way of indirectly refering to the 'Abbāsid caliph's mother, see al-Ṣabī', Hilāl, *Rusum dar al-khilafah: the rules and regulations of the 'Abbasid court*, trans. Salem, E. A., Beirut: Lebanese Commission for the Translation of Great Works, 1977, p. 50.

43 On the first consort being a Greek, see extracts from *Dustūr al-munajjimīn* in Casanova, P., 'Un nouveau manuscript de la secte des Assassins', *JA*, 19 (1922), pp. 129–30. On the second consort, see Ibn Muyassar, Tāj al-Dīn, *Akhbār Miṣr*, ed. Massé, H., as *Annales d'Égypte*, Cairo: IFAO, 1919, p. 67.

44 See Ibn Muyassar, *al-Muntaqā min akhbār Miṣr*, ed. Sayyid, A. F., Cairo: IFAO, 1981, pp. 70, 99; al-Maqrīzī, *Itti'āẓ*, vol. 3, p. 85.

45 al-Maqrīzī, *al-Muqaffā*, vol. 1, p. 667.
46 *al-Hidāya al-Āmiriyya fī ibṭāl da'wat al-Nizāriyya*, ed. Fyzee, A. A. A., London: OUP, 1938, p. 13. Fyzee doubts the dating of this wedding and the whole argument of the implicit 'new' *naṣṣ* in favour of al-Musta'lī (pp. 7–8). See also a very similar passage in Idrīs 'Imād al-Dīn, *'Uyūn*, vol. 7, p. 76 (Eng.), p. 192 (Ar.).
47 al-Maqrīzī, *Itti'āẓ*, vol. 3, p. 28.
48 Ibn Khaldūn, 'Abd al-Raḥmān, *Kitāb al-'Ibar*, Beirut: Dār al-'ilm li-'l-jāmi', n.d., vol. 4, p. 70.
49 Ibn al-Ṭuwayr, *Nuzha*, p. 6.
50 On Ibn Khallikān's account of al-Āmir appointing as his successor the foetus who then turned out to be a girl, see Ibn Khallikān, Aḥmad, *Kitāb Wafayāt al-a'yān*, trans. MacGuckin De Slane, W., *Biographical Dictionary*, Paris, 1842–71, repr. Beirut: Librairie du Liban, 1970, vol. 2, pp. 179–81.
51 On Qufayfa, see al-Maqrīzī, *Itti'āẓ*, vol. 3, p. 152.
52 Ibn al-Dawādārī, *Kanz*, vol. 6, p. 557 has al-Wafā'; Ibn Taghrībirdī, Jamāl al-Dīn Abu'l-Maḥāsin, *al-Nujūm al-zāhira fī mulūk Miṣr wa-'l-Qāhira*, Cairo: Dār al-Kutub al-Miṣriyya, 1353/1935, vol. 5, p. 288, has both al-Wafā' and al-Manā.
53 Ibn al-Dawādārī, *Kanz*, vol. 6, p. 566, and Ibn Taghrībirdī, *al-Nujūm*, vol. 5, p. 306, have Zayn al-kamāl; al-Maqrīzī, *Itti'āẓ*, vol. 3, p. 213, has Sitt.
54 In Ibn Taghrībirdī, *al-Nujūm*, vol. 5, p. 307. Also in Ibn al-Dawādārī, *Kanz*, vol. 7, p. 12.
55 William of Tyre, *A History of Deeds*, vol. 2, p. 321.
56 al-Maqrīzī, *Itti'āẓ*, vol. 3, p. 246.
57 al-Safadī, *al-Wafī*, vol. 29, no. 101, pp. 232–3.
58 Idris, H. R., *La Berbérie*, esp. vol. 1, pp. 73–225 passim. See also extensive coverage in Golovin, L., *Le Magrib central a l'époque des Zirides*, Paris: Arts et Metiers Graphiques, 1957. When dealing with the women of the Zīrīd dynasty, both authors rely extensively on Ibn 'Idhārī's *Bayān al-Mughrib*.
59 Idris, H. R., *La Berbérie*, vol. 2, p. 526.
60 Idris, H. R., *La Berbérie*, vol. 1, p. 274.
61 Ibn Khallikān, *Wafayāt*, vol. 2, pp. 351–2; and al-Maqrīzī, *al-Muqaffā*, vol. 4, pp. 42–3.
62 Ibn al-Athīr, 'Izz al-Dīn, *al-Kāmil fi'l ta'rīkh*, Beirut: Dār al-kitāb al-'arabī, 1967, vol. 10 , p. 217.
63 The Isma'īlī source *Dustūr al-munajjimīn* gives the names of the two sons of Nizār as Abū 'Abd Allāh Ḥusayn and Abū 'Alī Ḥasan: see Casanova, P., 'Un nouveau manuscript', pp. 129–30.
64 al-Maqrīzī, *Itti'āẓ*, vol. 3, pp. 112–13.
65 al-Maqrīzī, *al-Muqaffā*, vol. 3, p. 330.
66 Jūzjānī, 'Uthmān, *Ṭabaqāt-i Nāṣirī*, ed. Ḥabībī, 'A. H., Kabul: The Historical Society of Afghanistan, 1342–3/1963–4, vol. 2, p. 118.
67 See Mustawfī Qazvinī's *Ta'rīkh-i guzīdah*, trans. Defrémery, M., *Histoire des Seljukides et des Ismaéliens ou Assassins de l'Iran*, Paris: 1849, pp. 114–16; and Ibn al-Qalānisī as quoted in Dadoyan, S. B., *The Fatimid Armenians. Cultural and Political Interaction in the Near East*, Leiden: E. J. Brill, 1997, p. 130.
68 Hodgson, M. G. S., *The Order of Assassins, the Struggle of the Early Nizārī Ismā'īlīs Against the Islamic World*, The Hague: Mouton, 1955, p. 117. See Justi, F., *Iranisches Namenbuch*, Marburg: N. G. Elwertsche Verlagsbuchhandlung, 1895, p. 457; on Haṣan II's wife, Namwar, see p. 220.
69 Juvaynī, *History*, vol. 2, pp. 692–4. He also reports another version whereby Muḥammad b. Buzurg Ummīd, having found out that his wife had committed adultery and that the child was not his, killed the baby. On the basis of this version, Juvaynī claims, Muḥammad b. Buzurg Ummīd had in fact killed the imam! For variants of these accounts, see also Rashīd al-Dīn, Faḍl Allāh, *Jāmi' al-tawārīkh: qismat-i Ismā'īlīyān va-Fāṭimiyān va-Nizāriyān va-dā'īyān va-rafīqān*, ed. Dānishpazūh, M. T., Tehran: Bungāh-i tarjama va-nashr-i kitāb, 1338/1959, repr. 1977, p. 166.

70 For all these accounts on the Nizārīs, see Juvaynī, *History*, vol. 2, pp. 702–4; 709–10; 715; 722–3.
71 Shakir, M., *Sīrat al-Malik al-Mukarram: an edition and a study*, PhD thesis, SOAS, London: University of London, London, 1999, vol. 2, p. 39 (Ar.).
72 Idrīs 'Imād al-Dīn, *'Uyūn*, vol. 7, p. 54 (Eng.), p. 102 (Ar.); p. 53 (Eng.) p. 105 (Ar.); p. 56 (Eng.) p. 110 (Ar.).
73 'Umāra, Najm al-Dīn, *Ta'rīkh al-Yaman*, ed. Muḥammad b. 'Alī al-Akwa', Beirut: Maṭba'at al-sa'āda, 2nd edn, 1976, pp. 137–8, 153.
74 al-Maqrīzī, *al-Muqaffā*, vol. 3, p. 49.
75 Ibn Khallikān, *Wafayāt*, vol. 3, pp. 569–70; Ibn Kathīr, Abu'l-Fidā, *al-Bidāya wa-'l-nihāya*, Beirut: Dār iḥyā' al-turāth al-'arabī, 2nd edn, 1977, vol. 11, p. 311.
76 al-Maqrīzī, *al-Muqaffā*, vol. 3, p. 504.
77 Dadoyan, S. B., *Fatimid Armenians*, p. 160.
78 al-Anṭākī, Yaḥyā b. Sa'īd, *Ta'rīkh*, partial ed. and French trans., Kratchkovsky, I. and Vasiliev, A., 'Histoire de Yahya-ibn Sa'ïd d'Antioche', *Patrologia Orientalis*, 23 (1932), fascicule 3, p. 504.
79 al-Maqrīzī, *al-Muqaffā*, vol. 2, p. 306.
80 Ibn al-Qalānisī, *Ta'rīkh Dimashq*, p. 127.

CHAPTER

3

INSIDE THE PALACE WALLS: LIFE AT COURT

1. The Setting

Having successfully fought against the Aghlabids, in 297/909 the Fatimids established themselves in the Aghlabids' former royal city of Raqqada by taking over their palaces and all the other buildings the city contained: a large mosque, baths, markets and caravanserais. Raqqada was to be the Fatimids' first 'royal city'. Only a few years later, al-Mahdi took the decision to build a strategically more secure and appropriate seat for the growing needs of the newly-established dynasty. Having inherited from the Aghlabids a powerful navy, in 304/916 al-Mahdi ordered to build on the coast, 200 km south of Tunis, what was to become known as al-Mahdiyya, 'the city of the Mahdi'. When the city was completed five years later, al-Mahdi moved there and al-Mahdiyya, became the first purpose-built Fatimid capital. Built on an almost impregnable peninsula, al-Mahdiyya served as a natural port on the coastal trade route between al-Andalus and Egypt, and provided easy access to Sicily, an island the Fatimids had gained as part of their successful North African campaign. Defended by massive walls, a section of which is still extant today, the city had at least two royal palaces: one for the imam-caliph al-Mahdi, known as *qaṣr al-manār*, the 'lighthouse palace', facing west, and another for his son and heir al-Qa'im, facing east. Other buildings included a mosque (restored in the 1960s), storehouses, an arsenal and administrative edifices.

The second Fatimid capital city, which was to be the last in Ifriqiya, was Sabra, better known as al-Mansuriyya, built on the outskirts of Qayrawan by order of the imam-caliph al-Mansur, allegedly on the spot where, in 334/946, the imam-caliph had encamped when fighting against the Zenata leader Abu

Yazid. Al-Mansuriyya served as the dynasty's capital from 337/949 to 362/972–3. This city is now no longer extant except for a few remains unearthed by excavations. Literary sources, however, record that al-Mansuriyya was rich in water supply and had a caliph's palace named Khawarnaq almost at the centre of its circular layout, as well as a number of other palaces. It also featured three or more iron city gates and the city mosque (called, like the later and more famous Egyptian one, *al-Azhar*), which was the seat of the Friday public teaching sessions. Similarly to the royal palaces of other dynasties, those of al-Mansuriyya served administrative and diplomatic functions, and catered for all aspects of court life, as well as being the private dwellings of the Fatimid royals and their most important dignitaries.[1] Foreign visitors were impressed by the magnificence of al-Mansuriyya palaces, which were described as splendid structures, with waterpools and gardens. Most probably referring to the caliphal palace of al-Mansur, the contemporary Fatimid court poet ʿAli b. Muhammad al-ʿIyadi (who served in the courts of al-Mansur and al-Muʿizz) lauded its porticoes, its courtyard and the vast pool in the middle of which was the imam-caliph's audience-hall, while 'the secluded balconies around it were [like] virgins wearing girdled veils'.[2]

Finally, the last Fatimid capital, Cairo, was built after the 359/969 successful campaign in Egypt and became fully operative upon al-Muʿizz's arrival there in 362/972–3. Cairo was located on the east bank of the *Khalīj* (canal), north-east of the old Ikhshidid capital Fustat, which remained the largest city in the Mediterranean and a populous economic and commercial centre throughout the Fatimid period. Cairo underwent substantial changes and developments since its foundation. Originally, it was built on the orders of the Fatimid general Jawhar as a compound of barracks for the Fatimid troops and was surrounded by a fortification system of thick mud-brick walls and ditches. Cairo's original square layout was then enriched with the addition of a rather basic palace structure, which most probably consisted of a courtyard, a two-storey gateway and a mausoleum. It is reported that al-Muʿizz's relatives were given separate residences, and that a pavilion overlooking the Nile was erected for his wife Durzan. At around the same time, south of the palace, was built the original mosque of al-Azhar.

It was particularly under the imam-caliph al-ʿAziz that Cairo at last expanded into a royal city consisting of several palaces, an additional mosque, pavilions and bridges on the canal, bathhouses, gardens, fountains and the arsenal. The caliphate of al-ʿAziz was an eventful era in which the dynasty consolidated its political power while substantially developing the country's economy. It was also an era of creativity, when grand architectural activity served as a backdrop for increasingly sophisticated and elegant court ceremonial and celebrations. In time, Fatimid Cairo expanded within its original walls and beyond, towards the north and the south-west. Especially under the imam-caliphs al-Hakim and al-Mustansir new structures, such as the strong city gates, were added to the city landscape and existing monuments were enlarged or restored. Moreover, relatives of the imam-caliph sponsored, mostly outside the city gates, the construction and restoration of mosques, mausolea and bathhouses. New stone city walls were built by Badr al-Jamali, incorporating a larger area than the original mud walls erected by the general Jawhar. During the twelfth century, the mosque of al-Aqmar was built within the city compound upon the orders of al-Amir and his vizier al-Ma'mun, and a number of restoration works were undertaken both inside and outside the city walls.

From the time of al-ʿAziz onwards, Cairo featured two royal palaces that stood facing each other: the *qaṣr al-dhahab* ('the golden palace', henceforth the Great Palace) and *qaṣr al-baḥr* ('the Nile palace', henceforth the Small Palace). These stood in the large esplanade that was to become known as Bayn al-Qasrayn (lit. between the two palaces). Both palaces came to be described by al-Maqrizi in his *Khiṭaṭ* as compounds of several edifices, pavilions and courtyards.[3] Similarly to the model set since the ninth century by the ʿAbbasids for their court residence, the Egyptian Fatimid royal palaces – now no longer extant – were divided into two main sections, one for public audience and the other for private residence. Once fully developed, the Cairo royal palaces were multi-functional buildings, including all the main offices from the central treasury to the army complex, as well as a mausoleum.

From their splendid capital, the Fatimids sought to rival – but also to emulate – in wealth and opulence the ʿAbbasid caliphs in Baghdad, the Byzantine emperors in Constantinople and the Umayyad caliphs in al-Andalus. Rivalry among these courts took many forms: from being played out on the battlefield to being expressed through court ceremonials, including military parades and celebratory processions, as well as through the pomp that surrounded diplomatic visits. The Fatimids upstaged their ʿAbbasid, Byzantine and Umayyad counterparts in promoting the production of luxury textiles, jewellery, craftsmanship and architectural works, the quality and taste of which remained unrivalled for a long time throughout the Islamic world and beyond.

Rather than inhibiting exchanges between the major cities and countries of the Mediterranean and the Near East, international competition in fact created the circumstances under which commercial, human and intellectual exchanges prospered. If the trans-culturalism that derived from this movement of peoples was visible in towns, ports and markets, it was particularly noticeable in the palaces, where the varied personnel contributed, in its own way, to the sharing of taste, style and manners across the major courts of the period. This personnel consisted not only of dignitaries drawn from the military, scholars, jurists, court poets and talented musicians, but also of physicians, skilled artisans, chefs and even those slaves who succeded in becoming influential courtiers and concubines.[4]

2. The Sources

The court life at the Fatimid palaces is fairly well documented in a variety of written sources depicting caliphal splendor and impressive wealth and, at times, dwelling upon accounts of court ceremonies. The quality and quantity of information present in these narratives is a reflection of the diverse agendas and interests of the writers. By focusing on the public, visible and official characters of court life, the majority of these writers made only rare direct references to the lifestyle of women at court. However, when complemented with the copious indirect, incidental and anecdotal information scattered across a broad spectrum of sources, this body of material allows us to piece together some aspects of the palace women's lifestyles. These aspects include: the overall composition of the royal harems; the organisational structure of female palace staff; the wealth and attire the royal and elite court women displayed; their involvement in public and semi-public ceremonies and court protocol; the formal entertainment they enjoyed; and some pivotal personal events such as weddings and funerals.

Most of the artistic production of the Fatimid era could be classified as belonging to what has been defined as 'princely' art, focusing, as it did, on scenes of dance and courtly life. Such scenes are depicted in artefacts that were both sponsored by and made for the use of the Fatimid court.[5] Extant Fatimid pottery, woodcarvings, glass and metalwear, jewellery and textiles, which exhibit images of courtly life, add a visual dimension to narrative accounts and, in many cases, validate them. Caution in interpreting these iconographic representations is, however, de rigueur, as they could merely express formal stylistic types or conventions, rather than being faithful reflections of court life as it really was at the time. Nevertheless, some art historians have identified a degree of 'realism' in the way Fatimid artefacts depict courtly entertainment, as well as games and other activities.[6] For example, the 'realistic' character of representations of Fatimid courtly dance scenes, at times almost choreographed with both male and female dancers and musicians, is to an extent validated by the fact that very similar dances are still performed in Egypt today. Moreover, representations of courtiers or entertainers on pottery reflect the attire of women (and men) in fashion during the Fatimid period, including the use of *ṭirāz*, which is well documented in literary and documentary sources, as well as in archeological findings.

3. The Court Harems

The term *ḥarīm* is generally used to indicate the physical section of the palace reserved to women to which access was forbidden to most and limited to very few selected individuals, as well as its female and eunuch residents. The lack of documentary and archaeological evidence makes it difficult to establish where the women in al-Mahdi's family and entourage, who joined him in North Africa, came to be housed once they reached their destination. When al-Mahdi took possession of the Aghlabid palaces in Raqqada, he also inherited the harem (both as a physical space and its female residents) of the defeated ruler Ziyadat Allah. Presumably, arrangements were made to ensure that, on account of their status, al-Mahdi's women would be housed separately from those women of the former rulers who had been newly acquired as booty.

With the building of the first Fatimid royal palaces in North Africa, there is only limited evidence pointing to a space that, within a palace structure, would be used as the harem. One reference to the early Fatimid harem as physical space is indirectly provided by Idris 'Imad al-Din, who narrates that al-Mahdi, having once entered one of the rooms of his harem, found it untidy and with intruders; as a result, the imam-caliph dismissed all but one of those employed in his harem.[7] By the late tenth century, al-Qadi al-Nu'man was advising on how to furnish the women's quarters; they could be lavishly decorated and adorned with carpets, while, he adds, men's quarters should be simply furnished.[8] With reference to Cairo, as part of his description of the Great Palace, al-Maqrizi specifies that a section of it was used as residence for the harems of the imam-caliph *(maḥall ḥurumi-hi)*.[9] However, as al-Maqrizi provides only a general and vague historical context for the description of the development of the caliphal palaces' overall structure, his reference to the harem quarters does not allow us to determine when they were established or by which time they came to be fully developed.

As for the composition of the harem in the pre-dynastic period, we can only find vague references pointing to the existence in Syria of an unspecified harem belonging to 'Abd Allah, the future al-Mahdi. According to al-Mahdi's chamberlain Ja'far, upon leaving Syria for the journey which eventually took him with his master to North Africa, the 'harem' of al-Mahdi consisted of his mother, his two daughters, and two of his brother's daughters.[10] The caravan transporting the harem also included Umm Habib, who was to become the wife of al-Mahdi's son al-Qa'im, and Umm 'Ali al-Qahramana. During al-Mahdi's absence, while he was heading for North Africa, his harem had been taken care of by Abu Ahmad al-Su'luk, son of one of Ja'far's aunts, and by Abu Ja'far al-Khazari, who eventually had the task of rejoining the caravan transporting the harem with al-Mahdi, once he reached his destination.[11]

Following a long-established warfare custom of the Near and Middle East, al-Mahdi's harem was soon to be expanded thanks to the addition of all the concubines and female slaves who had belonged to the defeated Aghlabid ruler in Ifriqiya.[12] Similarly, al-Mansur annexed to his harem those of the defeated Abu Yazid, of his son and grandson. When in 362/972–3 al-Mu'izz moved from al-Mansuriyya to Cairo, he took with him all his family including his dead ancestors' relics. Idris 'Imad al-Din provides us with details about some of the women included in al-Mu'izz's caravan: four daughters of al-Mahdi, four daughters of al-Qa'im, and the five daughters of al-Mansur.[13] One can speculate that in the caravan was also Sitt al-Mulk, daughter of al-'Aziz, then just three years old. In Egypt, with the incorporation of the harems of the overthrown Ikhshidid rulers, the caliphal harem expanded further and so did those of the Fatimid high dignitaries, judging from the report that the vizier Ibn Killis had a harem of 800 women and 4,000 men as 'bodyguards'. In describing the composition of the caliphal harem in Cairo, the sources provide valuable information that reflects the complex and formal structure the harem had developed into, in all probability, by the late tenth century. Thus, the harem included the caliph's wives, his sons, his daughters, the mothers of his children, his concubines, and all their female attendants. Also part of the harem were the female members of the imam-caliph's extended family, including his mother, his aunts and his female cousins, as well as his unmarried, divorced or widowed sisters.

The expansion of the caliphal harem, paralleled by the growing complexity of the palace organisation, meant that an order of importance among its different members needed to be established. The existence of a hierarchy within the harem is reflected in the use and development of a specific, albeit not systematically applied, titulature to formally refer to its members. For example, in the eleventh century, the collective expression 'ladies of the court' was used to refer to the influential women among the caliph's female entourage. This would explain its occasional use in Geniza letters addressed to Fatimid officials asking for their intercession or thanking them for favours received. These letters included wishes for the officials concerned to find favour in the eyes of the ruler and of 'the ladies of the court'.[14]

In the context of harem hierarchy, the designation that most frequently occurs in the sources to indicate seniority is that of *sayyida*. As *al-sayyida al-malika* (lit. queen, sovereign) this title could apply to the most influential among the wives and concubines of the imam-caliph, specifically the mother of the designated heir, the queen mother, or even one of the elderly female members in his family. The other title used to indicate prominent royal women was *jiha*; as *al-jiha al-'ālīya* (lit. the high side, loosely Her Highness) the title usually designates acknowledgement of one or more royal consorts as being the most important.

a. Concubines and Slave-girls in the Harems

Irrespective of rank, as either *sayyida* or *jiha*, the ever-present figure in any medieval as well as modern representation of the harem, whether historical or literary, is that of the concubine. While there is almost no information on the identities of most of the Fatimid court concubines, on the lifestyles they enjoyed, even the language they spoke, there is a relative abundance of references to the few who became, or were perceived as being, the most famous or most important concubines. These references are interspersed in the historical narrative and, in most cases, presented in anecdotal form. Even though the historical value of these anecdotes is limited, they nevertheless reflect contemporary or retrospectively projected perceptions of what the concubines' roles and lives must have been like. Fadwa Malti-Douglas has identified three elements that characterise the anecdotal woman in medieval *adab* literature as a whole: eloquence, ruse and sexuality.[15] Broadly speaking, these elements transpire from those anecdotal narratives that refer to court women during the Fatimid period. Historically more valuable are the references to details included in the narrative, such as their ethnic or geographical origins, the way some of them were acquired, and the allocations and gifts bestowed on them.

The resorting to anecdotal accounts that feature emotional stories of love and sorrow between the powerful princely master and the concubine often serve the narrator the propagandist purpose of either exposing or revealing the personality of the male protagonist. For the detractor, the ruler would come across as the feeble-minded man who would concede easily to pleasure. The beautiful concubine would twist him around her little finger and he could therefore not be trusted with governance. For the supporter, such liaisons proved the ruler's sexual prowess and manliness, as well as his ability to be, among other things, a well-rounded human being with feelings and emotions.

Another interpretative key can be applied to the accounts relating to the acquisition of concubines and slave-girls as part of war booty, whereby the physical possession of the women signified the ultimate symbol of subjugation and humiliation for the defeated enemy, who would be symbolically emasculated and hurt at his most intimate level. Through possession, the victor would 'mark' the enemy's women with his dynastic imprint. And indeed, the early Fatimids imprinted a lot as they progressively annexed the women in the harems of those they defeated or succeeded. Typically portrayed as beautiful singers, dancers and musicians, court concubines come across as a coveted possession, a source of pleasant company and diversion for their masters and the recipients of their affection.

Somewhat romantically, the historian Ibn Khalliqan informs us that al-Mansur had a concubine named Qadib, of whom he was passionately fond.[16] Al-Maqrizi, referring to al-Mu'izz's sons, tells us of 'A'isha, the beloved concubine of 'Abd Allah, and reports a number of anecdotes on al-Mu'izz's eldest son, prince Tamim, reputed for devoting his life – and poetry – to courtly pleasures. One day Tamim was passing by a street when he heard a slave-girl singing expertly and playing the lute. Greatly impressed, he demanded that her master take her to his own palace. She was beautiful and on several occasions she had shown fondness for her ugly-looking, but kind, master by refusing to leave him when he was offered a high price for her. But this time it was the prince Tamim who wanted her, and who gave her master twice the amount of money he had asked for. Prince Tamim took the girl to the palace, manumitted her and married her. More emotionally charged is a second anecdote on Tamim. He once received from Baghdad a beautiful, exceptionally gifted slave-girl singer. He grew so fond of her that one day he asked her to express her most coveted wish, promising he would satisfy her demand. The girl pleaded to return to Baghdad and the prince, though full of sadness, kept his promise. He arranged for a convoy to take her back, but just before reaching Baghdad the girl vanished into thin air, never to be found again. The mysterious disappearance was reported back to Tamim, who never ceased thinking about her ever after.[17]

Both stories project traits of Tamim's personality – such as his fondness of singing girls, the means he used to get his object of desire, his being responsible for his own loss – that reveal a man guided by emotion rather than reason. In other words, more a fool than a leader! All in all, these anecdotes are part of a stereotypical portrayal of this first-born son of an imam-caliph who twice by-passed him by appointing his younger brothers as his successors.

Other anecdotes can be found regarding the concubines in the harems of Fatimid high court dignitaries. In Syria, Sa'd al-Dawla (d. 381/991), the local governor acting for al-'Aziz, had a slave-girl called Infirad, whom he preferred over his other 400 concubines. His bedroom antics with the beautiful Infirad brought the randy governor to an early death – indeed, having made love to her, he had a stroke, which left him half paralysed. He died three days later.[18] In the case of the vizier al-Afdal, it was the concubine who paid the price for excessive 'love'! The vizier is reported as having had some 800 slave-women, 50 of whom were his favourite concubines, each allocated a private room as well as a trousseau of clothes, brocades, gold, silver and jewels. He was so possessive that he had one of his favorite concubines beheaded, in an excess of jealousy, for simply seeing her gazing out towards the street. Presumably with some remorse, when he finally had her head in his hands, he wrote for her a beautiful elegy![19] Finally, for a high dignitary to see his concubines publicly 'exposed' could constitute the ultimate form of insult and humiliation at the hands of his opponents. In the Yemen, a group of Shafi'i jurists revolted against Sulayhid rule and seized the fortress of queen Arwa's high dignitary al-Mufaddal. They ordered his concubines to wear their finest clothes and to go and play their tambourines on the roof of his fortress. At the sight of his concubines playing and dancing 'in public', al-Mufaddal, wounded in his honour, had a fatal heart attack.[20]

Apart from concubines, either free-born or slave, and the female relatives of the master, the harem included female servants who attended to the needs of the other harem women. A caliph's daughter such as Sitt Misr would have thousands of *jāriyas* at her service and, even towards the end of the Fatimid dynasty, one of al-Amir's consorts, the high *jihat al-dār al-jadīda*, is reported to have had at least twenty. In turn, a highly placed *jāriya* would have *jāriyas* as attendants. Most of these female servants were slaves, many having arrived at the Fatimid court as part of booty. Among the earliest examples of enslavement of women as part of military campaigns, ostensibly carried out on behalf of the Fatimids, are the cases of two groups of women from two outposts of Isma'ili propaganda. In the Yemen, in 297/909, when the *dā'ī* Ibn al-Fadl conquered the city of Zabid, which was the seat of the 'Abbasid governor, he looted the city and took its women. In North Africa, in 302/914, the commander Hubasa, who advanced from Tripoli to Barqa on behalf of al-Qa'im, enslaved the consorts of the Mazata chieftains, after ordering the execution of their husbands and their sons.

Other female slaves arrived at the Fatimid court harems as part of lavish gifts that the powerful rulers of the time would exchange for diplomatic reasons to consolidate further political and economic ties. In 405/1014, the Zirid Badis sent magnificent presents to al-Hakim, which included twenty young slave-girls.[21] In 420/1029, and again in 424/1033, Badis's son, al-Mu'izz, sent the imam-caliph al-Zahir twenty beautiful slave-girls bejewelled with silver lockets over their breasts. Al-Zahir in turn sent the Zirid ruler other gifts among which were slave-girls known to have been expert singers and dancers. In 444/1052–3, the Byzantine emperor Michael IV sent al-Mustansir Turkish slaves; in 454/1062, al-Mustansir also received lavish and much-needed presents sent to him from the Yemen by 'Ali b. Muhammad al-Sulayhi, including eunuchs and slave-girls.[22] Some years later, in 462/1070, it was Iqbal al-Dawla, one of the rulers in al-Andalus, who sent al-Mustansir a gift of female as well as male slaves.[23]

To give slave-girls as gifts was part of international and domestic diplomatic exchanges. In North Africa, al-Mahdi gave some of Ziyad Allah's female slaves to the loyal Kutama high dignitaries,[24] while the imam-caliph al-Mu'izz is reported to have given slave-girls to al-Qadi al-Nu'man. Female slaves at the Fatimid court harem were also treated as a commodity, in that they could be bought or sold at the slave market.

This vast movement of women from court to court, from country to country, from continent to continent, meant that the Fatimid harems became a multi-ethnic, multi-cultural and religiously and linguistically diversified feminine universe. Many harem women were Christians and some are reported to have remained so; some were Jews and many others were Muslims or converts to Islam. Whether wives or concubines, relatives or servants, free-born or slaves, the women of the court harems were deemed as countless by several contemporary and later observers of the Fatimids. It certainly seemed so to the Persian poet and *dā'ī* Nasir-i Khusraw, who, having visited Cairo during the caliphate of al-Mustansir, stated that the women of the caliphal harem were so many that it was impossible to count them.[25] The same perception of numerical might transpires from the historical accounts on the Zirids: with regards to Buluggin, not only do sources tell us that he had 400 concubines, but also that he witnessed, in one day, the birth of as many as seventeen of his children.[26]

b. Women's Voices from the Harem

All the sources used in this section, whether including incidental references to the harems, anecdotal accounts on some of their women or reflecting commonly held perceptions about them, were written by men who, by virtue of their gender, had no access to the harem, and who wrote for a male audience. All in all, female voices are neither recorded nor directly heard. Occasionally, albeit mediated by a male narrator, there are records of these women's desires, their priorities, their fears, their versions of their personal stories. Even when their voices are heard, however, these women remain on the whole nameless. In Ifriqiya, once taken captive, the women formerly in the harem of the subjugated Aghlabid ruler voiced their requests to the new master, al-Mahdi, through their spokeswoman named Rawandu (or Ruwayla). Their priorities can be inferred from demands appropriate to their status: essentials such as good food and fine clothing, optionals such as sex and wine – the latter was, in fact, refused – and what ordinary people would have termed as luxuries: mattresses and soft blankets.[27]

We can also infer that, in everyday life, it was important for harem women to be together for company and social interaction, particularly in small palaces and courts. In al-Mansuriyya, the imam-caliph al-Muʿizz gave as a gift to al-Qadi al-Nuʿman a number of slave-girls whom the judge passed on to his sons as concubines. When, with the birth of children, the housing conditions in the *qāḍī*'s palace became impractical because of over-crowding, the slave-girls asked not to be scattered but to remain in each other's company so as not to feel lonely and isolated.[28] This is but a glimpse of the concerns of elite concubines and of their need for friendship and reciprocal support in an enclosed surrounding.

Finally, a direct testimony comes from the slave-girl of Abu Muhammad, son of Abu'l-Fadl Jaʿfar b. al-Furat (d. 392/1001), who had been an Ikhshidid vizier and remained a prominent figure under the Fatimids. Here is her testimony as reported by al-Maqrizi:

> I was living next door to him [Abu'l-Fadl] after the death of my master Abu Muhammad, with my daughter and a number of slave-girls at my service. One night a party came to summon me and I was taken, with my daughter and the slave-girls, to Abu'l-Fadl's house. Once we reached his place, both my daughter and myself kissed his hand. He ordered us to sit down and to

sing. I asked for a lute and began [singing] but I had just started when I saw him cover his face with a sleeve and cry. I stopped singing but he ordered me to continue. Once I finished, a servant took me by the hand and brought me, together with my daughter and my slave-girls, to a room full of the finest furnishings and food. However, once we entered, they locked the doors behind us, and by God, I did not set foot out of that room until he died.[29]

4. Female Staff at the Palace

The distinction is somewhat blurred between the personnel working specifically for the harem and female personnel working for the palace as a whole. Some female staff resided within the palace walls (*muqīmāt*), others were non-resident (*munqaṭiʿāt*) and must have lived either in Fustat or in commutable areas, such as the Qarafa, near to the royal city. The running of the court was dependent upon a vast staff. Most important in the Fatimid palace was the *ḥājib*, a chamberlain or master of ceremonies, whose main role was that of guarding and filtering access to the imam-caliph. Well known is the already-mentioned eunuch Jaʿfar, who was the *ḥājib* of al-Mahdi and who left a very useful record of the early Fatimid history. Once the seat of power moved to Cairo, the figure appears of the *sāḥib al-bāb*, or chief chamberlain, whose role developed, during the last phase of the dynasty, into that of a commander, a so-called 'man of the sword', who was second only to the vizier.[30] Vital for the running of the harem, as well as the many other palace sections, was the role played by the eunuchs. In the harem their function was to oversee the women, to guard them, to inform them and report on them. In other words, they were the link between the harem and the outside world.

Whether free or slave, the women who worked at the palace were broadly called *mustakhdimāt* or *quṣūriyyāt*, whereas those working in the factories serving the court were called *arbāb al-ṣanāʿi min al-quṣūriyyāt*. Rankwise, the most-highly placed employees were those attending to the personal needs of the caliph and his family, of the *jihāt* and high dignitaries. These were usually ladies of good social status, such as the wife of al-Sharif al-Musawi (d. 415/1024), who lived in the Akhdar Mosque and whose funeral service was led by the *dāʿī al-duʿāt* of the time. She resided at the palace while her sister-in-law had worked as a non-resident member of staff for Sitt al-Mulk.[31]

Twelfth century Fatimid records give us an insight into the organisation of female personnel employed in tailoring ateliers and food manufacture and preparation. As palace staff members, they came under the supervision of the palace head of personnel, called *ẓimām al-quṣūr*. There were two kinds of tailoring ateliers: the 'external' or public (*ẓāhir*); and the 'internal' or for the exclusive private (*khaṣṣa*) needs of the imam-caliph. The former was under the supervision of a eunuch, whereas the latter was supervised by a woman who held the title of *zayn al-khuzzān*. She would have some thirty women working under her and her responsibility was to deal with the most precious robes, such as those embroidered in gold, reserved for court use and, very importantly, also to organise the imam-caliph's private wardrobe. Because of her status, the *zayn al-khuzzān* would wear a gilt garment (*ḥulla*).[32] Nevertheless, the placing of the crown (a turban, in fact) on the head of the imam-caliph was a privilege reserved to a eunuch. Towards the end of the Fatimid dynasty, the *zayn al-khuzzān* was known to have been most likely a slave-girl of Greek/Byzantine origins.[33]

As for the palace kitchen, this consisted of the *maṭbakh al-qaṣr*, where meats and savoury products would be prepared; the *dār al-fiṭra*, destined for the preparation of patisserie, and the *dār al-tawābil*, used for the preparation of the seasonings. Women catered for most aspects of food acquisition, and its preparation as well as its presentation. Palace kitchen female personnel would include the supervisor of the table, the inspectors and the supervisors of the Treasury of the Drinks.[34] According to Nasir-i Khusraw, at the time of al-Mustansir the kitchen was just outside the palace and employed fifty people. Other sources specify that the kitchen was linked to the palace by an underground passage, through which the meals reserved to the caliph, the harem and the palace personnel would be promptly delivered. That many of the persons employed in the kitchen were women is indirectly confirmed by Ibn Saʿid al-Maghribi (d. 685/1286), who tells us of excellent women chefs who had learned their art at the Fatimid palace.[35]

In 516/1122, at the court of al-Amir, the presence is also attested of women in positions of responsibility at court, such as six lady treasures (*khuzzān*) and ten female standing attendants (*waqqāfāt*).[36] A curious anecdote on the vizier al-Afdal illustrates the extent of a ruler's fascination, in the Fatimid court of the twelfth century, with the idea of having female attendants. In a detailed description of al-Afdal's riches and possessions, Ibn Muyassar tells us that the vizier had a hall where he used to go to relax and drink. In it there were the mannequins (*ṣiwar*) of eight slave-girls facing each other, dressed in beautiful and expensive garments and bejewelled. Four of them were white and made of camphor, and four were black, made of amber. Al-Afdal's stepping into the room from the door of the audience hall would cause their heads to bow down, in a sign of respect, while his sitting in the room would make their heads rise.[37]

During the caliphate of al-Amir's successor, al-Hafiz, a woman, in flesh and blood, rose to the position of supervisor of the caliphal inkwell (*dawā*), which was one of the most important insignia of sovereignty. Her name was Sitt Ghazal and it is reported that, while she knew everything to do with pens, inkwells and cotton tufts, she was totally ignorant about everything else; she had a eunuch at her service. Another woman became al-Hafiz's standing-attendant. Both must have become wealthy, as they are acknowledged as patronesses of mosques.[38]

Also highly valued was the role of the wetnurses, who attended to the newborn babies of the imam-caliph. Working closer than anybody else to the royal infants, the job of wetnurse was a sensitive one and worth paying for. Wetnurses had to be completely trustworthy and their royal employers would have to make sure they would remain so, as the survival of the infant princes and, possibly, succession matters, could depend on their good work. The raising of the young princes in the healthiest possible way, in a context where infant mortality was high, remained the ruler's main concern to ensure succession. Being contractually bound to the father-cum-ruler, the nurse had also a 'broker' role in dynastic family matters. Coming, as she did, between mother and child, and in many cases taking the natural mother's place altogether, she was potentially an instrumental figure at the ruler's disposal to deflect power away from a given natural mother and allow him to exercise some control over a typically male-excluded zone.

As privileges could increase dramatically for a court nurse, should the child in her care be one day designated for succession, she would obviously have a vested interest in backing the succession claims of 'her' prince. For example, Salaf is reported to have had great influence in securing the succession of her milk-son, the imam-caliph al-Mansur. At the Zirid court, famous is the case of the influence attained by the nurse Fatima, known as Hadina Badis, a Christian slave converted to Islam who was eventually raised to the rank of Sanhaja princess.[39] Court nurses had plenty to gain from their position. It was probably because of the sensitive position they held that their work was handsomely compensated. In 415/1024, the house of ʿA'isha, the wealthy slave-girl who had belonged to al-Muʿizz's son ʿAbd Allah, was handed over to a nurse known as Zarqa. In the same year, another nurse called Safwat al-Raqama al-Nasraniyya was given a high-class house of al-Hakim, called al-Barjawaniyya, located to the side of the palace of al-Sayyida al-ʿAmma, that is Sitt al-Mulk.[40]

Also, as milk-brother of the future ruler, the son of a wetnurse would be well placed to bask one day in his milk-brother's power. Having almost equal rights to those of a blood brother, a ruler would potentially find in the milk-brother his perfect ally: a person legally committed to most family obligations but excluded from dynastic claims. Allegedly, Jaʿfar the chamberlain was the milk-brother of the imam-caliph al-Mahdi and remained one of his most trusted persons throughout his life.

Al-Maqrizi reports that, at the Fatimid palace in Cairo, there were also women employed as stablewomen (*shadādāt*) to work in the underground tunnels (*sarādīb*) that linked parts of the palace. These workers would operate a delivery service of goods and of people by using mules and donkeys.[41] The imam-caliph himself would resort to this system of transport to move in and out of the Great Palace to go to the Small Palace, to the Kafur gardens or to the pavilions along the canal, without exposing himself to the curiosity of onlookers. In time, the tunnels were used also by the viziers to go from their private palaces to their office in the Great Palace. The tunnels served as an escape route in time of siege, and also for gruesome events such as the delivery of corpses. It is through these tunnels that the corpses of three caliphs (al-Amir, al-Hafiz and al-Fa'iz), who in turn died while at a pavilion on the west bank of the Nile, called *manẓarat al-lu'lu'a* (the pearl pavilion), were returned to the palace.[42]

With such a complex and vast personnel, the court palaces were places pulsating with life and activity. The sources reflect such vibrancy by providing grand figures to provoke a sense of astonishment in the reader. These figures had mostly notional value but there is little doubt that the Fatimid palace male and female staff, must have been very numerous indeed. Towards the end of al-'Aziz's reign and in the earliest phase of al-Hakim's, the overall palace staff was reported to be in the region of 10,000. By al-Mustansir's time, there were in the palace allegedly 12,000 servants and a total of 30,000 people living there.[43] Even towards the end of the dynasty, the number of men and women working at the palace was estimated to be above 18,000. Al-Maqrizi states that when, in 567/1171, Saladin took the caliphal palace, its residents amounted to 12,000 persons.[44]

5. The Palace and the 'Politics' of Dress

Not long after his arrival in Egypt, the imam-caliph al-Mu'izz decreed that women should not wear large *sirwāls* (baggy trousers).[45] Issued during a year of economic crisis, and presumably intended as a measure to limit the amount of material needed to manufacture them, this seemingly unusual decree signals the Fatimids' keen interest in monitoring the output of the already well-established Egyptian textile industry. Indeed, throughout their rule, the Fatimid imam-caliphs greatly promoted the production and distribution of plain and embroidered fabrics. Not only were textiles exchanged as a valued commodity, but the Fatimids also used them on a grand scale in the manufacture of palace ceremonial costumes and bestowed them as gifts symbolic of royal favour, as in the case, under the imam-caliph al-'Aziz, of an unusually petite and cultivated woman from Syria. She was brought to the Cairo court, where she was given hospitality and, on a single occasion, received as a caliphal gift as many as 100 dresses of heavy material and silk, which had been specifically cut for her. This form of bestowal was not exclusive to the imam-caliph, but could also come from his wife. In 381/991, al-Sayyida al-'Aziziyya sent to the new-born son of a high dignitary 100 items of clothing, 500 *dīnārs* and two cots, in addition to the vast amount of clothes that had been already donated to him by her husband.[46]

The finest and most precious of fabrics was the so-called *ṭirāz*,[47] a type of linen embroidered with gold or silver threads featuring bands inscribed with the imam-caliph's name. Other fabrics included silk and brocade. The textile production took place in at least four factories in Egypt, the most renowned being that in the delta city of Tinnis. The manufacture of *ṭirāz*, in particular, was closely monitored by the palace because it was carried out under the auspices of the imam-caliph, whose name on this type of fabric could only be used after official approval. Moreover, the large quantities of gold and silver spun into thread required the presence *in situ* of loyal and trusted supervisors, appointed by the palace.[48]

As commodities, textiles formed part of the prized possessions of the Fatimid royals and their high dignitaries. Particularly since the early Egyptian days of the dynasty, vast quantities of the finest textiles and dresses are regularly noted by the sources as part of the wealth belonging to the royal princesses. Indeed, large amounts of clothing were listed in the inventory of the treasures left at their death by al-Mu'izz's daughters Rashida and 'Abda, as will be shown in Chapter 5.

The finest of fabrics were used in the imam-caliph's personal atelier. The imam-caliph's public attire was charged with symbolic meaning, conveyed through the choice of material, of colour (mostly white), of the number of pieces of his garment and of the insignia, such as the royal parasol. Also significant was the type of dress worn by the court dignitaries and the imam's entourage as a reflection or indication of their hierarchical status. From the reign of al-Mu'izz onwards, the wearing of specific clothes in specific fabrics reflected the ranks of high officials, thereby pointing to a strongly centralised hierarchical royal administration.[49]

By the twelfth century, Fatimid palace women are described as conforming to a formalised dress code that indicated not only their vicinity and kinship to the caliph, but also reflected the position and status of their fathers, brothers, husbands or masters. In reporting the budget records for the year 516/1122, al-Bata'ihi lists, in order of importance, the court women to whom the palace treasury had allocated expensive items of clothing. The value and complexity of the garments, of which he specifies each item, is proportional to the women's hierarchical status. With reference to al-Amir's consorts, al-Bata'ihi reports that the *jiha* al-'Aliya *bi-'l-dār al-jadīda*, at whose service was the eunuch Jawhar, was allocated a long, flowing gilt garment (*ḥulla mudhahhaba*) made of fifteen pieces and valued in Iraqi gold. The *jiha*, at whose service was the *qāḍī* Maknun, also known as 'Alam al-Amiriyya, was given a garment of the same value and style. That the *jiha* Murshid, *jiha* 'Anbar, the *sayyida jiha* Zill and the *jiha* Munjab held a lower status can be inferred by their allocation of a gilt garment each, made of fourteen pieces and lower in value. Other female members of al-Amir's family, the *sayyida 'amma* and the *sayyida* al-'Abida *al-'amma*, were only allotted a gilt garment each, with no indication of the number of pieces or its value. On the other hand, the daughters, the consorts and the senior ladies of less important clients of al-Amir were allocated a silk garment. Among them, the *jiha* of the client Abu'l-Fadl Ja'far, at whose service was the eunuch Rayhan, must have enjoyed a higher status, as her allocation consisted of a gilt garment. This lady may be the same as the *jiha* Rayhan, who became one of al-Hafiz's consorts. This list reveals how far the treasury went in recording details of and expenditure on female court garments, down to specifying the pairs of shoes they were entitled to![50]

The above description clearly reflects a twelfth-century situation. It is, however, not possible to indicate the time when, in the Fatimid court, a formalised dress code for women was introduced. What seems to be taking place during the twelfth century is an overall expansion of palace bureaucracy, which is reflected in the codification of female attire according to rank, in the increased use of formal hierarchical titulature, and in the formalisation of a complex court ceremonial. One could speculate that these developments in the palace coincided with the shift in the exercise of government from the hands of the caliph to those of the vizier. Accordingly, the growth of the office of the vizier brought about an expansion of the administrative apparatus and, with it, a fuller control of all aspects of court life, including the setting of treasury regulations on female attire and clothing allocation.

No other dynasty made better use of fine fabrics and *ṭirāz* as an expression of favour and patronage as did the Fatimids. Robes of honour (*khila'*) were bestowed in the name of the Fatimid imam-caliph upon clients and supporters of the dynasty, as well as worthy individuals, whether Muslims or non-Muslims.[51] All in all, such widespread and well-documented use indicated who was 'in charge' and who was close to and associated with power. The *ṭirāz* featured formulae of blessing upon the imam and his 'pure ancestors', or lists of the legitimate imams of the 'Alid line, thus stating and broadcasting the legitimacy of the imam, his genealogical claims and those of the dynasty as a whole.[52] High dignitaries, clients and their women were handsomely rewarded for their services and loyalty with gilt attires, whereas more distant supporters, both male and female, were mainly 'only' given silk garments. Though in theory the bestowal of robes of honour was the imam-caliph's prerogative, in practice it was also carried out by the vizier or other high dignitaries. Al-Maqrizi implicitly attests the political value attached to female attire when he reports the practice of extending the prestige of palace recognition to the women of the recipient of the robe of honour. When al-Mu'tamin, the vizier al-Ma'mun's brother, bestowed a robe of honour upon the *qāḍī* of Alexandria, al-Makin Abu Talib b. Hadid (d. 528/1133), he also sent two gilt garments to his women, together with a parcel containing silk women's wraps.[53]

The court set the fashion for the expanding wealthy strata of society who, in turn, reinterpreted the original meaning and purpose of court dress politics. They imitated the use of the embroidered *ṭirāz*, and even 'personalised' the clothes by having inscribed the names of the wearer. The fashion of *ṭirāz* was further popularised with the production of 'imitation' inscription bands, with fake writing!

6. The Entertainment

a. Court Poetry, Music and Dance

Throughout the medieval Muslim world, court poetry, while entertaining, was intended as a device to communicate ideas to audiences both inside and outside the court, as well as a vehicle of power legitimisation. Dependent for his livelihood upon patronage, the court poet worked for the ruler and against his enemies: he was an instrument of propaganda and an integral part of the palace machinery. In a nutshell, he was the court PR. As holder of a position that would bring him in physical contact with almost exclusively male audiences, the court poet would have to be a man. It is therefore not surprising that, in common with other contemporary dynasties, the output of Fatimid court poetry lacks the direct female voice. However, women do feature in Fatimid poetry. The Fatimid court poets honoured in their verses Fatima, whom they considered the exemplary female model and the best woman of all times. Through elegies or eulogies, poets such as Ibn Hani', al-Sultan al-Khattab and the lesser known al-Mutabbib also praised the prominent women of their time, both VIPs of the calibre of Sitt al-Mulk and queen Arwa, and elite women related to the imam-caliphs and high officials. Distinguished men would commission the composition of poems as a seduction technique, as did the page Farij, who asked the poet Abu Ja'far al-Bahraj to write a poem so that he could win over Husna, the slave he desired. Poetry was also used as an effective means to show familial love, as in the case of the poet Wajih al-Dawla Abu 'l-Mata' (d. 428/1036), who dedicated a poem to his elder sister.[54]

More often though, like their colleagues in other courts, poets 'invented' women for the pleasure of the patron. The woman would be represented in Fatimid poetical sources as beautiful, cunning, playful, teasing, seductive and decorative – typically a slave, a low-class woman or, at best, a mysterious and exotic creature. By contrast, 'the woman' as 'the bride' would serve as a powerful metaphor for what the institution of the imamate would be like in relation to the imam.[55] One of the best-known Fatimid poets is Tamim, son of the imam-caliph al-Mu'izz, whose poetry, populated by shapely girls, female dancers, musicians and wine-pouring women, epitomised and inspired a vision of what Fatimid court life might have been like.

Besides formal occasions, court poetry also circulated informally, as entertainment of the harem women, who on occasion were known to express their informed criticism. When, for example, the educated consorts of the Zirid al-Mu'izz criticised the delicate and feminine type of poetry that he had commissioned, he asked, as a result, two of his court poets to compose verses that would please his women.[56] At the same time, court women could express their appreciation of poetry by handsomely rewarding the poet. In the year 550/1155, the Fatimid princess al-Sayyida al-Sharifa, daughter of al-Hafiz, contributed to the donation of 500 *dīnārs* to the famous poet 'Umara, who had recited his poetry in the Golden Room in front of the caliph al-Fa'iz, his vizier Salih Tala'i' b. Ruzzik, the princes and others.[57]

If the typical 'professional' court poet was inevitably a man, this does not preclude the presence at court of a few poetesses, mostly amateur. The likes of princesses Wallada of Cordova and Umm al-Kiram of Almería, or slave-poetesses like Mut'a and Uns al-Qulub, of Hafsa al-Gharnatiyya, 'A'isha al-Qurtubiyya, the concubine Binan, and the pious Shuhda, entertained with their verses the Umayyad courts of al-Andalus and the 'Abbasid court in Baghdad.[58] As far as the Fatimid courts are concerned, the names of their poetesses have remained thus far unknown … except for the notable 'Aliya al-Badawiyya. She lived with her Arab Bedouin tribe in Upper Egypt during the caliphate of al-Amir. The fame of her beauty and poetical talent reached the caliph in Cairo and prompted him to go and meet her. He asked her to join him at court but she declined the offer. Disappointed, al-Amir returned to Cairo and made a request to her tribe to give her in marriage to him. Her tribesmen obliged and she finally married the caliph. City and palace life did not suit her as she longed for her free life in the open air, so to please her, al-Amir ordered that a pavilion be built for her on the banks of the Nile. Her longing was not only for her former free life but also for her former lover, her cousin Ibn Miyah! She wrote:

O Ibn Miyah, to you I raise a complaint
  The possessor has eventually been possessed
You were living the life of a free man
  Achieving what you wanted successfully
While, now, I am shut in a palace
  I know of naught but seclusion and constraint
How many times were our sinuous limbs inter-twined
  Where we did not fear for a glance to reach us
We played around at Ramalat al-Hima (lit. sands of passion)
  Whenever an unfettered person went his way[59]

It is reported that her cousin replied with verses that were intercepted by al-Amir, who, with aplomb and a dry sense of humour, stated that, had the quality

Fig. 2 Eleventh–twelfth-century ivory panel from Egypt, depicting merry-making scenes, with women playing a variety of wind and string instruments.
Inv. I.6375. Copyright © Bpk Berlin/Museum für Islamische Kunst, Staatliche Museen zu Berlin. Photo: Georg Niedermeiser.

of his verses been of a higher standard, he would have sent al-Badawiyya back to him. The love story of ʿAliya al-Badawiyya and Ibn Miyah became as famous as the 1,001 Nights and al-Amir's private affairs became the talk of the town. So did the verses of his wife![60]

Besides poetry, court entertainment included music and dance. Scenes of dance, music performances, games and other leisurely activities appear in ceramic paintings, ivories and wood carvings of the Fatimid period and confirm the poetical representation of the hedonistic lifestyle prevalent at court or, rather, the image of prosperity that the court intended to project of itself. Fatimid artefacts feature male and female dancers, as well as musicians, with some dancers seemingly singing and others playing castanets while performing (see Figs 2 and 3).[61] The range of instruments musicians are shown to play is wide and includes percussion, wind and string instruments, such as the drums and the *qānūn*, the oboe and the flute, as well as the harp and the lute. As for the context in which music and dance were perfomed, literary sources provide us with descriptions of family occasions and private parties, as well as more public events, where women were present both as performers and guests.

Jaʿfar the chamberlain reminisces in his memoires of the joyous occasion of al-Mahdi's wedding night in Salamiyya. He describes how, having stood in waiting outside the nuptial bedroom, he danced and played with some unveiled women to celebrate the consummation of the marriage.[62] During the dynastic period, music and dance performances were staged for private parties organised by the caliph in his palace, as well as in the houses of high dignitaries. In Cairo, al-ʿAziz staged a party in the hall of the Treasury, in which his mother Durzan, his closest slave-girls, the eunuchs and every woman musician (*mulhīya*) in the

palace participated. The Treasury room resounded with singing and the sound of all kinds of musical instruments. After singing and drinking, al-ʿAziz invited the slave-girls to take precious pearls he had ordered to be laid on a carpet, following the rediscovery of a treasure box of his father al-Muʿizz, which was thought to have been lost.[63] Among the high-ranking dignitaries, Barjawan was known occasionally to cut his work short to indulge in the pleasure of listening to music and singing. Male and female singers would gather at his house, he would join in the singing and the party would continue till late. One of the best-known female court singers of al-Hakim and al-Zahir's time was Malak al-Rasiya, who had been the *jāriya* of a prominent Cairine lady of the time.[64]

Dance and music also featured in some public events, such as processions and festivals. Al-Maqrizi reports the occasion when the imam-caliph al-Zahir, while solemnly going through Cairo, was preceded by a procession of dancers.[65] Nasir-i Khusraw noted that music accompanied the celebration of important festivities and civil occasions, such as the opening of the canal.[66] Notable is the presence at the time of al-Mustansir of a female palace drummer called Nasab, who played a public role in advertising the Fatimid victory of 450/1058 over the ʿAbbasids by celebrating the arrival in Cairo of the ʿAbbasids' insignia from Baghdad. According to al-Maqrizi, she used to stand under the palace and to march with her group (a band of musicians or singers), singing in procession.[67]

Court entertainment was not confined to the palace and encompassed other leisurely activities. It was not unusual for the imam-caliph or for high dignitaries to take their harems and servants to holiday residences built along the shores of the Nile. In the year 414/1023, the Fatimid court official al-Musabbihi organised an outing to his house on the shores of the Nile, taking with him his

Fig. 3 Eleventh–twelfth-century ivory plaque from casket, with dancing woman in an elaborately patterned outfit carrying a musical instrument.
Inv. 80c, Museo del Bargello, Florence, Italy. Courtesy of the Ministero dei Beni e le Attività Culturali. Reproduction by any means is forbidden. Photo: Paolo Tosi.

harem, which included his concubine, the *umm al-walad* al-ʿAziza, those close to him and his wife. The year after, the imam-caliph al-Zahir also took his harem and entourage to the resorts of al-Mushtaha and Rumayla.[68] Al-Mustansir is also known to have taken his female entourage out of town. By the twelfth century, retreating to holiday resorts had become a regular feature of court life. Al-Amir would depart for the pavilion of Lu'lu'a, on the Nile, with his *jihāts*, brothers, daughters and aunts. This destination was so sought after that his vizier, al-Ma'mun, had ordered the renovation of the pavilions opposite Lu'lu'a and the clearance of the houses built by the Sudanese troops in the eleventh century and later abandoned.[69]

b. A Few Weddings and Some Funerals

Functions and celebrations in the domestic or private sphere often have a distinctive 'public' character in providing an opportunity for officiants and participants to informally demonstrate to onlookers wealth, power and status. This is particularly the case with rituals of passage, such as births, weddings and funerals. The Fatimids, like other ruling dynasties, were obviously aware of the appeal that a public display of private life had to the crowd. An unusually high level of publicity was given to the marriage in 369/979 of the imam-caliph al-ʿAziz to a high-profile, presumably Egyptian, woman whose elevated status is indicated by the 200,000-*dīnār* dowry she received. After the wedding, the nuptial party is reported to have toured the city to the sound of drums and trumpets.[70] Within the framework of the events and developments characterising al-ʿAziz's caliphate, this nuptial tour fitted well within an overall policy to use Cairo as a public stage of power display, and confirm the focal role of Cairo and Egypt as the centre of an expanding Fatimid empire. Information on the ceremonies relating to the weddings of women in the royal family is non-existent. As far as the daughters of the imam-caliphs are concerned, such silence, matched by honomastic evidence, leads us to infer that, from the time of the imam-caliph al-Mansur onwards, they remained by and large celibate (see Chapter 5). With regard to more distant female relations in the caliphal family, references to their marriages, but not to the ceremonies, only occur when, as cousins, they marry the imam-caliph.

Paradoxically, weddings of elite, non-royal, court women receive marginally more attention. It is within the context of accounts on the lives and deeds of high court dignitaries that an insight can be gained into some wedding practices of their daughters and female relatives. We learn, for example, that weddings of distinguished members of the court could take place in the presence of the imam-caliph himself and that it would be arranged for the dowry to be paid by the state Treasury. Such was the case of the daughter of Ibrahim b. Dawwas

Hasan al-Islam (d. after 362/972), who had loyally followed al-Mu'izz to Egypt. She was given in marriage to a certain 'Abd Allah b. Isma'il al-Husayni in the presence of the imam-caliph himself.[71] The wealth of court officials and the extravagant expenditure they could indulge in, on the occasion of family weddings, is illustrated by the anecdote surrounding the marriage of the sister of al-'Aziz's wife's scribe. In 381/991, she was given in marriage to Buktikin al-Turki in Damascus, with a dowry of 100,000 *dīnār*s carried in boxes by thirty mules. For the banquet 20,000 animals were slaughtered, including stags, lambs, goats, ducks and other poultry. Twenty dome-shaped buildings were erected to host the banquet, which lasted for days until the groom fell ill. Not surprisingly, the bride was widowed only five months and eleven days after the wedding![72]

By contrast with the overall paucity of information on the Fatimid royal weddings, sources provide detailed descriptions of lavish nuptial celebrations of members of dynasties ruling on behalf of the Fatimids. In 413/1022–3, at the age of fifteen, the Zirid al-Mu'izz b. Badis married Umm Yusuf Zulaykha. The wedding was of a lavishness that had not been seen for any other monarch in Ifriqiya. Pavilions were built outside al-Mansuriyya and the wedding took place among a big deployment of artefacts, textiles and an incredible profusion of musical instruments. In 415/1024, another sumptuous marriage took place in Ifriqiya between Umm al-'Ulu, sister of al-Mu'izz, and her cousin 'Abd Allah b. Hammad al-Sanhaji. According to Ibn 'Idhari, the grand *īwān* of the royal palace was adorned in honour of the bride for the occasion. The crowd was admitted in to admire the precious stones, the textiles, the objects, and the golden and silver vases that had been given to her as presents. All the wedding gifts were transferred to purpose-built pavilions and tents. The amount of money given for the bride's dowry was so large that as many as ten mules, each surmounted by a beautiful young slave-girl, were required to transport it. A merchant who witnessed the cortège valued the goods at 1,000,000 *dīnār*s, something never seen before for a woman in Ifriqiya. The bridal cortège included the bride-to-be, preceded by black slaves owned by her brother, those of her father, those of her grandfather and of other court dignitaries. For the wedding celebrations, horsemen entertained the guests with memorable acrobatics.[73]

If weddings of Fatimid royal women were hardly described, their funerals were instead extensively reported, with embellishments so as to emphasise their opulence. When in 385/995 al-'Aziz's wife died, he had her wrapped in a shroud worth 10,000 *dīnār*s. The woman in charge of washing her corpse took for herself the linen of the bed where she was resting, along with her clothes, amounting to a value of 6,000 *dīnār*s. For seven days, 1,000 *dīnār*s were given to the poor, while the Qur'an reciters who were praying by her tomb received 3,000 *dīnār*s and the poets who composed elegies for her received rewards, some of which were of 500 *dīnār*s. Her daughter, Sitt al-Mulk, stayed at her tomb for a month, while al-'Aziz visited every day and people gathered every night around her grave, bringing food and sweets.[74] The palace acknowledged the services of Fatimid high dignitaries through display of wealth and charity on the occasion of their funerals. Court women took an active part in honouring these prominent dead. When the great general Jahwar al-Siqilli died in 381/991, al-Sayyida al-'Aziziyya sent embalming and burial equipment, as did al-'Aziz and the young al-Hakim. At around the same time, the famous vizier Ibn Killis died and his funeral was carefully staged, with slave-girls standing by his grave and feeding the mourning crowd by using silver spoons and cups.[75]

The imam-caliphs were buried in the mausoleum by the south-west corner of the palace.[76] Their wives, children and other members of the royal family were inhumed either in the same mausoleum or in the Qarafa cemetery. As a result of excavations at al-Qarafa begun in 1985, a number of tombs dating from the Fatimid period have been unearthed; some of them reflect the high status of their occupants, not only because of the tomb's size and architectural complexity, but also because of precious silk, cotton and linen *ṭirāz* found on the bodies. The recent discovery of a tomb containing twenty-seven female bodies, tentatively identified as belonging to the palace harem women, may yield interesting research outcomes on Fatimid female burial practices.[77]

In the provinces of the Empire, the funerals of Zirid royal women were equally impressive. Spectacular was that of the widow of Badis, which allegedly cost 100,000 *dīnārs*. The body of the deceased was placed in a coffin made of Indian wood encrusted with precious stones each worth 2,000 *dīnārs*, and buried in al-Mahdiyya. Badis's sister, Umm Mallal, was similarly honoured at her death in 414/1023. Her nephew al-Mu'izz recited the funeral prayer, and the procession was accompanied by flags and tambourines. Both al-Mu'izz's mother and his sister, Umm al-'Ulu, took part in the funeral. Al-Mu'izz destined 100,000 *dīnārs* for her inhumation; her coffin was also made of Indian wood and decorated with precious stones and gold leaf, its gold fittings weighing 1,000 *mithqāls*. The corpse was wrapped in 120 pieces of cloth, soaked with musk and camphor. To mark the solemn occasion, al-Mu'izz ordered the slaughtering of 50 young camels, 100 cows and 1,000 sheep, and the meat was distributed among the mourners. Poor women received 10,000 *dīnārs* and over 100 poets celebrated Umm Mallal in their elegies.[78] Perhaps the coming into possession of the inheritance left by these fabulously rich women was well worth celebrating!

c. *Religious and Secular Ceremonies: the Public and the Private*

Undeterred by the fact that the Egyptian population they ruled over had remained largely indifferent to Isma'ilism, the Fatimids fixed an official calendar of religious and secular public festivals. The main religious festivals celebrated the two traditional *'īds* (*'īd al-fiṭr* and *'īd al-aḍḥā*), the *'āshūrā'* day and the *mawlids*, which commemorated the birthdays of the Prophet Muhammad, 'Ali, Fatima, al-Hasan and al-Husayn, as well as the birthday of the imam of the time. A typically Shi'i festival the Fatimids introduced in Egypt was that of *Ghadīr*, celebrating the Prophet's naming of 'Ali as his successor at Ghadir Khumm.[79] Irrespective of their doctrinal significance, these festivals became very popular and attracted large crowds. On most occasions, the imam-caliph and his retinue would grace these events with their presence and, in some cases, courtly processions took place to and from the caliphal palace. Inside the palace, banquets were held and gifts bestowed, with court women being the recipients of presents and delicacies, as documented on the occasions of the *mawlids*, when they received the best pistachios on the market, and at the beginning and the end of Ramadan, when, besides new garments, each woman of the palace was given a plate of rare and exotic assorted sweets.[80] The participation of court women in the ceremonies marking these religious festivals is hardly recorded. Al-Musabbihi provides us with one precious reference. In describing the 'memorable' celebrations held during the night of the middle of Rajab of 415/1024, he specifies that the imam-caliph al-Zahir took part in them with the women of the palace and other court personnel. During this night vast quantities of oil and perfume were used as fuel to light the mosques and mausolea of Cairo, Fustat and Qarafa. This celebration of Shi'i character, often associated with the festival of lights, also involved fasting and a ritual bath.[81]

As for festivals to mark secular events, they included seasonal festivities, such as the New Year and those associated with the Nile, as well as the completion of main engineering works and parades to celebrate military victories. During the New Year celebrations, the imam-caliph would give the first newly minted golden coins of the year to his wives, his brothers, his female slaves and the high-ranking eunuchs.[82] This Fatimid custom echoes that of the 'Abbasid court, where, on the occasion of the Christian New Year, the caliph lavishly bestowed precious gifts upon all the palace servants.[83] There is no direct indication of active participation of Fatimid court women at secular festivals. However, when sources list the extensive palace personnel taking part in celebratory parades, they include drummers and other musicians, as well as the carriers of the caliphal insignia.[84] The existence during the Fatimid period of female palace drummers and female insignia-carriers is undisputed and this leads us to infer that, at some point, these palace women must have had a public profile at such events. As for the mere appearance of court women at public functions, a reference to distinctively patterned garments made exclusively for the vizier and his consort on the occasion of special public events might indicate that, at least in theory, the presence was envisaged in public of both, and not only of the vizier.[85]

On the occasion of festivals and ceremonies, the public space of the Fatimid capital became a ritual stage that was crossed throughout the year by processions that, as convincingly shown by Paula Sanders, were used by the dynasty to make visible and advertise its own power and authority.[86] The parading of the caliphal insignia was one of the most easily identifiable signs of dynastic advertising. Whether or not court women physically participated in such processions, there were nevertheless reminders of their contribution to the acquisition of some of these insignia. According to al-Qadi al-Nuʿman, it was apparently thanks to a woman that the famous and potent sword of Muhammad, known as Dhu'l-Faqar, reached the Fatimids. It had come into the possession of the ʿAbbasids but, following the death of the caliph Jaʿfar al-Muqtadir (d. 295/908), one of his concubines handed it to an ʿAlid supporter as recompense for his act of chivalry towards her. As a result, al-Qadi al-Nuʿman claims that the invincible sword was during his time in the hands of al-Muʿizz.[87] In a figurative manner, al-Qadi al-Nuʿman is tracing the line of legitimacy from al-Muʿizz through al-Mansur and back to ʿAli and the Prophet himself. Dhu'l-Faqar is symbolic of the might, both military and spiritual, of the Fatimids and, together with the crown, was paraded at solemn processions as one of the imam-caliph's insignia.[88]

To the religious and secular ceremonies just described, one should add those functions and formal occasions that took place within the private space of the palace. They included ceremonials staged to welcome foreign envoys and ambassadors, formal banquets at which the palace elite entertained each other and the caliph, as well as the formalities required for the daily rounds, which consisted of audiences given by the caliph to his officers and by the vizier to the public. There is evidence of palace women being present at some of these semi-private functions. For instance, when in 471/1078 the Coptic patriarch Kirillus II visited the imam-caliph al-Mustansir, both the caliph's mother and his sister took part in the welcoming of this esteemed guest. According to a biography of Kirillus II describing the visit, the two women and the Fatimid caliph were sitting in the Golden Hall next to each other amidst a profusion of perfume, some of which they offered to the patriarch. They then asked him to bless them and their palace; he did so, prayed for them and they reciprocated on their behalf and that of the whole dynasty.[89]

Even if not physically present at religious festivals within the palace, court women could nevertheless be formally represented by their servants, as on the occasion of the *khatima*, the celebration for the completion of the recitation of the whole Qur'an, which coincided with the last night of Ramadan. A twelfth-century eye-witness to the event reports that the caliph, his brothers, uncles and other important personalities gathered for the *khatima* celebrations, ready to receive the blessings of this eventful occasion. The servants of the *jihāts*, the ladies and 'the most distinguished ladies among the people of the palace' were also present, and carried before the caliph and the other participants dates (ice?) and containers filled with water, wrapped in cotton, so that the blessing of the *khatima* would pervade them. After the ceremony was over, the servants would bring these containers back to their mistresses.[90]

Historical, literary and archeological sources all contribute to form a picture of the increasingly complex nature of palace life under the Fatimids. The gradual growth in size and varied composition of the harem went hand in hand with the expansion of the political and economic power that the Fatimid dynasty was able to exercise over and beyond the territories that recognised its sovereignty. The ladies of the caliphal family, as well as female palace staff, when mentioned, are included in the narratives to serve a function: they all performed their ideal or allocated tasks. For historians and chroniclers, to record the size of the harem, the hierarchy within it, as well as the specific roles of individual categories of palace staff, gave a measure of the efficiency of the Fatimid palace organisation and its bureaucratic apparatus. At the same time, references to the Fatimids' penchant for refined court entertainment are indicative of the cultivated and luxurious climate that prevailed at their court; this, enjoyed by powerful men and their women, put the Fatimid court on a par with those of other important dynasties of the time.

The above considerations are based on the interpretation of short but telling references. From them glimpses can be gained of a variety of women: those living in the palace and receiving foreign envoys, those working for the palace, some powerful and many passive, a few lasting and many ephemeral, but still recorded. To the powerful, strong and influential few are devoted more than passing references in the sources and they will be the subjects of the next chapter.

Notes

1 For the Fāṭimid royal cities in Ifrīqiyā, see Talbi, M., 'Sabra or al-Manṣūriyya', *EI2*nd, vol. 8, pp. 688–9; Talbi, M., 'al-Mahdiyya', *EI2*nd, vol. 5, pp. 1246–7.

2 See al-'Iyadī's poem translated into English by Bloom, J. M., in his *Meaning in early Fatimid architecture: Islamic Art in North Africa and Egypt in the Fourth Century* AH/*10* c. AD, PhD thesis, Cambridge, MA: Harvard University, 1980, p. 42.

3 al-Maqrīzī Taqī al-Dīn, *al-Mawā'iẓ wa-'l-i'tibār bi-dhikr al-khiṭaṭ wa-'l-āthār*, Beirut: Dār al-ṣādir, n.d., offset of Būlāq 1324 edn, vol. 1, p. 362. On the development of the *qaṣr* in Fāṭimid Cairo, see Bloom, J. M., *Meaning*, esp. pp. 75–85.

4 The famous Andalusian poet Ibn Hāni' migrated to North Africa to become the court poet of the Fāṭimids and 'Umāra arrived from the Yemen, via Makka, to Cairo in 550/ 1155, see al-Maqrīzī, Taqī al-Dīn, *Itti'āẓ al-ḥunafā' bi-akhbār al-a'imma al-Fāṭimiyyīn al-khulafā'*, ed. al-Shayyāl, J. and Ḥilmī, M., Cairo: Lajnat iḥyā' al-turāth al-islāmī, 1387–93/1967–73, vol. 3, p. 224. An example of human exchanges leading to shared fashion and taste across the courts is the ninth-century musician Ziryāb the Persian, who fled from the 'Abbāsid court to the Cordovan palace of 'Abd al-Raḥmān II, where 'he became the arbiter of good taste and fashion, introducing eastern refinements in dress, hair styles, table manners, and social

intercourse', in O'Callaghan, F., *A History of Medieval Spain*, Ithaca and London: Cornell University Press, 1975, p. 158.

5 For a discussion on a 'princely cycle in Islamic art' under the Umayyads and the 'Abbāsids, see Shoshan, B., 'High Culture and Popular Culture in Medieval Islam', *SI*, 73 (1991), 1, pp. 73–4.

6 See especially Ettinghausen's theory that one of the innovations of Fāṭimid art was in its 'realistic' depictions: Ettinghausen, A. S. R., 'Early realism in Islamic art', in *Studi orientalistici in onore di Giorgio Levi Della Vida*, vol. 1, Rome: Istituto per l'Oriente, 1956, pp. 250–73. His theory has been criticised by Grube, E. J., 'Realism or formalism: notes on some Fāṭimid luster-painted ceramic vessels', in Traini, R. (ed.), *Studi in onore di Francesco Gabrieli nel suo ottantesimo compleanno*, Rome: Università di Roma 'La Sapienza', 1984, pp. 423–32. A study of wood carvings from fragments believed to be from the Small Palace points to their documentary role on dances practised and known during the artist's time, as Fāṭimid art reveals 'a keen observation of reality': see Khemir, S., *The Palace of Sitt al-Mulk and Fāṭimid Imagery*, PhD thesis, SOAS, London: University of London, 1990, vol. 1, p. 156. On figurative representation in Fāṭimid art, see also George Marçais' seminal work.

7 Idrīs 'Imād al-Dīn, *'Uyūn al-akhbār wa-funūn al-athār*, ed. Ghālib, M., vols 4–6, Beirut: Dār al-Andalus, 1973–8, vol. 5, p. 115.

8 On the basis of al-Qāḍī al-Nu'mān, *Da'ā'im* and *Mukhtaṣar al-athār*, see Fyzee, A. A. A., *Compendium of Fatimid Law*, Simla: Indian Institute of Advanced Study, 1969, p. 149.

9 al-Maqrīzī, *Khiṭaṭ*, vol. 1, p. 362.

10 The two daughters mentioned could have been Sakīna and Rāshida, two of the four daughters indicated as having died in North Africa. The other two, Umm al-Ḥusayn and Umm 'Alī, being married, must have been part of another caravan.

11 al-Yamānī, Muḥammad b. Muḥammad, *Sīrat al-ḥājib Ja'far*, ed. and trans. Ivanow, W., *Rise*, pp.189–90; al-Qāḍī al-Nu'mān, *Kitāb Iftitāḥ al-da'wa*, ed. Dachraoui, F., Tunis: al-Sharika al-Tūnisiyya li-'l-tawzī', 1975, pp. 261–2 (Ar.). Al-Nu'mān states that the arrival of the harem coincided with the investiture in Raqqāda on 21 Rabī' al-thānī 297/7th January 910 (p. 299 Ar.). In fact, al-Khazarī arrived beforehand, while al-Mahdī was still in Sijilmasa.

12 Ibn 'Idhārī, Aḥmad, *Kitāb al-Bayān al-mughrib*, ed. Colin, G. S. and Lévi-Provençal, E., Leiden: E. J. Brill, 1948, p. 151; cf. al-Qāḍī al-Nu'mān, *Iftitāḥ*, pp. 246–7.

13 Idrīs 'Imād al-Dīn, *'Uyūn*, vol. 6, p. 185. From other sources we can infer that in the caravan there was also a daughter of al-Mu'izz, Rāshida, who travelled in the convoy carrying precious carpets, which were eventually used by al-Ḥākim to adorn the *īwān* of the caliphal palace. Ibn al-Zubayr, *Kitāb al-Dhakhā'ir wa-'l-tuḥaf*, ed. Muḥammad Ḥamīd Allāh, Kuwait: Kuwait Government Press, 1959, p. 150.

14 Goitein, S. D., *A Mediterranean Society* (henceforth *MS*), Berkeley: University of California Press, 1971, vol. 2: The Community, p. 352 and p. 604, n. 32.

15 Malti-Douglas, F., *Woman's Body, Woman's Word: Gender and Discourse in Arabo-Islamic Writing*, Princeton: Princeton University Press, 1991, pp. 29–53.

16 Ibn Khallikān, Aḥmad, *Kitāb Wafayāt al-a'yān*, ed. Iḥsān 'Abbās, Beirut: Dār al-thaqāfa, n.d. [1968], vol. 1, p. 235.

17 al-Maqrīzī, Taqī al-Dīn, *Kitāb al-Muqaffā al-kabīr*, ed. al-Ya'lāwī, M., Beirut: Dār al-gharb al-islāmī, 7 vols, 1991, vol. 2, pp. 596–600.

18 Ibn al-Qalānisī, Ḥamza b. Asad, *Ta'rīkh Dimashq*, ed. Zakār, S., Damascus: Dār Ḥassān, 1983, pp. 66–7.

19 Ibn Muyassar, Tāj al-Dīn, *Akhbār Miṣr*, ed. Massé, H., as *Annales d'Égypte*, Cairo: IFAO, 1919, p. 60.

20 Idrīs 'Imād al-Dīn, *'Uyūn*, vol. 7, p. 80 (Eng.), pp. 232–3 (Ar.).

21 Ibn 'Idhārī al-Marrākushī, Aḥmad, *Kitāb al-Bayān al-mughrib, Histoire de l'Afrique et de l'Espagne*

intitulée al-Bayano'l-Mogrib, French trans. Fagnan, E. R., Algiers: Imprimerie Orientale P. Fontana, 1901, vol. 2, pp. 386–7.

22 Idrīs 'Imād al-Dīn, *'Uyūn*, vol. 7, p. 50 (Eng.), p. 86 (Ar.).

23 Ibn al-Zubayr, *Kitāb al-Dhakhā'ir, Kitāb al-Hadāyā wa-'l-tuḥaf*, ed. and trans. al-Hijjāwī al-Qaddūmī, G., *Book of Gifts and Rarities*, Cambridge, MA: Harvard University Press, 1996, pp. 104–5, 110, 113. Almería was one of the most important ports of tenth–eleventh-century al-Andalus for the export of slaves. There are references to schools or institutions for the training of female slaves to be employed by Andalusian aristocratic families as *qiyān* for the entertainment of their masters, see Guichard , P., 'The Social History of Muslim Spain', in Jayyusi, S. K. (ed.), *The Legacy of Muslim Spain*, Leiden: Brill, 1994, pp. 692–3, 696.

24 al-Maqrīzī, *Khiṭaṭ*, vol. 1, p. 350.

25 Nāṣir-i Khusraw, *Sefer nameh: Relation du Voyage de Nassiri Khosrau*, ed. and French trans. Schefer, C., Amsterdam: Philo Press, 1970, p. 128.

26 Ibn Khallikān, Aḥmad, *Kitāb Wafayāt al-a'yān*, trans. MacGuckin De Slane, W., *Biographical Dictionary*, Paris: 1842–71, repr. Beirut: Librairie du Liban, 1970, vol. 1, p. 268.

27 al-Qāḍī al-Nu'mān, *Iftitāḥ*, p. 248 (Ar.); see also Halm, H., *The Empire of the Mahdi. The Rise of the Fatimids*, trans. Bonner, M., Leiden: E. J. Brill, 1996, p. 122.

28 al-Qāḍī al-Nu'mān, *Kitāb al-Majālis wa-'l-musāyarāt*, ed. al-Faqī, Ḥ. et al., Tunis: al-Maṭba'a al-rasmiyya li-'l-jumhūriyya al-tūnisiyya, 1978, pp. 545–6; see also Halm, H., *Empire*, p. 341.

29 al-Maqrīzī, *al-Muqaffā*, vol. 3, pp. 47–8.

30 On the *sāḥib al-bāb* in the Fāṭimid court see Ibn al-Ṭuwayr, al-Murtaḍā, *Nuzhat al-muqlatayn fī akhbār al-dawlatayn*, ed. Sayyid, A. F., Stuttgart and Beirut: F. Steiner, 1992, pp. 122–3.

31 al-Musabbiḥī, Muḥammad b. 'Ubayd Allāh, *Akhbār Miṣr*, vol. 1, ed. Sayyid, A. F. and Bianquis, T., Cairo: IFAO, 1978, pp. 110–11. An alternative reading for *muqīma* could be *muqayyina*, a lady's maid.

32 Ibn al-Ma'mūn al-Baṭā'iḥī, Jamāl al-Dīn, *Nuṣūṣ min akhbār Miṣr*, ed. Sayyid, A. F., Cairo: IFAO, 1983, pp. 50–1.

33 Lev, Y., 'Tinnīs: an industrial medieval town', in Barrucand, M. (ed.), *L'Égypte Fatimide: son art et son histoire*, Paris: Presses de l'Université de Paris-Sorbonne, 1999, p. 88.

34 Ibn al-Ma'mūn al-Baṭā'iḥī, *Nuṣūṣ*, pp. 50–1.

35 Sayyid, A. F., *La capitale de l'Égypte jusqu'à l'époque Fatimide*, Beirut/Stuttgart: F. Steiner, 1998, pp. 238–9.

36 Ibn al-Ma'mūn al-Baṭā'iḥī, *Nuṣūṣ*, p. 51.

37 Ibn Muyassar, *Akhbār Miṣr*, p. 58.

38 al-Maqrīzī, *Khiṭaṭ*, vol. 2, p. 449 ; see also Lev, Y., 'Tinnīs', p. 89.

39 Golovin, L., *Le Magrib central a l'époque des Zirides*, Paris: Arts et Metiers Graphiques, 1957, p. 179.

40 al-Musabbiḥī, *Akhbār Miṣr*, vol. 1, p. 89.

41 al-Maqrīzī, *Khiṭaṭ*, vol. 1, p. 386.

42 Sayyid, A. F., *La capitale*, pp. 215–16 and 480.

43 al-Maqrīzī, *Itti'āẓ*, vol. 1, p. 295; Ibn al-Qalānisī, *Ta'rīkh Dimashq*, p. 75 (10,000 concubines and eunuchs) and Nāṣir-i Khusraw, *Sefer nameh*, p. 128.

44 al-Maqrīzī, *Khiṭaṭ*, vol. 1, p. 384. As a term of comparison, during the sixteenth and seventeenth centuries, the Ottoman harem consisted respectively of c. 150 and 400 women. See Peirce, L. P., *The Imperial Harem: Women and Sovereignty in the Ottoman Empire*, New York, Oxford: OUP, 1993, p. 290, note 6.

45 al-Maqrīzī, *Itti'āẓ*, vol. 1, p. 214.

46 al-Maqrīzī, *Itti'āẓ*, vol. 2, p. 20; and vol. 1, p. 271.

47 On the *ṭirāẓ* and its developments since the Umayyad times, see Stillman Y. K. and Sanders, P., '*Ṭirāẓ*' *EI2*nd, vol. 10, pp. 534–8. On Fāṭimid *ṭirāẓ* in particular, see Stillman, Y. K., *Female*

Attire of Medieval Egypt According to the Trousseau Lists and Cognate Material from the Cairo Geniza, PhD thesis, Philadelphia: University of Pennsylvania, 1972; and Bierman, I. A., *Art and politics: the impact of Fatimid uses of ṭirāz fabrics*, PhD thesis, Chicago: University of Chicago Press, 1980.

48 The thirteenth-century Ibn Māmātī specifies the position of some employees in the *ṭirāz* production: a controller (*nāẓir*), a supervisor (*mushārif*), a fiscal agent (*'āmil*) and a notary (*shāhid*), see Cooper, R. S., *Ibn Māmmatī's Rules for the Ministries: Translation with Commentary of the Qawānīn al-Dawāwīn*, PhD thesis, Berkeley: University of California, 1973, p. 279.

49 Bierman, I. A., *Art*, pp. 76–9.

50 See Ibn al-Ma'mūn al-Baṭā'iḥī, *Nuṣūṣ*, pp. 49–50 and p. 94, on the *jihāt* getting from the Treasury of Leather forty pairs of 'shoes' per month.

51 See Stillman, Y. K., *Female*, p. 16. For an example of a robe of honour bestowed upon a Jewish court physician and one donated to a rich Jewish merchant, see Goitein, S. D., MS, vol. 2, pp. 347 and 604, n. 28.

52 See Bierman, I. A., *Art*, pp. 62–4.

53 al-Maqrīzī, *al-Muqaffā*, vol. 1, p. 507.

54 al-Musabbiḥī, *Akhbār Miṣr*, vol. 2, ed. Ḥusayn Naṣṣār, Cairo: IFAO, 1984, pp. 34–5.

55 Smoor, P., '"The Master of the Century": Fāṭimid Poets in Cairo', in Vermeulen, U. and De Smet, D. (eds), *ESFAME*, 1995, pp. 139–62; in particular, pp. 153–5; 159.

56 Idris, H. R., *La Berbérie*, vol. 1, p. 134.

57 al-Maqrīzī, *Itti'āẓ*, vol. 3, p. 226.

58 al-Safadī, Ṣalāḥ al-Dīn, *Kitāb al-Wafī bi-'l-wafāyāt*, Wiesbaden: F. Steiner, 1981–, vol. 10, n. 4799, p. 290; vol. 13, n. 113, p. 107; vol. 16, n. 224, pp. 190–2. On educated Andalusian women, see Viguera, M. J., '*Aṣluhu li'l-Ma'ālī*: on the social status of Andalusī women', in Jayyusi, S. K. (ed.), *Legacy*, pp. 709–24.

59 al-Maqrīzī, Taqī al-Dīn, *al-Mawā'iẓ wa-'l-i'tibār bi-dhikr al-khiṭaṭ wa-'l-āthār*, ed. al-Sharqāwī, Beirut: Maktabat madbūla, 1998, vol. 2, pp. 797–8.

60 al-Maqrīzī, ed. al-Sharqāwī, *Khiṭaṭ*, vol. 2, pp. 796–9. The narrative continues with a story hinting at al-Āmir's questionable sexual prowess with his wife, 'with whom he spent the nights in conversation'!

61 On the castanets held by a dancer in one of the wood carvings from the palace of Sitt al-Mulk and their link to the 'Fāṭimid ivory dolls' excavated at Fusṭāṭ, see Khemir, S., *The Palace*, vol. 1, pp. 157–9.

62 al-Yamānī, *Sīra*, in Ivanow,W., *Rise*, pp. 186–7.

63 Ibn al-Zubayr, *Kitāb al-Dhakhā'ir*, *Kitāb al-Hadāyā wa-'l-tuḥaf*, ed. and trans. al-Hijjāwī al-Qaddūmī, p. 14, Eng. trans., pp. 67–8.

64 For Barjawān, see al-Maqrīzī, *al-Muqaffā*, vol. 2, pp. 574–5; for the singer Malak; see al-Musabbiḥī, *Akhbār Miṣr*, vol. 1, p. 96.

65 al-Maqrīzī, *Itti'āẓ*, vol. 2, p. 164. The procession did not impress the onlookers, who booed the imam-caliph, crying from hunger.

66 Nāṣir-i Khusraw, *Sefer nameh*, p. 137; the occasion celebrated the opening of dams aptly placed along the Nile to allow its waters to flood the lands in its proximity.

67 Cf. Lev, Y., 'Aspects of Egyptian society', in Vermeulen, U. and van Steenbergen, J. (eds), *ESFAME*, Leuven: Peeters, 2001, p. 17, n. 31 based on al-Maqrīzī's *Khiṭaṭ*.

68 al-Musabbiḥī, *Akhbār Miṣr*, vol. 1, pp. 16, 41–2.

69 Ibn al-Ma'mūn al-Baṭā'iḥī, *Nuṣūṣ*, p. 98.

70 al-Maqrīzī, *Itti'āẓ*, vol. 1, p. 252.

71 al-Maqrīzī, *al-Muqaffā*, vol. 1, p. 153.

72 Ibn Muyassar, *Akhbār Miṣr*, p. 49; see also al-Maqrīzī, *Itti'āẓ*, vol. 1, p. 271.

73 Idris, H. R., *La Berbérie*, vol. 1, pp. 135–6, p. 142.

74 Ibn Muyassar, *Akhbār Miṣr*, p. 288–9.

75 For Jawhar, see al-Maqrīzī, *al-Muqaffā*, vol. 3, p. 111; for Ibn Killis, see Lane-Poole, S., *A History of Egypt in the Middle Ages*, London: Methuen, 1925, vol. 6, p. 121.

76 Thomas Leisten argues instead that the *turba* in the palace was the burial chamber for the imam-caliphs alone and that their relatives were buried elsewhere: see his 'Dynastic tomb or private mausolea: observations on the concept of funerary structures of the Fāṭimid and 'Abbāsid caliphs' in Barrucand, M. (ed.), *L'Égypte Fatimide*, pp. 465–79.

77 Gayraud, R-P., 'Le *Qarafa al-kubra*, dernière demeure des Fatimides' in Barrucand, M. (ed.), *L'Égypte Fatimide*, pp. 443–64, in particular pp. 460–1 and 464.

78 Idris, H. R., *La Berbérie*, vol. 1, p. 141–2.

79 For the dynastic and propaganda uses which these festivals served, see Sanders, P., 'Claiming the past: Ghadīr Khumm and the rise of Ḥāfiẓī historiography in late Fāṭimid Egypt', *SI*, 75 (1992), pp. 81–104.

80 Ibn al-Ma'mūn al-Baṭā'iḥī, *Nuṣūṣ*, p. 93; and al-Maqrīzī, *Itti'āẓ*, vol. 3, p. 343.

81 al-Musabbiḥī, *Akhbār Miṣr*, vol. 1, p. 48; and al-Maqrīzī, *Itti'āẓ*, vol. 2, p. 151. For a Ṭayyibī interpretation of the rituals associated with the middle of the Rajab festival, see Idrīs 'Imād al-Dīn, *Risalat al-Bayān li-mā wajab min ma'rifat al-ṣalāt*, MS 132 in Cortese, D., *Arabic Ismaili Manuscripts, The Zāhid 'Alī Collection in the Library of the Institute of Ismaili Studies*, London: I. B. Tauris, 2003.

82 Ibn al-Ma'mūn al-Baṭā'iḥī, *Nuṣūṣ*, pp. 58, 81.

83 al-Ṣabī', Hilāl, *Rusum dar al-Khilafah: the rules and regulations of the 'Abbasid court*, trans. Salem, E. A., Beirut: Lebanese Commission for the Translation of Great Works, 1977, p. 24, n. 5.

84 al-Qalqashandī, Shihāb al-Dīn, *Subḥ al-a'shā fī ṣinā'at al-inshā'*, ed. Ibrāhīm, Cairo: Dār al-Kutub al-Miṣriyya, 1331–8/1913–20, vol. 3, pp. 503–7.

85 See reference to such garments in Ibn al-Ma'mūn al-Baṭā'iḥī, *Nuṣūṣ*, p. 55.

86 Sanders, P., *Ritual, Politics, and the City in Fatimid Cairo*, Albany: SUNY Press, 1994, in particular pp. 5–11.

87 al-Qāḍī al-Nu'mān, *al-Majālis*, pp. 114–15.

88 For Dhu'l-Faqār's power and fame celebrated by the poet Ibn Hāni' al-Andalusī, see Yalaoui, M., *Un poète chiite d'occident au IVème/Xème siècle: Ibn Hāni' al-Andalusī*, Tunis: Publications de l'Université de Tunis, 1976, pp. 139–40.

89 Heijer, J. den, 'Considérations sur les communautés chrétiennes en Égypte Fatimide: l'État et l'Église sous le vizirat de Badr al-Jamālī (1074–1094)', in Barrucand, M., *L'Égypte Fatimide*, p. 572.

90 Ibn al-Ma'mūn al-Baṭā'iḥī, *Nuṣūṣ*, p. 83; and al-Maqrīzī, *Khiṭaṭ*, vol. 1, p. 452. The texts feature two different terms regarding what was carried before the caliph, with dates seeming the most likely explanation, as they are the typical fruit eaten at the end of the fasting. *Thalj* (ice), however, is not unheard of, as the term is used in a list of annual expenditure of the 'Abbāsid caliphs.

CHAPTER

4

BATTLEAXES AND FORMIDABLE AUNTIES

The protagonists of this chapter are the influential and powerful women at the Fatimid courts and at the courts of the Fatimids' vassal dynasties. Their rise to a position of influence was often a by-product of wider dynastic and palace power struggles; moreover, by consolidating and extending their influence, a few women were able to exercise some degree of power. While this power was exclusively confined to the secular domain, the case of one woman, the Yemeni queen Arwa, stands out as the only example thus far of a female ruler who might have held a position of religious authority in addition to her status as a secular sovereign.

Besides the Fatimids, during the period between the tenth and twelfth centuries, other Muslim dynasties were experiencing the strong influence of women belonging to the ruling family. In al-Andalus, during the Umayyad caliphate of al-Hakam al-Mustansir (r. 350–62/961–76), in one instance female influence turned into the sharing of outright power. Upon becoming the *umm al-walad* of two of al-Hakam's sons, the caliph's singing slave-girl, Subh al-Bashkunsiyya, saw her wealth and status significantly increased. Furthermore, at her consort's death, as mother of his minor heir, she was able to rule in conjunction with the vizier and her treasurer, only to be out-manoeuvered by the latter, who became the effective ruler of the region. Similarly, within the 'Abbasid dynasty, several wives and mothers of caliphs-to-be were known to have influenced dynastic politics by supporting the succession claims of one or the other of their sons.[1]

Further east, in Saljuq Persia, during the eleventh century, the sultan Malik Shah's queen consort, known as Terken Khatun, had so great an influence at court as to prompt one of the most notorious outright condemnations of women's involvement in politics. On the basis of a selective choice of Qur'anic passages and *ḥadīths*, Malik Shah's vizier Nizam al-Mulk argued that women could not be rulers because of their lack of experience of social matters resulting in a 'limited' development of their rationality and intellect.[2] He held that, as wives and mothers, women could not judge situations objectively and would fall easy prey to the advice of their inferiors. Nizam al-Mulk saw female involvement in government as catastrophic for all strata of society: the sovereign's name and dignity would suffer, society at large would experience no less than chaos and even the state financial reserves would be affected and eventually dissipated. It is evident that he was not talking from a purely theoretical and dispassionately objective perspective but was voicing real concerns, mostly dictated by self-interest, about the succession to his master, as his object was to undermine Terken Khatun's support for her son Mahmud's claims to the succession. It is in the light of this climate that some sources link Nizam al-Mulk's assassination in 485/1092 to court intrigue masterminded by Terken herself.[3] In medieval sources, Terken came to embody the negative aspects of female influence: court intrigue, political and social chaos, and the division within society (*fitna*), along with money embezzlement.

Female influence and power are also documented in relation to the Byzantine court. Some women rose to prominence as consorts, such as the empress Zoe (d. 1050) or Eirene, wife of Alexis I Comnenus (d. 1118), while others ruled as regents or, briefly, as sovereigns like the empress Theodora (d. 1056). The Fatimids felt first-hand the full force of Theodora's power. In 446/1054, following a major economic crisis, al-Mustansir had asked the Byzantine emperor to send him large quantities of crops. The emperor agreed but died before being able to have the consignment delivered. Upon her taking over the reins of the empire, Theodora wrote to al-Mustansir demanding a Fatimid–Byzantine military alliance should she come under attack and at the same time withheld the delivery of the crops. Furious, al-Mustansir responded with military intervention, thus setting, according to al-Maqrizi, the conditions that were to be a major contributing cause to the greatest ecomomic, social and political collapse that Egypt ever suffered under the Fatimids: the *shidda al-Mustanṣiriyya*.[4]

Beyond their specific historical, dynastic and local contexts, common denominators can be detected in the circumstances that made it possible for these royal women to become influential. All of them were powerful by virtue of their connections to powerful men: they were the mothers of, the consorts of, the daughters of, the sisters of, the aunts of or even the slaves of past or present rulers. The power of court women was proportional to that of their men. In the absence of husbands, sons or other male relatives, their retention of influence or power still needed, at least formally, the endorsement of a male authority beyond the family per se, be it a vizier or an allied ruler. Within the Fatimid context, an example of status and influence gained through birth is that of Sitt al-Mulk, the daughter of the imam-caliph al-ʿAziz. Power could also come by giving birth to the designated heir, as in the case of the slave Rasad, who, as *umm al-walad*, became regent for her son, the imam-caliph al-Mustansir. Dominance could also be gained through marriage, as in the case of the Sulayhid queen Arwa.

Another common denominator across dynasties was the importance given to seniority, as demonstrated in the influential roles played by grandmothers, widowed mothers of Fatimid caliphs and other senior ladies – 'the old ladies of the palace' within the court hierarchy. The slave origins of several Fatimid royal consorts and concubines meant that the figure of what would typically be an important senior woman, the caliph's mother-in-law, was conspicuously absent from the sources. By contrast, in the accounts of the influential senior women at the Byzantine court, the emperor's mother-in-law was portrayed as a potent force to be reckoned with.[5]

However, while the Byzantine emperors and – to some extent – the ʿAbbasid caliphs sought to forge matrimonial alliances to strengthen their own power, the Fatimid imam-caliphs did not make use of dynastic marriages to consolidate international connections. On the contrary, there is evidence that they discouraged such types of unions by preventing their own daughters from getting married altogether. It is only during the last phase of the Fatimid era that marriages of men in the caliphal family are mentioned in the sources, and not to daughters of foreign rulers but to the daughters of viziers and military commanders.

Unlike other dynasties, with the Fatimids the male collaterals of the imam-caliph – his brothers, his cousins, and so on – are seldom mentioned as holding any position of power. Fear that they could make succession counter-claims, or secure a degree of power for themselves, no doubt contributed to their relegation to marginal passive roles within the court. Looking at the power struggles among brothers that preceded the accession to the throne of some imam-caliphs, such concerns were more than justified. As sons of the caliph, his children were all potentially influential by virtue of their filiation, until the day one of them would be designated as successor, an event that meant power for the chosen one and marginalisation for the others.[6] Notable is the case of the caliph al-Hafiz who, not trusting his viziers, appointed his own sons as ministers, only to discover the dangers of giving a power base to his sons when, having chosen one as his successor, in-fighting broke out among them. To end the quarrel, in 529/1135, al-Hafiz had no alternative but to order the killing of Hasan, one of his sons, accused of fomenting sectors of the army against the brother designated as heir apparent.

This caliph's disengagement from power of his male kin and non-designated princes is reflected in the overall silence about their activities in the sources. Paradoxically, this silence renders more noticeable and, in many ways, astonishing the coverage, at times greatly detailed, of the wealth and influence of the imam-caliph's female close relatives. Unlike their male counterparts, some women of the Fatimid caliphal family were given not mere allowances (a double-edged sword when representing the main source of income) but were also allocated annual revenues from rents and land, as well as material assets they could sell (see Chapter 5). Hence, women of the caliph's family became repositories of wealth, and with wealth came influence. With the exception of al-Hakim in relation to his half-sister Sitt al-Mulk, the gaining of influence on the part of some women in the imam-caliph's entourage did not constitute a source of concern for the imam-caliph himself. No matter how powerful, royal women could not challenge caliphal power by themselves and in their own name. However, their influence and power was substantial enough to deserve apprehensive monitoring by the movers and shakers of palace politics, and to attract the attention of the chroniclers of the time.

The subdivision of the present chapter into two main sections dealing with women's influence and women's power should not lead to the assumption that these were two separate modes pertaining to two distinct and self-sufficient spheres: the private-domestic on the one hand, and the public and political on the other. Even more misleading would be the neat identification of the private with the female and the public with the male domain. When it comes to the ruling elite, what could seem like a private matter, once it was known, recorded or alluded to, became public in scope. Consequently, private and public are to be seen in their interaction as fluid, rather than unconnected, modes and they will be considered in their 'reciprocity of influence in interactive situations', rather than in isolation.[7]

1. Between Authority and Power

Shiʿi Jaʿfarite teachings on the status of the imam as supreme spiritual and secular leader were the basis of the Ismaʿili doctrine on the imamate. With the establishment of the Fatimids as an Ismaʿili dynasty, spiritual and temporal authority became embodied in the person of the imam-caliph. As imam, he was the spiritual leader of the elect Ismaʿilis (*amīr al-muʾminīn*); as caliph, he was the leader of the rest of the Muslim community (*amīr al-muslimīn*).

Both Sunnis and Shiʿis perceived secular power, and even more so, the spiritual authority that legitimised it, as male domains; an overt challenge to the axiom that the caliph and the imam could only be men was unthinkable. However, historical and meta-historical examples of famous queens and women rulers show that it was not impossible for a woman to hold a position of power, albeit only secular. Medieval Muslim theologians and scholars argued against the idea of a woman in power on the basis of their interpretation of selected Qur'anic passages, as well as *ḥadīths*. They often invoked the most notorious *ḥadīth* in this respect: 'those who entrust their affairs to women, will never know prosperity'.[8] The significance that scholars attach to this *ḥadīth* varied according to the historical context in which they placed it and their interpretation changed according to their particular agendas. Some commentators interpreted this *ḥadīth* as referring to queen Buran (r. 630–1 CE), who ruled Persia at the onset of the Arab conquest. Hence, it came to be read as a 'prophetic' reference to the sweeping Arab military victory (as an expression of God's favour) over the Sasanian empire, contrasting the 'feminine' weakness of her country with the 'virile' motivation and strength of the Arab army.[9] Other scholars, particularly Shiʿi, read it instead as an implicit reference to ʿA'isha, the favourite wife of the Prophet, when she opposed ʿAli's accession to the caliphate, thus causing the first *fitna* of Islam.

It is within the context of this *fitna*, and the role ʿA'isha played in it, that medieval Shiʿi scholars expressed their most heartfelt reservations about women in positions of influence or power. The principal aim of these scholars was not, nevertheless, to pass judgement on women as such, but to endorse a specifically Shiʿi interpretation of past history. For instance, the Imami Muhammad al-Mufid (d. 413/1032) expressed his view that female involvement in public matters was irreconcilable with the preservation of female modesty. How could women address men, give them orders, or even become military leaders, while remaining modest and hiding away 'behind the curtain', as was prescribed to them (in fact, to the Prophet's wives) in the Holy Qur'an? Al-Mufid's stance on the matter is clear enough: his section devoted to women and veiling in his *Compendium* is conveniently located within the narrative of ʿA'isha's opposition to ʿAli. Had ʿA'isha conformed to the divine revelation concerning the Prophet's wives, no *fitna* would ever have happened.[10] By contrast, Shiʿi authors praised women such as Umm Salama, another wife of the Prophet, whom they portrayed as displaying the virtues of piety, obedience and modesty, and who naturally delegated to men all political and military decisions.

Al-Mufid, like most Shiʿi scholars, saw ʿA'isha as the prime leader of the opposition to ʿAli and therefore as fully responsible for the consequences of her stance. As the anti-heroine, she is the example of the disobedient wife/widow who puts her own ambition before her responsibilities to the whole community. For the Shiʿi chronicler al-Masʿudi, she even dared to wish to become caliph herself![11] Paradoxically, despite (or because of) the negative connotations cast on ʿA'isha, she emerges in Shiʿi works as a more active and influential character than she does in Sunni texts. With ʿA'isha being portrayed as a negative example of a woman who became personally involved in leadership contests, Shiʿi scholars could have easily extended their condemnation of female participation in power-related matters to the whole female gender, but this was not to be the case; had they done so, they would have ultimately devalued the status of Fatima, the woman they credited with the highest spiritual charisma, as active defender of justice over the rights of the *Ahl al-Bayt*.

Fatimid scholars, historians, missionaries, poets and the like, shared with other Shiʿis their negative attitude towards ʿA'isha. Unlike them, however, they did not use the case of ʿA'isha's opposition to ʿAli as an expedient to pass judgement on female involvement in leadership and public matters. Perhaps this is because they portrayed Fatima also as a public figure to whom they attributed public statements made to voice her support for ʿAli and for the Prophet's family. In Shiʿi as well as Fatimid works, she is consistently referred to as a member of the *Ahl al-Bayt*, sharing with her male counterparts, Muhammad, ʿAli, al-Hasan and al-Husayn, qualities such as purity and infallibility. However, as al-Qadi al-Nuʿman points out: Fatima plays 'no part in the imamate, she being the "Mother of the imams"'.[12] Despite her centrality in the genealogical claims made in support of the Fatimids, despite mothering imams, despite the later mystical elaborations on her piety and perfection, she was still a woman who could not aspire to, let alone hold, the highest position of authority: that of imam.

2. Public Signs of Women's Influence and Power

To have their name inscribed on coins is, for any ruler, one of the most potent visual symbols of power. The name often appears within the context of a legend that functions as a doctrinal and political statement in support of the bearer's authority. Given the paramount importance of the choice of wording on coins, it is remarkable that one Fatimid imam-caliph ordered the minting of a coin bearing a reference to a woman. He was arguably the first caliph in the history of Islam to have done so. While still in al-Mansuriyya, the imam-caliph al-Muʿizz inaugurated his caliphate with the minting in 341/953 of *dīnār*s bearing his name on one side and reading on the other:

> … ʿAli ibn Abi Talib is the Nominee of the Prophet and the Most Excellent Representative and the Husband of the Radiant Chaste One (*zawj al-zahrā' al-batūl*) [that is, Fatima].[13]

The adoption of such legend marked a break from previous styles of wording in Fatimid coinage and served as an unequivocal statement about the ʿAlid descent of the Fatimids, through Fatima, at a time of genealogical disputes. Its uncompromising nature offended the Sunni scholars and jurists of Ifriqiya and after only two years a new overall phrasing for the coinage had to be devised that left out, among other statements, any direct references to Fatima. Through the use of Fatima's epithets, al-Mu'izz had symbolically and publicly acknowledged, although for a limited number of years, the role of a woman in the legitimisation of Fatimid power. If no longer used on coins, the name of Fatima was nevertheless included in the blessing formula adopted by the Fatimids for their *khuṭba*. When the general Jawhar conquered Egypt, he ordered the removal of any mention of the 'Abbasid rulers from the Friday sermon, to recite instead: 'Praise be on Muhammad, on 'Ali and on Fatima the virgin, on al-Hasan and al-Husayn, and on the imams, forefathers of the chief commander of believers [that is, al-Mu'izz bi-'llāh].'[14]

There are a number of well-known recorded instances of ruling Muslim women whose names appeared on coins. One is the late eighth-century Zubayda Umm Ja'far of the Barmakid dynasty of Rayy. The other is the famous Ayyubid sultana Shajar al-Durr, whose titles were borne both on *dīnārs* and *dirhams*.[15] None of the Fatimid royal women who exercised power went as far as displaying it through coins. Whether regents of a minor ruler or actual queens, the coins minted during their times continued to carry the name of the Fatimid imam-caliph, or even the name of the long-deceased consort-ruler, as in the case of the Yemeni queen Arwa.

Another public sign of power is for the ruler to have his name included, as a recipient of blessings, in the *khuṭba* of the Friday congregational prayer. The most famous Muslim woman to have been bestowed this honour was the sultana Shajar al-Durr. Rather than directly referring to her by name, her titles instead were broadcast from the Cairo pulpits in the *khuṭba* after the blessing upon the 'Abbasid caliph. In it, she was referred to as the 'queen of the Muslims, the defender of this world and the next, the mother of Khalil, the Mu'tasimiyya [the (subject) of the 'Abbasid caliphal-Mu'tasim], and the companion to the sultan Malik al-Salih'.[16] Her status is formally defined by her links to powerful men: her son, the 'Abbasid caliph, and her husband. There is no direct reference to date of a Fatimid royal woman's name or titles being included in the Friday *khuṭba*. However, there is evidence of formal acknowledgement of Fatimid women's authority in official addresses and public speeches. In 411/1021, after the disappearance of the imam-caliph al-Hakim, the vizier Khatir al-Mulk announced in a public speech al-Zahir's nomination as the new imam-caliph on the authority of Sitt al-Mulk. In the Yemen, the titles and epithets of queen Arwa prominently featured in the speech delivered in mourning of the Fatimid caliph al-Amir; one can safely assume that, at least in her capital Dhu Jibla, her name might have been included in the *khuṭba*, after that of the Fatimid imam-caliph.[17]

The strongest sign pointing to the power, or empowerment, of some Fatimid royal women is in the fact that they were often the signatories and the recipients of official correspondence and numerous diplomatic missives. Already, in the early eleventh century, Sitt al-Mulk and the Zirid Umm Mallal were known to have exchanged official correspondence. It is, however, particularly during the reign of al-Mustansir that an intense epistolary exchange took place between the Fatimid royal women in Cairo and the Sulayhid sovereigns in the Yemen. Letters marked salient moments in the life of the two dynasties; announcements were made of seemingly personal events such as marriages, births (of baby boys, of course!) and deaths, all of which were in fact charged with genealogical and political implications. At times, the signatory of these missives was the imam-caliph himself, and this constituted the most obvious sign of recognition of the recipient's status. For instance, as queen-consort, Arwa received a *sijill* sent by the Fatimid imam-caliph al-Mustansir congratulating her on the birth of a male heir.[18]

Fatimid royal women also exchanged official correspondence with Arwa during periods when support was needed, both in emotional and political terms. In 471/1078, less than two years after Badr al-Jamali had assumed the direction of the *da'wa*, and when the Yemen had become an essential outpost for the credibility of the Fatimid missionary effort, al-Mustansir's mother wrote to queen Arwa to reassure her of the unabated support for the Sulayhids on the part of the Fatimid caliph.[19] Moreover, when the Sulayhid al-Mukarram died in 459/1067, Arwa received a letter of condolences from the daughter of the imam al-Zahir, in which the latter confirmed that official correspondence had been sent to confirm the appointment of Arwa's son as successor, and to enjoin the princes and believers of the Yemen to pay obeisance to both the queen and her son.[20]

At times, the wording used by Fatimid royal women to refer to themselves in the official correspondence they sent served to convey endorsement and legitimisation of their sons' right to rule, as well as to formally announce their new status as mothers of the chosen heir. When the imam-caliph al-Mustansir died, one of his wives wrote to Arwa and, instead of using her name or titles, she presented herself as 'al-Musta'li's mother' to stress her newly acquired status as the mother of the appointed heir.[21] Finally, official correspondence from Fatimid royal women could also deal with the quintessentially male domain of war. In a letter written by the sister of al-Mustansir to al-Mukarram in the Yemen, she congratulates him over his military victory against rebellious tribes.[22] The use of diplomatic correspondence between royal women was to become more established a few centuries later at the Ottoman court, where the Walide sultan, or sultana mother, exchanged letters with rulers of foreign countries. Famous in this respect are the letters to Queen Elizabeth I of England sent in the late 1590s by Safiye, the sultana mother of Mehmet III.[23]

Some royal women, although de facto ruling, chose not to alter in their favour the names and titles appearing in official documents, decrees, or coins issued under their rule. Besides Arwa, who kept the name of her husband on coins long after his death, there is also the instance of Sitt al-Mulk. Although the effective ruler after al-Hakim's death and before al-Zahir's investiture, she nevertheless ordered the then head of the Chancery, Khatir al-Mulk, to see that official documents and decrees were still sent in al-Hakim's name. This was, however, but a way for her to legitimise her decisions in the absence of an imam-caliph on the throne.[24]

The bestowal and use of titles was another indication of the status of royal women. The title *malika* (sovereign, queen), while in theory referring to a woman exercising sovereignty, in practice mainly indicated her membership of the royal family (that is, queen consort or queen mother). In Cairo, it was applied to the caliph's mother, such as in the cases of al-Mustansir's and al-Musta'li's mothers, or to the caliph's daughters, such as al-Zahir's daughter. Naturally, it was employed in the formal addressing of queen Arwa. It seems that, at first, the title referred to her role as queen consort, as indicated by the fact that she inherited the title *malika* after her mother in-law's death. However, after her husband's demise, *al-malika* came to indicate her exercise of power.

Finally, for a royal lady to have a private army was yet another clear sign of empowerment, or at least of her ability to build a potential power base for herself or her protégés. As we will see, Sitt al-Mulk disposed of a special military corps at her service. Al-Mustansir's mother, Rasad, filled the Fatimid army with an enormous number of black slaves, whom she purchased to counterbalance the influence of other ethnic-based military sectors. Eventually, Rasad's move turned out to be a double-edged sword. While, on the one hand, her black troops showed her loyalty by executing her orders, on the other, their sheer number prompted viziers to recruit more 'Eastern' soldiers to limit the influence of the army contingent she sponsored, thus leading to the inability of the Treasury to cope with the increased demand for funds to pay the soldiers' salaries.

3. Women's Influence

A royal woman could exercise her influence (*nufūdh*, *ta'thīr*) at court in several ways: in succession matters, palace appointments, finance and, in specific contexts, by being the force behind – or the front person for – conspiracy plans aimed at undermining existing power networks. Since the ninth century, changes in the 'Abbasid caliphs' marriage practices led to growing competition among the mothers of potential caliphs-to-be. This meant that the mother's power and influence grew once her own son had assumed office, as did the power of the palace harem, which had become an arena for succession battles.[25] An example of a prominent 'Abbasid royal mother is that of the caliph al-Muqtadir's (d. 320/932), who became queen regent and whose name was mentioned alongside that of her son in official eulogies.[26]

As for the Fatimids, when they were still in Ifriqiya, it was the pressure over succession exercised by Karima, supported by the harem and court clique that ensured, for example, the accession to the caliphate of her son, al-Mansur. Heinz Halm remarks that court political influence in this case, as in the case of al-Mansur's own son al-Muʿizz, must have been fairly pervasive, as well as effective, as shown by the fact that al-Muʿizz 'was never designated in public as successor by his father, and probably not internally either' and that, like his father, he could succeed thanks to the support of the court clique.[27] Particularly during the first century of the dynasty's Egyptian phase, the imam-caliphs' mothers and those consorts who were to be the mothers of future imams became the most recognisable influential women at the Fatimid court. An example is provided by al-Zahir's mother, who is reported as having solicited the dismissal of a Fatimid high officer from Damascus.[28] The culmination of this maternal influence can be seen in al-Mustansir's mother, Rasad. With Rasad come to the fore some of the characteristics stereotypically associated with female influence: court intrigue, nepotism and personal vengeance.

From the late eleventh century to the end of the dynasty, with changed internal palace organisation and with a new power balance between the caliph and his vizier, the influence of royal mothers appears to have diminished, while other women of the caliph's family were able to rise.

a. The Mother: Rasad, Between Influence and Power

For almost forty years, Rasad was a force to be reckoned with. Her support was instrumental in the making and breaking of ministers, and she influenced court politics, especially to do with the running of palace departments and the Fatimid army. She was one of the 'Cinderellas' of the Fatimid dynasty: from slave to regent. Rasad is variously reported as having been a slave of Sudani, Abyssinian or Nubian origins, whom the imam-caliph al-Zahir had bought from a rich Jewish merchant called Abu Saʿd al-Tustari. When in 427/1036 the imam-caliph al-Zahir died, he was succeeded by his and Rasad's seven-year-old son, al-Mustansir. Due to the imam-caliph's young age, effective power was in the hands of the experienced vizier ʿAli b. Ahmad al-Jarjara'i. It is following the death of this vizier in 436/1044–5 that the figure of al-Mustansir's mother becomes more and more prominent. Even though the imam-caliph was, by then, already fifteen, Rasad 'ruled over the "state"' (*ḥakamat … ʿalā al-dawla*) in her position as queen regent for her son.[29]

Rasad turned to her advantage the power vacuum created by the death of al-Jarjara'i, while his successors, among them the vizier al-Fallahi (also a Jewish notable who had converted to Islam), were taking office. She did so by nominating her previous master, Abu Saʿd al-Tustari, to head her *dīwāns*, a sector of the palace which increasingly gained political weight until it became, in the words of the Persian *dāʿī* al-Shirazi, 'the gate to power'. Al-Shirazi goes as far as to say that al-Tustari had become the brain behind all things related to the *dawla*, while the vizier al-Fallahi held only nominal power.[30] Al-Shirazi's assessment is corroborated by references in some Jewish documents of the Geniza collection, addressing al-Tustari as viceroy or 'superintendent of all the affairs of the state'.[31]

The rivalry between al-Tustari and the vizier al-Fallahi came to a head over the control of the army, the regiments of which were divided along ethnic lines. While al-Tustari sided with the *maghāriba*, al-Fallahi endorsed the *mashāriqa*, some of whom he allegedly instructed in 439/1047 to kill al-Tustari. Nobody was charged for al-Tustari's murder and Rasad, furious about the affair and the *laissez faire* attitude of her son al-Mustansir, worked on avenging the death of her former master.[32] She had al-Fallahi incarcerated and he was killed a year after al-Tustari's death. Al-Shirazi, without mentioning her name, clearly refers to Rasad when he states that al-Fallahi's death was an act of retaliation by the palace women, who were inflamed by hatred and rancour, and that the 'high *jiha*' had promoted one man and dismissed others to make him do what she wanted. Possibly in an attempt to redress the delicate power balance in the army and to limit the influence of the Turks, al-Maqrizi reports, on the authority of Ibn Muyassar, that Rasad, besides the black troops, had 5,000 slaves at her personal service.[33]

Having strengthened her power base, Rasad became more and more influential in manipulating the appointment of government officials or indeed worthy of manipulation on their part. Her influence was exerted not only through the backing of her own 'candidates' but also in her ability to seemingly resist pressure to accept other people's choices. In a climate of highly volatile political alliances, to be appointed to high positions as Rasad's protégé had its benefits but it also involved high risks, so much so that her offers of highly desirable jobs at her service were occasionally politely turned down. For instance, when Rasad sought to employ Abu Nasr al-Tustari, the brother of her former master, she asked him and his wife to serve in her *dīwān*, but they refused. Even when, after some time, Rasad asked them again, still they refused. At last, she made Abu Nasr work for her for three months.[34] The sources state that Abu Nasr had declined the offer, fearing reprisal from other high officials and from the Turks, but it is also reported that it was the ambitious Abu Muhammad al-Yazuri who plotted to avert Abu Nasr's employment on Rasad's part, as he had an interest in retaining that position either for himself or his entourage. When in 441/1049 the vizier Abu'l-Barakat appointed al-Yazuri to the post of *qāḍī* as part of a plan to keep him busy so as to entice him away from Rasad's service and to break his collusion with her, al-Yazuri tried to have one of his sons appointed to work for her. He was met with her 'firm refusal', which was most likely conditioned by the fact that, in that year, Abu'l-Barakat, keen to control Rasad's *dīwān* himself, had already appointed his son, Khatir al-Mulk, to work for her in substitution of al-Yazuri.[35] That Rasad's *dīwān* was indeed 'a gate to power', and that its control was crucial, is shown by the fact that even when, in 442/1050, al-Yazuri became the vizier, he regained charge of her *dīwān*, while also holding the post of chief judge as well as chief *dāʿī*. A further sign of the bond between al-Yazuri and Rasad was the fact that the vizier appointed one of her relatives or protégés, Abu'l-Faraj b. al-Maghribi, as head of the military administration. Abu'l-Faraj eventually became vizier himself.[36] Rasad's influence extended to the appointment of the Fatimid *daʿwa* leadership. Al-Shirazi, who had himself successfully resorted to Rasad's intercession on behalf of some of his friends, was hoping to use his friendship with al-Yazuri to have the post of chief *dāʿī*, but Rasad had the upper hand and convinced the vizier to re-appoint the aged but experienced Qasim b. al-Nuʿman, who had already held the position in the past.[37]

In 450/1058 al-Yazuri, who was to be the last 'civil' vizier or 'minister of the pen' of note, died. Numerous weak viziers succeeded him, but they were unable to solve the deepening factional rivalries within the army. While, in the east, the Fatimids had lost Baghdad for good, at home the army was out of control, with the Sudani and Turkish factions openly at war: numbers versus expertise, commanders versus commanders. In this midst, Rasad did what she could to influence the shift of power in the army through networking and money. In 454/1062 she actively backed military riots against the Turks by providing the black slaves with money and arms.[38] In her campaign against the Turks, Rasad tried to gain the support of the viziers Abu-'l-Barakāt and al-Nazwi, only to dismiss them once they refused to back the Sudanis. At last, she found an ally in the vizier al-Babili, who, by accepting to side with the blacks, prompted what Ibn Muyassar, echoed by al-Maqrizi, regarded as the beginning of the decline of the dynasty. Predictably, contemporary and later observers depicted female interference in matters of government and *fitna* as intertwined, or even bed-fellows. Once again, the nightmare scenario predicted by Nizam al-Mulk as to the dire repercussions on government, economy and society of women's involvement in politics seemed to come true in the case of Rasad.

Between 457/1064 and 464/1071, country-wide army and civil rebellions, coupled with a low Nile, made the country, and especially Cairo, a hard place to live in. By 459/1067, the combination of military alliances and strong army leadership brought about the defeat of the Sudani troops, following the anti-Turk military resistance backed by Rasad in that year. The victorious Turkish commander, Nasir al-Dawla, was left with vast numbers of soldiers to pay, and when he asked the imam-caliph for more money, he had it denied because of the lack of cash reserves. As a last resort, the soldiers and their commanders looted the palace treasure vaults. In 464/1071, Rasad was arrested and all her assets confiscated; however, some sources state that, by 462/1069, with her daughters, she had fled to Baghdad, though this is unlikely.[39] In 465/1073, Nasir al-Dawla was assassinated in Fustat; a year later Badr al-Jamali, in his capacity as commander-in-chief, became vizier and restored order, this time with a military power base. The arrival of Badr al-Jamali effectively marked the end of Rasad's overall influence; but she was still the queen mother after all, and it is in her 'diplomatic' capacity that she reappears, as late as 471/1078, cited as welcoming at the palace the Coptic patriarch and as exchanging official letters with the Yemeni queen Arwa.[40] Despite her long involvement in palace politics, Rasad was, with the exception of the partial al-Shirazi, overlooked by Isma'ili authors. Idris 'Imad al-Din does mention her in *'Uyūn al-akhbār* but only as the witness of the supernatural gift of 'foreknowledge' possessed by her son, the imam al-Mustansir, who had informed her of the death of 'Ali al-Sulayhi's son al-A'azz before the news had reached Cairo.[41]

How did Rasad come to exert such an influence on state affairs? Was she really responsible for the *fitna* and subsequent economic crisis, as medieval and modern sources argue?[42] Or was she just a tool in the hands of others against the background of internal and external palace rivalries? Was Rasad really such a powerful woman that she stood up against other strong personalities of the time, as the historian Ibn Muyassar contends? Or were historians trying to give a clear-cut account of events for their readers by using the narrative device of heroes versus villains?

To understand Rasad's rise to prominence, it is essential to identify the conditions that made it possible. After al-Jarjara'i's death, she could exercise her influence as queen mother directly, apparently unchallenged. Her *dīwān*s became a power base within the palace. As al-Yazuri owed his position as vizier partly to Rasad, he could monitor her but could not restrict her influence. During the fifteen years between al-Yazuri's death and Badr al-Jamali's rise to power, as many as 54 viziers and 42 *qāḍī*s succeeded one another. This unsettled climate, culminating in the civil war, represents a period of transition for the administrative and political apparatus, as reflected by the increasing importance of army politics. From Badr al-Jamali onwards, the viziers would no longer gain office as a result of palace patronage, but rather in their capacity as military commanders. Rasad was possibly one of the last royals who attempted to retain the system of palace patronage by backing her own protégés to the highest government positions.

It is just possible that, rather than provoking the civil war, Rasad's intervention in administration and military affairs delayed the inevitable shift in the nature of the vizier's power base. After Rasad, the influence of the Cairo palace women was never to be the same, as the mothers of under-age imam-caliphs were never again to become regents. Instead, the viziers took over that role. The only means palace women had to limit the viziers' power was to act as an oppositional and conspiratorial force. For some sources, this was just another proof of the irrational and subversive characteristics of female involvement in politics.

b. The Aunts: The 'Clouds of Red Revenge'

At no other time is the conspiratorial influence of palace women more visible than during the final twenty years of the Fatimid caliphate. The last three caliphs, al-Zafir, al-Fa'iz and al-'Adid, were too young and too weak to assert their own will over their all-powerful viziers. The latter two were merely five and nine years of age when they were placed on the throne, only nominally under the tutelage (*fī amān*) of their aunts, but effectively under that of the vizier. The Fatimid army was used by a succession of viziers, as well as by the palace clique, as a power base, with the blacks remaining closely linked to harem politics.

It is within this context that the women of the harem became the resistance bastion to the power of some viziers. They did so by invoking the help of other ambitious individuals who, in turn, exploited the opportunity to rise to power themselves. The most cogent example is that of al-Zafir's sister, *al-sayyida al-'amma* Sitt al-Qusur. Seeking revenge for the murder of her brother in 549/1154, she appealed for help by writing to ask the Franks in Ascalon to intervene against the vizier 'Abbas.[43] But the person who took full advantage of the turmoil surrounding al-Zafir's death was to be the Armenian governor of Asyut, the general al-Salih Tala'i' b. Ruzzik, who was a Twelver Shi'i sympathiser. He marched through the civil unrest of Cairo and soon afterwards became the new Fatimid vizier and the regent of the caliph al-Fa'iz. Sitt al-Qusur's revenge was not only for al-Zafir's murder, but also for the execution of his two brothers, whom 'Abbas had accused of fratricide. She held responsible for al-Zafir's murder none other than 'Abbas himself, and his son Nasr, and she is reported to have paid a substantial amount of money to have them killed. In her desperate cry for reprisal, Sitt al-Qusur had been backed by the women and the personnel of the harem, who are reported to have savagely retaliated against Nasr.[44] The Fatimid sympathiser poet 'Umara, who visited Cairo soon after Nasr's murder, figuratively speaks of 'the clouds of red revenge' descending copiously upon 'Abbas and his son Nasr from the vizier al-Salih. In another poem in honour of the caliph-child al-Fa'iz and his 'protective' vizier al-Salih, 'Umara alludes to the role of the palace women and praises their indomitable spirit, by stating:

Hence her spirit [that is, woman] can never be stolen,
nor can anyone witness her money being devoured.[45]

However, only a few years later, history repeated itself at the palace. The harem was dissatisfied with the vizier al-Salih and was accusing him of mismanagement, as well as abuse of power.[46] After the death of the sickly and heirless al-Fa'iz in 555/1160, al-Salih had placed al-ʿAdid, the nine-year-old cousin of the deceased caliph, on the throne, and had him married to his own daughter. Some sources noted that the vizier left the caliph with no authority whatsoever and that he transferred the money reserves from the palace to his own headquarters. This was too much for the women of the palace to bear! Sitt al-Qusur is named, yet again, as being responsible for planning al-Salih's removal (permanently) and she is reported to have paid 15,000 *dīnār*s for his assassination.[47] The sources present us with a rather confusing succession of the events leading to al-Salih's killing and its immediate aftermath. In 556/1161, al-Salih was ambushed by palace personnel and killed, with the gory details of his assassination scrupulously provided by al-Maqrizi. Al-Zafir's sister was killed too, but it is unclear whether by the dying al-Salih or by the vengeful hand of his son. The figure of a younger sister of Sitt al-Qusur then enters the plot, disclaiming any knowledge of her sister's conspiracy and blaming her sister's associates.[48] What transpires from these accounts is that the sister or sisters of the murdered caliph, who were also the aunts of the caliph-child al-Fa'iz, opposed, with the support of the harem, the growing power of viziers such as ʿAbbas and later al-Salih. A number of sources do not mention the sisters at all and place al-Salih's murder within the context of the Fatimid princes' revolt over his curtailing of their allowances.[49]

Opposition to the viziers was not only coming from the blood relatives of the young caliphs but also from their acquired relatives, such as their spouses. It seems that some viziers developed such paranoia towards the harem as a cauldron of plots against their authority that the vizier al-Salih went as far as to arrest high dignitaries (and their children) found to have exchanged correspondence with suspected plotters such as al-Zafir's sisters.[50] Moreover, it appears that viziers did not refrain from murdering their kin. In 557/1161, al-Salih's son al-ʿAdil allegedly killed his own sister, who was married to the caliph al-ʿAdid, when he suspected her of being among the conspirators in his father's murder.[51]

Whether mothers, sisters or aunts, the exercise of influence by court women in palace politics seems, apart from notable exceptions, to have been characterised by a common denominator: it was at its highest when the effective power of viziers (or other courtiers) grew disproportionally at the expense of the caliph's control of governance. This occurrence was not unique to the Fatimids: in the east, towards the end of the Ghaznavid sultan Masʿud's reign (421–31/1030–40), at a time when the Saljuqs had increased their military and political power, sources report the ascendant influence of the Ghaznavid court women, particularly the sultan's aunt Hurrih-i Khuttali. She advised Mas'ud and incited him to regain power and then, after a heavy Ghaznavid military defeat, she was there to pick up the pieces.[52] In times of low spirits, some royal women were able to stir the men of their family and provide, by way of emotional or other means, the motivation to attempt a reversal of fortune. However, for the Fatimid caliphs it was all too late, and the conspiratorial efforts of the royal ladies were to be of no avail.

4. From Influence to Power: Women Rulers

The eleventh-century Byzantine historian Michael Psellus, in writing about the rule of the empress Theodora, stated: 'everyone was agreed that for the Roman Empire to be governed by a woman, instead of a man, was improper, and even if the people did not think so, it certainly seemed that they did. But if one removes this single objection, one must say that in everything else the Empire prospered and its glory increased'.[53] Psellus' assessment was that of an insider who admired the firm hand of Theodora. Most historians would confirm that her administration was indeed effective in controlling unruly aristocrats, in curbing abuses of power, and, as shown by her handling of al-Mustansir, in negotiating international deals to the Byzantine advantage.

Within the Fatimid domains, two women who lived within twenty years of Theodora's rule stood out for their exercise of power, their handling of diplomatic relations and their control over ambitious high dignitaries or tribal warlords. One was Sitt al-Mulk, the daughter of al-'Aziz and half-sister of al-Hakim; the other was Arwa, the Sulayhid queen of the Yemen. The former exercised her influence before and during the reign of al-Hakim. In the aftermath of his death, Sitt al-Mulk held outright power and continued to wield it in several ways during the reign of al-Zahir until her death. The latter, Arwa, was the wife of the Sulayhid ruler of the Yemen and, after his death, became the acknowledged sovereign of the Sulayhid territories for over fifty years. In the same way Theodora impressed Psellus, both Sitt al-Mulk and Arwa made such an impact on contemporary and later chroniclers that they could not fail to record their deeds and the circumstances that led to their exercising of power. Even when typically hostile to the Fatimids, these chroniclers often spoke of these women, notwithstanding their gender, in favourable terms.

Both Sitt al-Mulk and Arwa belonged to reigning families either by birth or by marriage; in both cases their status, combined with particular historical circumstances, contributed to their acquisition of power. Sitt al-Mulk's influence and power at court rose as sister and aunt of under-age imam-caliphs; Arwa's sovereignty was at first shared with her incapacitated husband and, once widowed, she exercised it in her own right – not without some reluctance – almost as a continuation of her late husband's authority. Therefore both women emerged in support or in lieu of an adolescent or a weakened man, with their 'careers' seemingly developing by accident or default.

a. The Daughter, the Sister and the Aunt: Sitt al-Mulk

Court maverick, daddy's girl, a fratricide to some, to many the brain behind some high-profile murders, Sitt al-Mulk stands out as one of those few women who are extensively written about in medieval Islamic sources.[54] The fact that many chroniclers chose to write on Sitt al-Mulk, whatever their specific agendas, as a personality in her own right, rather than treating her as a collateral figure within their narratives, raises legitimate questions: why her, why then? Mostly praised and occasionally slandered by medieval non-Isma'ili chroniclers, yet virtually ignored by Isma'ili sources, Sitt al-Mulk's 'career' can be appraised in the light of the volatile political and economic climate during al-Hakim's reign. The full extent of Sitt al-Mulk's rise to power ought to be measured against the background of the shifting balance of power amongst the fiercely rival factions who aimed to retain control of the court, along with its administrative and political institutions.

Sitt al-Mulk was born in al-Mansuriyya in Dhu'l-Qa'da 359/970, the daughter of al-'Aziz and of a Christian *umm al-walad*. At the age of about five, and by now living in Cairo, a twist of fate propelled Sitt al-Mulk into a life of prestige from what would have otherwise been one spent in historical obscurity. Having bypassed his eldest (and childless) son Tamim, al-Mu'izz had nominated his second son, 'Abd Allah, as his successor. But in 364/975 'Abd Allah died and it is at this point that, almost by default, the third son was finally designated to succeed to the throne. He took the name of al-'Aziz and, as his own destiny changed, so did that of his family, his entourage and the whole dynasty. Sitt al-Mulk's first name was possibly Sultana but she is more commonly referred to by a variety of titles such as *Sayyidat al-Mulk*, *Sitt al-Kull*, *al-Sayyida al-Sharīfa* and *al-Sitt al-'Amma*.

Much is made by the sources of the love that her father bestowed upon her. He assigned her the use of the Small Palace, located opposite the main royal residence. Within the palace complex, Sitt al-Mulk had at her disposal a living quarter consisting of a structure including four *īwāns* with water pools.[55] Some of the exquisite wood carvings that decorated her palace are still extant to this day and are among the most prized artefacts held in the Islamic Art Museum in Cairo. She is reported as having had some 4,000 slave-girls working for her. Her fame reflected upon some of the women who worked closely for her, so that some biographical information can be found about them. Her most famous slave was Taqarrub (d. 415/1024), formerly owned by Sitt al-Mulk's mother, al-Sayyida al-ʿAziziyya. Taqarrub is described as Sitt al-Mulk's chief informant, and as a very zealous, good-mannered and good-natured woman. Taqarrub died a very wealthy woman, was buried in al-Qarafa and her wealth entrusted to al-Maliha, another slave of Sitt al-Mulk. Al-Maliha was possibly the same black slave featured in a poem by Abu 'l-Fath Mansur al-Bini (d. 415/1024), where he gives an erotic rendition of their courtship on the shores of the Nile.[56] Another woman known to have worked for Sitt al-Mulk was the already mentioned sister of a prominent *shaykh* of the time, and her entourage further included a black slave called ʿAtuf, founder of an army division, *al-ʿaṭūfiyya*, stationed in a quarter of Cairo named after this troop.[57] It is very likely that, like ʿAtuf, this army division was also loyal to Sitt al-Mulk. She also had a military squadron, known as *al-qayṣariyya*, to escort her outside the palace. However, in the light of the events of her life, one wonders whether the true function of her military personnel was actually to 'observe' her rather than serve her.

As she grew up, Sitt al-Mulk witnessed the flourishing of court life, as well as the complexities and challenges of a world in transformation. The eldest daughter of al-ʿAziz, Sitt al-Mulk was to be the last known offspring of an imam-caliph to have been born in North Africa. She was brought up in a Cairo court where – to the detriment of the *maghāriba*'s monopoly of key offices – the imam-caliph was now pursuing a policy of ethnic diversification in the management of important areas of the palace administration, as well as the army. In 367/977, an Iraqi Jew who had converted to Islam became the first vizier of the Fatimids in Egypt. He was Ibn Killis, who had served the Ikhshidids as a fiscal administrator. Another non-Berber was Barjawan, a eunuch slave of uncertain origins, who, at first as an intendant at the court of al-ʿAziz and later as the guardian to al-Hakim, was to become – albeit for a short period – the most powerful man in office in the Fatimid empire. In order to consolidate the Fatimid control over Syria and Palestine, al-ʿAziz encouraged employement of the *mashāriqa*, especially Turks, within the Fatimid army. In the face of this move, the *maghāriba*, who had loyally supported the dynasty since its early period, managed nevertheless to retain control of high military posts.

In Egypt, the private sphere of court life was not exempt from a process of 'localisation' of the dynasty. With the blessing of the powerful Ibn Killis, a clever public relations operation took place to signal to the populace the commitment of the Fatimids to the 'locals'. Around 366/976, prominent court women of the 'old stock', such as the grandmother of Sitt al-Mulk, her aunt, her mother and, eventually, Sitt al-Mulk herself, became – or were encouraged to become – involved in patronage of highly visible public buildings, both secular and religious. In 369/979, al-ʿAziz remarried. The ceremony received an unusually high public profile, which was meant to impress the locals as well as to show the dynasty as having a common touch. In 375/986, the brothers of Sitt al-Mulk's mother were respectively appointed Melkite Metropolite of Cairo and Fustat, and Patriarch of Jerusalem.[58] This was a nepotistic move that, nevertheless, must have reassured the Christian population of Egypt and beyond, as to the tolerant intentions of the Fatimid imam-caliph.

The polarisation of powers between 'old' and 'new' forces inevitably caused members of the royal family to switch their support to players in either camps, depending on the benefits they could derive from this or that alliance. In turn, collusion with a prominent member of royalty meant, for each force at play, the realistic chance of manipulating events in one's favour. In this game, as the eldest beloved offspring of al-ʿAziz and, for some time, apparently the sole one, to 'win' Sitt al-Mulk must have become a coveted prize. And Sitt al-Mulk, knowing her worth, quickly learned to use her position to her advantage, keeping various powerful men on their toes. She employed a North African agent, Abu 'l-ʿAbbas Ahmad b. al-Maghribi (d. 415/1024), who had previously worked for her mother.[59] The celebrated Maghribi chief *qāḍī* and *dāʿī*, Malik b. Saʿid al-Fariqi, who was to serve under al-Hakim, held her in high esteem. The Iraqi ʿAli al-Jarjara'i, who was to become one of the most famous Fatimid viziers, initially worked at her service, although eventually she became dissatisfied with his performance and dismissed him. Sitt al-Mulk, however, was to re-employ him as manager of her *dīwāns* in 414/1023, when he became 'her tongue and hand'.[60] When in 385/995 the Christian vizier ʿIsa b. Nasturus, accused of misconduct, was ousted by the imam-caliph al-ʿAziz, he sought, with success, her intercession to be reinstated in his post.[61]

However, Sitt al-Mulk's influence would have probably been limited to that of a medium-calibre court broker had another twist of fate not intervened. The death of Ibn Killis in 380/991 had created a political vacuum, as witnessed by the quick succession of mainly Christians viziers, six of them over a period of six years! Crucially, in 383/993, Sitt al-Mulk's half-brother or brother Muhammad, al-ʿAziz's designated heir apparent, died. Al-ʿAziz's younger son al-Mansur, aged eight, was designated instead as the heir to the throne and was to succeed his father with the dynastic name of al-Hakim bi-Amr Allah. Al-Hakim, the first Egypt-born Fatimid imam-caliph, was born in 375/985 and had been placed under the guardianship of the eunuch Barjawan. With his designation as heir, al-Hakim's status shifted from irrelevance to paramount importance, while Barjawan's position changed from small-scale dignitary to major player, with all the winning cards in his hand. The full force of Barjawan's entrance into the political scene had profound consequences for Sitt al-Mulk as to the direction her allegiances would take at a time when the 'easterner' and 'westerner' factions within the court were set on a full collision course. Matters finally came to a head when, in 386/996, al-ʿAziz died in Bilbays, on his way to Syria. His succession did not run smoothly, though, to the extent that the events that followed al-ʿAziz's death led chroniclers, such as Ibn al-Qalanisi, to talk of an attempted palace-based coup d'état, ostensibly led by Sitt al-Mulk, who intended to secure the enthronement of the son of her paternal uncle ʿAbd Allah. This episode is variously reported by a number of sources that state that, immediately after her father's death, Sitt al-Mulk arrived at around midnight at the palace in Cairo, accompanied by the *qāḍī* Muhammad b. al-Nuʿman, a figurehead of the North African 'old guard' of Fatimid dignitaries, by the Bearer of the Parasol Abu 'l-Fadl Raydan al-Saqalibi, by other courtiers and backed by the *qayṣariyya* squadron. Barjawan's handling of Sitt al-Mulk on this occasion seems to corroborate the coup d'état theory. Not only did Barjawan prevent her from entering the palace, he also placed her under house arrest, having her guarded by as many as 1,000 horsemen.[62] Not surprisingly, Barjawan hurried on to proclaim al-Hakim as the new imam-caliph.

A closer look at the dynamics of these events reveals that the attempted coup was not so much the result of Sitt al-Mulk's sole initiative to take control over her father's succession, but rather the more probable outcome of the *maghāriba*'s political manoeuvring of the position the princess held at court. The person who halted Sitt al-Mulk's entrance to the caliphal palace was not one of the holders of power – that is, the vizier, the *wāsiṭa* or the military chief commander – but rather Barjawan, who, up until this point, was 'only' the guardian of the imam-caliph-to-be. Indeed, as shown above, the power-holders appeared to have been on Sitt al-Mulk's side. Although the highest among the holders of power, the Berber *wāsiṭa* Ibn ʿAmmar al-Kutami, does not appear to have been overtly implicated in the coup attempt; both his position as military commander of the Berber troops and the fact than he, more than anyone else, had the power to stop Sitt al-Mulk, but did not do so, lead us to believe that he might have played some role in this event.

According to at least two sources, Sitt al-Mulk was in love with her cousin, in whose favour the coup had allegedly been staged.[63] The hints of a romantic liaison between her and her cousin remain unsubstantiated, as the princess never married, probably forced into spinsterhood by dynastic dictates. However, it is not too far fetched to conceive that, in order to retain the 'North African' character of the dynasty, the Berber leadership might have favoured a union between Sitt al-Mulk and her cousin. As the son of ʿAbd Allah, an Ifriqiyan through and through, who had initially been designated to succeed al-Muʿizz while the dynasty was still in al-Mansuriyya, the heart of this young prince must have been in the right place with regards to the defence of the Berbers' interests. It is perhaps around this time, and within this context, that we can appraise the curious episode, reported by a number of sources, of al-Hakim (but de facto Barjawan) suspecting his sister Sitt al-Mulk of having sex with men in her palace. The imam-caliph is reported to have sent trustworthy women to check her virginity; however, rather than being preoccupied with the honour of his sister, al-Hakim might have been primarily concerned with ensuring that Sitt al-Mulk was not pregnant, a condition that would bring havoc to future dynastic succession plans.[64]

Within a year of al-Hakim's succession to the throne, Barjawan managed fatally to break the power of the Berbers by defeating Ibn 'Ammar and taking his post as *wāsiṭa*, thus making himself the effective master of the regime. By this time, the Christian vizier Ibn Nasturus was overshadowed once and for all. The formal establishment of an 'easterner' as *wāsiṭa*, and the undermining of Christian officials, signalled the need for a U-turn in Sitt al-Mulk's choice of allies. It is within this context that her generosity towards her half-brother may be appraised. Already in 387/997, the by-now twenty-seven-year-old Sitt al-Mulk had dispensed lavish donations upon the eleven-year-old al-Hakim. He received from her 30 horses with gold stirrups, including one inlaid and one made of crystal, 20 mules with saddles and bridles, 50 eunuchs (*khādim*), 100 trunks of fine clothes, a crown embedded with precious stones, a headdress with precious stones, baskets with different types of spices and fine herbs. She also presented him with a miniature garden made of silver, complete with replicas of different plants carrying fruits made of precious stones.[65]

As long as Barjawan was in power, Sitt al-Mulk either kept a low profile or was sidelined. She reappears on the scene in 390/1000, when her former ally in the alleged coup, Abu 'l-Fadl Raydan al-Saqalibi, killed Barjawan, ostensibly by order of al-Hakim.

In 390/1000 al-Hakim, now about fifteen and with Barjawan out of the way, took effective control of the government, a move that had positive repercussions for Sitt al-Mulk. In that same year, she received from her brother highly profitable *iqṭāʿāts*, land grants and real estates. Within two years she became a trusted advisor to al-Hakim, who 'was consulting her in the affairs [of the 'state'] (*kāna yushāwiru-hā fī 'l-umūr*), acted according to her opinion, and did not oppose her advice'.[66] According to Ibn Zafir, Sitt al-Mulk had been guiding al-Hakim in his best policies by pointing him in the right direction and the imam-caliph valued her opinion so much that he would change his mind on matters at the last moment on account of her advice.[67] In 392/1002, grievances arose in Syria because of oppressive work legislation and tax increases introduced by al-Hakim's representatives. It was Sitt al-Mulk who, alerted in writing by a former Christian employee and protégé of hers, successfully persuaded her imam-caliph brother to address the people's demands directly and take action against the perpetrators of such injustice, thus trying to promote his popularity in this elusive province. A few years later, Sitt al-Mulk's interference in public affairs was still evident, as it was she who uncovered a plot against the Christian secretary Fahd

b. Ibrahim, whom two administrative officials had falsely accused of theft.

Though resolved, the crisis in Syria was to be the first of many and more serious crises that marred al-Hakim's reign. In 395/1004, a certain Abu Rakwa started in North Africa an anti-Fatimid revolt – possibly instigated by the Umayads of Spain – that took three years to suppress. In Egypt, the running of the judiciary was proving problematic, with *qāḍī*s hired and fired in short order. Between 397/1006 and 399/1008, adverse economic circumstances, partly caused by the immense expenditure involved in quashing the Abu Rakwa revolt, brought about a dramatic monetary crisis, leading al-Hakim to resort to a series of drastic and unpopular financial measures. These included the targeting of Christian-owned assets and the confiscation of the possessions belonging to his mother, his sister, his wives, his concubines and others.[68] Just as things seemed to be back on an even keel, in 402/1011 the Jarrahid revolt broke out in Palestine, threatening further the fragile Fatimid hold over the eastern Mediterranean. Some years later, in 408/1017, a profound doctrinal crisis brought about the emergence of the Druze movement, whose adherents – despite al-Hakim's reported protestation – upheld the belief in his divinity.

It is over this decade that the relationship between Sitt al-Mulk and al-Hakim begins to show clear signs of friction. In 401/1010, Sitt al-Mulk's servant ʿAtuf was killed by a group of Turks reportedly at al-Hakim's command. The following year the princess ensured that the revenues and presents from Tinnis came into her possession. She had contacted the governor of Tinnis on behalf of al-Hakim and ordered him to bring all the revenues of the previous three years. Although al-Hakim's order had originally been for the governor to bring these revenues to him, the governor brought them instead directly to Sitt al-Mulk and 'she made use of them as she pleased'.[69] The episode is indicative of the command that she – more than her brother – could exercise over reminding a 'forgetful' governor of his duties and of her hold on a commercial 'piazza' as important as the delta town of Tinnis, with its substantial Christian population.

Dynastic rifts added further strain to the relationship between Sitt al-Mulk and the royal women on the one hand, and the imam-caliph on the other. In 404/1013, al-Hakim took the controversial decision to designate a great-grandson of al-Mahdi, Abu Hashim al-ʿAbbas, as the next imam (*walī ʿahd al-mu'minīn*), and his cousin, Abu 'l-Qasim ʿAbd al-Rahim b. Ilyas, the son of a Christian woman, as the next caliph (*walī ʿahd al-muslimīn*), thus bypassing his own son. The fact that Abu 'l-Qasim became the governor of Damascus points to a strategy by al-Hakim to strengthen the Fatimid hold on the eastern regions of the empire. To bypass his own offspring in favour of relatives must have caused more than a frisson among the consorts of the imam-caliph; al-Hakim's eagerness to avoid any opposition to his succession plans may be one of the reasons behind his resorting, during the same year, to draconian measures against palace women. He is reported to have sent away from the palace a large number of his concubines and mothers of his children. Sources adverse to al-Hakim go as far as to say that he placed some of them in crates that were then sealed and thrown into the Nile.[70] Isma'ili sources are silent about al-Hakim's anti-female measures, except for a rare explicit hint regarding problems linked to his palace women found in a twelfth-century Isma'ili source referring to the occurrence of female 'intrigues' during the caliphate of al-Hakim.[71] Sitt al-Mulk, by now an ageing spinster with no chance of having children of her own, took it upon herself to defend the direct bloodline of the dynasty by giving refuge in her residence to al-Hakim's wife Amina and their son 'Ali, who, according to Ibn Taghribirdi, were both fleeing from the caliph's persecution.[72]

The strain in the relationship between Sitt al-Mulk and al-Hakim was also reflected in the imam-caliph's targeting of high dignitaries who had belonged to Sitt al-Mulk's entourage. In 404/1013, the vizier al-Jarjara'i had his hands amputated and, a year later, the *qāḍī al-quḍāt* Malik b. Sa'id was killed upon the caliph's order. Al-Maqrizi points to the friendship between the judge and Sitt al-Mulk as the motive that led al-Hakim to order the *qāḍī*'s killing and explicitely states that, by that time, 'al-Hakim had split up with her'.[73] By 409/1018, 'Isa b. Nasturus, another of Sitt al-Mulk's 'allies', was also killed. Judging by the lack of references to her in the sources, for a few years Sitt al-Mulk was indeed once again laying low. She eventually reappeared as the central figure in one of the greatest causes célèbres in medieval Islamic history. During the night of 27 Shawwal 411/13 February 1021, al-Hakim mysteriously disappeared or, to go with Ibn Sa'id's reading of the event, the finding of his clothes stained with blood and torn by knives left no doubt that he had been killed.[74] A number of well-known medieval historians pointed at Sitt al-Mulk as the main instigator of a conspiracy against her brother. Ever since, the shadow of suspicion has been hanging over her and, alas, it is to her reputation as a possible fratricidal murderer that ultimately she owes her fame. Several reasons have been adduced for her supposed action; fear for her personal safety; the increasingly bizarre behaviour of her brother, especially against women; his elimination of several of her closest collaborators; and her disapproval of her brother's succession plans.

Nevertheless, despite all allegations, there appears with be no conclusive evidence against Sitt al-Mulk. The majority of chroniclers, both those almost contemporary with the events in question, such as al-Antaki, al-Rudhbari, al-Musabbihi, Ibn Abi Tayy, al-Ruhi, Ibn Sa'id, al-Futi down to William of Tyre, and those well informed about the vicissitudes of the Fatimid court, such as Ibn Hammad, do not mention Sitt al-Mulk in reporting the circumstances of her brother's death. Al-Quda'i, who during 454–7/1062–4 worked at the Fatimid court, does not mention Sitt al-Mulk's involvement in the killing of al-Hakim either. However, he states that Sitt al-Mulk was instrumental in exposing the

Berber chief, Ibn Dawwas, as the murderer of al-Hakim and, as a result, in having him killed by a group of the late imam-caliph's loyal servants.[75] Some other sources, instead, are unequivocal in denouncing Sitt al-Mulk's involvement in al-Hakim's murder. Accounts are, however, contradictory.[76] All in all, the mere allegation of her involvement in organising the plot, and in succeeding to eliminate the imam-caliph, reveals the perception of her contemporaries that she was a woman who had both the ability and the means to change dynastic history.

The most famous source pointing at Sitt al-Mulk's involvement is the almost-contemporary 'Abbasid and anti-Fatimid historian al-Sabi' (d. 448/1056). In his version of events, the 'intelligent and energetic' Sitt al-Mulk plotted to murder her brother with the help of the Berber chief Ibn Dawwas. According to the historian, after the killing, Ibn Dawwas brought al-Hakim's corpse to Sitt al-Mulk, who then buried it in her *majlis*, hid the whole thing and gave money and robes of honour to Ibn Dawwas. Apparently, she also promised him the post of regent on behalf of her nephew. Al-Sabi' adds that eventually Sitt al-Mulk killed Ibn Dawwas and those who were involved in the conspiracy, as she was afraid that her involvement in the murder would become known.[77] This narrative became so popular that it was acritically quoted by a number of subsequent historians who, in so doing, contributed in forging the myth of 'Sitt al-Mulk the fratricide'. A notable exception was Ibn Taghribirdi, who, while using al-Sabi' when portraying Sitt al-Mulk and her supposed involvement, tells us that these were the rumours spread at the time and denies she had any role in the murder.

If put on trial today, Sitt al-Mulk would be acquitted of the charge of fratricide for lack of hard evidence, as demonstrated by discrepancies and inconsistencies found in the narratives chronicling this episode. These narratives, however, agree on Sitt al-Mulk being the mind behind the killing of Ibn Dawwas and his associates in the regicide. Indeed, it can be inferred that, within the context of the ever-growing influence the *mashāriqa* had gained at court to the detriment of the *maghāriba* factions, Ibn Dawwas as a Berber had plenty of motives to wish the caliph dead.

Following al-Hakim's death, the palace dignitaries gathered around Sitt al-Mulk, who, as the protector of the under-age heir al-Zahir, now had in her hands the reins of power. But this time, rather than being open to manipulation, Sitt al-Mulk, now mature and experienced, found herself in the position of manipulating the powerful men of the court to her advantage. The news of the caliph-imam's 'disappearance' was officially brought to her first (and not to the caliph's mother, as customary). More significantly in his speech the vizier Khatir al-Mulk thus announced on Sitt al-Mulk's authority the succession to the caliphate of al-Hakim's son: 'Our Lady [that is, Sitt al-Mulk] says that this is your master' and, as a sign of her authority, it was she who bestowed upon the neo-caliph the crown that had belonged to al-Mu'izz.[78]

In the one month that elapsed between al-Hakim's 'disappearance' and the appointment of al-Zahir on 10 Dhu 'l-Hijja 411/27 March 1021, Sitt al-Mulk was nominally the uncontested ruler of the Fatimid regime.[79] Even when the young al-Zahir was formally appointed, it was Sitt al-Mulk who acted as regent. She resorted to political purges as part of a strenuous effort to protect the caliph's hold on power from palace political machinations. Purges consisted of the systematic execution of those viziers who had worked in her service but allegedly showed disloyalty, as well as of those dignitaries who attempted to prevail over her. Besides determining the killing of the Kutama Ibn Dawwas,[80] she ordered the execution of her Kutama vizier Abu 'l-Hasan 'Ammar b. Muhammad (d. 411/1021), whose task had been to inspect offices and estates. After the latter's killing, she personally oversaw all aspects of administration and no project could be carried out without her authorisation, which was put in writing by her slave Abu 'l-Bayan.[81] She also removed Abu Hashim al-'Abbas, formerly designated by al-Hakim as *walī al-'ahd*, and was instrumental in the death of 'Abd al-Rahim b. Ilyas.[82] On a pretext, Sitt al-Mulk invited 'Abd al-Rahim to Cairo from Damascus and, having managed to take 200 *dīnārs* from him, she had him arrested and eventually murdered. Likewise, she instigated the execution of the vizier Musa b. al-Hasan (d. 413/1022), who was police prefect and governor of the Sa'id region during al-Hakim's reign. Her pragmatism stretched as far as dismissing her black servant Raydan, surnamed 'Anbar, who had been a doorkeeper of al-Hakim, because he talked too much.[83] In the light of these purges, it is perhaps not surprising that the chronicler al-Musabbihi, who had worked at court under al-Hakim, regarded Sitt al-Mulk's entourage with considerable suspicion and regretted the passing of al-Hakim's time.

During her years as regent, as far as domestic affairs were concerned, Sitt al-Mulk adopted a policy of détente and abolished many of the restrictions imposed by her half-brother. She allowed women to leave their houses again and to wear jewels; she re-introduced the drinking of wine, as well as listening to and playing music. She reformed the tax system, redistributed land and property that al-Hakim had confiscated from the original owners (particularly Christians), and reformed the state finances. In the words of Ibn Hammad, 'she protected the empire and directed the government',[84] a comment reminiscent of the words of the Byzantine historian Psellus with reference to Theodora!

On the international front, she is credited with having conducted diplomatic negotiations with Byzantium. In 408/1017, al-Hakim had appointed an Armenian officer, Fatik, as Fatimid governor of Aleppo. Before al-Hakim's death, Fatik had made himself somewhat independent and showed leanings towards Byzantium as a possible ally. As at this time the direction of Byzantium expansionistic policy was not clear (possibly towards Georgia and Armenia or towards Syria), Sitt al-Mulk sent lavish presents to Fatik to entice him to restore his allegiance to Cairo and sought to improve relations with the Byzantine emperor. Sitt al-Mulk's 'courting' of Fatik triggered al-Sabi''s imagination once more as, according to him, Sitt al-Mulk 'fawned upon' Fatik so much that she corresponded with him and sent him robes and horses with gold mounts.[85]

Whether we believe al-Sabi''s version of events or not, the climate in the region was certainly one that demanded some careful negotiations between Fatimids and Byzantines to clarify the terms of economic and political control of the eastern Mediterranean. In 411/1021–2, the Byzantine emperor was in Trabsond as a result of a campaign to take Georgia. Heinz Halm suggests that Sitt al-Mulk sent the patriarch of Jerusalem, Nikephoros, on a diplomatic mission to the emperor to propose a deal: the Fatimids would restore the churches and treat the Christians well, if the Byzantine emperor would lift trade sanctions and allow the free circulation of Muslims in the lands under his control. At the end of the Georgian campaign, the emperor brought Nikephoros back with him to Constantinople. The negotiations went on for a long time because of the ambivalent alliance policy carried out by Fatik in Aleppo and came to a standstill when, following the killing of Fatik in 412/1022, the Turkish Badr brought the region back under Fatimid control. Sitt al-Mulk might have had a role in the killing of Fatik in Aleppo.[86] After her death, the Byzantine emperor no longer saw the need to continue the negotiations and sent Nikephoros back to Cairo.[87]

After an intense and eventful life, the circumstances of Sitt al-Mulk's death were obscure and – to say the least – not edifying: she died of diarrhoea in 414/1023.[88] In his elegy written in her honour, the eleventh-century poet 'Abd al-Rahman al-Mutabbib sung her praise thus:

> … Living under the sovereignty (*fi ẓill*) of Sitt al-Mulk
> We have shared the comfort of its shadows.
> … The utmost fortune of wellbeing – came from the lower
> To the open-handedness of her palm.
> … As if the lands had not prospered yesterday
> Until the eye saw their emptiness.
> …
> Don't be surprised by the night-like gloom of today
> [from] what were yesterday's gifts from her.[89]

Elsewhere, her supposed beauty and efficiency in running the state inspired the popular lore of her time, as she was associated with one of the then best living quarters in Cairo, al-'Atufiyya, named after her black servant 'Atuf. A verse by Ibrahim al-Mi'mar reads:

> In al-Jawdariyya, I saw a crescent-moon face
> Leaning towards al-Batuliyya instead of al-'Atufiyya.

She has two rows of pearly teeth
If they move, her face [is] Bint al-Husayniyya [Sitt al-Mulk].[90]

Sitt al-Mulk's authority and stature impressed other artists of her time. A lustre painted pottery plate, kept at the Museum of Islamic Art in Cairo and dated to her period, shows what could be her portrait: a woman with a crown on her head.[91]

Sitt al-Mulk had been a beloved, and spoilt, daughter, the most famous and most fastidious of sisters and the formidable aunt par excellence. From being a tool in the hands of rival factions, Sitt al-Mulk eventually affirmed herself as chief manipulator of events much to her personal, dynastic and public advantage. In North Africa, Sitt al-Mulk's example was mirrored by the actions of another formidable aunt. She was Umm Mallal, the aunt of the Zirid al-Mu'izz b. Badis, who acted as a mother to him, raised him and chose the Maliki scholar Abu 'l-Hasan 'Ali b. Abi 'l-Rijal as his tutor.[92] She also became his regent until her death, which, like that of Sitt al-Mulk, occurred in 414/1023.

b. The Wife, the Widow, the Mother: Queen Arwa al-Sayyida al-Hurra

Almost twenty years after Sitt al-Mulk's death, a woman was born in the Yemen who would become queen consort for ten years and then queen in her own right for another fifty. Here was another strong personality struggling to maintain order over fighting tribal factions, and depicted as a loyal advocate of the Fatimid cause. Unlike Sitt al-Mulk, she was extensively referred to in Isma'ili literature, ostensibly for her own merits, but in reality as a device to play the legitimising link in doctrinal disputes. She was Arwa b. Ahmad al-Sulayhi, also known as al-Sayyida al-Hurra (lit. the free lady), the wife of the Sulayhid *dā'ī* and leader, al-Mukarram Ahmad. Since the last years of her husband's rule, she had effectively exercised power over southern Yemen, as well as overseeing the affairs of Oman and Bahrayn. With her husband's death, as queen mother, she continued to rule in the name of her son and, at his death, she remained in power until her long life (she lived to be almost ninety) came to an end in 532/1138 – and, with it, the Sulayhid dynasty as a whole.

b. i. Her Background and Asma', her Mother-in-Law

The Sulayhid dynasty, which recognised Fatimid authority and ruled over parts of the Yemen for almost a century, was founded by al-Mukarram's father, the *dā'ī* 'Ali b. Muhammad al-Sulayhi. The son of a well-reputed Yemeni Shafi'i judge, 'Ali espoused the Fatimid cause and gained the military support of important Yemeni tribes, such as the Hamdani and the Himyari. At the height of his power, he became the sovereign of a territory that, from San'a', stretched westwards to Zabid and southwards to Aden, although recurrent tribal rebellions threatened, during and after 'Ali's reign, the Sulayhid hold on important cities and fortresses. 'Ali achieved political supremacy through military and diplomatic means and exercised personal as well as family rule by giving important administrative and military offices to members of the Sulayhid family, but he is not reported to have had a vizier as such. Idris 'Imad al-Din states that when, in 454/1062, 'Ali went on *ḥajj*, on the way to which he was to be killed, he left his wife Asma' and their son al-A'azz in San'a', presumably to keep control of the city. Asma', who was addressed as *mawlātu-nā* by her husband, was highly influential to the extent of possibly sharing power with her consort. She secured the appointment of her brother As'ad b. Shihab as governor of the Tihama, who would receive orders jointly from 'Ali al-Sulayhi and queen Asma'. The fact that she was also entrusted with the delivery of vast amounts of money, which her brother sent to her husband, also points to her prestige.[93]

The Yemen was an important military, political and commercial outpost for the Fatimids. Particularly from the mid-450/1060s onwards, the Fatimids' hold on the Yemen as their province became of paramount importance in keeping alive their imperial dream in the face of territorial losses elsewhere. Not only did the Yemen turn out to be the last significant territorial hold for the Fatimids but, as the intense correspondence from the Cairo headquarters shows, it came to be seen as an essential outpost for the *da'wa* activities as a whole. The Yemen's geographical location on the trade route to India, the control of which meant a political as well as economic advantage for the Fatimids over the 'Abbasids, indeed proved to be crucial for the spreading of Fatimid Isma'ilism to the Indian subcontinent and for its survival there in the post-Fatimid era.

The source upon which most accounts about the Sulayhids rely is the *History of the Yemen* by the Yemeni chronicler and panegyrist Najm al-Din 'Umara (d. 569/1174). A partial observer, 'Umara portrays the Sulayhids as a dynasty that took pride in educating its women to high standards and that valued their judgement.[94] To illustrate his view, 'Umara refers to 'Ali consulting with his consort Asma' and favouring her opinion. Moreover, after his father's murder, al-Mukarram is reported to have perpetuated his father's attitude by taking advice from his mother. Ibn Khaldun (d. 784/1382), however, takes a different view of this mother–son relation by stating candidly, but perhaps not inaccurately, that it was the queen mother Asma' who was in charge of the affairs of government during the first part of al-Mukarram's reign.[95]

It appears that Asma' was able to influence her son, if we believe 'Umara's account of her clever ploy to convince al-Mukarram to take up arms against a rival tribe. In 459/1067, 'Ali and his wife Asma' were ambushed by the Najahids; the king was decapitated while Asma', her daughter Fatima and other women were taken prisoner to Zabid, where they were held captive by the Najahid leader Sa'id for a whole year.[96] Asma' acted as intermediary to spare the other women's lives, begging Sa'id to allow them back to San'a', but he refused and, having forced them to march behind the severed heads of 'Ali and his brother, kept them imprisoned, with Asma''s cell in full view of her husband's impaled head. These were dire times for the Sulayhids, as they suffered from widespread inter-tribal conflicts and consequent territorial loss. According to a story reported by Idris 'Imad al-Din, Asma', while captive, cunningly hid in a loaf of bread a letter that, by way of a beggar, eventually reached her son. In it, she invoked his intervention to free her and the other Sulayhid women caught by the Najahids.[97] In relation to Asma''s call for help, 'Umara adds that, in the epistle, she had asked her son to liberate her before she gave birth to her captor's child. Outraged, al-Mukarram gathered his men and set to rescue her by fighting the Najahids back.[98] Beyond their veracity, these stories present Asma' as the resourceful heroine who, in time of despair, is able to play on her son's emotions and motivate him into action.

During al-Mukarram's reign, we can infer Asma''s actual involvement in the affairs of the Sulayhid governance from reports about her knowledge of sensitive strategic information and her dealing with financial matters, such as the control and distribution of tributes from the provinces. Significantly, her daughter-in-law, Arwa, did not hold any public role until after Asma''s death in 467/1074–5. Queen Asma' is portrayed as a generous and noble lady, and a patroness of court poets, one of whom praised her thus:

> I say, when people magnified the throne of Bilqis,
> 'Asma' hath obscured the name of the loftiest among the stars'.[9]

In other words, the splendour of the queen of Sheba (Bilqis) would pale in comparison to Asma's. We are told that, as a sign of distinction, Asma' did not wear the veil in public either before or after her husband's death.[100]

b. ii. al-Sayyida Arwa bint Ahmad b. Muhammad al-Sulayhi

Arwa, daughter of Ahmad, son of Muhammad, was born, possibly in 440/1045, within the Sulayhid clan and, after her father's death, was brought up in 'Ali and Asma''s palace.[101] In his account, 'Umara introduces his readers to her future role by showing her father-in-law 'Ali's appreciation and support of her.[102] By building up her character within the narrative, he also implies that her innate qualities justified her future status and gave it greater 'legitimacy' than that of a mere royal consort. 'Umara also tells us of her education: her knowledge of the Qur'an, her ability to read and write, to memorise chronicles, poetry and historical events, and her excellence in glossing and interpreting texts.[103]

In 458/1065 (for 'Umara, in 461/1069), at the age of eighteen, upon her marriage to the Sulayhid king's son al-Mukarram Ahmad b. 'Ali, Arwa received as dowry from her father-in-law Aden's net yearly revenue, which amounted to

c. 100,000 *dīnārs*. However, upon ʿAli's death in 459/1067, the Maʿnid dynasty in charge of the port-city suspended this payment to Arwa. It was only after al-Mukarram's restoration of Sulayhid authority there that the tribute to his queen consort was resumed. Following al-Mukarram's death, its payment ended. Arwa's marital bliss did not last long. In 458/1066 al-Muwaffaq, ʿAli's elder son and heir, died and his younger brother al-Mukarram was appointed as ʿAli's successor, hence Arwa's status shifted to the rank of queen-consort-to-be. Shortly after al-Mukarram's appointment, ʿAli al-Sulayhi was killed. Then, sometime around 467/1074–5, shortly after the death of his mother, al-Mukarram was hit by paraplegia. This event marks the beginning of Arwa's effective take-over of power in the Yemen, as queen consort. Meanwhile, rebellions had been mushrooming throughout the Yemen, in the Haraz region, in the Tihama, and even in the Sulayhid capital Sanʿa', where the rebel Zaydis had made several attempts to seize the city. As the sick al-Mukarram moved out from Sanʿa', ostensibly for medical reasons, to the remote hill town of Dhu Jibla, in central Yemen, an apparently reluctant Arwa took charge of the affairs of 'state' and made Dhu Jibla the new Sulayhid capital. Rather than for its salubrious air, Arwa's choice of Dhu Jibla was more likely dictated by the need to find a more suitable alternative to Sanʿa', where Sulayhid sovereignty was being eroded.

As in the case of the Byzantine Theodora, to have a woman as sovereign needed some kind of apology, even though in Arwa's case her sovereignty was at first exercised as queen consort of a disabled husband. According to ʿUmara, it was al-Mukarram who transferred the responsibility of the affairs of government onto his wife, to which Arwa, by now in her late twenties, objected: 'A woman, who is [still] desirable in bed, is not suitable for running a "state".'[104] While this statement is presented as an expression of her personal reservations, one suspects that it was indeed constructed by the panegyrist ʿUmara as a device to praise her modesty by showing her reluctance to being thrown into the spotlight. In addition, the link here between sexual desirability and inadequacy to rule echoed not so much a reservation with female leadership per se, but rather with leadership made vulnerable by being embodied in a fertile woman potentially exposed to sexual subjugation. The broader implication here is that, in theory, it would have been acceptable for a senior woman, of post-childbearing age, to hold a public office or, more generally, to have a public social role.[105] Finally, it has been suggested that, in the case of Arwa, having a woman as ruler may have been perceived as a potential weakness, which, in turn, might have encouraged the loosening of alliances and the emergence of autonomous tendencies within the Yemen.[106] Whether this is plausible for a country characterised by recurrent shifting of tribal alliances, is far from being proven.

Meanwhile, Egypt was particularly attentive to the state of affairs in the Yemen, with the imam-caliph al-Mustansir sending letters to the Sulayhids emphasising the importance of the Yemeni *dāʿīs* in promoting the spreading of the Ismaʿili mission to India. In 469/1076, the chief *dāʿī*, al-Mu'ayyad fi'l-Din al-Shirazi, died in Cairo, his post being taken over by the Armenian vizier Badr al-Jamali, along with his other high offices as commander-in-chief and chief *qāḍī*. From this time onwards, until Badr's death, the official correspondence exchanged by al-Mustansir and his family with the Sulayhid queen often includes praises of Badr and mentions his numerous titles and offices.[107] As head of the *daʿwa*, Badr worked in Egypt to promote the dynasty – and himself– through, among other means, the building and restoration of public edifices. Abroad, he saw the Yemen as the last remaining base for the expansion and consolidation of the *daʿwa* to western India and, possibly, for strengthening the allegiance of the holy cities of Makka and Madina to the Fatimids.

Upon al-Mukarram's demise in 477/1084, a letter addressed to Arwa soon reached her from Cairo, confirming the appointment as ruler of their son ʿAli ʿAbd al-Mustansir, known as al-Mukarram junior.[108] Some two years later, the imam-caliph al-Zahir's daughter sent Arwa another letter, in which she enjoined the pro-Fatimid Yemeni tribal leaders to obey both ʿAbd al-Mustansir and his mother Arwa. Beyond formal recognition, however, Arwa's son does not seem to make much of an impact on the Yemeni scene,[109] and when al-Mustansir talks business, especially *daʿwa* business, it is to Arwa that he turns. In a *sijill* dated 481/1089, it is she whom the imam-caliph encourages to supervise the *daʿwa* in the provinces, and it was around this time that Tayyibi Ismaʿilis claimed that her rank in the *daʿwa* was elevated to that of *ḥujja* (lit. proof).

The Sulayhid men did not enjoy a long life and around the mid-480s/early 1090s al-Mukarram junior also died. Arwa found herself to be the sole Sulayhid ruler. This time she was no longer, not even formally, queen consort, nor queen regent, just queen. By now, at least from the point of view of the Fatimid headquarters in Cairo, it seemed more difficult to sustain the acceptability of a single, widowed and most probably son-less woman ruling over a vassal country. As a widow with young sons, through her role as acting queen-regent, Rasad represented a precedent to warrant formal acceptance of Arwa's status on the part of the Fatimids. Instead, having lost the son on whose behalf she reigned, Arwa was formally asked to comply with the orders to marry the Fatimid *dāʿī* Saba' b. Ahmad al-Sulayhi, a relative on Arwa's paternal side, with whom marriage links had already been established, his sons having married, respectively, Arwa's daughter and sister. 'Umara tells us that, on paper, she obliged but that she refused to consummate or even stage the marriage.[110] Was Cairo interested in keeping up appearances, or was the instruction to marry the *dāʿī* Saba' an expedient to monitor Arwa's allegiance to the Fatimid cause? The politically naïve 'Umara does not reflect any concerns of this type, but what his narrative conveys is that, in the Yemen, the queen did not really need a husband to rule.

Therefore, the formality of a marriage on paper might have been more a concern of the Cairo leadership than of the local Yemeni tribal leaders.

It is significant that, when al-Mustansir instructed Arwa in writing to marry the *dāʿī* Saba', she could not refuse. According to Idris ʿImad al-Din, Arwa had appointed Saba' as regent (*nā'ib*) over her son, al-Mukarran junior.[111] ʿUmara draws a parallel with the Qur'anic passage of the queen of Sheba receiving a letter from King Solomon. Indeed, on receiving al-Mustansir's epistle, queen Arwa is reported to have quoted from the Qur'an: 'It [the letter] is from Solomon and it says: "In the name of Allah."' (Qur. 22–30/2), thus implying that royal and divine-based authority could not be contradicted.[112] The eleventh-century al-Thaʿlabi's coverage of narratives on the queen of Sheba in his *Arā'is al-majālis* makes us suggest an additional interpretative key. In one story, once Sheba converted to Islam, Solomon decided to marry her off. He asked her to marry one of her own men, to which Sheba responded that she was a woman in authority over her own people, hence voicing her uneasiness. To this, Solomon replied: 'Submission to Islam requires that you do not prohibit what God has declared as lawful.' In turn, the queen of Sheba said: 'If there is no other way … marry me off to Tubbaʿ the Elder, king of Hamdan.'[113] Implicit in al-Thaʿlabi's passage is a correspondence between divine and social order, between submission to God and submission to male authority. Accordingly, whether the queen marries Solomon or one of her own tribesmen, she in fact submits to both the divine and the natural order.[114] In ʿUmara's account, while queen Arwa bows to the imam's authority, in practice she does not submit to the will of her new husband; and, being 'the master of her own people',[115] she maintains her acknowledged high status among them.

Once she became a sole ruler, Arwa faced difficult times. The tribal fighting in the Yemen eventually led to the establishment of autonomous dynasties in strategically and economically important cities such as Sanʿa' and Aden. In 491/1097, Saba', her nominal husband and her loyal commander-in-chief, died. Queen Arwa had to wait over ten years before she found another close supporter in ʿAli b. Najib al-Dawla, whom, having arrived to the Yemen from Cairo in 513/1119, she appointed as commander-in-chief of the army and of civil affairs. Their relationship turned sour, though, and she had him captured; he died disgraced while on his way back to Egypt.

Ironically, Arwa's biggest challenge came from the very authority she was representing. In 487/1094, the imam-caliph al-Mustansir and his vizier Badr al-Jamali died in quick succession. Arwa had faithfully served the Fatimid imam, for whom she provided, from a distant province, preferential trade links, logistic support and also intelligence on the *daʿwa* affairs of the Yemen, Oman and India.[116] From the time of al-Mustansir's death, she continued to support for over three decades the rights of his successors al-Mustaʿli and al-Amir against

Nizari claims. When in 524/1130 the caliph al-Amir was murdered, in the claimed absence of a male heir,[117] al-Amir's cousin 'Abd al-Majid eventually rose to the throne with the name of al-Hafiz. His controversial succession, however, was challenged by those who upheld the rights of a son of al-Amir called al-Tayyib, who had allegedly been born a few months before his father's death, but whose existence had been doubted by some. Queen Arwa, with a number of other Musta'lian supporters in Egypt and Syria, did not acknowledge al-Hafiz's sovereignty and endorsed the legitimacy of al-Tayyib. Not all the Isma'ilis in the Yemen backed her choice of dynastic allegiance and, in keeping with old rivalries, the rulers of San'a' and Aden supported instead the legitimacy of al-Hafiz.[118]

Tayyibi sources state that Arwa had proof of al-Tayyib's existence, having received an official letter in 524/1130 from the caliph al-Amir announcing his son's birth.[119] Even though this letter is not the only source attesting the existence of al-Tayyib, this document proved crucial for the future of the Tayyibi branch of Isma'ilism. Not only was this letter a testimony of the child's existence, but it was also to be interpreted, by later Tayyibis, as implicitly confirming the legitimacy of Arwa's spiritual authority. On the strength of this authority, Tayyibi sources state that in 520/1126 Arwa had appointed the *dā'ī* al-Dhu'ayb b. Musa as the first of what was to become a chain of Tayyibi *dā'ī muṭlaqs* (lit. absolute *dā'ī*). By virtue of Arwa's spiritual status, the *dā'ī muṭlaqs* retrospectively established a link between their own spiritual authority and the Fatimid imam-caliphs.

From 'Umara's account, we can glimpse traits ascribed to Arwa in terms of her style in the exercise of power: the preference for diplomacy over direct military confrontation; the centralisation of power in her person; her pragmatism in the face of territorial losses; and finally, of great importance for the identity, development and survival of Yemeni Isma'ilism, her acumen vis-à-vis her relationship with the Cairo headquarters following the death of al-Amir. 'Umara also reveals her vindictive side when he narrates that, in retaliation for displaying 'Ali al-Sulayhi's severed head to his wife Asma', Arwa exposed the head of her mother-in-law's captor to his imprisoned wife Umm al-Ma'arik.[120] 'Umara's portrayal of Arwa also includes the traditional role of woman as a daughter's mother. When Shams al-Ma'ali, the husband of Arwa's daughter, Fatima, took another wife, the girl wrote to her mother seeking help. In response, Arwa sent an army against the straying son-in-law. Dressed as a man, Fatima was able to camouflage herself among the army men sent to her rescue and to return to her mother while Shams al-Ma'ali remained under siege until he was expelled from his domains.[121] Hell hath no fury ...

Arwa's long life came to an end in 532/1138, and with it the Sulayhid dynasty. As al-Sultan al-Khattab sang in her praise: 'She was the Banu Sulayhi's

Fig. 4 Dhu Jibla, Yemen: the shrine of queen Arwa in the western corner of the Friday Mosque, built in Fatimid style under her orders in 480/1087. *Photo: Delia Cortese*.

pearl, who brought light to a place of darkness.'[122] She was buried in the Friday Mosque at Dhu Jibla, where her shrine can still be visited today (see Figs 4 and 5). Several sources record her as a great patron of architecture in the Yemen, specifically in San'a' and Dhu Jibla. Despite her role as queen, her status was not acknowledged in Yemeni coinage. As late as 501/1107, that is more than twenty years after her husband's death and at least seven years after the death of her son, al-Mukarram junior, Arwa's name does not appear on coins that, as though 'frozen' in time, still bear the name 'al-Mukarram'.[123] In today's Yemen, Arwa is still remembered as a great and much loved sovereign, as attested in Yemeni contemporary historiography, literature and popular lore, where this daughter of the Yemen is referred to as *Bilqīs al-ṣughrā* – that is, the junior queen of Sheba.

In his *'Uyūn al-akhbār*, Idris 'Imad al-Din informs us that Arwa, in her will, reiterated her allegiance to the imam al-Tayyib by bequeathing her treasure to him and prohibiting anybody else from using any of its items 'lest they incur Allah's wrath!' This bequest to al-Tayyib ought to be interpreted as symbolic, that is, intended for the cause in his name, given that, according to Tayyibi belief, al-Tayyib had gone into concealment as an infant. Be that as it may, the

Fig. 5 Dhu Jibla, Yemen: interior of the Friday Mosque: the *miḥrāb*. *Photo: Delia Cortese*.

will listed forty-four items, including golden tiaras, swords, necklaces, bracelets and anklets, brooches, rings, gold panes and seals, as well as precious stones ranging from topaz and sapphire to rubies, not to mention beautiful and valuable pearls.[124] Indeed, queen Arwa might have inherited some of these precious stones from her father-in-law, who is reported to have owned a large number of them.[125]

In one of the codicils to her will, quoted in full by Idris ʿImad al-Din, Arwa bears witness to Fatima, the 'radiant and the pure', as the fifth among the elected *aṣḥāb*, or People of the House. Beyond its formulaic use, the occurrence of this statement in the context of this particular will raises a number of questions. Was this a doctrinal statement by the queen to reiterate the Ismaʿili legacy of the Sulayhid dynasty? Was it a final affirmation of her Ismaʿili identity, not only through political allegiance but also through conviction? Or was instead Idris ʿImad al-Din, a Tayyibi *dāʿī muṭlaq* himself, keen to highlight Arwa's homage to al-Tayyib and to Fatima, to stress the position of the *dāʿī muṭlaq* as the spiritual executor of her legacy? Was, then, the reference to Fatima a Tayyibi 'sectarian' device to ultimately link the queen and Tayyibi leadership to the holiest of Shiʿi female figures?

b. iii. Political and … Religious Authority?

A full evaluation of Arwa's role would not be complete without an analysis of the nature of her authority. While Arwa's political authority is clearly acknowledged by all the sources, an assessment of whether or not she held spiritual authority is influenced by the sources used and the doctrinal stance of their respective writers. The four most important sources for the life and times of Arwa provide rather different portrayals of the queen and are somehow more revealing of their authors' perspectives than the events or characters they intend to portray.

The earliest primary source to mention Arwa is *al-Sijillāt al-Mustanṣiriyya*, a collection of official correspondence exchanged mainly between the Fatimid caliph al-Mustansir, or his closest entourage (his mother, his sister, his wife), and the leaders of the Sulahyid dynasty.[126] On reading this correspondence, Arwa emerges not only as the effective leader of the Yemen in her role as representative of the Fatimid imam there, but also as the promoter and supervisor of the *daʿwa* affairs in the region, as well as the defender of its *dāʿīs*.[127] While in this correspondence she is consistently addressed as *malika*, the spiritually charged term *ḥujja* is never used in relation to her.[128]

The second source, also contemporary, consists of two works: a collection of poetry, the *Dīwān*, and a doctrinal treatise, the *Ghāyat al-mawālīd*, both by al-Sultan al-Khattab, a Tayyibi poet and scholar who was converted to Ismaʿilism by the *dāʿī* Dhu'ayb b. Musa al-Wadi'i, and murdered in 533/1138–9, shortly after Arwa's death. As al-Khattab became an apprentice *dāʿī* under the instruction of Dhu'ayb, the first *dāʿī muṭlaq*, his perspective is that of an insider witness and transmitter who was personally and directly involved in legitimising the claims of the Yemeni Tayyibi hierarchy.

In his *Dīwān*, al-Khattab, while eulogising Arwa for her deeds, her allegiance and service to the imams, and while lauding her everlasting significance, mentions on two occasions that Arwa was a *ḥujja*.[129] In his *Ghāya*, after a theoretical discussion about the necessity of the presence of *ḥujjas* as guides in the twelve 'regions' of the world, al-Khattab states that Arwa is one of these *ḥujjas*. This statement occurs within a full theoretical discussion about whether being male or female affects the essence of a person and the level of perfection this person can achieve. Al-Khattab provides specific examples of women who attained levels (and ranks) of excellence, far superior to those achieved by men, such as Fatima *al-Zahrā'* and Khadija. He concludes that it is not the external form that gives an indication about the quality of a person, but rather the person's acts of devotion and good deeds.[130]

Rather than the words of a feminist *ante-litteram*, or of a disinterested appraiser of the spiritual potential and achievements of womankind, al-Khattab's long-winded and elaborate argument might have instead served the purpose of defending the legitimacy of the line of the Yemeni *dā'īs* down to his own master, Dhu'ayb. As Dhu'ayb had been appointed *dā'ī muṭlaq* on the authority of Arwa, a woman, al-Khattab had a vested interest in arguing in favour of female spiritual attainments. However, the very extent to which al-Khattab goes in building a convincing argument, implicitely validating Arwa's status as *ḥujja*, might just point to the lengths he had to stretch to in order to persuade his audience to accept a woman in such a high position of spiritual authority.

The third, and most puzzling, source is the already mentioned *Ta'rīkh al-Yaman* by 'Umara, which he wrote in 563/1167–8, therefore some thirty years after Arwa's death, for the chief secretary of the last Fatimid caliph, al-'Adid. According to some scholars, 'Umara, originally a Shafi'i, either remained a Sunni throughout his life or became a supporter of the Cairo-endorsed Hafizi line of caliphs. Be that as it may, he was put to death by Saladin for his supposed part in an attempted coup to restore Fatimid power in Egypt.

On the evidence of al-Akwa''s edition of 'Umara's text, at the death of al-Mukarram the leadership of the *da'wa* passed into the hands of the *dā'ī* Saba' and, by implication Arwa exercised only temporal authority.[131] However, in the Kay edition of 'Umara, Arwa is also invested with spiritual authority by being called *ḥujja*, here intended as a rank inferior only to that of the imam. This discrepancy between the two editions of 'Umara's text was analysed by Samuel Stern, who, on the basis of comparative analysis with similar passages by the historian al-Janadi (d. 732/1331–2), who used 'Umara as his source, concluded that only the passages in which 'Umara attributes to Arwa temporal authority are original. Those passages referring to Arwa as a *ḥujja* being, in Stern's view, the result of subsequent Tayyibi interpolations.[132]

Doctrinal considerations underlie the account of Arwa featured in the fourth source: the fifteenth-century Tayyibi historiography, *'Uyūn al-akhbār*, by Idris 'Imad al-Din. As the nineteenth *dā'ī muṭlaq*, Idris provides a reconstruction of Tayyibi history according to his partial perspective by emphasising the continuity and legitimacy of the *da'wa*, while downplaying internal dissent. In such a reconstruction, in creating the new rank of *dā'ī muṭlaq* Arwa becomes the watershed between Fatimid and Tayyibi Yemeni history. Prior to her appointment of Dhu'ayb as the first *dā'ī muṭlaq*, Idris is concerned with showing the legitimacy of the Cairo-endorsed Yemeni *da'wa* leadership, starting from al-Mukarram junior and proceeding with the chief *qāḍī* and *dā'ī* Lamak and his son Yahya. To prove his point, Idris affirms that al-Mustansir held Arwa in special regard, that he raised her to the rank of *ḥujja* in the *da'wa* and that the imam-caliph ordered the *dā'īs* to follow her orders. In these tasks, Arwa was aided by the chief *dā'ī* and *waṣī* in the Yemen, Lamak and his son, who had the function of 'guarantors of the *sharī'a*' but were still obedient to Arwa in all matters pertaining to the *da'wa*. The same Idris informs us that subsequently al-Musta'li appointed both Arwa and Lamak to being in charge of the Yemeni *daʿwa*.[133] With Arwa's appointment of the *dāʿī* Dhu'ayb, in her capacity as representative of the concealed imam al-Tayyib, Tayyibi history proper begins and Idris presents us with a continuous chain of succession of *dāʿī muṭlaqs* from Dhu'ayb down to his own times.

Idris interprets statements from the official correspondence from Cairo to validate his contention that Arwa was indeed a *ḥujja*, hence in a position of spiritual authority, which warranted her appointment of *dāʿīs*. Thus, Idris portrays the queen as a qualified trainer of *dāʿīs*, who was able to explain to them difficult doctrinal issues and, by describing her as being thoroughly familiar with the science of revelation and allegoric interpretation, he makes her fully qualified to hold such a high position in the *daʿwa* hierarchy. However, when checked against the text of the *sijills* to which Idris refers, one finds that statements in those documents are not quite as explicit as Idris suggests. In the *Sijillāt*, Arwa is indeed addressed with titles *suggestive* of the spiritual dimension attached to the important role to which, as supervisor of the *daʿwa*, she had been appointed. But is this enough to infer the conferment to her of the title of *ḥujja*? To further support his argument, Idris also quotes from the *Tuḥfat al-qulūb*, by the twelfth-century *dāʿī muṭlaq*, Hatim b. Ibrahim al-Hamidi, who stated that the chief *qāḍī* and *dāʿī* Lamak, on his return to the Yemen from Cairo, imparted the knowledge of some of the eternal esoteric truths (*ḥaqāʾiq*) to both al-Mukarram and Arwa.[134] Thus, according to Idris, Arwa, in her capacity as spiritual leader, becomes the *trait d'union* with the hidden imam al-Tayyib: a woman, a queen and the highest spiritual rank after the imam himself!

Owing to the uniqueness in Islamic history of a woman who was believed to have been formally bestowed with spiritual authority, the question of whether or not Arwa was a *ḥujja* has aroused the interest of a number of contemporary scholars. Their conclusions, conditioned by their respective standpoints, range from the acknowledgement of her de facto *ḥujja*-ship, the interpretation of her title of *ḥujja* as being only honorific and non-executive, the recognition that she held an unspecified high spiritual status, to the placing of her authority exclusively within the temporal domain.[135] The ultimate difficulty in reaching a definitive conclusion lies with the acknowledgement of the variety of meanings, functions and roles that the term *ḥujja* conveys when used in different Shiʿi historical, doctrinal and geographical contexts. While medieval Ismaʿili authors used the term *ḥujja* according to their own doctrinal, missionary or cosmological discourse, their Tayyibi counterparts had a vested interest in using the term in relation to Arwa. For her, a tailor-made type of *ḥujja*-ship was retrospectively devised to lend authority to the introduction of a new rank, that of *dāʿī muṭlaq*, which was specific to the Tayyibi *daʿwa* hierarchy, and to fill the hierarchical vacuum between the rank of the hidden imam and that of such a *dāʿī muṭlaq*.

Powerful and influential women such as queen Arwa and princess Sitt al-Mulk were appraised for fulfilling their roles as sovereigns, regents, good administrators and skilful diplomats. The acknowledgement of their qualities, even by detractors, contrasts with the recurrent portrayal of influential women as 'interfering' in state affairs only by means of intrigues, assassination plots and the resort to extreme measures in the face of hardship. This is the image that transpires from accounts touching upon the royal women during the last years of the Fatimid rule. As the caliph was losing control of the political situation, so the caliphal women were losing their means of exercising influence, even by way of palace intrigue. Their only resort was to appeal for help from outside the palace walls. They practically did so, with the enticement of money and, symbolically, by sacrificing the outermost sign of their femininity: their hair.

In 549/1154, the ladies of the palace cut their hair and sent the locks to Salih Tala'iʿ b. Ruzzik in Upper Egypt, to invoke his intervention against the much-hated minister ʿAbbas. The poignant gesture was such an effective sign of distress that Salih, attracted by financial and political gain, soon responded to the call and, with his troops, marched to Cairo, the locks of the royal women's hair waving in the air from the tops of their spears.[136] While Salih took care of ʿAbbas, the palace women personally took revenge upon his son Nasr, who had been captured by the Franks and returned to Cairo upon payment of a ransom. The sources compete in providing the most bloodthirsty account of the women's vindictiveness: Nasr was mutilated, forced to eat his own torn flesh, hanged while still alive and, for good measure, crucified. The sources report a 'gender-specific' rendition of the tortures Nasr was subjected to at the hands of the palace women, who are reported as having used not fine armoury, such as the engraved silver swords kept in the palace vaults, but common everyday utensils, such as scissors, knives and even their own wooden clogs and shoes (*qabāqīb*, *zarābīl*).[137] The reference to the uncontrolled use of these tools conveys a powerful image of the irrational behaviour of enraged women, who could switch from domesticity to wildness. To refer to the use of basic tools of torture, particularly the clogs, also served the narrator as a device to add a greater sense of humiliation to Nasr's already undignified death. All in all, these accounts of female revenge point to the writers' perception of the women's role in affairs, which should have been a male domain, as being 'unnatural', as emphasised by the ultimate reversal of their accepted (or expected) female submissive and compassionate roles.

The same type of distress call once received by Salih was dispatched again in 558/1162, when the shaved hair of the palace women and children was sent in a nosebag to the Zangid ruler of Aleppo, Nur al-Din, as a call for help. The dramatic haircut had allegedly been ordered by the young caliph al-ʿAdid, out of concern for the repeated attempts by the Franks to invade Egypt.[138] These, and more practically compelling measures, though effective in the short term, did nothing to save the Fatimids, whose power, by now literally hanging by the hair, came to an end in 567/1171.

Notes

1 On powerful 'Abbāsid royal women see Levy, R., A *Baghdad Chronicle*, Cambridge: CUP, 1929, p. 140; Holt, P. M., et al. (eds), *The Cambridge History of Islam*, Cambridge: CUP, 1970, vol. 1, p. 114; Roded, R. *Women in Islamic Biographical Collections*, Boulder and London: Lynne Rienner, 1994, pp. 115–23.

2 Niẓām al-Mulk, Abū 'Alī Ḥasan, *The Book of Government or Rules for Kings*, trans. Darke, H., London, Henley and Boston: Routledge & Kegan Paul, 1978, 2nd edn, p. 179; his main Qur'anic reference is 4.34. On Niẓām al-Mulk's careful selection of sources, see Spellberg, D., 'Niẓām al-Mulk's manipulation of tradition: 'Ā'isha and the role of women in the Islamic government', *MW*, 78 (1988), 2, pp. 111–17.

3 Bowen, H., 'Niẓām al-Mulk', *EI2nd*, vol. 8, p. 72; and Lambton, A. K., 'The internal structure of the Saljuq empire', *The Cambridge History of Iran*, Cambridge: CUP, 1968, vol. 5, p. 255. Niẓām al-Mulk's depiction of the grave consequences of female involvement in politics rings suspiciously prophetic in view of the events after Malik Shāh's death. Did he see through the politics of the court-harem and historical events supported his views, or did contemporary and future historians find a ready-made explanation for the decline of the Saljūqs?

4 al-Maqrīzī, Taqī al-Dīn, *al-Mawā'iẓ wa-'l-i'tibār bi-dhikr al-khiṭaṭ wa-'l-āthār*, Beirut: Dār al-ṣādir, n.d., offset of Būlāq, 1324 edn, vol.1, p. 335. For a twelfth-century negative portrayal of Theodora, see El-Cheikh, N. M., 'Describing the Other to get at the self: Byzantine women in Arabic sources (8th–11th centuries), *JESHO*, 40 (1997), p. 244.

5 On the power and influence of mothers-in-law in the Byzantine Comnenus and Ducas dynasties, see Buckler, G., *Anna Comnena: a study*, Oxford: Clarendon, 1968, pp. 124–5; on powerful Byzantine women, see Garland, L., *Byzantine Empresses: Women and Power in Byzantium* AD *527–1204*, London: 1999.

6 See the case of Tamīm, the son of al-Mu'izz, suspected of plotting with other male relatives against his own father, in Daftary, F., *The Ismā'īlīs: Their History and Doctrines*, Cambridge: CUP, 1990, p. 181.

7 See Nelson, C., 'Public and Private Politics: Women in the Middle Eastern World', *American Ethnologist*, 1 (1974), 3, pp. 551–63, in particular p. 553.

8 On the historical validity and authority of this *ḥadīth* see Mernissi, F., *The Forgotten Queens of Islam*, London: Polity, 1993.

9 Contrary to this view, al-Ṭabarī considered her a good, effective and just ruler, see Noeldeke, Th., *Geschichte der Perser und Araber zur Zeit der Sasaniden*, Leiden: E. J. Brill, 1879, p. 391. On Buran, see Rose, J., 'Three Queens, Two Wives and a Goddess: Roles and Images of Women in Sasanian Iran', in Hambly, R. G. (ed.), *Women in the Medieval Islamic World: Power, Patronage and Piety*, London: Macmillan, 1998, pp. 43–5.

10 In his argument, al-Mufīd refers to Qur. 33:53: 'And [as for the Prophet's wives], whenever you ask them for anything, ask them from behind a screen (*ḥijāb*): this will but deepen the purity of your hearts and theirs'. See al-Mufīd, Muḥammad, *al-Jumal aw al-naṣra fī ḥarb al-Baṣra*, Qum: Maktabat al-dawārī, 1963, pp. 79–81.

11 See Spellberg, D., *Politics, Gender and the Islamic Past: the Legacy of 'Ā'isha bint Abi Bakr*, New York: Columbia University Press, 1994, p. 129.

12 al-Qāḍī al-Nu'mān, *Da'ā'im al-Islām fī dhikr al-ḥalāl*, trans. Fyzee, A. A. A., *The Pillars of Islam:*

Vol. 1, Acts of Devotion and Religious Observances, revised and annotated by Poonawala, I. K. H., New Delhi and Oxford: OUP, 2002, p. 48.

13 For the full wording of the legend, see Kazan, W., *The Coinage of Islam: Collection of William Kazan*, Beirut: Bank of Beirut, 1404/1983, p. 299, no. 446. See also Falk, T. (ed.), *Treasures of Islam*, Geneva: Artline Editions, 1985, p. 370, no. 441: the main opposition to al-Mu'izz's wording for his coins came from the Mālikīs of Qayrawan. In their 'Additional Evidence of the Fāṭimid Use of Dīnārs for Propaganda Purposes' in Sharon, M. (ed.), *Studies in Islamic History and Civilization in Honour of Professor David Ayalon*, Jerusalem, Cana and Leiden: E. J. Brill, 1986, pp. 145–51, A. S. Ehrenkreutz and G. W. Heck argue that the recurrent mention in Fāṭimid coins of particular months in which they were supposedly issued might have served a propagandist purpose. They link the occurrence of specific dates to Fāṭima's life events: Jumādā II to the month of her presumed birth, Jumādā I to her death and Rajab to her marriage to 'Alī.

14 al-Safadī, Ṣalāḥ al-Dīn, *Kitāb al-Wafi bi-'l-wafāyāt*, Wiesbaden: F. Steiner, 1981–, vol. 11, no. 320, p. 225.

15 For Zubayda Umm Ja'far, see Miles, C. G., *The Numismatic History of Rayy*, New York: American Numismatic Society, 1938, p. 81; for Shajar al-Durr, see al-Safadī, *al-Wafi*, vol. 16, no. 133, p. 120. Other examples include the fifteenth-century Tadū, who ruled in southern Iraq, had coins struck in her name and was mentioned in the Friday prayer. In India, a century later, the Moghul empress Nūr Jahān, wife of Jahān Gīr, had become the actual ruler and had also coins minted in her name.

16 al-Safadī, *al-Wafi*, vol. 16, no. 133, p. 120.

17 For queen Arwā, see Idrīs 'Imād al-Dīn, *'Uyūn al-akhbār*, vol. 7, ed. and trans. A. F. Sayyid, *The Fatimids and their Successors in Yaman*, London: I. B. Tauris, 2002, vol. 7, pp. 260–1 (Ar.).

18 al-Mustanṣir bi-'llāh, Abū Tamīm Ma'add, *al-Sijillāt al-Mustanṣiriyya*, ed. 'Abd al-Mun'im Mājid, Cairo: Dār al-fikr al-'arabī, 1954, no. 65, pp. 209–10.

19 *Sijillāt*, no. 51, p. 169.

20 *Sijillāt*, no. 52, p. 172.

21 *Sijillāt*, no. 35, pp. 109–11.

22 *Sijillāt*, no. 28, pp. 96–7.

23 See Skilliter, S. A., 'Three letters from the Ottoman "Sultana" Ṣāfiye to Queen Elizabeth I', in Stern, S. M. (ed.), *Documents from Islamic Chanceries*, Oxford: Bruno Cassirer, 1965, pp. 119–57.

24 Stern, S. M., *Fatimid Decrees, Original Documents from the Fatimid Chancery*, London: Faber & Faber, 1964, p. 128: 'it was convenient for al-Ḥākim's sister Sitt al-Mulk, who assumed the government, to rule in the dead caliph's name'.

25 On the dynastic and financial complications resulting from the change in marriage patterns among the 'Abbāsid caliphs, and the draconian ways by which they were resolved, see Bosworth, C. E., 'Notes on the lives of some 'Abbāsid princes and descendants', in Bosworth, C. E. (ed.), *The Arabs, Byzantium and Iran*, Aldershot: Variorum, 1996, p. 278.

26 Significantly, it was al-Muqtadir's mother, rather than the caliph, who held public audience. Ibn Jubayr also reports that, in Baghdad, court mothers attended the public Thursday morning lecture, together with the caliph and other women of the palace, and that the preacher 'would eulogise the caliph and his mother, addressing her as "the Most Noble Veil" and the "Most Compassionate Presence"': see Levy, R., *A Baghdad Chronicle*, pp. 140, 235.

27 Halm, H., *The Empire of the Mahdi. The Rise of the Fatimids*, trans. M. Bonner, Leiden: E. J. Brill, 1996, pp. 311, 342.

28 al-Musabbiḥī, Muḥammad b. 'Ubayd Allāh, *Akhbār Miṣr*, ed. Sayyid, A. F. and Bianquis, T., Cairo: IFAO, 1978, vol. 1, p. 15.

29 Ibn Muyassar, Tāj al-Dīn, *Akhbār Miṣr*, ed. Massé, H., as *Annales d'Égypte*, Cairo: IFAO, 1919, p. 14.

30 al-Mu'ayyad fi'l-Dīn al-Shīrāzī, *Sīrat al-Mu'ayyad fi'l-Dīn dā'ī al-du'āt*, ed. Kāmil Ḥusayn, M., Cairo: Dār al-kātib al-miṣrī, 1949, p. 81.

31 Goitein, S. D., *A Mediterranean Society*, Berkeley: University of California Press, 1967–88, vol. 2, p. 377, see also n. 12, p. 610.

32 Ibn Muyassar, *Akhbār Miṣr*, pp. 1–2.

33 For al-Mu'ayyad fi'l-Dīn al-Shīrāzī's statement on palace women, see his *Sīra*, p. 84; for al-Maqrīzī's report, see his *Khiṭaṭ*, French trans. Bouriant, M. U., *Description topographique et historique de l'Égypte*, Paris and Cairo: Mission Archéologique Française du Caire and E. Leroux, 1895, part 1, p. 270.

34 al-Maqrīzī, Taqī al-Dīn, *Kitāb al-Muqaffā al-kabīr*, ed. al-Ya'lāwī, M., Beirut: Dār al-gharb al-islāmī, 1991, vol. 1, p. 251.

35 Ibn Muyassar, *Akhbār Miṣr*, p. 4; and al-Maqrīzī, Taqī al-Dīn, *Itti'āẓ al-ḥunafā' bi-akhbār al-a'imma al-Fāṭimiyyīn al-khulafā'*, ed. al-Shayyāl, J. and Ḥilmī, M., Cairo: Lajnat iḥyā al-turāth al-islāmī, 1387–93/1967–73, vol. 2, pp. 199–200, 208.

36 Ibn Muyassar, *Akhbār Miṣr*, p. 5. According to al-Maqrīzī, *al-Muqaffā*, vol. 3, p. 367, al-Yāzūrī gained access to the service of al-Mustanṣir's mother and devoted himself to her service and that of her courtiers. For Abu 'l-Faraj, see al-Maqrīzī, *al-Muqaffā*, vol. 5, p. 502. See also Lev, Y., *State and society in Fatimid Egypt*, Leiden: E. J. Brill, 1991, pp. 42–3.

37 See al-Shīrāzī's harsh evaluation of Qāsim's competence and his strongly hinted reference to Rasad as being behind his appointment in his *Sīra*, p. 82.

38 Ibn Muyassar, *Akhbār Miṣr*, p. 13.

39 Ibn Muyassar, *Akhbār Miṣr*, p. 21; and Ibn Ẓāfir, Jamāl al-Dīn, *Akhbār al-duwal al-munqaṭi'a*, ed. Ferré, A., Cairo: IFAO, 1972, p. 75.

40 *Sijillāt*, no. 51, p. 169.

41 Idrīs 'Imād al-Dīn, *'Uyūn*, vol. 7, p. 102 (Ar.).

42 See Sayyid, A. F., *al-Dawla al-Fāṭimiyya fī Miṣr: tafsīr jadīd*, Cairo: al-Dār al-Miṣriyya al-Lubnāniyya, 1992, pp. 197–8; see also the overall negative image given by 'Abd al-Karīm Aḥmad, Nurīmān, *al-Mar'a fī Miṣr fi'l-'aṣr al-Fāṭimī*, Cairo: al-Hay'a al-miṣriyya al-'āmma li-'l-kitāb, 1993, pp. 209–21.

43 al-Maqrīzī, *Iti'āẓ*, vol. 3, p. 220; and Ibn Ẓāfir, *Akhbār*, p. 109.

44 In addition to the primary sources referred to in Sayyid, A. F., *La capitale de l'Égypte jusqu' à l'époque Fatimide*, Beirut/Stuttgart: F. Steiner, 1998, p. 540, see Ibn al-Athīr, 'Izz al-Dīn, *al-Kāmil fi'l-ta'rīkh*, Beirut: Dār al-kitāb al-'arabī, 1967, vol. 9, p. 44; and al-Safadī, *al-Wafī*, vol. 27, no. 31 pp. 68–9.

45 Smoor, P., 'Umāra's odes describing the imām', *AI*, 35 (2001), 2, p. 566.

46 Ibn al-Athīr, *al-Kāmil*, vol. 9, p. 75.

47 al-Maqrīzī, *Itti'āẓ*, vol. 3, pp. 231, 239.

48 al-Maqrīzī, *Itti'āẓ*, vol. 3, pp. 246–8, 253. For the two sisters as leaders of conspiracy see also Smoor, P. ,''Umāra's Elegies and the Lamp of Loyalty', *AI*, 34 (2000), pp. 472–3.

49 For a number of extracts from a variety of primary sources, see Smoor, P., ''Umāra's Elegies', pp. 474, 479–80.

50 al-Maqrīzī, *Itti'āẓ* , vol. 3, p. 231.

51 Ibn al-Dawādārī, Abū Bakr b. 'Abd Allāh, *Kanz al-durar wa-jāmi' al-ghurar: al-durra al-muḍiya fī akhbār al-dawla al-Fāṭimiyya*, al-juz' al-sādis, ed. al-Munajjid, Ṣ., Cairo: O. Harrassowitz, 1961, vol. 7, p. 19. According to Ibn al-Athīr, however, al-Ṣāliḥ's daughter outlived al-'Āḍid, and even remarried: see Ibn al-Athīr, *al-Kāmil*, vol. 9, Beirut edn, p. 68.

52 See Amirsoleimani, S., 'Women in Tārīkh-i Bayhaqī', *Der Islam*, 78 (2001), 2, pp. 232–4.

53 Psellus, M., *Chronographia*, trans. Sewter, E. R. A., *Fourteen Byzantine Rulers*, Harmondsworth: Penguin, 1966, p. 262.

54 With Arwā, Sitt al-Mulk is the only woman in Ismāʿīlī history to whom scholars have devoted specific studies. See Lev, Y., 'The Fatimid Princess Sitt al-Mulk', *JSS*, 32 (1987), pp. 319–28; Halm, H., 'Sitt al-Mulk', *EI2nd*, vol. 9, pp. 685–6; Halm, H., 'Le destin de la princesse Sitt al-Mulk' in Barrucand, M. (ed.), *L'Égypte Fatimide: son art et son histoire*, Paris: Presses de l'Université de Paris-Sorbonne, 1999, pp. 69–72; Halm, H., 'Die regentschaft der Prinzessin Sitt al-Mulk' in *Die Kalifen von Kairo*, Munchen: C. H. Beck, 2003, pp. 305–11; and ʿAbd al-Karīm Aḥmad, *al-Mar'a*, pp. 195–205.

55 al-Maqrīzī, *Khiṭaṭ*, vol. 1, p. 457.

56 al-Musabbiḥī, *Akhbār Miṣr*, vol. 2, pp. 11–12.

57 al-Maqrīzī, *Khiṭaṭ*, vol. 2, p. 13.

58 al-Anṭākī, Yaḥyā b. Saʿīd, *Ta'rīkh*, partial ed. and French trans. Kratchkovsky, I. and Vasiliev, A., 'Histoire de Yahya-ibn Saʿīd d'Antioche', *Patrologia Orientalis*, 23 (1932), p. 415.

59 al-Musabbiḥī, *Akhbār Miṣr*, vol. 1, p. 94.

60 Al-Maqrīzī's expression could be tongue in cheek given, that in 404/1013 al-Jarjarā'ī had his hands amputated on al-Ḥākim's orders. As reported by al-Maqrīzī, the punishment had been instigated by Sitt al-Mulk, who had become suspicious of al-Jarjarā'ī when he sent her a conciliatory note after their falling out: al-Maqrīzī, *Ittiʿāẓ*, vol. 2, pp. 102, 183.

61 Ibn Ẓāfir, *Akhbār*, p. 41; Ibn al-Qalānisī, Ḥamza b. Asad, *Ta'rīkh Dimashq*, ed. Zakār, S., Damascus: Dār Ḥassān, 1983, p. 57.

62 In his article 'Le destin', p. 70, Halm discusses statements in a variety of primary sources referring to her possible involvement in this coup.

63 See Ibn al-Qalānisī's extract quoted in Halm, H., 'Le destin', p. 70, and Ibn al-Athīr, *al-Kāmil*, vol. 7, p. 177.

64 In his *Ittiʿāẓ*, al-Maqrīzī reports for the year 410/1016 that a quarrel took place between al-Ḥākim and his sister, during which the imam-caliph accused Sitt al-Mulk of debauchery and of being pregnant, but by that time the princess was about fifty. The episode is further discussed in Halm, H., 'Le destin', p. 71.

65 Ibn al-Zubayr, *Kitāb al-Dhakhā'ir, Kitāb al-Hadāyā wa-'l-tuḥaf*, ed. and trans. al-Hijjāwī al-Qaddūmī, G., *Book of Gifts and Rarities*, Cambridge, MA: Harvard University Press, 1996, p. 104.

66 Ibn al-Qalānisī, *Ta'rīkh Dimashq*, p. 97.

67 Ibn Ẓāfir, *Akhbār*, p. 57.

68 P. Vatikiotis argues that al-Ḥākim confiscated the property of the women in his family as a way of preventing them from intriguing against him. Vatikiotis, P., *The Fatimid Theory of State*, Lahore: Orientalia Publishers, 1957, p. 153.

69 al-Musabbiḥī, Muḥammad b. ʿUbayd Allāh, *Nuṣūṣ ḍā'iʿa min akhbār Miṣr*, ed. Sayyid, A. F., Cairo: IFAO, n.d. [1981], p. 30.

70 al-Anṭākī, 'Histoire', p. 518.

71 *Majlis* 117 from the *Majālis* by al-Ḥāmidī, in Ivanow, W., *Ismaili Tradition Concerning the Rise of the Fatimids*, London: OUP, 1942, p. 309.

72 Ibn Taghrībirdī, Jamāl al-Dīn Abu 'l-Maḥāsin, *al-Nujūm al-Zāhira fī mulūk Miṣr wa-'l-Qāhira*, Cairo: Dār al-kutub al-Miṣriyya, 1351/1933, vol. 4, pp. 193–4.

73 al-Maqrīzī, *Ittiʿāẓ* , vol. 2, p. 107.

74 Ibn Saʿīd, ʿAlī b. Mūsā, *al-Nujūm al-ẓāhira fī ḥulā ḥadhrat al-Qāhira*, ed. Ḥusayn Naṣṣār, Cairo: Dār al-Kutub al-Miṣriyya, 1970, p. 50.

75 As reported by Ibn Taghrībirdī, *al-Nujūm*, 1933 edn, vol. 4, pp. 191–2.

76 On the contradictory character of the sources see Lev, Y., 'The Fatimid Princess Sitt al-Mulk', pp. 324–5.

77 Reported by Ibn Taghrībirdī, *al-Nujūm*, 1933 edn, vol. 4, p. 192.

78 al-Maqrīzī, *Ittiʿāẓ* , vol. 2, p. 125.

79 al-Anṭākī emphasises the influence Sitt al-Mulk had on al-Ẓāhir: he lived at her palace until al-Ḥākim's disappearance, she supervised his development and, even after his appointment, she looked after the affairs of state and appointed viziers. See also Ibn Ḥammād, Abū 'Abd Allāh, *Akhbār mulūk banī 'Ubayd*, ed. and French trans. Vonderheyden, M., *Histoire des Rois 'Obaïdites (Les Califes Fatimides)*, Algiers: J. Carbonel; Paris: P. Geuthner, 1927, p. 58 (Ar.) and p. 87 (Fr.).

80 al-Maqrīzī, *Itti'āẓ*, vol. 2, pp. 117, 127–8, 183.

81 Ibn 'Idhārī, al-Marrāhushī, Aḥmad, *Kitāb al-Bayān al-mughrib, Histoire de l'Afrique et de l'Espagne intitulée al Bayano 'l-Mogrib*, French trans. Fagnan, E. R., Algiers: Imprimerie Orientale P. Fontane, 1901, vol. 1, p. 404.

82 al-Maqrīzī, *Itti'āẓ*, vol. 2, pp. 182–3.

83 'Anbar was related to the Abu'l-Faḍl Rayḍān, an ally of Sitt al-Mulk and the killer of Barjawān, see al-Musabbiḥī, *Akhbār Miṣr*, vol. 1, p. 45.

84 Ibn Ḥammād, *Histoire*, p. 58 (Ar.) and p. 87 (Fr.), and al-Maqrīzī, *Itti'āẓ*, vol. 2, p. 174. al-Anṭākī notes Sitt al-Mulk's generosity towards the Christian patriarch of Alexandria and towards the Christian community as a whole; Ibn Taghrībirdī also acknowledges her political and administrative skills in his *al-Nujūm*, 1933 edn, vol. 4, p. 248.

85 Ibn Taghrībirdī, *al-Nujūm*, 1933 edn, vol. 4, pp. 194–5.

86 al-Maqrīzī, *Itti'āẓ*, vol. 2, p. 130.

87 Halm, H., *Kalifen*, p. 311.

88 The date of Sitt al-Mulk's death is discussed in Halm, H., 'Le destine', pp. 71–2.

89 al-Musabbiḥī, *Akhbār Miṣr*, vol. 2, pp. 89–90.

90 al-Maqrīzī, *Khiṭaṭ*, vol. 2, p. 13.

91 Cairo, Museum of Islamic Art, no. 17–22765, 4–22812 as referred to in Khemir, S., *The Palace of Sitt al-Mulk and Fāṭimid Imagery*, PhD thesis, SOAS, London: University of London, 1990, vol. 1, p. 31.

92 Idris, H. R., *La Berbérie*, vol. 1, p. 141.

93 'Umāra, Najm al-Dīn, *Ta'rīkh al-Yaman*, ed. Muḥammad b. 'Alī al-Akwa', Beirut: Maṭba'at al-sa'āda, 2nd edn, 1976, pp. 120, 123. See also Stookey, R. W., *Yemen: The Politics of the Yemen Arab Republic*, Boulder: Westview Press, 1978, p. 63, based on H. C. Kay's ed. and trans. of 'Umāra's *Ta'rīkh* entitled, *Yaman: its early medieval history*, London: E. Arnold, 1892, p. 19 (Ar.). On Asmā' and A'azz in San'a' and on As'ad's appointment as ruler of Zabīd, see Idrīs 'Imād al-Dīn, *'Uyūn*, vol. 7, p. 38 (Eng.), p. 26 (Ar.).

94 See for example the Qur'anic passages that both Asmā' and Arwā are reported to have appropriately quoted: 'Umāra, *Ta'rīkh*, ed. al-Akwa', p. 120, refers to the exchange of Qur'anic verses between Asmā' and her husband, thus showing her sagacity and sense of humour; cf. a very similar passage in al-Safadī, *al-Wafi*, vol. 22, no. 27, pp. 77–8.

95 Ibn Khaldūn, 'Abd al-Raḥmān, *Kitāb al-'Ibar*, Beirut: Dār al-kitāb al-lubnānī, 1958, vol. 4, p. 459.

96 While 'Umāra has Asmā' imprisoned for a year, the twelfth-century (?) *Sīrat al-Malik al-Mukarram* has her captive for less than four months, see Shakir, M., *Sīrat al-Malik al-Mukarram: an edition and a study*, PhD thesis, SOAS, London: University of London, 1999, vol. 1 (Ar.), pp. 83–4, and vol. 2 (Eng.), pp. 139–41.

97 Idrīs 'Imād al-Dīn, *'Uyūn*, vol. 7, p. 116 (Ar.), pp. 57–8 (Eng.); and p. 122 (Ar.), 60 (Eng.).

98 'Umāra, *Ta'rīkh*, ed. al-Akwa', p. 128 and ff. In *Sīrat al-Malik al-Mukarram* there is no mention of such a letter. M. Shakir (vol. 2, p. 140) argues that it would have been highly unlikely for a woman of her rank to 'write such blameworthy words about her own honour, even to arouse the rancour' and for her son to have even thought of 'telling such shameful things to someone', let alone publicly announcing it as stated by 'Umāra.

99 Quoted in al-Hamdānī, Ḥ. F., 'The Life and Times of Queen Saiyidah Arwā the Ṣulaiḥid of the Yemen', *JRCAS*, 18 (1931), p. 508.

100 Idrīs 'Imād al-Dīn, *'Uyūn*, vol. 7, p. 132 (Ar.), p. 64 (Eng.); 'Umāra, *Ta'rīkh*, ed. al-Akwa', p. 133. For one of the poets at Asmā's palace, his career and the (unfounded) suspicion of improper acquisition of wealth, see Shakir, M., *Sīra*, vol. 2, p. 175.

101 The queen's official title was al-Sayyida or al-Ḥurra al-Malika, Arwā being her proper name according to 'Umāra. For a discussion on her name, see Shakir, M., *Sīra*, vol. 2, pp. 118–20. Arwā's legacy is strongly reflected in contemporary Yemeni popular culture: Arwā is a very widespread female name and queen Arwā's lifestory has been fictionalised.

102 'Alī is said to have had premonitions about Arwā's future role in preserving the dynasty: see Stookey, R. W., *Yemen*, pp. 67–8. 'Alī chose her as wife for his son, al-Mukarram, see Shakir, M., *Sīra*, vol. 1, p. 22 (Ar.); and vol. 2, n. 55, pp. 118–20.

103 'Umāra, *Ta'rīkh*, ed. al-Akwa', p. 137, and ed. Kay, p. 39; see also Ḥ. al-Hamdānī's interpretation in his 'The Life', p. 509, but cf. Stookey's translation, p. 68.

104 'Umāra, *Ta'rīkh*, ed. Kay, p. 29, ed. al-Akwa', p. 138.

105 In this respect, L. Peirce argues that in the seventeenth-century Ottoman court, royal concubines would not normally assume public roles before the age of thirty-three. When they did, as in the case of 25-year-old Turhān Sulṭān, who in 1651 acted as regent for her nine-year-old son, it provoked uneasiness because of the perceived threat to the political, as well as social stability of the state. In Peirce, L. P., *The Imperial Harem: Women and Sovereignty in the Ottoman Empire*, New York, Oxford: OUP, 1993, pp. 279–85. After the menopause, women were felt to be less of a liability for the honour of the family, and could therefore socialise more freely. On an Ottoman sixteenth-century legal ruling on attendance of Friday prayer for older women, see Peirce, L. , 'Seniority, sexuality, and social order: the vocabulary of gender in early modern Ottoman society' in Zilfi, M. C. (ed.), *Women in the Ottoman Empire*, Leiden: E. J. Brill, 1997, pp. 170, 186.

106 See Stookey, R. W., *Yemen*, pp. 69–70. Female leadership in another reported case seems to have encouraged more peaceful policies. The eleventh-century Ghaznavid Sulṭān Maḥmūd remarked thus about a female governor in Rayy: 'If that woman were a man, we would have to have a lot of troops in Nishapur', implying a less aggressive nature in a woman in power, quoted in Amirsoleimani, S., 'Women', pp. 245–6.

107 See *Sijillāt*, *sijill* 26 in Idrīs 'Imād al-Dīn, *'Uyūn*, vol. 7, p. 158.

108 See *Sijillāt*, *sijill* 26, in Idrīs 'Imād al-Dīn, *'Uyūn*, vol. 7, p. 156. Different dates are given by writers for al-Mukarram's death, the one in the text is that suggested by Idrīs 'Imād al-Dīn.

109 Information on Arwā's male offspring is contradictory. 'Umāra, *Ta'rīkh*, ed. al-Akwa', p. 137, tells us that she had four children from al-Mukarram: two daughters and two sons, adding that the boys, named Muḥammad and 'Alī , died in infancy in San'a'. According to the *Sijillāt*, ed. Mājid, p. 210, in 461/1068 the imam-caliph al-Mustanṣir congratulates Arwāh upon the birth of a son. In 478/1085, after the death of al-Mukarram, in *Sijillāt*, pp. 90–3, al-Mustanṣir appoints al-Mukarram's son 'Alī as his successor. If this is the same as the child born in 461/ 1068, he would have been around seventeen and therefore no longer an infant. While 'Umāra hardly acknowledges 'Alī, Idrīs 'Imād al-Dīn makes him a warrior fighting, like his father, the unruly warlords of the Yemen. As for Muḥammad, he is reported to have died while his brother was still alive, see al-Hamdānī, Ḥ. F., 'The Life', p. 511.

110 'Umāra, *Ta'rīkh*, ed. al-Akwa', pp. 52–3. Stookey, R. W., *Yemen*, pp. 69–71. Both 'Umāra (ed. Kay) and Idrīs 'Imād al-Dīn agree that the 'official' regent for her minor son 'Alī was Sabā' himself, until his death in 491/1098.

111 Idrīs 'Imād al-Dīn, *'Uyūn*, vol. 7, p. 162 (Ar.), p. 71 (Eng.).

112 'Umāra, *Ta'rīkh*, ed. al-Akwa', p. 151.

113 For al-Tha'labī, see Lassner, J., *Demonizing the Queen of Sheba*, Chicago and London: University of Chicago Press, 1993, p. 201.
114 For Lassner's argument on natural and divine order, see his *Demonizing*, pp. 79–87.
115 'Umāra, *Ta'rīkh*: 'All her people used to say: our lady is our master', ed. Kay, p. 36, ed. al-Akwa', p. 152.
116 *Sijillāt*, pp. 167–9 where al-Mustanṣir praises Arwā over her intelligence work on the state of the *da'wa*.
117 On the claim that al-Āmir had revoked his designation of al-Ṭayyib, cf. Daftary, *Ismā'īlīs*, n. 23, pp. 656–7.
118 Hamdani, A., 'The Dā'ī Ḥātim ibn Ibrāhīm al-Ḥāmidī (d. 596H. 1199AD) and his book *Tuḥfat al-qulūb*', *Oriens*, 23–4 (1974), p. 259.
119 The *sijill* with the birth announcement is reported by 'Umāra, *Ta'rīkh*, ed. Kay, pp. 100–2 (Ar.), and is also included in Idrīs 'Imād al-Dīn, *'Uyūn*, vol. 7, pp. 247–8 (Ar.). Al-Akwa''s edition of 'Umāra does not contain this passage.
120 'Umāra, *Ta'rīkh*, ed. al-Akwa', pp. 144–5, narrating the event of the killing of her captor and the exposure of his head in 481/1087 (Asmā' died 467/1075). However, in *Sīrat al-Mukarram*, the head of Asmā's captor was presented to her during her lifetime, by her own son al-Mukarram, in 460/1067, see Shakir, M., *Sīra*, vol. 1, pp. 151–2 and 154, and vol. 2, pp. 168–9.
121 'Umāra, *Ta'rīkh*, ed. al-Akwa', p. 153.
122 In Poonawala, I. K. (ed.), *al-Sulṭān al-Khaṭṭāb: ḥayātu-hu wa-shi'ru-hu*, Beirut: Dār al-gharb al-islāmī, 1999, *qaṣīda* no. 8, p. 295.
123 Darley-Doran, R., 'Examples of Islamic Coinage from Yemen', in Daum, W. (ed.), *Yemen: 3000 Years of Art and Civilization in Arabia Felix*, Innsbruck: Pinguin/Frankfurt: Umschau, 1988, p. 201, with pictures and legendae of two Sulayḥid gold *dīnārs* of the period of queen Arwā minted in Aden and Dhū Jibla. There circulated also coins minted in Zabīd bearing the name of the Fāṭimid imam-caliph in Cairo: see the coin dated 447/1055–6 in Falk, T. (ed.), *Treasures*, p. 371, no. 445.
124 Idrīs 'Imād al-Dīn, *'Uyūn*, pp. 279–90 (Ar.).
125 Ibn al-Zubayr, *Kitāb al-Dhakhā'ir*, p. 194.
126 Beside 'A. M. Mājid's 1954 edition, additional *sijillāt* are quoted and reported by Idrīs 'Imād al-Dīn, *'Uyūn*, vol. 7.
127 *Sijillāt*, no. 50, pp. 168–9.
128 *Sijillāt*, no. 36, pp. 118 and no. 45, p. 154, both dated 480/1087, use the term *malika*; the same title is used by the caliph al-Musta'lī's mother writing to her in 489/1095, as in *sijill* no. 35, p. 110.
129 al-Sulṭān al-Khaṭṭāb, *Dīwān* in Poonawala, I. K. (ed.), *al-Sulṭān*, *qaṣīda* no. 8, p. 226, verse 7: 'oh *ḥujja* of the master through whose explanation (*bayān*) God guided the one whom the doubts confused'; *qaṣīda* no. 5, p. 283, verse 6: 'the *ḥujja* in front of whom the majority of slaves are humbled'.
130 From *Ghāyat al-mawālīd*, *apud* Poonawala, I. K., *al-Sulṭān*, Appendix 1, pp. 433–6. W. Ivanow in *Rise*, pp. 22–3, doubted the attribution of this work to al-Sulṭān al-Khaṭṭāb but Poonawala, I. K., in his *Biobibliography of Ismā'īlī Literature*, Malibu: Undena Publications, 1977, p. 135, dismisses these doubts. Cf. Stern, S. M., 'The Succession to the Fatimid Imam al-Āmir, the Claims of the later Fatimids to the Imamaṭe, and the Rise of Ṭayyibī Ismā'īlism', *Oriens*, 4 (1951), part 2, pp. 227–8.
131 'Umāra, *Ta'rīkh*, ed. al-Akwa', p. 146, confirmed by al-Janādī, see Kay edition, p. 254, n. 37.
132 Stern, S. M., 'The Succession', pp. 217–19, 221. For a concise response to Stern, see Poonawala, I. K., *Biobibliography*, pp. 137–8, n. 1.
133 Idrīs 'Imād al-Dīn, *'Uyūn*, vol. 7, pp. 161–2 and p. 213 (Ar.), pp. 70–1, 78 (Eng.).

134 In Idrīs 'Imād al-Dīn, *'Uyūn*, vol. 7, p. 130 (Ar.).

135 See, respectively, Daftary, F., 'Sayyida Ḥurra: The Ismā'īlī Ṣulayḥid Queen of Yemen', in Hambly, G. R. G., (ed.), *Women in the Medieval Islamic World*, pp. 117, 122; Hamdani, A., 'The Dā 'ī Ḥātim', p. 271; al-Imad, L., 'Women and Religion in the Fatimid Caliphate: The Case of al-Sayyidah al-Hurrah, Queen of Yemen', in Mazzaoui, M. M. and Moreen, V. B. (eds), *Intellectual Studies on Islam: Essays Written in Honor of Martin B. Dickson*, Salt Lake City: University of Utah Press, 1990, pp. 137–44; Mernissi, F., *Forgotten*, Chapter 8, in particular pp. 193–8.

136 In addition to the primary sources mentioned by Sayyid, A. F., *La capitale*, p. 540, see Ibn al-Athīr, *al-Kāmil*, vol. 9, p. 44.

137 Ibn Taghrībirdī, *al-Nujūm*, 1935 edn, vol. 5, p. 311; for the revenge exacted on Naṣr, see al-Safadī, *al-Wafi*, vol. 27, no. 31 pp. 68–9, where, after all the tortures, his corpse is finally burnt.

138 Ibn al-Dawādārī, *Kanz*, vol. 7, p. 30.

CHAPTER

5

WOMEN OF SUBSTANCE IN THE FATIMID COURTS

A tour through the interior of the Fatimid caliphal palace in early eleventh-century Cairo would have been a truly unforgettable experience. One would walk through room upon room furnished with precious objects, to eventually face a golden throne studded with precious stones. Gleaming fine silverware, some even reproducing miniature gardens with fruits made of precious stones, would shine; dainty gilt vases filled with expensive violet, rose and other exotic oils would abound. Violets, narcissi, roses and water-lilies would be on view to please the senses with their vibrant colours and with their scent freshening the air. Exquisitely carved rock-crystal chess pieces and other games would be available as favourite pasttimes for both palace ladies and men. Ivory caskets would guard the fine jewellery worn by the royal women. One would perhaps enter the vaults of famed princesses, such as ʿAbda and Rashida, or of queen mothers like Rasad, and find them piled with embroidered linen and colourful silks, dusty silver shields and saddles, gold coins and ingots. Or stroll across some forty rooms to browse through rare and precious illuminated manuscripts. One would witness the opulence and style of a court where sophistication was at its height: a court where women's wealth and riches would be recorded in history books.

The opulence of the court extended beyond the palace walls. Were we to continue our imaginary tour heading some two and a half kilometres south-west of the palace, we would enter the Qarafa area. There, the money of the court women went a long way indeed in sponsoring the construction of buildings: from splendid palaces to mosques; from mausolea to fountains, baths and wells. These were places of prayer, and of remembrance, that the palace ladies, although spending their wealth to build and maintain them, perhaps never even visited! The names of these patronesses lived on thanks to inscriptions on monuments or were perpetuated in books or through popular lore.

However, were we to undertake our palace tour in the second half of the eleventh century, we would face a different scenario. In 461/1068, the hungry Turkish contingent of the multi-ethnic Fatimid army stormed the treasury vaults. Deprived of their salaries, and with families to feed, enraged by the court display of opulence, the Turks melted down and turned into cash the products of years of expert and painstaking workmanship, art, culture and beauty. At the Qarafa, too, monuments were not to last for ever. One hundred years on, many magnificent buildings were razed to the ground, some as a result of fires set in the senseless hope of diverting attacks by enemy troops, others as a result of new laws that, for example, declared ostentatious funerary monuments unlawful. Not all was lost, though; treasury items resurfaced as spoils in the hands of high officials, and wealth at court was eventually reconstituted. Some monuments were built or restored, and with them other palace women rose to fame as sponsors.

Although the present chapter will focus on female wealth and patronage at the Fatimid court in Cairo, references will also be made to Zirid and Sulayhid royal women. The affluence of Fatimid royal ladies will be discussed within the context of international rivalry and exchanges between the courts of the time, especially the Byzantine and 'Abbasid, from whose domains some of the Fatimid palace women and their courtiers had originally come.

1. Women of Substance at the Fatimid Courts

While there are references pointing to a lively court life during the North African period of the Fatimid dynasty, and to the wealth of the caliph and his close associates, evidence of women as noticeable recipients of wealth and riches only emerges during the Egyptian phase of the dynasty. The greater availability of evidence on female wealth in the Cairo court could be an indication of a change in the financial attitude of the imam-caliph towards supporting and maintaining his own family. As one may infer from Michael Brett's discussion of changing trade practices among the members of the Fatimid caliphal family in North Africa, women and male relatives of the early imam-caliphs were fully dependent upon the allowances that the imams bestowed on them.[1] In Egypt, however, while the male relatives of the imam-caliph continued to remain fully dependant on these allowances, the royal women were able to acquire much wealth through a diversified system of salaries, allocations and gifts, as well as revenues and land grants.

In addition to entering into possession of the wealth of the dynasties they had supplanted, the Fatimids arrived in Egypt already wealthy in their own right.

Through trade, they had built a sound financial basis since the Salamiyya days, and, once in Ifriqiya, they had increased it further thanks to expanding trade, inclusive of gold, as well as revenues from agriculture, duties and taxation.[2] With the establishment of the Fatimid dynasty in Egypt, the acquisition of revenues from its already developed agricultural economy, from tolls on commerce, from the export of flax, combined with the flourishing of the Mediterranean trade, all contributed to the financial success of the Fatimid *dawla* in what has been defined as 'an economic miracle'.[3]

The beneficiaries of such a prosperity were the caliph, his family, the court, the land contractors, the provincial officials, the mercantile classes and, though intermittently, a relatively large section of the Egyptian population. The royal family led the way in the accumulation of wealth, with the imam-caliph having his own private treasury (*khizānat al-khāṣṣ*), as did other members of his family, including prominent women.[4] Benefiting from their royal status, Fatimid women were able to accumulate wealth and riches that, unlike most women in the medieval Muslim world, they could also manage with, ostensibly, a degree of autonomy.

The women who benefited most from this prosperity were those whose links with the caliph were most permanent. Nothing is stronger and more durable than blood ties. Consequently, the imam-caliph's daughters, his mother, his aunts and other close relatives figure prominently among the ladies of substance. Testimony to this is the wealth enjoyed, for instance, by the female relatives of the imam-caliph al-Hakim. His mother was already known for her considerable personal wealth when, according to al-Maqrizi, she received from her son 500,000 *dīnārs* just before his 'disappearance'.[5] The overall extent of her assets can be gauged by al-Maqrizi's reference in his report for the year 415/1024 – that is, three years after al-Hakim's death – concerning the vizier al-Jarjara'i's plan to ask al-Hakim's mother and aunt for money to rescue the state economy, a plan that, nevertheless, the vizier did not pursue.[6] Al-Hakim's half-sister, Sitt al-Mulk, is reported to have received in the year 390/1000 land grants that would provide her with an annual income of 100,000 *dīnārs* – a revenue she gained from her estates, which included lands in higher and lower Egypt and neighbouring regions, houses, orchards and from taxation.[7] Besides estates and land, Sitt al-Mulk's personal fortune is described by several writers as including assets such as perfumes, spices, precious stones, thousands of slaves and, possibly, animal stock. Finally, al-Hakim's daughter, Sitt Misr, besides commodities and jewellery, owned land yielding her a yearly revenue of 50,000 *dīnārs*, and could also afford as many as 8,000 slaves at her service.[8]

In addition to direct blood ties, relation to the caliphal family could be established through marriage or concubinage, ideally made more solid by the birth of son-heirs. As royal consorts, women would typically receive substantial dowries, be entitled to stipends or allowances, and be lavished by their husbands, as well as becoming the recipients of gifts while their husbands were in office. For instance, among the possessions of Rasad, consort of the imam-caliph al-Zahir and mother of his successor al-Mustansir, are included diplomatic gifts given to her by the Byzantine emperor Michael and a rare precious stone with healing powers given to her by the grandmother of the vizier Khatir al-Mulk, as well as family heirlooms such as 4,000 saddles with silver ornaments.[9] Some favoured concubines became famous for their wealth. ʿA'isha, the concubine of ʿAbd Allah, son of al-Muʿizz, left at her death a personal fortune of 400,000 *dīnārs*. Sources state that she had become one of the most influential women of the palace, as reflected, among other details, by the fact that her funeral was led by the head of the *daʿwa* and the judiciary, Qasim b. ʿAbd al-ʿAziz, of al-Qadi al-Nuʿman's descent.[10]

Marriage or concubinage were not the only gateways to personal wealth. As it turned out, the wealthiest Fatimid royal women were not the wives but, by and large, the unmarried daughters of the caliphs, princesses such as Rashida, ʿAbda and Sitt al-Mulk. One wonders if the large donations that formed the basis of their fabulous wealth were bestowed upon them as a form of compensation for remaining celibate, to counteract their loss of dowry. Celibacy was most likely enforced upon them for dynastic reasons, so as to curb parallel genealogical counter-claims,[11] but also to avoid political and diplomatic disputes, as, once married out, these princesses could become 'hostages' in the hands of other powerful rulers. Finally, financial considerations must have played a part in keeping these princesses unmarried, due to the potential loss of family patrimony that marriage would entail. However, one cannot exclude that in some cases celibacy could have been a choice made out of loyalty to one's family, as it appears to have been in the case of some princesses at the Safavid court in sixteenth-century Persia.[12]

Beside the women of the imam-caliph's family, close female relatives of viziers and high palace dignitaries were also known for their wealth and riches. A daughter of the powerful and immensely wealthy Fatimid vizier Ibn Killis was reported to have received a dowry of over 200,000 *dīnārs*.[13] The wife of al-Hakim's chief commander, Ibna Abi ʿAbd Allah al-Husayn b. Ahmad b. Nasr, left at her death assets ranging from gold and silver to clothes and furniture, as well as cash from estate revenues. Her daughter inherited all her fortune.[14] Female palace employees could also become wealthy, especially through the imam-caliph's favours in recompense for their loyalty or their service, as in the case of Sitt Ghazal, the woman in charge of one of the imam-caliph's most precious insignia, the royal ink well.[15] Finally, faithful servants, ladies-in-waiting and other personnel very close to the imam-caliph's family were also able to accumulate wealth, as in the case of Sitt al-Mulk's slave-informant Taqarrub.[16]

2. Wealth and Riches

Palace ladies were wealthy, some were also rich. Their wealth consisted of land, real estates and valuables such as jewellery and textiles. Their riches came from disposable income in the form of monthly or yearly salaries, or of allowances for personal expenditure and for investment. In reading about the valuables and riches recorded in their wills, one cannot fail to notice a variety that reveals a basic, yet clever, investment strategy of diversification, no doubt aimed at spreading financial risk. Next to gold and silver items, could be found textiles, perfumes and coins, as well as more 'liquid' assets such as revenues from land-taxes, custom duties, rents from estates, houses, orchards and *ḥammāms* (bath-houses).[17]

Assets could be converted into cash, especially in times of need, or function in lieu of cash, notably in the case of textiles, above all silk, as well as gold and silver items.[18] Particularly in the case of unmarried, widowed or divorced women, the assets served as security, a kind of pension for old age and insurance against rainy days. Naturally, wealth, as a status symbol, was there to be displayed to impress relatives, neighbours and friends, as well as, on a larger scale, subjects and foreign envoys.[19] By flaunting the wealth of their many women, the men of the dynasty projected an image of personal affluence that was in itself a sign of their individual prowess, as well as of the *dawla*'s financial well-being. Outside the palace walls, some well-to-do urban women also acquired, invested and displayed their wealth and riches, which, although on a smaller scale, paralleled those enjoyed by their royal counterparts.

The figures reported in this chapter are mainly derived from literary, rather than documentary, sources. Hence, they are by and large notional figures that reflect literary conventions and the writers' own perception of the ladies' wealth, rather than the real value of their assets. Figures are generally rounded up, that is, 1,000 trousers or 30,000 silk robes, and, in the case of dowry, standard amounts are indicated, such as the 100,000-*dīnār* dowry that seems to have been the standard *mahr* (dowry) for 'royal brides' over a few centuries and across several dynasties![20]

a. Wealth

The articles most frequently recorded in connection to female wealth consisted of textiles and clothes, especially those made of linen and silk but also cotton and wool, patterned or plain, multi-coloured or monochrome. Textiles were among the main produce of Egypt, and were one of the people's preferred commodities and forms of investment, as shown by both literary and documentary sources. As evidenced by medieval Arabic papyri, textiles were the most

Fig. 6 Eleventh–twelfth-century pair of Fatimid silver armlets from Egypt or Syria. *Private collection.*

consistently listed commodity among the Egyptian exports, as well as one of the most frequently plundered goods in attacks on caravans. Other evidence shows that textiles were used to their utmost limit and even disinterred from burial sites to be sold to the paper-makers of Cairo.

That Fatimid royals and courtiers highly valued textiles as a commodity is evidenced by the inventories of the goods in their possession. Princess Rashida's wardrobe included thousands upon thousands of multi-coloured and monochrome dresses, while the dowry of the vizier al-Afdal's daughter included 100 robes of honours worth 500 *dīnārs* each.[21] Among the Fatimid high dignitaries, the vizier Ibn Killis is reported to have left at his death 500,000 *dīnārs* worth of linen of different types, while the vizier Barjawan left as many as 1,000 trousers with, attached in their upper seam, 1,000 silk waistbands, as well as other innumerable garments. The vizier al-Afdal seemed to have had a preference for silk brocade tunics (*dībāj*), as he is reported to have owned up to 75,000 of them.[22] These large amounts of textiles might well be an indication of the viziers' involvement in large-scale trading and financial enterprises.

Fig. 7 Tenth–eleventh-century Fatimid enamelled-gold jewellery element from Egypt or Syria. *Private collection.*

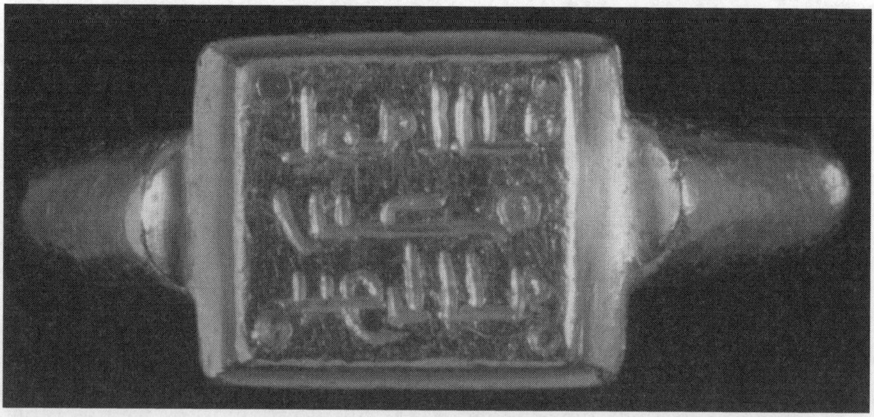

Fig. 8 Twelfth-century Egyptian cast gold, engraved, niello ring inscribed 'Zubayda, God's slave, trusts in Him'. This is a very rare example of an Islamic signet revealing the name of a woman as its owner.
JLY 1809. Courtesy of The Nasser D. Khalili Collection of Islamic Art, Nour Foundation, London.

Another expression of wealth in valuables, and as popular a form of investment as textiles, were fine gold coins, especially Muʿizzi and ʿAzizi *dīnārs*, noted worldwide for the quality of their manufacture and purity of their gold.[23] Besides coins, gold and silver were issued as ingots, or used in the production of items such as vessels, thread for the embroidery of *ṭirāz* and robes of honours, and of various ornaments, including ornaments on saddles and ships.[24] The refinement of gold and silver jewellery of the Fatimid period, ranging from rings, pendants and brooches to tiaras and bracelets, has remained unrivalled (see Figs 6 and 7). The special care the Fatimids devoted to outward appearance and the attention they paid to the wearing of jewellery was embedded in Ismaʿili law, which formally encouraged women to wear jewellery while praying. In fact, both men and women wore jewellery that, particularly in the case of finger rings, featured inscribed formulae and the names of their owners. However, of the hundreds of Fatimid rings that have been preserved to this day, only a handful bear dedications or inscriptions naming women, one rare example being a golden ring bearing the name of 'Zubayda'[25] (see Fig. 8). Precious and semi-precious stones also featured among the royal treasures. We are told of rubies, emeralds, sapphires and pearls, of the personal preferences of the imam-caliph al-ʿAziz for rock crystal or of al-Zahir for precious stones; and of rare gems, as well as carafes of pure rock crystal, included among the possessions of princess ʿAbda.

Camphor, rose water, musk and violet oil feature among the extensive possessions of the palace ladies, along with vast quantities of perfumes that, like the spices, were given to court ladies as part of their allowance. Both served various functions, from personal and domestic use as ingredients for the preparation of medicines, preservatives, cosmetics and contraceptives, to commercial use, as spices and perfumes with a specific, yet variable, market value.[26]

Moreover, wealth could be measured by the large number of servants or soldiers at one's service, as well as the many slaves owned by men and women of substance. Ownership of slaves and eunuchs was indeed a sign of wealth and status not only because of their market value but also because of the money needed to maintain them, including the payment of the *zakāt* on the part of their master or mistress.[27] Finally, wealthy courtiers invested in livestock such as horses and mules, and possibly (in the case of Sitt al-Mulk) so did a royal woman.

An illustration of the diversified nature of royal women's wealth and riches is to be found in comparing the treasures of the two celibate princesses Rashida and ʿAbda, the imam-caliph al-Muʿizz's daughters, who lived to a venerable old age. Besides 30,000 pieces of pure silk and 12,000 pieces of fabric in various colours, Rashida also owned 100 large jars full of camphor, and in totality her possessions were worth 1,700,000 *dīnārs*. She is also reported to have owned the black pure silk tent in which the ʿAbbasid caliph Harun al-Rashid had died in Tus. Her sister ʿAbda had possessions to match. It took forty Egyptian *raṭl* of wax to seal her treasury vaults, her private chambers, chests and whatever belongings had to be sealed at her death. Even allowing for a narrative degree of exaggeration, sources state that the inventory of her household effects was recorded on thirty bundles of paper. ʿAbda's possessions included 1,300 pieces of niello and enamelled silver, 400 gilt-decorated swords, 30,000 pieces of Sicilian cloth and an unlimited number of jewels and emeralds. ʿAbda had also a basin and a ewer made of rock crystal that were greatly admired by the vizier al-Yazuri, who eventually came to possess them, probably through confiscation, along with ʿAbda's precious ruby scent-container.[28]

Sources portray Rashida and ʿAbda as having led a frugal lifestyle despite their immense wealth: according to Ibn Zubayr, ʿAbda's diet consisted of a simple meal based on broth, meat and bread, while Rashida is reported as having 'earned her living from spinning yarn and never laid a hand on anything that belonged to the royal treasury for her subsistence'.[29] It is doubtful whether the same statement could be applicable to other royal women whose status was not secured by birth, as in the case, for example, of one of the caliph al-Amir's favourite consorts, ʿAliya al-Badawiyya, who loved beautiful objects and coveted those in the possession of others.[30]

Having lived long lives, spanning over the reigns of five imam-caliphs, ʿAbda and Rashida were able to accumulate wealth and riches from different sources: inheritance, gifts and revenues. More than to her moral rectitude, the reference to Rashida earning her living through spinning could point to the fact that having wealth did not necessarily mean ability to dispose of it. Indeed, we can assume that ʿAbda and Rashida may have served the role of human 'deposit banks' to guard family wealth and that their renowned treasures were in fact family and dynastic rather than their own. Their noble attitude to wealth seemed not to have been shared by some of their male relatives, namely the descendants of al-Muʿizz, who are reported as having eagerly awaited the sisters' deaths, so they could get hold of 'their' treasures.[31]

The safe-keeping associated to elite women in the Fatimid period is somewhat confirmed by the course of action taken by Muʿizz al-Dawla (d. 454/1062), *walī* (governor) of Aleppo, in dispatching revenues to al-Mustansir. Muʿizz sent the local dues to the imam-caliph by way of a delegation that included al-Sayyida ʿAlawiyya b. Waththab, wife of Muʿizz's son. The source specifies that 'she had with her from the castle 40,000 *dīnār*s and precious presents' and that al-Mustansir treated her reverently.[32]

b. Riches

The best-known example of a Fatimid royal lady whose wealth generated disposable income is Sitt al-Mulk. In 390/1000, Sitt al-Mulk received from al-Hakim a conspicuous allocation in the form of custom duties (*rusūm*), as well as tax farms (*iqṭāʿ*).[33] *Iqṭāʿāt* were a form of administrative grant on agricultural land or other estates, the property of which remained legally in the hands of the imam-caliph, but the income from which was given to a nominated recipient. That a royal woman would expressly be named by an imam-caliph as the recipient of revenues from taxes and duties is indeed indicative of Sitt al-Mulk's high status within the court. She is also known to have owned land, estates and orchards that generated income from produce, rents and duties. The occasional 'diversion' into her coffers of revenues originally intended for the imam-caliph added further to Sitt al-Mulk's access to cash. She must have used her disposable income not only to meet personal expenditure and for the maintenance of her palace personnel but also for investment in privately owned works such as the public baths, the building of which she is reported to have commissioned.[34] In turn, investments such as bathhouses generated further income for her benefit. While Sitt al-Mulk is known to have been engaged in diplomatic negotiations with the Byzantines to favour Fatimid trading activities, there is no direct reference to date to her involvement in trade for her personal gain. Indeed, the overall extent and modality of Fatimid caliphal women's engagement in commercial transactions is unclear. Two examples from North Africa give us an insight as to the women's use of agents and the 'international' dimension of their trading activities. Al-Muʿizz's consort Durzan appears to have sold through an agent (*wakīl*) a slave who was brought from Ifriqiya to Egypt.[35] The aunt of the Zirid al-Muʿizz b. Badis, Umm Mallal, is retrospectively reported, in a Geniza document dated 1059–60, to have been actively involved in maritime trade.[36]

Another means by which the women (and the men) of the court acquired riches was through legal entitlements such as annual or monthly salaries and allowances. This was by no means an exclusively Fatimid custom, as there is evidence that in the tenth-century 'Abbasid court the closest female members of the caliph's family were paid monthly salaries all accounted for in official chancery documents.[37] Similarly, a record of the Fatimid palace budget and accounts dating to the caliphate of al-Amir details the allowances of goods and produce destined to the royal women, as well as specific categories of courtiers and employees. For example, the Treasury of Spices and Medical Remedies (*khizānat al-tawābil*) allocated substantial quantities of amber, camphor, musk and rose water to royal women.[38]

In addition to regular entitlements, Fatimid royal and court ladies were the recipients of occasional or celebratory gifts from the imam-caliph in person, as well as from ambassadors and high dignitaries. Gifts could range from finely embroidered robes of honour to jewels, gold or silver objects, cash, land and houses. At times, gift packages included slaves and, more rarely – for royals and their like – eunuchs.[39] In commenting on caliphal gift-giving to women, al-Maqrizi did not miss the opportunity to report romantic and witty anecdotal accounts. The consort of al-Amir would lock the door to her chamber in the evening, only to open it after her husband had given her gifts. Al-Maqrizi comments that, in this way, she accumulated 100,000 *dīnārs*. Was she greedy or was al-Amir a frequent visitor? Upon hearing his concubine Jihat Bayyan play the lute, the caliph al-Hafiz dreamt of going to the Treasury to take a box for her containing a gem. On waking up, he indeed went to the vault, found the gem he had dreamt of and gave it to her, promising that every year, on the same day, he would repeat the gesture.[40] Ordinary people employed by the palace could also be the recipients of royal donations, as in the case of much-esteemed wet nurses and loyal servants. In 450/1058, al-Mustansir donated land to Nasab, the female palace drummer, for her effort in praising and advertising the Fatimids' victory over the ʿAbbasids in that year.

Neither gender nor status could stop the taxman and even the wealth and riches of the Fatimid royal ladies were not immune. Like everyone else, royal women sought to devise ways to reduce the impact of taxes on their patrimony. All main taxes were applicable to women as well as men: first, the *zakāt*, levied on the capital of every sane and free Muslim, be it treasures, revenues or money, livestock or land produce; second, the taxes due from private estates and other types of properties; third, the so-called incidental taxes (*aḥdāth*), usually paid on the profits of sales and on general merchandise. However, women were exempt from the *jizya*, a personal tax to be paid by all non-Muslims, so presumably the Christian and Jewish ladies of the palace were, at least in theory, not required to pay.[41]

Investing in projects that could be turned into charitable foundations (*waqf*) constituted a clever strategy to gain revenues while enjoying tax relief. As charitable foundation, an estate or a valuable object was neither subject to patrimonial tax nor to state confiscation. *Waqf*s could be given as gifts to beneficiaries, be they individuals, families or categories of people; once formally donated, these gifts could normally not be revoked. The beneficiaries were usually members of the family, such as children or typically, unmarried daughters, who could therefore look forward to enjoying revenues from *waqf*s lasting for a lifetime (provided the *waqf* was well-managed). It is a matter of legal contention whether the founder of a *waqf* could also nominate himself or herself as its beneficiary without rendering it invalid; however, the founder could become its administrator and therefore use its revenues and profits during his or her lifetime. For instance, in the case of Sitt al-Mulk's bathhouses (a typical charitable foundation), she would have benefited from a regular and safe revenue, most likely through the intermediation of an administrator. In fact, by law, a *waqf* administrator (*nāẓir*, *mutawallī*) had to be an adult male, that is a competent person with full capacity to act and administer. Indeed, we will see a number of instances of male administrators whose names were recorded in association with building projects sponsored and founded by women.

c. How Wealth and Riches were Acquired

Women of the caliphal family and entourage acquired their wealth and riches through a combination of means: by inheritance, salaries and allowances, dowries, gifts and donations, as well as through profits from revenues, rents, land and, very likely, though not openly stated, from trade. The formulation by the Fatimids of a Shi'i-based legal code, which was generally more favourable to women in matters of inheritance than the Sunni one, eased, in theory, women's access to money as well as to real estates. Fatimid jurists such as al-Qadi al-Nu'man elaborated an Isma'ili law of inheritance, according to which a woman as sole offspring could not only inherit the whole property of her parents, at the exclusion of their agnates, but she could even inherit or own land and estates. A woman's right to inherit or own land and real estates was partially linked to, and justified on the basis of, the position of Fatima as sole heir after Muhammad's death, with particular reference to the illustrious precedent of Fatima as inheritor of the Fadak orchard. That Fatimid women did indeed benefit from this right can be seen by the presence of land and real estates, and the revenues derived from them, listed among court women's wealth and riches. Already during the North African period of the dynasty we have a reference to a prominent woman sharing with her eunuch the ownership of a piece of land, she was the wife of the best-known of all Fatimid chief generals: Jawhar b. 'Abd Allah.[42] Inheritance was acquired not only directly, from fathers or husbands, but also from mothers to daughters, as in the case of Bint Abi Ja'far, the granddaughter of al-Husayn b. Jawhar, al-Hakim's chief commander and *wāsiṭa*, who inherited, at her mother's death in 415/1024, not only her valuables and revenues but also her real estates.[43]

d. How Wealth and Riches were Lost: The Damoclean Sword of Confiscation

Once acquired, wealth and riches needed securing, managing and protection from the effects of financial odds and shifting court politics. As easily as a ruler would donate, he or his viziers would also confiscate irrespective of – and at times because of – the owner's status. It has been suggested that confiscation was rooted in an understanding of wealth, which, although accumulated by the ruler's associates or employees, was ultimately perceived by the ruler as belonging to himself, as he, in the first instance, had created the circumstances for it to be gathered.[44] An aspect of a wider remedial financial state policy, particularly directed against government officials, the resorting to confiscation represented a source of occasional revenue. If carried out while the officials were still in office, the curtailing of their wealth through confiscation represented an effective measure to limit their influence. If implemented against officials who had either been dismissed or were no longer in office, mulcting was a means for the Treasury to recoup the wealth gained legally, or at the margin of legality, by officers who, by a system of favours or outright bribery, could secure for themselves and their families substantial additional revenues. Ever since the times of the early ʿAbbasid caliphs, especially al-Mansur (d. 158/775), confiscation of assets was a well-established practice. It was adopted by the Fatimids and it was to be routinely resorted to, as a very useful source of revenue, under the Mamluks and beyond.[45]

Women of the Fatimid court, irrespective of their status, were never safe from confiscation. Under al-Hakim in the year 399/1008–9, at a time of severe monetary crisis, the Treasury confiscated the assets of the imam-caliph's mother, his sister, his aunts, wives and concubines. The extent of the assets seized was such that a new *dīwān* had to be created in order to manage all the confiscated goods.[46] As inheritors of the wealth of important men, court women were particularly exposed to confiscation. In 415/1024, again a year of high inflation, the Head of Treasury impounded the inheritance of a prominent court woman, Bint Abi ʿAbd Allah, the daughter-in-law of al-Hakim's chief commander and *wāsiṭa,* al-Husayn b. Jawhar, as a result of his assessment that the woman's possessions had been multiplied threefold.[47] Nevertheless, Bint Abi ʿAbd Allah's wealth was eventually inherited by her daughter.

In a number of cases, for the ʿAbbasids, the Fatimids and other dynasties, confiscation of elite women's assets was not exclusively a matter of money. The women targeted were influential and were often the representatives of an *ancien régime* that the new caliph intended to replace.[48] From this perspective, the resorting to confiscation served to make a strong statement about changes in politics, power base and influence. For example, the ʿAbbasid caliph al-Qahir, who acceded to the throne in 321/933, having blamed his predecessor al-Muqtadir and his entourage for having allowed a 'government of women and eunuchs', confiscated all the wealth and riches of Shaghab, the former caliph's mother, of his wife, his children and his allies, and he instituted a new *dīwān* for the management of all the goods. Along similar lines, it could be argued that al-Hakim's confiscation strategy of 399/1008–9 against the palace harem could be seen not just as a financial statement but as a political one as well. With less money, the influence of the harem would be reduced and the ability of its members to plot against the imam-caliph himself curtailed. Fatimid palace ladies were not only victims but, at times, instigators of confiscation, which they used to curtail the influence of ministers and palace officials whom they deemed their antagonists. Such was the case of Rasad, al-Mustansir's mother, who showed her influence by appointing and dismissing viziers and by using confiscation against them, only to become herself the victim of confiscation at the hands of the rebel governor of Alexandria, Nasir al-Dawla.[49]

Despite their perceived vulnerability, court women were no more likely than men to be subjected to the confiscation of their assets. In contrast with men, however, leniency would normally be shown in carrying out the mulcting of women's possessions. Prominent women would not be tortured or imprisoned and, in the very rare cases in which they were, sources record a public outcry of condemnation for resorting to the use of force against them.

The most infamous case of violence against a royal woman relates to Shaghab, the influential mother of the ʿAbbasid caliph al-Muqtadir. Upon her son's death in 321/933, and the subsequent enthronement of al-Qahir, she had all her assets confiscated and even her charitable foundations, for which she was much praised, were to be dismantled. In order to change the deeds of her *waqf*s, the new caliph needed her legal consent and the testimony of witnesses. When she refused, Shaghab was imprisoned, tortured and eventually died in captivity the same year.

During the late eleventh century, Egypt was devastated by the most serious of famines, along with economic hardship and political as well as civil unrest. The *shidda al-Mustanṣiriyya* affected everybody, irrespective of status; some palace ladies fled to other countries, others died of consumption, and yet many, against all the odds, survived. From 439/1074 onwards, stability was restored to Egypt and, gradually, palace women were able to reconstitute their wealth. As custodians of assets, royal and elite women continued to be a safer choice than their men: they did not take up arms, they did not hold potentially dangerous positions in the government, they lived a more sheltered life and, above all, they kept the property within the family. As unmarried daughters or aunts, but also as widows, wives and daughters, they could own and transfer property within the family to their children or their siblings' children, whether male or female. Women could also be the beneficiaries, even the trustees, of charitable foundations. *Waqf*s could serve several purposes, among which was investment in non-taxable projects, a way to ensure that property was preserved in its integrity and not divided up through inheritance, creating a safe refuge from confiscation. As Shaghab is reported to have stated when pressed to give her charitable foundations to the new caliph: 'something that I donated as *waqf* to Allah I cannot claim back, take all my money [instead]!'[50]

e. Management and Spending Strategies

Their revenues being so varied and complex, palace ladies did not manage their wealth all by themselves. They resorted to the services of representatives, deputies and agents, whose names are often recorded in conjunction with the management of palace women's *dīwāns* and estates, as well as with the enterprises they financed. This was the case not only in the Fatimid court but, for instance, in the Zirid court as well, where the name is recorded of the adminisator of the wealth and riches of al-Muʿizz b. Badis's mother.[51] As for the Cairo court, in the case of prominent women such as the queen mother, the main consort of the imam-caliph, or the likes of a Sitt al-Mulk, the responsibility for the management of the royal ladies' wealth and riches fell upon high dignitaries. One was Sharif b. Hamza, who was in charge of the *dīwāns* of al-Zahir's mother; but while he remained an obscure figure, other dignitaries holding similar posts rose to the ranks of *wāsiṭa* and even vizier. Examples of the phenomenal careers of viziers who started as stewards of a royal lady's wealth are those of al-Jarjara'i, who worked in the service of Sitt al-Mulk and, three decades later, of al-Yazuri, who had been in charge of the *dīwān* of Rasad. Alternatively, men who had had prestigious careers could find themselves 'reduced' to the role of glorified lackey. Such was the case of Ibrahim al-Bazzaz, who, having served as chief commander for al-Husayn b. Jawhar, ended up working as factotum for al-Husayn's daughter in Tanta.[52] Deputies would supervise projects and take care of enterprises outside the palace walls on behalf of the royal ladies. During the twelfth century in particular, one notices the part that the eunuchs played at the Fatimid court as deputies and main intermediaries between royal women and the different departments of the palace. Such a mediating role was so prominent that some of the royal *jihāt* came to be known after the name of their chief eunuchs. The honorific titles borne by these deputies show their high status at the palace: for example the Qadi Maknun al-Hafizi, who worked at the service of ʿAlam, one of al-Amir's consorts, and who oversaw on her behalf the construction work of the mosque of Sayyida Ruqayya; or the Shaykh Abu Turab al-Sawaf, who supervised for the same woman the building works of al-Andalus mosque.[53]

There is little doubt that the use palace women made of their wealth was multi-faceted. Part was invested in commodities, land, real estates and charitable foundations, and part was destined to satisfy personal needs, however, a large part was also devolved to the management of their entourage. Sources are keen to show that royal women dispensed money and gifts to high dignitaries to ensure their support and friendship; when these means of persuasion did not work, large sums were used to secure specific court alliances. Given the diversity and 'fluidity' of their assets, state viziers, even the ruler himself, would not shy away from asking these ladies of substance for help to support the state finances. On more than one occasion, when the Treasury could not afford to meet one of the largest areas of expenditure – that is, military wages – the seemingly most unlikely of financial reserves were called upon for help. Across the centuries and across dynasties, military wages and the uncertainty of their regular payment have been the Achilles' heel in the stability of governments. Widely recorded are the cases of mothers or close female relatives of claimants to power and their connivance with the military: from al-Khayzuran, the 'Abbasid widow of the caliph al-Mahdi, to the fourteenth-century Yemeni Jiha Tayy, the widow of a Rasulid sultan.[54] As already shown in Chapter 4, some Fatimid elite ladies also became sponsors of one section or another of the military. Not surprisingly, soldiers did not need much persuasion to placate their discontent once offered financial incentives. Additional bonuses were always a good means of securing support from particular troops, as evidenced by the case of Rasad. These types of 'investments' through bonuses were not invented by the Fatimids nor did they cease with them, and are a valuable indication of women's financial status and the extent of their involvement in palace politics.

3. Architectural Patronage and its Female Champions

For elite and affluent women in the medieval Islamic world a spiritually edifying way to use their wealth, and at the same time leave their permanent mark in history, was through charity and patronage. As far as charitable donations are concerned, there are some remarkable examples of prominent women of the Fatimid period showing their generosity to the populace in times of particular hardship. For example during the plague that affected Ifriqiya in 425/1033, Umm Yusuf Zulaykha, the wife of al-Mu'izz b. Badis, is reported to have donated 60,000 shrouds. Under al-Mustansir, a descendant of the Prophet and daughter of the person in charge of alms distributed vast quantities of alms and all her considerable personal wealth during the *shidda*. Another meritorious act was performed by al-Zahir's mother, who, in 415/1024, partly financed the caravan carrying the *kiswa* (the embroidered covering of the Ka'ba) to Makka.[55] As for patronage, while very few royal women are referred to as patronesses of the arts, several are noted as having been important architectural patronesses. Even a cursory reading of the works by an architecture and topography enthusiast like al-Maqrizi reveal that, during the Fatimid era, a significant number of building works were commissioned and sponsored by palace ladies.

Women, however, were by no means the main architectural patrons during the Fatimid period. Particularly in Cairo, the most prolific sponsors of construction works were naturally those men endowed with authority, power and wealth: the imam-caliphs and their viziers. Among the most frequently sponsored works were mosques, with all their annexes; public buildings such as baths, water fountains, wells, mills, ovens and funerary monuments, and commercial outlets such as shops and markets. Building and restoration of public edifices occurred throughout the dynasty, but was more intense during specific periods within Fatimid history. The imam-caliphs and viziers chose their timing and location very carefully, to put to maximum use the amount of money and work invested. Architectural patronage served mainly political and doctrinal purposes, even in the case of buildings commissioned seemingly in response to private needs, but which nevertheless still functioned as visible enough signs to make public statements about the individual patrons and the dynasty as a whole.

The political as well as doctrinal use of architectural patronage is reflected, for example, in the styles of *minbars* (mosque pulpits). The carved wooden *minbar* in the mosque in Fez, known as the Andalusian Mosque, was built in unmistakably Fatimid style in 369/980 to signal the authority in the city of Buluggin, the founder of the Zirid dynasty, who at the time ruled Ifriqiya on behalf of the Fatimids. When the Umayyads of Spain took possession of Fez, they marked their presence and authority, among other ways, by destroying the Fatimid-styled pulpit.[56] In turn, when the imam-caliph al-ʿAziz, during one of the most intense periods of architectural activity in Fatimid history, replaced the old *minbar* from the Sunni mosque of ʿAmr b. al-ʿAs (that is the Old Mosque) with a new *minbar*, he signalled, in the capital's ritual space, the authority of the Fatimid dynasty.[57]

As part of their architectural patronage, the imam-caliphs and powerful officials commissioned building and restoration works to honour, remember, or show their devotion to prominent women of the past or their contemporaries. For example, during one of the Fatimid spurs of building activity under the caliph al-Hafiz, a number of mosques and mausolea were built or restored to honour famous female figures who occupied a special space in Shiʿi sacred history. Moreover, imam-caliphs ordered the construction of palaces, promenades and pavilions for their wives and concubines. They also allocated palaces for the exclusive use of their daughters, as in the case of Sitt al-Mulk.[58]

However, the main emphasis in this section is not on architectural patronage by men for women, but rather on patronage by Fatimid court women who commissioned and sponsored important construction works. Architectural patronage was not unique to Fatimid royal women, but was a pursuit shared with other royal ladies across the Mediterranean, including North Africa and beyond, in the ʿAbbasid domains. Although the majority of female patrons belonged to the ruling family, a relatively small number of patronesses came from the circles of court officials. Indeed, during the last three decades of the Fatimid rule, ladies from the vizier's family are recorded as having been architectural sponsors. Other patronesses came from the *ʿulamā'* families, but this does not seem to have been the case under the Fatimids. At the ʿAbbasid court, there were celebrated instances of patronesses such as Harun al-Rashid's influential mother al-Khayzuran, who was credited with promoting public building works, and Harun's wife Zubayda (d. 216/831–2), who sponsored the construction of an extensive water-supply network along the pilgrimage route to Makka, for the benefit of the holy city and its pilgrims.[59]

At the Byzantine court, high-ranking women, contemporary with the Fatimids, directed their patronage particularly towards religious institutions such as nunneries and convents. Above all places of prayer, but also of protection and refuge, at times these institutions served as centres of intellectual and literary activity. For instance, under the early phase of the Comnenus family's rule, Eirene Doukaina, who was the wife of Emperor Alexius I Comnenus (1081–1118), founded the convent of Our Lady of Grace in Constantinople, where her daughter Anna and granddaughter Eirene engaged in literary patronage. Anna sponsored research on commentaries on Aristotle and on the field of philosophy as a whole. She was renowned in her own right as the author of the *Alexiad*, being her insight into the history of her father's reign.[60] Similarly to the female patronage of religious buildings in Fatimid times, Byzantine female patronage of monasteries, hospitals, almshouses and so on was not only a display of power and a call for lasting fame, but also an expression of piety: that is, a charitable action from which spiritual merit was believed to be gained.

In North Africa we find another splendid example of female architectural patronage. One of the most famous and oldest mosques of Morocco, the Qarawiyyin mosque in Fez, was built in the mid-ninth century by order of Fatima, the daughter of Muhammad al-Qayrawani, from whom she had inherited a fortune that she devoted to charitable works.[61] In the early eleventh century, female patronage in North Africa took the shape of donations of splendid Qur'anic manuscripts especially commissioned by Zirid court ladies for the Great Mosque of Qayrawan. Particularly notable is the one commissioned by Umm Mallal, partly still extant today.[62]

The spending habits of the Fatimid royal ladies did not differ substantially from those of royal Byzantine and ʿAbbasid court women of similar rank in other dynasties and other epochs. However, as far as architectural patronage is concerned, it is significant to note that Fatimid court women mainly devolved money for works of public religious use and, more specifically, mausolea associated with ʿAli's family and his descendants.[63] The pursuit of architectural patronage by court women was by no means to remain unique to the Fatimids. It was to be continued, in Egypt and beyond, under the Sunni Ayyubids[64] and the Mamluks, when, as in the case of their predecessors, the patronage of religious and secular public works was directed towards projects which, beside their practical function, served as advertisements for broader dynastic policies.

Two main phases of Fatimid female architectural patronage can be identified: the first was inaugurated in 366/976 with the building of the Jamiʿ al-Qarafa by Durzan, al-Muʿizz's widow and mother of the imam-caliph al-ʿAziz. The second, almost 150 years later, coincides with the time of Sayyida ʿAlam al-Amiriyya, the widow of the caliph al-Amir, who is known to have restored and built a number of mosques also in the Qarafa area. The architectural activities during these two phases were informed by distinctive circumstances pertaining to the history of the Fatimid dynasty. Durzan's sponsorship fitted well with al-ʿAziz and his vizier Ibn Killis's concerted effort to celebrate the dynasty's achievements in Egypt and to assert an Ismaʿili character upon the landscape not only of Cairo but also of its surroundings. The patronage of al-Sayyida al-Amiriyya, however, ought to be evaluated within the context of the caliph al-Hafiz's efforts to advertise the legitimacy of his accession to the Fatimid throne. In both cases the women involved were extremely wealthy widows of former imam-caliphs and in receipt of large inheritances, which they partly invested in charitable acts.

a. Phase One: Architectural Patronage under al-ʿAziz

The relatively long caliphate of al-ʿAziz has been singled out by Fatimid and non-Fatimid historians as one of the most prosperous of the dynasty. This success was, to a large extent, the outcome of taxation reforms carried out under his father, al-Muʿizz, and the result of the rationalisation of the *dawla* administrative apparatus under the vizierate of Ibn Killis. One of the expressions of such affluence was the flourishing of building activity in Cairo as reported by al-Maqrizi, who credits al-ʿAziz with ordering as many as thirteen major building works, ranging from the Golden Palace and the Cairo Mosque to an oratory, a fortress, a belvedere, a bridge and public baths.[65] As was customary, many of these buildings would be established as *waqfs*, thus making them excellent forms of investment for the imam and for his family. The mention in the sources of both the names of the imam and his vizier in conjunction with these building and restoration activities shows that they must have worked in tandem in such projects.[66] Moreover, the fact that Ibn Killis was in charge, of among other departments, the one dealing with *waqf* explains further his involvement in these architectural enterprises.[67]

This flurry of building activity coincided with what Yaacov Lev identifies as a crucial period in the 'Ismaʿilisation of Egypt', during which both the imam-caliph and his vizier applied a bold policy towards the implementation of the Ismaʿili legal system in Cairo and other urban centres within Egypt.[68] It was due to the initiative of Ibn Killis that regular weekly lectures and scholarly workshops on Ismaʿili law, philosophy and theology were held in al-Azhar mosque and other locations, where salaried *fuqahāʾ* would conduct sessions in which both Ismaʿili and non-Ismaʿili scholars would participate.[69] The furthering of Ismaʿili education to a wider public went hand in hand with ensuring adequate physical provisions for places of worship, where doctrinal as well as legal instruction could take place. Al-ʿAziz's sponsoring of building activity continued on a grand scale even after the death of Ibn Killis in 380/991. In that year, al-ʿAziz gave orders to start the building of what was to become one of the great congregational mosques of Cairo. Situated outside al-Muʿizz's north gates, this mosque was much bigger than al-Azhar, measuring more than 120 metres by 115; it came to be known as al-Hakim Mosque.

a. i. Durzan: Patronage as Status Symbol of Female Influence

The first, most famous and most prolific Fatimid architectural patroness was Durzan, the imam-caliph al-Muʿizz's consort, also known as al-Sayyida al-Muʿizziyya or as Taghrid. Durzan rose to prominence following the death of ʿAbd Allah, the heir apparent of al-Muʿizz, in 363/973–4, when, as the mother of the newly designated heir, al-ʿAziz, she earned a position of paramount importance at court. With the death of al-Muʿizz in 365/975, her status rose even higher following the enthronement of her son as imam-caliph. An expression of her status within the court, Durzan's architectural patronage was linked to those two salient events.

In 366/976, Durzan, together with her daughter Sitt al-Malik, ordered, in the Qarafa area, the building of her first and greatest architectural project: the congregational mosque, the Jamiʿ al-Qarafa, eventually rebuilt as the 'Friends of God' Mosque. Erected on the site of a previous mosque, the Jamiʿ al-Qarafa is described by a number of historians, among them al-Maqrizi, as one of the most beautiful edifices of its time. It was the second mosque built by the Fatimids in Egypt, after al-Azhar, which dates back to 359–61/970–2, and was similar to al-Azhar in its design and large proportions, with as many as fourteen gates. Jamiʿ al-Qarafa was to become the locus of state festival celebrations involving the distribution of food to Fatimid notables as well as the capital's poor. Al-Maqrizi specifies that Fatimid high dignitaries spent their summer nights in its courtyard, while, in the winter, they would sleep by its pulpit.[70] At the end of the Fatimid era, a fire destroyed this mosque and only the so-called 'green *miḥrāb*' survived.

In Cairo, Durzan commissioned the building of a pavilion overlooking the Nile, called *Manāzil al-ʿizz*,[71] which, during the Ayyubid period, was to be transformed into a Shafiʿi *madrasa*. This was her only legacy in Cairo itself, as her main construction location remained the Qarafa area. The buildings she sponsored here were varied: the Qarafa palace (*qaṣr*), a public bath, a cistern or pool (*ḥawḍ*)[72] and, in the Abu 'l-Ma'lum fortress, the royal garden and a hydraulic pump, which fed the ablution hall of that palace. Moreover, a well was built upon her orders in the centre of the courtyard of the famous Ibn Tulun Mosque. Installed during the month of Muharram 385/February 995, this well replaced a previous one that had been destroyed in a fire. More importantly, Durzan is credited with the building of a mausoleum in Qarafa, where she is believed to have been buried. Among the monuments attributed to her, this is thus far the only one from which a limestone plaque has survived, which bears an inscription in which she is expressly mentioned as its patroness. At a later stage, this mausoleum was used to bury other female members of the caliphal family, possibly including one of al-ʿAziz's wives.[73] The person in charge of most of the building work commissioned by Durzan was the *muḥtasib* (lit. superintendent) al-Hasan (or al-Husayn) b. ʿAbd al-ʿAziz al-Farisi.

The timing of Durzan's patronage is significant in many ways: it begins one year after her husband's death and, even keeping in mind the time that elapses between the inception of a building project and its completion, this may point to the fact that it was only as a widow that she had full access to the money necessary for the project. The modern Egyptian scholar Nuriman ʿAbd al-Karim Ahmad suggests, in this regard, that, as al-Muʿizz preferred a modest and ascetic lifestyle, his wife was not given 'the opportunity' to spend great sums of money during his lifetime.[74] Ahmad adds that another possible reason for the timing of Durzan's patronage lies with al-ʿAziz's generosity in allowing his mother to keep her inherited money! In fact, her patronage should be viewed within the context of al-ʿAziz's Ismaʿilisation policy mentioned above, whereby his use of architectural patronage would tally well with his mother's motivations and financial capability. Moreover, one cannot overlook the role that the powerful Ibn Killis might have played in 'guiding' Durzan in the use of her wealth. By the time the Qarafa mosque was completed, Ibn Killis had been in charge of both the state and the caliphal family finances for almost three years and, as seen already, was personally involved in promoting the Ismaʿilisation programme in various ways, including architectural patronage.

The location of most of Durzan's projects – al-Qarafa – deserves special attention, as its choice for her sponsorship there of a *qaṣr*, a mosque, a bath, a watering pool and a mausoleum appears not to have been accidental. As far as the *qaṣr* is concerned, ʿAbd al- Karim Ahmad notes that her choice of location for the Qarafa palace was possibly due to the fact that it was along a promenade route outside Cairo, which was the seat of government, and she adds that the location chosen might have been particularly suitable after Durzan's husband's death.[75] It is questionable, however, whether, in this and other cases, the choice of location was really hers, or, rather the vizier's or other officials in charge of land allocations.[76] One could speculate that this 'suitability' was linked to the financial benefit she could derive from such building activity. Built in a convenient and upmarket location, the palace might have indeed been a good investment for the potential of its real-estate value to increase, an aspect that a widow who relied on inherited money would have to take into consideration as security for her old age.

As for the choice of site for the Jamiʿ al-Qarafa, it seems highly probable that it was the result of a deliberate plan that continued to be implemented after

Durzan, when a number of Fatimid imam-caliphs, viziers and several palace women built monuments there. Al-Azhar and its annexes were constructed to serve Cairo, a city built by the Fatimids, Isma'ili in character and predominantly inhabited by the Fatimid elite. The 'Amr b. al-'As mosque had been serving the overcrowded Fustat. Durzan's mosque was therefore built in al-Qarafa to cater for its growing number of residents and visitors attracted to the area by its position between 'establishment' Cairo and 'trading' Fustat. The Qarafa area, described by the eleventh-century Egyptian physician Ibn Ridwan as particularly salubrious, was indeed lived in and frequented by a wide spectrum of the population: Sunnis and Shi'is, residents and pilgrims, Christians and Jews, the wealthy and the poor. Fatimid-sponsored building activity in al-Qarafa served the purpose of affirming the Fatimid rule, as well as promoting the dynasty to the Egyptian and non-Egyptian public at large. It was with Durzan's sponsorship of the Jami' al-Qarafa that this construction activity was inaugurated, at a time when the above-mentioned Isma'ilisation programme was extended to areas outside Cairo.[77] In time, the Jami' al-Qarafa came to be especially associated with womenfolk as a funerary mosque.[78] An extensive section of the Qarafa area had been, was – and still is – occupied by the cemetery that carries its name and that, as it will be shown later, had long been connected with the popular cult of 'saints', including female 'saints' of 'Alid descent.

Al-Hakim followed in his father's footsteps in promoting building activity. In 393/1002, two years after the death of Barjawan, al-Hakim ordered the building of the Rashida mosque in al-Qarafa as a way of displaying his authority as imam-caliph. In spite of, or in response to, the economic and political upheavals that marked the early period of his reign, al-Hakim in 400/1009 made a conspicuous endowment to the mosque of al-Azhar for its upkeep, as witnessed by his *waqfiyya*.[79] By 403/1012, the building of the al-Hakim mosque was at last completed! There are no specific references in the sources to female patronage during al-Hakim's reign, but the limited role of female royal patronage at this time could be linked to the imam-caliph resorting to a confiscation policy targeting palace women. One exception is al-Hakim's half-sister Sitt al-Mulk's patronage of bathhouses. The object of her patronage points, at one level, to the importance of the *ḥammām* in the lifestyle of women in general; not only were bathhouses places that all women, irrespective of their religious affiliation, were allowed to attend, but, according to Isma'ili ritual purity laws for women, regular visits to the public baths were in fact mandatory.[80] At another, more prosaic, level, for Sitt al-Mulk to invest in the building of *ḥammāms* represented a secure source of constant revenue.

Given the evident participation of some Fatimid royal women in architectural sponsorship during the early years of the Egyptian phase of the dynasty, the almost total absence of female patronage in the period between al-Hakim's death and that, just over a century later, of al-Amir, is indeed conspicuous. The only recorded patroness of a mosque built near al-Qarafa, in 430–1/1038–9, is the otherwise unknown wife of one ʿAli b. Yahya b. Tahir al-Mawsili, who might have been a royal courtier but was certainly not a member of the imam's family.[81] During this hundred years lapse, the Fatimid royal family was not short of a few immensely wealthy women such ʿAbda and Rashida, al-Hakim's daughter Sitt Misr, and Rasad. However, none of them is known to have used her wealth to sponsor architectural works. In the face of the political and economic instability of the period, the wealth and assets of these royal women were used to meet more pressing needs such as financing the treasury or subsidising the factional army. Moreover, the royal women themselves might have chosen, or been encouraged, to diversify their forms of investments beyond bricks and mortar. Another major obstacle to the promotion of any major 'state'-sponsored building activity, let alone by women, was the occurrence of the *shidda al-Mustanṣiriyya*, which lasted from 457/1065 to 464/1072.

In the aftermath of this crisis, the person called to save the day was Badr al-Jamali. It is following his arrival in Cairo in 466/1074 that 'state'-sponsored architectural projects and restoration works resume on a grand scale. Many of these projects bore blatant witness to Badr's status and power. In several monumental inscriptions, Badr's name duly appears after that of al-Mustansir; however, the addition to the vizier's name of lines upon lines of his titles, alongside a consequent shrinking of the space reserved for the acknowledgement of the imam-caliph, show a marked change of emphasis in the balance of power.[82] During the twenty years of Badr's vizierate, architectural works carried out in his name and that of al-Mustansir's range from restoration of minarets in Upper Egypt to the building of mosques in Lower Egypt and, in the capital, from extending the city walls to the construction of new city gates.[83] Badr was responsible for paving the way to what Yaacov Lev terms the 'de-Ismaʿilisation of the legal system', which would more clearly manifest itself during the twelfth century.[84] At this time, Sunni schools flourished in Alexandria and Sunni *qāḍī*s were sitting side by side with Ismaʿili judges to reach legal decisions in the Egyptian capital. Architectural activity served to mark the landscape in accordance with dynastic and doctrinal changes.

Elsewhere in the Fatimid domains, female sponsorship of major architectural projects found its champion in Arwa. She is recorded as having commissioned, in the Sulayhid capital Dhu Jibla, the construction of her palace (see Fig. 9) and, after her husband's death, the building in 480/1087 of the Friday Mosque, where she is still buried. Arwa is also credited with the building, in or around San'a', of at least two mosques, one of which, known as Masjid al-Hurra, has been ascribed either to her or to her mother-in-law Asma'.[85] These mosques are no longer extant and their original location is uncertain; it seems that one was erected by

Fig. 9 Queen Arwa's capital, Dhu Jibla, Yemen, with a view of the ruins of the castle built over the site of the royal palace she commissioned in the late eleventh century. *Photo: Delia Cortese.*

one of the city gates, while the other was outside the city on the road to Hadda.[86] Also in San'a', Arwa is recorded as having ordered repairs and extensions to the Great Mosque and the masterly decoration (carving, gilding and painting) of its eastern-side ceiling.[87] Finally, Arwa's name is associated with the foundation of the Great Mosque at 'Ibb. Noteworthy is the hypothesis that Arwa might have 'introduced' into Yemen a 'Fatimid' architectural feature in mosque design, notably the courtyard mosque with a *ḥaram* exhibiting a widened central nave.[88]

b. Phase Two: Architectural Patronage under al-Amir and al-Hafiz, Restoration and Politico-Doctrinal Landscaping

It is under the caliphate of al-Amir that Fatimid female architectural patronage resurfaces with renewed vigour. This impetus is a reflection of broader architectural activity sponsored by the caliph himself, who, following the death in 515/1121 of his vizier al-Afdal, the son of Badr al-Jamali, was keen to make visible statements about his own authority. Al-Afdal's power had been all-pervasive, encompassing dynastic policies and religious rituals. He had abolished Shi'i and

Isma'ili festivals, and played down the ritual role of the caliph in the important celebrations of *'id al-fiṭr* and *'āshūrā'*.[89] Al-Amir's response was not only to reinstate the festivals but also to add a new *mawlid*: the birthday of the imam-caliph of the time. Besides the festivals, al-Amir's and his new vizier al-Bata'ihi's renewed emphasis on promoting religious unity (Shi'i, Sunni and non-Muslim) was manifested through ordering the restoration of as many as seven mosques in the capital, especially in the Qarafa area, including Durzan's mosque.[90] The restorations extended to mausolea of 'Alid female figures, such as Sayyida Nafisa, Sayyida Zaynab and Umm Kulthum al-'Alawiyya.[91] Within the Cairo walls, in 519/1125 al-Amir and al-Bata'ihi commissioned the building of al-Aqmar mosque, which, with its innovative design, was intended to become a new focus for the celebration of religious festivals led by the caliph. The building of this new mosque, with its famed circular inscriptions, served to honour both the caliph al-Amir and al-Bata'ihi, who was to be the last Isma'ili vizier.[92] Despite their call for unity among Shi'is, it was the internal Isma'ili rivalry between Musta'lis and Nizaris that most concerned the caliph and his vizier. This would be justified by the fact that, in 524/1130, al-Amir was to be assassinated at the hands of the Nizaris.

A number of al-Amir's numerous consorts are credited with having followed his example as architectural patrons. In 522/1128, the year that the vizier al-Bata'ihi died, al-Amir's consort known as *jiha al-dār al-jadīda* generously sponsored the building of a mosque named the Bitter Orange Mosque near the Qarafa Kubra, by the Ibn Tulun aqueduct.[93] His best-known consort and prolific architectural sponsor was, however, Sayyida 'Alam al-Amiriyya, also known as Jiha Maknun. Al-Maqrizi states that, in 526/1132, that is two years after al-Amir's death, Sayyida 'Alam sponsored the restoration and building of the following monuments: a mosque in the Qarafa area (later known as al-Andalus Mosque), the oratory al-Mughafir, and, possibly, the entire al-Andalus complex, including the *ribāṭ* for elderly and widowed women.[94] The same source associates Sayyida 'Alam with the construction of another important mosque, the Sayyida Ruqayya.

The relevance of such an association rests with the legitimacy claims to the caliphate of al-Amir's successor, his cousin al-Hafiz. In a climate filled with internal dissent and revolt, the new caliph al-Hafiz had to face the reality of reduced numbers of Isma'ilis both within and outside the palace. Not surprisingly, al-Hafiz harboured mistrust for his non-Isma'ili viziers, all of whom lasted in office only for short periods. The debates that arose concerning al-Hafiz's accession to the caliphate led him to devote considerable effort to the elaboration of a clear argument in support of his claims to legitimacy while, at the same time, appealing for a broader Shi'i or Muslim unity. In the alleged absence of a son of al-Amir, al-Hafiz, who was his cousin, mounted a doctrinal campaign to support his somewhat unusual accession to the caliphate by recalling as precedent the example of the Prophet's designation of his cousin 'Ali as his legitimate successor. In a *sijill* issued upon his accession, al-Hafiz claimed that al-Amir had personally transmitted the imamate to him.[95]

In her study of 'Alid shrines in the Qarafa cemetery, Caroline Williams places the intense building activity related to these shrines within the context of the succession debates that characterised this period of Fatimid history.[96] In her view, the 'Alid shrines – whether erected, expanded or restored – served as powerful visual advertisements in the hands of claimants within the Fatimid dynasty. Williams's argument provides a useful framework to interpret the architectural patronage that occurred during al-Hafiz's time as being an expression of a campaign in support of his legitimacy claims. Moreover, the building and restoration of 'Alid monuments he sponsored could be linked to his attempts to win back dissatisfied Shi'is.

Already during al-Amir's caliphate, a number of tombs of persons linked to the *Ahl al-Bayt* had been built or restored. During the reign of al-Hafiz the restoration programme of religious monuments continued: for example, in 532/1137 the *mashhad* of the Sayyida Nafisa was repaired, while a year later major works were done on the mosque of the Sayyida Ruqayya; in 542/1147, the Masjid Jihat Rayhan was built. An anecdote drawn from Fatimid sources links al-Hafiz with the building of a shrine known as *Mashhad al-Nūr* (the Shrine of Light). It is reported that, during al-Hafiz's caliphate, one night the people of Fustat saw a column of light (*ignis fatuus*?) rising from the area near al-Qarafa and informed the caliph. He verified the reports, ordered excavations of the spot in question and found the funerary stone of an 'Alid woman, Maryam b. 'Abd Allah, whose ancestor was Ibrahim Tabataba'i, a descendant of the Prophet's grandson al-Hasan. The caliph ordered that *Mashhad al-Nūr* be built on that very spot.[97] Al-Hafiz's architectural patronage, linked in this anecdote to a miraculous event centred around an 'Alid woman, served the caliph the purpose of supporting his own ancestry, of legitimising his caliphate and enhancing his prestige. Other portentous events linking al-Hafiz to 'Alid sacred history are reported to involve women, both as honoured figures of the past and wealthy, elite patronesses of his time.

A female figure of the past with a distinguished ancestry is recalled with reference to al-Hafiz's architectural patronage of the Ruqayya shrine. By recounting the miraculous circumstances which prompted al-Hafiz to order the building of this shrine, Muhammad al-Jawwani (d. 588/1192), an almost contemporary observer of al-Hafiz's reign, provides further literary evidence suggestive of the caliph's use of patronage as a legitimacy tool. According to al-Jawwani, the shrine was built upon the orders of al-Hafiz himself, as a result of a dream he had, in which a woman had appeared to him enveloped in a cloak.

When, in the dream, he asked her to disclose her identity, she answered that she was Ruqayya, 'Ali's daughter by a woman other than Fatima. As a result of his vision, al-Hafiz summoned two courtiers, informed them of the dream, and ordered the excavation of the place where he reckoned the woman had appeared to him. Miraculously, a tomb of a woman identified as Ruqayya, was unearthed, and al-Hafiz, this time a direct witness to a miracle performed not by a distant 'Alid female descendant but by the very daughter of the first imam himself, ordered the construction of the shrine.[98] Through its anecdotal appeal, this story aimed at enhancing al-Hafiz's status to a broad spectrum of the population. As eminent a woman as 'Ali's own daughter, Ruqayya, appeared in a dream *to him*, and the veracious nature of such a dream was shown by the finding of her tomb. As in the case of the *Mashhad al-Nūr*, the Sayyida Ruqayya mosque is made to witness to the 'Alid credentials al-Hafiz intended to display, which aimed at seeking the support of the Twelver Shi'is but also at appealing to the common roots of the schismatic Isma'ili groups.

Yet al-Maqrizi provides another account of the circumstances surrounding the foundation of the Ruqayya complex, by linking it to a well-known woman of al-Hafiz's own time. As a wealthy and eminent widow of the caliph al-Amir, with no male offspring, 'Alam al-Amiriyya became a potentially perfect match for al-Hafiz as architectural sponsor to tally with his dynastic campaigning. Her involvement in architectural projects had begun with the patronage of buildings for charitable purposes and ended with the construction of the Sayyida Ruqayya mosque, containing the tomb of Ruqayya, the main *miḥrāb* of which is still extant, indeed known as one of the finest examples of stucco decoration in the whole of Egypt. Noted for its beauty, the shrine carried a number of inscriptions, one of which is a Qur'anic passage mentioning the *Ahl al-Bayt* (Qur. 33:33), a verse that pilgrims are expected to recite upon visiting an 'Alid shrine. Another inscription, in the interior of its dome, dates the building to 527/1133.[99] Under the dome is a superbly arabesque-decorated wooden cenotaph (*tābūt*), carrying an inscription that states that the tomb itself was made in 533/1138–9 by order of 'Alam al-Amiriyya, whose agent was the Qadi Maknun, to whose name is added: 'the servant of al-Hafiz'.[100]

The presence in one site of inscriptions featuring the name of al-Hafiz, the Qur'anic reference to the *Ahl al-Bayt*, the alleged presence of Ruqayya's relics and the name of the patroness as al-Sayyida al-Amiriyya lend themselves to interpretations as to the function of this site that go beyond the immediate concern of honouring the memory of one of 'Ali's lesser-known daughters. The inscriptions at this shrine would make it clear to the visitor or the pilgrim that the caliph al-Hafiz was linked to 'Ali's progeny, that, like 'Ali, he was appointed by his predecessor, and that the implicit witness of this appointment was al-Amir's widow, who, through her patronage of the shrine, was indirectly validating al-

Hafiz's claim that he had been appointed by her husband. In other words, this wealthy widow was the *trait d'union* between the past and the present caliph, and her name, forever preserved on the tomb, provided the proof of such a continuity.

After 'Alam al-Amiriyya there are further references to Fatimid female patronage of religious buildings. Two of al-Hafiz's consorts are singled out as patronesses of mosques in the Qarafa: Jiha Bayyan, a singing concubine credited with the building of the *Masjid Jihat Bayyān* and Jiha Rayhan, who built another mosque subsequently restored by her eunuch Rayhan in 542/1147.[101] Unlike their more famous predecessors, these patronesses were neither widows nor spinsters but consorts who did not wait for their husband's death to invest their money in architectural projects. While their patronage could be seen as a form of investment, beyond financial return or security, there could have been other benefits to be gained in sponsoring pious works. Their patronage of building activities occurred within the context of over a decade of intense power struggles involving at least four sons of al-Hafiz, one of whom was eventually killed by order of his own father for his opposition to the appointment of one of his brothers as heir apparent. Were these consorts also the mothers of any of these potential heirs, who sought to carve in stone their ambition of becoming queen mothers? Family and palace in-fighting extended to the army and it is within the context of rivalry between different power bases, involving claimants to the succession to al-Hafiz's throne, possibly their mothers, influential eunuchs and military viziers, that the restoration in 542/1147 of the Jihat Rayhan mosque carried out by Rayhan, the eunuch of the caliphal consort, could be assessed. The heavy clashes between the two infantry corps of the Rayhaniyya and the Juyushiyya, which, since 529/1133–4, had marred the running of the Fatimid army, culminated in outright military confrontation in 544/1149–50, coinciding with al-Hafiz's death.[102]

During al-Hafiz's caliphate, particularly noticeable is the rise in engagement in architectural patronage by wealthy courtiers, both male and female. For example, the already mentioned Sitt Ghazal, who had been the carrier of the caliphal inkwell, commissioned, in 536/1141, a mosque (*Masjid Sitt Ghazāl*) in the Qarafa area. In 541/1146, another mosque (*Masjid Shaqīq al-Mulk*) was sponsored by the Manager of the Treasury. The female standing attendant of al-Hafiz is also reported to have built a mosque. Furthermore, the carrier of the parasol, a Slav man, built a mosque (*Masjid 'Azīm al-Dawla*) but – according to popular lore – he brought misfortune upon himself by cutting off a lotus tree in the cemetery. Under the caliphate of al-Zafir, another patroness was the Maghribi Ballara, who, as wife and mother of viziers, ordered in 547/1152 the building of the mosque known as *Masjid Umm 'Abbās*.[103]

The Umm 'Abbas mosque is thus far the last known building to be linked to female patronage in Fatimid Egypt. Once again, with this mosque, architecture mirrored historical circumstances – and how much had these changed since the times of Durzan, the first Fatimid patroness! Durzan had been the wealthy widow and mother of two of the greatest Fatimid imam-caliphs. Ballara, on the other hand, was the wife and mother of two of the most scheming Fatimid viziers, who rose to their rank with blood on their hands.

The above examples of female architectural patronage during the Fatimid era lead us to a broader discussion on this phenomenon. Was it different from male patronage and, if so, to what extent? Was it devoted to particular types of buildings and, if so, was this targeting of any particular relevance? Could female patronage be distinguished from 'state'-sponsored patronage? To what extent were the patronesses really in control (logistic or financial) of the projects ascribed to them?[104]

The availability of information, or indeed the lack of it, emerging from literary and archaeological data calls for some reflection. When referring to Fatimid patronesses, late medieval Muslim historians and chroniclers made a selective use of Fatimid sources, most of which are no longer extant. As the main aim of their narratives was far from providing a record of female patronage, their references to Fatimid female architectural sponsors were by and large incidental. For example, in reconstructing the topographical history of Cairo, al-Maqrizi's main interest was in the buildings per se, rather than their sponsors. Indeed, more than one scholar has doubted al-Maqrizi's accuracy in ascribing the patronage of some buildings to specific individuals, and has claimed that he based his information more on popular knowledge than, for example, on evidence from monumental inscriptions.

As for the edifices themselves, over time they underwent adaptation, demolition, reconstruction and, especially if public, intentional acts of effacement to reflect changing religious or political circumstances. Although references in literary sources can occasionally help a topographical reconstruction, it is nevertheless unlikely that we will ever know the full extent of, and circumstances informing, Fatimid female patronage.

4. Reasons for Patronage: Beyond Generosity and Piety

The famous thirteenth-century mystical poet Jalal al-Din Rumi said about patronage of religious buildings: 'Every man puts up these sacred edifices with a particular intention: either to display his generosity, or for the sake of fame, or to gain a reward in heaven'.[105] Beyond gender qualifications, these three main reasons could apply to the patronesses of the Fatimid era, with the addition of a few significant motives. Ladies of the Fatimid palace could indeed afford to be generous, as they were wealthy enough to spend some of their fortunes in charity works. The buildings they sponsored did give them fame, and their names were recorded not only, occasionally, on the buildings themselves, but also in the history books and chronicles. Together with their names, their status at court as women of importance and influence was also acknowledged. By sponsoring buildings related to religious rituals, these women promoted the performance of prayer, recitation of the Qur'an and alms-giving, as well as the charitable activities connected to them, such as feeding the poor and sheltering the needy. Through such pious deeds, these patronesses might have indeed hoped to gain heavenly rewards, as witnessed by the inscriptions commissioned by the Zirid nurse Fatima for the Great Mosque of Qayrawan: 'in the hope of God's recompense and in the desire of His satisfaction'.[106]

Additional motives for patronage were the result of personal and family reasons, and responses to local cultural and religious practices, as well as to 'international' expectations. Personal reasons for sponsoring were linked not only to these patronesses' individual status but also the politico-dynastic apparatus to which they belonged. Socio-geographical motives were inextricably linked to the local Egyptian cultural and religious context these ladies were operating in, while the external reasons were related to the international scene as a means of emulation of practices by other dynasties, or to impress foreign envoys or visitors.

The overwhelming majority of Fatimid patronesses were widows of former imam-caliphs and were of mature age, and many were queen mothers, whose secure status within the caliphal family and the palace was based on seniority. Upon the death of the imam-caliph, his main consort's wealth would increase once she received her full share of inheritance. If she was also the mother of the imam-caliph in office, she would command great respect as one of the most senior members of the caliphal family – the one representing continuity with the past and also a continued influence upon her son. Hence, she would be ideally suited to endorse the charitable activities promoted by the dynasty, and to become the representative of the *noblesse oblige* of wealth and status. In most cases, her wealth and status remained uncontested, as she would also hold the key to furthering officials' careers; after all, she was the person at court with the longest contact with the experienced members of the administrative and financial elite, including viziers, some of whom had started their careers as managers of the queen-mother's private treasury. Through visible charitable actions, palace ladies could perpetuate their names and also make a statement about their position. In the case of mothers of potential heirs, to commission a building was a way of endorsing their son's claims and showing readiness to take on the role of the principal lady in the palace. Seniority and maturity also allowed royal women greater freedom of movement and social interaction than younger women, who, at least in theory, were expected to follow more literally the modesty rules. Patronage of charitable works, including buildings for ritual functions (waterworks for drinking but also for ablutions, for example), would have been the ideal means by which to show their accomplishments and to become role models of piety and generosity, two characteristics much suited to their status and age. Moreover, for women of all ages and status, to become patrons of charitable buildings by means of *waqf* endowments would have added to their own financial security, or, if they chose, to that of other family members or beneficiaries.[107]

Female patronage was also motivated by political and genealogical considerations. Imam-caliphs and viziers were the natural policy-makers and the most obvious users of architectural patronage to visualise, support and advertise their policies. Typical examples were the imam-caliph al-ʿAziz and his vizier Ibn Killis. Royal female patronage was also part of this policy: the royal ladies had the money, the status, the personal motivations and the credentials. One suspects that, in some cases, their wealth might have come in handy to imam-caliphs and viziers for the implementation of their own aims, and that royal ladies might have been (willingly or unwillingly) 'used' to support genealogical and other claims through their architectural patronage. Though in theory financially secure, these women's positions depended to a great extent upon their ability to retain their wealth, as imams and viziers could still confiscate their assets, banish them from the court or even exile them. The example of Qabiha al-Rumiyya, the *jāriya* of the ʿAbbasid caliph al-Mutawakkil (d. 247/861) and mother of the caliph al-Muʿtazz (d. 255/869) must have been a powerful reminder of how much a woman, even the caliph's mother, could lose: her own son, her wealth, her status and her country.[108]

During the Fatimid era, when choosing the location for their patronage and the particular type of edifice, royal patronesses, or the high-ranking courtiers acting on their behalf or indeed in their name, took into account the local, both social and geographical, context. In medieval Egypt, the visitation of tombs and shrines of Muslim (as well as Christian and Jewish) holy people was a well-established practice, as revealed by extant pilgrimage guides illustrating both local and 'national' pilgrimages. Building edifices on hills or having domes over them, constructing near the sites of existing tombs and shrines or restoring old structures – these were all means of making the caliphal family visible to the worshippers and the numerous pilgrims attending the sites. Particularly if the sponsored edifices were ʿAlid shrines and places of pilgrimage, they also represented a means of generating revenues from alms and donations, from ritual objects as well as various trading activities that would develop around them.[109] Through building and restoration of existing edifices in the capital and beyond, the Fatimids re-interpreted the use of space to the benefit of the dynasty: the more visible and the more widespread their presence, the more effective this re-interpretation.

Finally, external and more wide-ranging considerations for female architectural patronage during the Fatimids ought to be taken into account. With the establishment of the dynasty in Cairo, and the expansionist plans towards the eastern Mediterranean regions, the Fatimids found themselves face to face with one of their greatest rivals in the region: the Byzantines. The Fatimids rivalled in prestige, style and splendour the refined Byzantine court and it is in this context that the prominent position acquired by the women of the Fatimid court ought to be examined. Like the women of the Cairo caliphal family, the royal female members of Byzantium were by and large commoners, even slaves, who gained prestige through marrying emperors or princes, and by becoming mothers of their heirs.[110]

Between the eighth and twelfth centuries, the Byzantine imperial ladies were able to acquire a power they rarely turned down. News of the political, social and economic independence of the Byzantine royal women filtered through to Cairo via Byzantine concubines who entered the Fatimid royal harems, as well as via the well-travelled and fashion-inspiring court poets and other courtiers. Through the display of wealth and architectural patronage, the Fatimid caliphal ladies, backed by their male kin, took it upon themselves to match their counterparts in Constantinople: some historians, including Ibn Taghribirdi, do not fail to notice this 'competition' when providing accounts of the wealth displayed by Fatimid ladies during official visits by Byzantine envoys.[111]

The recording and showing of palace ladies' wealth and female patronage coincide with the coming of age of the Fatimid dynasty on the world political stage. The dynasty's imperial aims were fought at every level, including the opulence of the courts and through their ritual and artistic expressions. The display of palace ladies' wealth and their visibility through patronage were just two of the several means by which the Fatimids rivalled their main competitors around the Mediterranean and beyond.

Notes

1 Brett, M., *The Rise of the Fatimids: the World of the Mediterranean & the Middle East in the Tenth Century* CE, Leiden: Brill, 2001, pp. 261–2.

2 Brett, M., *Rise*, pp. 257–66. Brett, p. 336, states that al-Mu'izz brought the North African gold with him to Egypt for *dīnār* minting. According to Halm, some 1,500 coffers filled with money were carried over the bridge to Giza in 358/969: Halm, H., *The Empire of the Mahdi. The Rise of the Fatimids*, trans. M. Bonner, Leiden: E. J. Brill, 1996, p. 414.

3 See S. D. Goitein and H. Kennedy as referred to in Brett, M., *Rise*, p. 333. For a general discussion on the Fāṭimid caliphal family's wealth, see Lev, Y., *State and Society in Fāṭimid Egypt*, Leiden: E. J. Brill, 1991, pp. 65–7.

4 al-Musabbiḥī, Muḥammad b. 'Ubayd Allāh, *Akhbār Miṣr*, ed. Sayyid, A. F. and Bianquis, T., Cairo: IFAO, 1978, vol. 1, p. 108, refers to the *dīwān al-sayyida wālida mawlā-nā*, that is, the *dīwān* of the queen mother of our master, al-Ẓāhir al-Maqrīzī, Taqī al-Dīn, *Itti'āẓ al-ḥunafā' bi-*

akhbār al-a'imma al-Fāṭimiyyīn al-khulafā', ed. al-Shayyāl, J. and Ḥilmī, M., Cairo: Lajnat iḥyā' al-turāth al-islāmī, 1387–93/1967–1973, vol. 2, pp. 200 and 212 refers, for the years 439/1047 and 442/1050, to the *dīwān* of al-Mustanṣir's mother.

5 al-Maqrīzī, *Itti'āẓ*, vol. 2, p. 116. The anecdote points to the choice of a senior, reliable figure, such as the queen mother, as the most trustworthy safe-keeper of large amounts of money.

6 al-Maqrīzī, *Itti'āẓ*, vol. 2, p. 154. It was not unusual for viziers to ask, in times of financial crisis, for a loan from the imam-caliph or his family. The vizier was expected to return the money once the crisis was over.

7 al-Maqrīzī, *Itti'āẓ*, vol. 2, p. 33. Elsewhere in the *Itti'āẓ* (vol. 2, p. 458), al-Maqrīzī indicates 50,000 *dīnārs* per year. al-Musabbiḥī also refers to an orchard of the *sayyida 'amma*, that is Sitt al-Mulk, in *Akhbār Miṣr*, vol. 1, p. 43.

8 Ibn al-Zubayr, *Kitāb al-Hadāyā wa-'l-tuḥaf*, ed. and trans. al-Hijjāwī al-Qaddūmī, G., *Book of Gifts and Rarities*, Cambridge, MA: Harvard University Press, 1996, pp. 222–3. See also Ibn Taghrībirdī, Jamāl al-Dīn Abu 'l-Maḥāsin, *al-Nujūm al-Zāhira fī mulūk Miṣr wa-'l-Qāhire*, Cairo: Dār al-Kutub al-Miṣriyya, 1351/1933, vol. 4, p. 192.

9 In addition to al-Zubayr's listing, see al-Maqrīzī, *Itti'āẓ*, vol. 2, p. 289.

10 al-Musabbiḥī, *Akhbār Miṣr*, vol. 1, p. 105; and al-Maqrīzī, *Itti'āẓ*, vol. 2, p. 173.

11 The celibate status of the daughters of Fāṭimid imam-caliphs has also been noted by H. Halm, who sees this celibacy as part of a deliberate royal policy to avoid dynastic counter-claims. See Halm, H., 'Le destin de la princesse Sitt al-Mulk', in Barrucand, M. (ed.), *L'Égypte Fatimide: son art et son histoire*, Paris: Presses de l'Université de Paris-Sorbonne, 1999, pp. 70–1. See also Halm's statement in his *Die Kalifen von Kairo*, Munchen: C. H. Beck, 2003, p. 314.

12 Fairchild Ruggles, D., 'Vision and Power: An Introduction', in Fairchild Ruggles, D. (ed.), *Women, Patronage, and Self-representation in Islamic Societies*, Albany: SUNY, 2000, pp. 6–10.

13 Lane-Poole, S., *A History of Egypt in the Middle Ages*, London: Methuen, 1925, vol. 6, p. 121.

14 al-Musabbiḥī, *Akhbār Miṣr*, vol. 1, pp. 92–3.

15 al-Maqrīzī, Taqī al-Dīn, *al-Mawā'iẓ wa-'l-i'tibār bi-dhikr al-khiṭaṭ wa-'l-āthār*, Beirut: Dār al-ṣādir, n.d., offset of Būlāq, 1324 edn, vol.1, p. 449.

16 al-Musabbiḥī, *Akhbār Miṣr*, vol. 1, p. 111.

17 See the list of items that al-Ḥākim confiscated in 399/1009 from the women in his family, in al-Anṭākī, Yaḥyā b. Sa'īd, *Ta'rīkh*, partial ed. and French trans. Kratchkovsky, I. and Vasiliev, A., 'Histoire de Yahya-ibn Sa'īd d'Antioche', *Patrologia Orientalis*, 23 (1932), p. 491.

18 When famine hit Egypt during al-Mustanṣir's reign, the women of the household (*arbāb al-buyūt*) resolved to sell their jewellery in exchange for food. Al-Maqrīzī tells us of a woman who sold a necklace worth 1,000 *dīnārs* in exchange for a sack of flour. However, she was pillaged by other hungry people and managed to save only a handful of flour for herself. With it, she made a flat piece of bread, then turned up at al-Mustanṣir's palace and called for the caliph to see a piece of bread worth 1,000 *dīnārs*. During the year 461/1069, numerous riches were removed from the palace treasuries (among them, the Treasury of the queen Mother) and sold in order to pay the wages of the Turkish troops: al-Maqrīzī, *Itti'āẓ*, vol. 2, pp. 289, 299. Evidence of the use of silk as cash comes from bills of exchange issued against silk rather than against *dīnārs*: see Goitein, S. D., A *Mediterranean Society*, Berkeley: University of California Press, 5 vols, 1967–88, vol. 1, pp. 222–3, 245.

19 On al-Ḥākim's aunt Sayyida Rāshida and her display of wealth during the visit of the Byzantine envoyees, see Ibn Taghrībirdī, *al-Nujūm*, 1933 edn, vol. 4, p. 192.

20 See Rabī'a (d. 686/1287), who 'married al-malik Harūn b. al-Ṣāḥib Shams al-dīn … her dowry (*ṣadāq*) was 100,000 *dīnārs* … '; the eleventh-century 'Abbāsid caliph al-Qā'im bi-Amr Allāh gave his wife Khadīja al-Saljuqiyya a dowry of 100,000 *dīnārs*. Al-Muqtafī, who reigned after him, married away his daughter Zubayda to the sulṭān Mas'ūd b. Muḥammad b. Malik Shāh

for a dowry of 100,000 *dīnārs*.' al-Safadī, Ṣalāḥ al-Dīn, *Kitāb al-Wafī bi-'l-wafāyāt*, Wiesbaden: F. Steiner, 1981–, vol. 14, no. 51, pp. 52–3. For figures in literary sources, see Conrad, L. I., 'Seven and the Tasbī'. On the Implications of Numerical Symbolism for the Study of Medieval Islamic History', *JESHO*, 31 (1988), pp. 42–73.

21 Ibn al-Ṭuwayr, al-Murtaḍā, *Nuzhat al-muqlatayn fī akhbār al-dawlatayn*, ed. Sayyid, A. F., Stuttgart and Beirut: F. Steiner, 1992, p. 6.

22 See Ibn al-Ṣayrafī, Abu'l-Qāsim, *al-Ishāra ilā man nāla al-wizāra*, *BIFAO*, 25 (1925): on Ibn Killis, p. 90, on Barjawān, p. 85; on the wealth of al-Afḍal at his death, see the review of Ibn Muyassar's *Annales* by Wiet, G., in *JA*, 18 (1921), p. 107, where a comparison is drawn between different sources reporting on the vizier's silk brocade tunics: 700 in Ibn Muyassar, 75,000 in Ibn Khallikān and 65,000 in al-Abshihī!

23 The purchasing value of the Fāṭimid *dīnār* varied; for example, one *dīnār* would buy c. 110 kg of grain in 396/1005 but only 11 kg towards the last decades of the dynasty, with the proviso that the fluctuation in grain prices depended greatly on the flooding of the Nile. The price of silk, instead, was more stable, at c. 20 *dīnārs* per c. 6 kg (10 *raṭl*). See Lowe, J. D., *Monetary Development in Fatimid Egypt and Syria*, MA thesis, University of Arizona, 1985, table p. 80 for grain prices and p. 83 for silk.

24 See Arwā's treasure in Idrīs 'Imād al-Dīn, *'Uyūn al-akhbār*, ed. and trans. A. F. Sayyid, *The Fatimids and their Successors in Yemen*, London: I. B. Tauris, 2002, vol. 7, pp. 279–94 (Ar.). Among her silver treasure, al-Mustanṣir's mother is reported to have owned a silver-decorated Nile boat made for her by her former master al-Tustarī when he was in charge of the *wisāṭa* in 436/1044: al-Maqrīzī, *Itti'āẓ*, vol. 2, pp. 293–4. According to 'Abd al-Karīm Aḥmad, Nurīmān, *al-Mar'a fī Miṣr fī'l-'aṣr al-Fāṭimī*, Cairo: al-Hay'a al-miṣriyya al-'āmma li-'l-kitāb, 1993, p. 58 this type of boat was used in official ceremonies.

25 Khalili collection: Wenzel, M., *Ornament and Amulet, Rings of the Islamic Lands*. *The Nasser D. Khalili Collection of Islamic Art*, vol. 14, London and Oxford: Azimuth Editions and OUP, 1993, p. 56, no. 163.

26 For the rise in price of violet oil in 399/1008, see Ibn al-Dawādārī, Abū Bakr b. 'Abd Allāh, *Kanz al-durar wa-jāmi' al-ghurar: al-durra al-muḍīya fī akhbār al-dawla al-Fāṭimiyya*, al-juz' al-sādis, ed. al-Munajjid, Ṣ., Cairo: O. Harrassowitz, 1961, vol. 6, p. 279.

27 On Ibn Killis receiving from al-'Azīz c. 374/984, 500 young girls and 1,000 young boys from the *maghāriba*, see Ibn al-Ṣayrafī, *al-Ishāra*, p. 92. On the master's legal obligation to pay the *zakāt* on behalf of his/her slaves, see al-Qāḍī al-Nu'mān, *Da'ā'im al-Islām fī dhikr al-ḥalāl*, trans. Fyzee, A. A. A., *The Pillars of Islam: Vol. 1, Acts of Devotion and Religious Observances*, revised and annotated by Poonawala, I. K. H., New Delhi and Oxford: OUP, 2002, vol. 1, p. 332. For livestock possibly owned by Sitt al-Mulk and donated to her half-brother, see al-Maqrīzī, *Khiṭaṭ*, vol. 1, p. 458.

28 Ibn al-Zubayr, *al-Dhakhā'ir*, Gh., pp. 223–4; al-Maqrīzī, *Khiṭaṭ*, vol. 1, p. 415 and al-Maqrīzī, *Itti'āẓ*, vol. 2, p. 294. See a similar account of Rāshida and 'Abda's wealth in Ibn Taghrībirdī, *al-Nujūm*, 1933 edn, vol. 4, pp. 192–3.

29 Ibn al-Zubayr, *al-Dhakhā'ir*. See also Ibn Taghrībirdī, *al-Nujūm*, 1933 edn, p. 193.

30 According to al-Maqrīzī, she demanded a rare marble basin proudly owned by the *qāḍī* Abū Ṭālib b. Ḥadīd, who, reluctantly, gave it to her.

31 Ibn al-Zubayr, *al-Dhakhā'ir*, p. 223.

32 al-Maqrīzī, Taqī al-Dīn, *Kitāb al-Muqaffā al-kabīr*, ed. al-Ya'lāwī, M., Beirut: Dār al-gharb al-islāmī, 7 vols, 1991, vol. 2, p. 643.

33 See al-Maqrīzī, *Itti'āẓ*, vol. 2, p. 33 passim.

34 On Sitt al-Mulk's bathhouses, see Lev, Y., *State*, p. 65, n. 3.

35 al-Maqrīzī, *Khiṭaṭ*, vol. 1, p. 353.

36 Ben-Sasson, M., *The Jews of Sicily, 825–1068*, Jerusalem, 1991, document 11 (in Hebrew). We are grateful to Prof. Yaacov Lev for providing us with this reference.

37 The overall monthly allowance to the caliph al-Muqtadir's mother, the princes, the female relatives and the servants for the year 306/918 was 61,930 *dīnārs*, see al-Ṣabī', Hilāl, *Rusum dar al-Khilafah: the rules and regulations of the 'Abbasid court*, trans. Salem, E. A., Beirut: Lebanese Commission for the Translation of Great Works, 1977, p. 24.

38 Ibn al-Ma'mūn al-Baṭā'iḥī, Jamāl al-Dīn, *Nuṣūṣ min akhbār Miṣr*, ed. Sayyid, A. F., Cairo: IFAO, 1983, pp. 90–2; also al-Maqrīzī, *Khiṭaṭ*, vol. 1, pp. 420–2.

39 On the extremely high value of eunuchs given to imam-caliphs as gifts, see Lev, Y., *State*, pp. 77–8.

40 al-Maqrīzī, *Khiṭaṭ*, vol. 2, pp. 446, 448.

41 Based on Ibn Māmātī, where the *jizya* was required from all non-Muslim free and adult men: see Levy, R., *The Social Structure of Islam*, Cambridge: CUP, 1957, p. 392; and Rabie, H., *The Financial System of Egypt*, London: OUP, 1972, pp. 108–9, where evidence is reported that Fāṭimids did not always collect the *jizya* tax at a flat ratio.

42 *Sīrat al-ustādh Jawdhar*, ed. Ḥusayn, M. K., and Sha'īra, M. 'A. H., Cairo: Dār al-fikr al-'arabī, 1954, p. 122.

43 al-Musabbiḥī, *Akhbār Miṣr*, vol. 1, pp. 92–3.

44 Lev, Y., *State*, p. 72 and ff.

45 Al-Manṣūr is credited with having established the *bayt māl al-maẓālim* (the Treasury of Wrongful Exaction) to safe-keep the money he confiscated from ministers accused of extortion. The caliph al-Muqtadir made an agent extract the sum of 700,000 *dīnārs* from the widow of a former minister: see Levy, R., *Social Structure*, pp. 307–8, and Rabie, H., *Financial*, pp. 121–7; for the practice under the Mamlūks, see Petry, C. F., 'Class solidarity versus gender gain: Women as custodians of property in later medieval Egypt', in Keddie, N. R. and Baron, B. (eds), *Women in Middle Eastern History*, New Haven and London: Yale University Press, 1991, pp. 127–8.

46 al-Anṭākī, 'Histoire', p. 491.

47 al-Musabbiḥī, *Akhbār Miṣr*, vol. 1, pp. 32–3.

48 Sourdel, D., *Le Vizirat 'Abbāside de 749 a 939*, Damascus: IFD, 1960, vol. 2, pp. 388, 391 and 471–5 (based on Miskawayh). For other instances of influential palace ladies and mulcting in the 'Abbāsid, Saljūq and Ayyūbid courts, see al-Safadī, *al-Wāfī*: on the *jāriya* of the 'Abbāsid caliph al-Mutawakkil and mother of al-Mu'tazz, vol. 24, no. 188, pp. 186–7; on a Saljūq court woman, vol. 24, no. 430, p. 376; and on the Ayyūbid princess Rabī'a Khātūn, vol. 14, no. 122, pp. 97–9.

49 Ibn Sa'īd, 'Alī b. Mūsā, *al-Nujūm al-ẓāhira fī ḥulā ḥadhrat al-Qāhira*, ed. Ḥusayn Naṣṣār, Cairo: Dār al-Kutub al-Miṣriyya, 1970, p. 360.

50 On her numerous charitable works for Makka and Madina, see al-Safadī, *al-Wāfī*, vol. 16, no. 197, pp. 167–8.

51 See Idris, H. R., *La Berbérie Orientale sous les Zīrīdes*, Paris: A. Maisonneuve, 1962, vol. 2, p. 547.

52 al-Musabbiḥī, *Akhbār Miṣr*, vol. 1, p. 108.

53 See al-Maqrīzī, *Khiṭaṭ*, vol. 2, p. 446.

54 Ed: 'al-Khayzurān', in *EI2nd*, vol. 4, p. 1164, where, on the basis of al-Ṭabarī, it is reported that, in order to secure support for her son as al-Mahdī's successor to the caliphate, she 'made arrangements to appease the mutineers'. For a number of examples from Rasūlid Yemen, see Sadek, N., 'Rasūlid women and patronage', *PSAS*, 19 (1989), p. 123.

55 Idris, H. R., *La Berbérie*, vol. 1, p. 136, and al-Maqrīzī's *Ighāthat al-umma fī kashf al-ghumma*, French trans. Wiet, G., 'Le Traité des famines de Maqrīzī', *JESHO*, 5 (1962), p. 26; al-Musabbiḥī, *Akhbār Miṣr*, vol. 1, p. 77.

56 Terrasse, H., 'Fās: monuments', *EI2nd*, vol. 2, p. 821.

57 Ibn Duqmāq, Ibrāhīm b. Muḥammad, *Kitāb al-Intiṣār li-wāsiṭa 'aqd al-amṣār*, ed. Vollers, Beirut:

al-Maktab al-Tijārī, 1893, section 1, p. 64. He specifies (p. 68) that this and subsequent works were made upon the order of al-ʿAzīz, during the vizirate of (and the supervision of?) Ibn Killis. Restoration works to this mosque were further carried out under al-Ḥākim as a statement of changed ownership.

58 An instance in the Fāṭimid period of an edifice purposely built for a woman was Hawdaj (lit. sedan chair), an odd-shaped building erected near the garden of *jazīrat al-rawḍa*, on the Nile, for al-Āmir's consort, ʿĀlīya al-Badawiyya.

59 On Zubayda's generosity, piety and endurance in pursuing the construction project see al-Safadī, *al-Wafi*, vol. 14, no. 242, pp. 176–8. On her political influence due to her wealth and status, see Roded, R., *Women in Islamic Biographical Collections*, Boulder and London: Lynne Rienner, 1994, pp. 123–5.

60 For an English translation, see Sewter, E. R. A., *The Alexiad of Anna Comnena*, Harmondsworth: Penguin Classics, 1969. On Anna's turning to literary activity as a compensation for being excluded from politics after her father's death, see Angold, M., *The Byzantine Empire (1025–1204): a political history*, London and New York: Longman, 1997, 2nd edn, pp. 246–7.

61 See Golovin, L., *Essai sur l'architecture religieuse musulmane*, vol. 4: L'art Hispano-Musulman, Paris: Klincksieck, 1979, vol. 4, pp. 191–2, where two accounts are given on the identity of Fāṭima, one linking her to Islamic Spain.

62 On documentary evidence for the donations by al-Muʿizz b. Bādīs's nurse Fāṭima, see Roy, B. and Poinssot, P., *Inscriptions Arabes de Kairouan*, Paris: O. Klincksieck, 1950, vol. 2, fasc. 1, pp. 27–32. On those of Umm Mallāl and Umm al-ʿUlū, see Idris, H. R., *La Berbérie*, vol. 1, p. 141 and vol. 2, pp. 417, 771; and Golovin, L., *Le Magrib central a l'époque des Zirides*, Paris: Arts et Metiers Graphiques, 1957, pp. 159–61.

63 For an early study on building work sponsored and commissioned by Fāṭimid royal women see Bloom, J. M., 'The Mosque of the Qarāfa in Cairo', *Muqarnas*, 4 (1987), pp. 7–20.

64 See Humphreys, S. R., 'Women as Patrons of Religious Architecture in Ayyūbid Damascus', *Muqarnas*, 11 (1994), pp. 35–54.

65 al-Maqrīzī, *Ittiʿāẓ*, vol. 1, pp. 294–5.

66 Ibn Duqmāq, *al-Intiṣār*, vol. 1, pp. 64, 68; cf. Ibn Ẓahīra, Ibrāhīm, *al-Faḍā'il al-bāhira fī maḥāsin Miṣr wa-'l-Qāhira*, al-Saqā, M., and al-Muhandis, K. (eds), Cairo: Dār al-Kutub al-Miṣriyya, 1969, pp. 105–6.

67 Ibn Muyassar, *Akhbār Miṣr*, p. 45.

68 At around this time, the al-Nuʿmān family began its monopoly of the judiciary, which, despite the occasional friction with the vizier in charge, remained continuous for almost a century: see Lev, Y., *State*, pp. 133–7.

69 Lev, Y., 'The Fatimid vizier Yaʿqub ibn Killis and the Beginning of the Fatimid Administration in Egypt', *Der Islam*, 58 (1981), pp. 245–7. On Ibn Killis and his intellectual circle where Ismāʿīlīs engaged in learned discussions with Jewish scholars, see Cohen, M., 'In the court of Yaʿqūb ibn Killis: a fragment from the Cairo Genizah', *JQR*, 80 (1990), 3–4, pp. 283–314 .

70 al-Maqrīzī, *Khiṭaṭ*, vol. 2, pp. 245, 318–20.

71 In al-Maqrīzī, *Khiṭaṭ*, vol. 2, pp. 364–5. See also Bloom, J. M., 'The Mosque of the Qarāfa', p. 19, n. 57.

72 al-Maqrīzī states that the patroness of this cistern was Sitt al-Malik, 'aunt of al-Ḥākim and daughter of al-Muʿizz', presumably Durzān's daughter. However, there is disagreement in the sources as to who sponsored this construction: see al-Maqrīzī, *Khiṭaṭ*, vol. 2, pp. 459–60.

73 Originally, the burial place for Fāṭimid caliphs, their spouses and children was the 'Saffron' mausoleum within the caliphal palace; for the plaque, see Rāghib, Y., 'Sur deux mouments funéraires du cimitière d'al-Qarāfa al-Kubrā au Caire', *AI*, 12 (1974), pp. 68–72.

74 ʿAbd al-Karīm Aḥmad, N., *al-Mar'a*, p. 60.

75 'Abd al-Karīm Aḥmad, N., *al-Mar'a*, p. 68.
76 On female patronage and land allocations in Ottoman Turkey, see a brief reference in Thys-Senocak, L., 'The Yeni Valide Mosque complex at Eminönü', *Muqarnas*, 15 (1998), p. 61.
77 This programme began under al-'Azīz through the appointment of Ismā'īlī *qāḍīs* in Fusṭāṭ, Tinnīs and Damietta: cf. Lev, Y., *State*, pp. 134–5.
78 Bloom, J. M., 'The Mosque of the Qarāfa', pp. 7–20; and his 'The mosque of al-Ḥākim in Cairo', *Muqarnas*, 1 (1983), p. 29.
79 Rabbat, N., 'Al-Azhar mosque: an Architectural Chronicle of Cairo's History', *Muqarnas*, 13 (1996), p. 55.
80 On the *ḥammāms* during the Fāṭimids, see Sayyid, A. F., *La capitale de l'Égypte jusqu' à l'époque Fatimide*, Beirut/Stuttgart: F. Steiner, 1998, pp. 323–6.
81 Bloom, J. M., 'The mosque of the Qarāfa', p. 17.
82 See, for example, Wiet, G., 'Une nouvelle inscription Fatimide au Caire', *JA*, 249 (1961), p. 14 (Ar.), 15 (Fr.); the imam is given only three short titles, against Badr's six titles, plus the description of his achievements.
83 For building works carried out by Badr al-Jamālī, see Creswell, K. A. C., *The Muslim architecture of Egypt: Vol. 1, Ikhshīds and Fāṭimids*, AD *939–1171*, Oxford: Clarendon Press, 1952, repr. New York: Hacker, 1978, pp. 146–219. On Badr's mausoleum, see Rāghib, Y., 'Le mausolée de Yūnus al-Sa'dī est-il celui de Badr al-Gamālī?', *Arabica*, 20 (1973), pp. 305–7.
84 Lev, Y., *State*, p. 197, pp. 138ff.
85 For the Friday Mosque and Arwā's tomb in Dhū Jibla, see Daum, W. (ed.), *Yemen: 3000 years of art and civilization in Arabia felix*, Innsbruck: Pinguin/Frankfurt: Umschau, 1988, p. 209; for San'a', see Lewcock, R., Rex Smith, G., et al., 'The architectural history and description of San'a' mosques: the great Mosque', in Serjeant, R. B. (ed.), *San'a': an Arabian Islamic city*, London: The World of Islam Festival Trust, 1983, p. 324.
86 Shakir, M., *Sīrat al-Malik al-Mukarram: an edition and a study*, PhD thesis, SOAS, London: University of London, 1999, vol. 1, p. 123; and vol. 2, pp. 163–5.
87 Lewcock, R., 'The architectural', p. 324.
88 Finster, B., 'An outline of the history of Islamic religious architecture in Yemen', *Muqarnas*, 9 (1992), p. 128 and n. 24.
89 Lev, Y., *State*, p. 146, inferred from al-Maqrīzī; the policy of reducing the imam's visibility at public festivals had already started under Badr al-Jamālī, who stopped processions led by the imam to the *muṣallā*: see Sanders, P., *Ritual, Politics, and the City in Fatimid Cairo*, Albany: SUNY Press, 1994, pp. 67–9; and Bierman, I. A., *Writing Signs: the Fatimid Public Text*, Berkeley: University of California Press, 1998, p. 108.
90 In 520/1126, a *masṭaba* was added to the mosque for the use of Ṣūfīs whom al-Āmir would watch dancing from the belvedere built on the upper part of the Qarāfa palace: see al-Maqrīzī, *Khiṭaṭ*, vol. 2, p. 453.
91 For a description of the *mashhad* of Umm Kulthūm and the Aqmar Mosque see, Creswell, K. A. C., *Muslim Architecture*, vol. 1, pp. 239–46. On the sanctuary of Sayyida Nafīsa, and its history during and after the Fāṭimids, see Rāghib, Y., 'Al-Sayyida Nafīsa, sa légende, son culte et son cimetière', *SI*, 44 (1976), pp. 61–86; 45 (1977), pp. 27–55.
92 On the propaganda purposes of al-Aqmar Mosque, see Bierman, I. A., *Writing Signs*, pp. 108–16. See also Behrens-Abouseif, D., 'The Façade of the Aqmar Mosque in the Context of Fatimid Ceremonial', *Muqarnas*, 9 (1992), pp. 29–38.
93 On the meanings of the titles of this consort of al-Āmir, see 'Abd al-Karīm Aḥmad, N., *al-Mar'a*, p. 43. For the money she spent on building this mosque, see al-Maqrīzī, *Khiṭaṭ*, vol. 2, p. 446.
94 al-Maqrīzī, *Khiṭaṭ*, vol. 2, p. 454.

95 See al-Qalqashandī, Shihāb al-Dīn, *Subḥ al-aʿshā fī ṣināʿat al-inshā*ʾ, ed. Ibrāhīm, Cairo: Dār al-Kutub al-Miṣriyya, 1331–8/1913–20, vol. 9, pp. 291–7; see Stern, S. M., 'The Succession to the Fatimid Imam al-Āmir, the Claims of the later Fatimids to the Imamate, and the Rise of Ṭayyibī Ismailism', *Oriens*, 4 (1951), part 2, pp. 270 and ff.

96 Williams, C., 'The cult of ʿAlid Saints in the Fatimid Monuments of Cairo – part II: the Mausolea', *Muqarnas*, 3 (1985), p. 47. Doubts have been raised about her chronology of some of the buildings discussed in the article. For the purpose of this discussion, the date of completion of the mausoleum of Sayyida Ruqayya is not disputed.

97 See Rāghib, Y., 'Deux monuments Fatimides au pied du Muqaṭṭam', *REI*, 46 (1978), pp. 99–101, where the account given by Ibn al-Zayyāt and al-Sakhāwī is drawn from no longer extant Fāṭimid sources such as al-Quḍāʿī and al-Jawwānī.

98 In Rāghib, Y., 'Les mausolées Fatimides du quartier d'al-Mašāhid', *AI*, 17 (1981), pp. 18–26, based on a MS copy of a text by Muḥammad al-Jawwānī kept in Cairo's Dār al-Kutub.

99 See Creswell, K. A. C., *Muslim Architecture*, vol. 1, tex, p. 250, plate 86c. Rāghib, Y., in 'Les mausolées', pp. 26–7, argues that the complex was built in three stages and that either ʿAlam built the complex together with al-Ḥāfiẓ, or that he was responsible for the building and ʿAlam subsequently commissioned the stucco *miḥrāb* and the wooden cenotaph.

100 'The building of this blessed tomb was ordered by the noble [female] personage, the Āmiriyya, whose agent was the Qāḍī Maknūn, servant of al-Ḥāfiẓ, by the hand of the excellent Abū Turāb Haydara b. Abi 'l-Fatḥ … in the year 533 [1138–9]' – from the cenotaph under the dome of the *mashhad* of Sayyida Ruqayya, quoted from Williams, C., 'The cult', p. 47; see also Russell, D., *Medieval Cairo and the Monasteries of the Wādi Natrūn*, London: Weidenfeld and Nicolson, 1962, pp. 127, 295.

101 al-Maqrīzī, *Khiṭaṭ*, vol. 2, p. 448.

102 For the origins of the Rayḥāniyya and the Juyūshiyya, and their rivalry, see Lev, Y., *State*, pp. 127–9.

103 al-Maqrīzī, *Khiṭaṭ*, vol. 2, p. 447, 449.

104 Besides the study on Ottoman female architecture by Thys-Senocak, L., 'The Yeni Valide Mosque', pp. 58–70, see Baer, G., 'Women and *waqf*: an analysis of the Istanbul *Tahrir* of 1546', in Warburg, G. R. and Gilbar, G. G. (eds), *Studies in Islamic Society*, Haifa: Haifa University Press/Leiden: E. J. Brill, 1984, pp. 9–27.

105 In [Rūmī, Jalāl al-Dīn], *Discourses of Rūmī*, trans. Arberry, A. J., London: John Murray, 1961, p. 114.

106 The inscriptions refer to Fāṭima's constitution into *waqf* in the year 410/1019–20 of a casket and a magnificent bound Qur'an, quoted in Roy, B. and Poinssot, P., *Inscriptions Arabes*, vol. 2, fasc. 1, pp. 27–32.

107 Female investment strategy through *waqfs* was used not only in widowhood but, as in the case of the fifteenth-century wife of a Mamlūk sulṭān, also upon showing signs of the husband's failing fortunes: see Petry, C., 'Class', pp. 135–6.

108 al-Safadī, *al-Wafi*, vol. 24, no. 188, pp. 186–7.

109 For shrines as places of 'national' pilgrimages, see a reference to the twelfth-century pilgrimage guide by al-Harawī, *Kitāb al-Ishārāt*, in Taylor, C. S., *In the Vicinity of the Righteous: Ziyara and the Veneration of Muslim Saints in Late Medieval Egypt*, Leiden: E. J. Brill, 1999, p. 4, n. 10. For revenues from ʿAlīd shrines, see Rāghib, Y., 'Al-Sayyida Nafīsa', pp. 32–3.

110 On the social mobility of female court entourage in Byzantium, see Talbot Rice, D., *The Byzantines*, London: Thames and Hudson, 1962, pp. 103–4.

111 Ibn Taghrībirdī, *al-Nujūm*, 1933 edn, vol. 4, p. 192.

CHAPTER

6

OUTSIDE THE PALACE WALLS: DAILY LIFE

1. 'Sects' and the City: Landscape and Religious Diversity in the Fatimid Capital and its Environs

For almost a century following the foundation of Cairo, Egypt enjoyed a period of economic prosperity that, coupled with political and administrative stability, contributed, notwithstanding a broader demographic decline that had affected Egypt and Syria since the eighth century, to a relative growth in urban population. The famous Fatimid physician Ibn Ridwan provides us with a vivid description of eleventh-century living conditions amongst the people inhabiting the main sections of the Fatimid capital: Fustat, al-Qarafa and Cairo. Fustat is portrayed as the most crowded and worst part of the city to live in, owing to the poor quality of air made stagnant by the narrowness of the alleys flanked by high-storey buildings, particularly around the 'Amr b. al-'As Mosque, and contaminated by rotting carcasses of animals and rubbish in the streets. Pollution extended to the water supply, as people would deposit animal faeces and sewage into the stretch of the Nile nearer to Fustat, to the extent of affecting the flow of the river. If Ibn Ridwan was unimpressed by the sanitary conditions of Fustat, Nasir-i Khusraw was by contrast enthusiastic about its vibrancy. He described the market of the lamps by the 'Amr mosque as unequalled in any country, with some of its alleys covered and lit by lamps during the day. Almost 200 warehouses sold works of art from all parts of the world, including inlaid artefacts, rock crystal, delicate pottery, metallic lustreware, transparent green glass, elephant tusks, exotic birds, all sorts of fruits and vegetables and abundant honey and sugar. Traders were reported to sell at fixed prices and moved around on rented donkeys.[1] As for Cairo, Ibn Ridwan considered it a better place than

Fustat because the buildings were not so high, and the lanes were cleaner and broader and less littered with rubbish. As Cairo was remote from the main course of the Nile, people would drink mainly well water, arguably cleaner than that of the river.[2]

Ibn Ridwan describes al-Qarafa as one of the best areas of the capital to live in because of the good quality of the air. Although typically associated with its famed cemetery, it would be limiting to assume that al-Qarafa was simply a place for the dead. Especially since the ninth-century construction of the Ibn Tulun aqueduct and the addition of new water works initiated by, or expanded under, the Fatimids, the Qarafa was a place for the living, too, so much so that its permanent population was referred to as Qarafiyya. The building of mosques, palace-like pavilions, water cisterns, public fountains, ovens and mills[3] added to the living and residential component that is still witnessed today, further north, in the Northern Cemetery's densely populated 'City of the Dead' (almost one million people at the end of the 1990s). An indication of al-Qarafa as a lively gathering place is offered by al-Maqrizi, who reports that in Fatimid times the area around the Qarafa *qaṣr* built by Durzan became a favourite meeting point during festivals and celebrations for the caliphal palace entourage, as well as the owners of the houses of the 'non-resident palace employees', male and female.[4]

Outside the Fatimid capital, the physical landscape reflected the religious diversity of the population. In Fustat, a number of churches enjoyed periods of relative wealth and a few, sporadic, periods of destruction and desecration. Synagogues and at least a Jewish slaughterhouse were legally protected. In the Qarafa area, there were Christian monasteries and tombs, while the shrines of 'saints' were visited by Christians as well as Muslims. The interaction in Fatimid Egypt between Christians and Jews, and between them and Muslims, was therefore more widespread and complex than the sources may at first lead us to believe. On the one hand, the voices are recorded of religious and legal personalities from each community who disapproved of inter-religious mixing and strove to keep physical, dietary and ritual boundaries among the urban population in order to safeguard religious identity. Whether for theological or political reasons, the historians who reported such voices took the opportunity to express their own implicit or explicit rebuke of instances of Muslim women mixing with Christian or Jewish men, and vice versa.[5] In the marketplace, one of the tasks of the *muḥtasib* (market inspector) was indeed to enforce the law of gender and religious separation and segregation at every level. Within the context of ritual purity, al-Qadi al-Nuʿman, on the basis of Jaʿfarite tradition, even remarked that it was inappropriate for Muslims to perform *ṣalāt* in clothes tailored by non-Muslims.[6] By the same account, an eleventh-century Jewish Community Statute dealing with the pilgrimage site of Dammuh, south of Fustat, formally prohibited Jewish men and women to take with them non-Jews to the site.[7] During the time of al-Hakim, laws were issued to enforce religious separation in cemeteries and other public areas, such as the *ḥammāms*, which non-Muslims could attend only on specific days. An extreme expression of enforcement of religious boundaries was the imposition on Christians and Jews to wear identity badges, to keep to the use of specific colours, and in general to maintain a low profile by wearing modest clothes. However, apart from these exceptional measures, in practice, it was hard to distinguish a Jew or a Christian from a Muslim, whether man or woman.[8]

Inter-mingling between Muslims and non-Muslims was widespread indeed. Within the court, the imam-caliphs occasionally married non-Muslims and their children were breast-fed by non-Muslim nurses. Positions such as those of vizier, military commander and court physician were often filled by Christians and Jews. Non-Muslim secretaries, attendants and servants were among the extensive palace personnel. Outside the court, Jewish and Christian merchants and artisans, as well as the many Christians employed in the prosperous textile industries in the delta region, were in regular contact with court officials and, at times, with the most powerful members of the caliphal family. Interaction did not stop at the formal level of employment: the Fatimid imam-caliphs are reported to have publicly attended Christian festivals with their women and to have by-passed in some cases even the religious rules of separation at burial.[9] In turn, Jewish and Christian officials would act as intermediaries between the court and the populace, to the extent that they would generously give charity to the Muslim population in times of hardship. For instance, in 450/1058, Ibn 'Usfura, the Jewish *wakīl* of Rasad, devolved charity and clothes to the poor and destitute who were living in the Qarafa. They assumed that the donations were coming from al-Mustansir and his mother but, on discovering the identity of their true benefactor, they expressed amazement and gratefully prayed for God to bestow blessings upon him.[10]

Whether the result of religious tolerance or political opportunism,[11] the overall benign attitude of the Fatimids towards religious minorities did not pass unnoticed among the Egyptian Muslim population. In more than one instance the people publicly showed dissatisfaction at the appointment of Christians and Jews to high offices, and occasionally, but fiercely, retaliated against them. The harsh persecutory measures of the imam-caliph al-Hakim towards religious minorities ought to be evaluated also within the context of such manifestations of popular discontent. Be that as it may, from documentary and legal sources we learn that in Fatimid Egypt Muslims, Christians and Jews did indeed live side by side, rented houses and shops from one another, shared ownership of houses[12] and were business and trade partners, with Jewish physicians treating Muslim and Christian patients and vice versa. This is not to say that the members of each community did not keep to ritual and dietary laws, as proven, for example, by the existence of Jewish slaughterhouses in Fustat. Neither does it mean that they intermarried; in fact, there are no references to inter-faith marriages between Christians and Jews, as they were, and in some cases theoretically still are, prohibited by their respective religious laws. Conversions across Christianity and Judaism were also not allowed, even though there were some famous exceptions. Much more numerous are the cases of conversion to Islam, for instance, that of a Jewish man who had converted but remained married to his Jewish wife, who, according to the *sharī'a*, could keep her own religion.[13]

The indigenous Christian community of Egypt, the Copts, had been granted, ever since the seventh century, the status of a protected community (*ahl al-dhimma*). With the expansion of the textile industry in the delta region during the ninth century, the Copts became increasingly associated with the manufacture '... of linen which our women spin and we weave'.[14] During the Fatimid era, the textile cities of Tinnis and Damietta continued to have a majority Christian population. Like the Jews, the Copts underwent the inexorable process of Arabisation and, even though they continued to use Coptic as their liturgical language, by the tenth century both started to use Arabic for their literary production. By the thirteenth century, Arabic had overtaken Coptic in literature and correspondence, while, in everyday spoken language, Copts remained bilingual.[15]

Under the Fatimids, Copts reached their zenith during al-'Aziz's caliphate, with one of his wives known to have been a Melchite Copt. The Muslim population resented al-'Aziz giving permission to rebuild ruined churches outside Fustat[16] and, more broadly, his employment of high dignitaries from among Christians and Jews. Under al-'Aziz's successor came also the Copts' nadir. Between the years 394/1004 and 404/1013, al-Hakim pursued a policy of persecution of Christians and Jews, characterised by forced conversions, the razing to the ground of places of worship and confiscation. But Copts were not the only Christians in Fatimid Egypt. A recent study of Fatimid Armenians has uncovered the interplay of another minority, allegedly some 30,000, which differed from the Copts in being a community of immigrants, many of whom converted to Islam. Islamisation must have been particularly high among the Armenian troops, who had entered Egypt with Badr al-Jamali; but a record pointing to their Christian identity is only found from the time of al-Hafiz.[17]

There is much wider and more detailed information about the Jewish communities in Egypt during the Fatimid era, thanks to the nineteenth-century discovery of thousands of documents, mainly dated from between the eleventh and thirteenth centuries, which were preserved in the Ben Ezra synagogue in Cairo. Known as the Geniza collection, these documents provide an invaluable contribution to the history of the Fustat community of Jewish merchants, numbering perhaps a few hundred families. Analysis of these records is still in progress but a wealth of information can be gathered from the seminal work of

Solomon Goitein. By revealing the social, commercial, legal and ritual history of the community as a whole, these records also shed light, through marriage contracts, legal correspondence and private letters, on the everyday life and activities of Jewish women living in Fatimid and Ayyubid Fustat. We are informed about the items of their dowry trousseaux, their wishes, marriage clauses and professions. Given the mercantile nature of the Jewish community in Fustat, there were a number of Jewish marriages contracted with spouses away from Egypt, as far as the Yemen and Spain. Some Jewish women were in a good enough position to stipulate conditions in their contracts about monogamy and the right to ask for divorce, but others must have considered themselves lucky to find a husband at all.[18] What hanged over them all was the Jewish practice of *agunah*, the condition of a separated wife who is not officially divorced, hence cannot re-marry because her husband is withdrawing the divorce document. Another legal difference between Jewish wives and their Muslim neighbours refers to the stipulations about their earnings derived from employment, which traditionally in Jewish law belong to the husband.

Like Muslim and Christian women, Jewesses must have spent a good deal of their time spinning and embroidering: the items of marriage trousseaux contained many plain textiles, which were presumably meant to be embroidered after marriage. Female professions varied from the essential services of 'doctor', midwife and nurse to other services such as that of the *muʿallima* (usually embroidery teacher) or trader. As with Muslim women, there were Jewess body-washers to take care of Jewish rites of death and burial. Jewish women were not housebound, and seclusion applied almost exclusively to the elite. Jewesses were out and about in the markets; they went at least once a week to the bathhouse, travelled to attend the synagogue, to visit the shrines and to go to court.[19]

Notwithstanding their negative attitudes towards women in waged professions, most Jews looked favourably on women entrepreneurs. The most famous, and the most often mentioned in the Geniza documents, was Karima, the daughter of Amram, also known as al-Wuhsha (lit. the broker). The daughter of a 'banker' who had moved from Alexandria to Fustat, her life was an eventful one. Married at an early age to a man of limited means, in 490/1095 she divorced him while pregnant by another man. Because of her illicit liaison, she was expelled from her local synagogue. She also had a daughter, who is reported to have owned a house. For business, al-Wuhsha mixed with men and women and, judging from her will, she acquired considerable wealth during her lifetime. She left gold and money to her relatives and piously bestowed a tenth of her estate to charitable institutions. The lion's share of her wealth, however, went to her only son; to his natural father, she left nothing, except for 'two promissory notes on debts … of 80 *dīnārs*'.[20] She also left a very large sum of money for her funeral provisions. She certainly knew her worth!

2. Ideal Homes and Harsh Realities

In Cairo the houses, shops, baths and caravanserais belonged to the imam-caliph, who charged monthly rents.[21] In areas adjacent to the capital living space was plentiful, rents were low but house maintenance was expensive. Many houses were privately owned and, according to several Geniza documents, for most upper- and middle-class women owning houses represented an important form of investment. In fact, rather than being traded as a physical unit, houses changed hands as if they were divided into numerical shares of which a private investor, whether male or female, could buy as many as were available and depending on how much he or she intended to invest. Most houses would have kitchens, a few would have bathing facilities and almost none would have a fixed bedroom, as sleeping arrangements would change according to the season. A well-to-do dwelling would have a 'secret door' opening onto a back alley, through which the women of the house would go in and out.[22]

Ibn Ridwan provides a list of good housekeeping guidelines that gives an insight into the ideal living conditions to which his upper- and middle-class contemporaries aspired. He recommends that houses and living rooms should be spacious, to allow good air circulation and sunlight, that they should be tiled with marble and paved or plastered with gypsum. Floors should be cleaned regularly and, while in hot weather they ought to be covered with cool mats, in winter they should be covered with warm carpets, felts, silk brocade and wool. The less privileged could use affordable lining such as tattered mats and pelts of rams. In hot weather, water should be profusely sprinkled around the house, fountains and pools should be filled and water-skin containers as well as silver, lead, ceramic and earthenware vessels should be placed in different corners of the house. As a cooling device, the outside of the house should be sheltered with many fans and canvas tents. The living rooms ought to face north and furnishing should include cooling aromatics such as violet, rose, narcissus, wild thyme and mandrake. The interiors should ideally be perfumed with camphor, rose water, sandalwood and fragrant oils. In cold weather, rooms should be equipped with stoves and furnished with branches of 'warm' flowers such as narcissus, thyme, citron, camomile, lily of the valley and jasmine. The most appropriate home deodorants would be ambergris, wood of aloe and spices like cardamom, frankincense and mastik.[23]

The expansion of international commerce in the Mediterranean and beyond meant that city markets afforded a greater availability, variety and turnover of products, thus affecting the balance of the local economy as well as, broadly speaking, the state of people's health and quality of life. By the same account, however, the affluence of the Fatimid elite belied a fragile domestic economy. Indeed, Egypt's urban prosperity was also regularly dented by the effects of short-term but vicious political and economic crises that, when combined with, or provoked by, unfavourable circumstances such as poor climate, poor performance of the Nile and revolts, precipitated the country into famines and epidemics. Because such occurrences hit large sections of the population irrespective of gender, age and status, the imam-caliph and his viziers resorted at times to the ad hoc implementation of draconian economic, social and health measures in order to either respond to these crises, or to prevent their reoccurrence.

a. Women's Restrictions under al-Hakim

One of the most intriguing aspects of Fatimid history relates to al-Hakim's imposition of severe restrictions on the mobility and visibility of women, ranging from limiting their use of public baths to going out altogether. Often depicted as a 'Nero of the Islamic world', many anti-Isma'ili historians reported, out of context and with exaggerations, al-Hakim's seemingly odd decrees targeting women, Jews and Christians, and prohibiting the consumption of specific food products and the celebration of Christian festivals. Their emphasis on such measures contributed to an interpretation of al-Hakim's domestic policies as being dictated by insanity. By contrast, Isma'ili sources cast an ominous silence on this controversial aspect of al-Hakim's reign. Recently, however, scholars have sought to reappraise his reign in more objective terms and to evaluate al-Hakim's policies against the economic, social and doctrinal complexities of his time.

Al-Hakim's earliest-known set of restrictions imposed on women dates to 391/1000–1, when the imam-caliph forbade them to go out in the evening, as he perceived the streets of Cairo at night to be more crowded with women than men. In 394/1003–4, women were ordered not to unveil and not to cry at tombs and during funerals. A year later they were forbidden to adorn themselves, to go to the *ḥammām* unless completely covered and to show their faces during funerals. In 399/1008–9, al-Hakim forbade the installation of grids used by women during their visits to the cemetery and two years later he prohibited them to go to the *ḥammām* altogether. In 402/1012, the imam-caliph prevented women from going out after the evening prayer, from going to the cemetery, gathering on the shores of the Nile and going on boats with men. The following year he barred women from singing and sitting along the street and, in 404/1013, he freed all his male and female slaves, but also forbade all women, young and old, to go out at all. To ensure compliance with his orders, he is reported to have banned in the same year the manufacture of women's shoes. Again in 405/1014, al-Hakim imposed strict restrictions on the mobility of women and, intermittently, restrictions must have remained in place until the end of his reign. Chroniclers reported stories of women who, having disobeyed the caliphal orders, were walled alive inside public baths, as well as stories about some of al-Hakim's concubines and *umm al-walads* being placed in crates and drowned in the Nile.

The sanctions targeting women went hand in hand with a series of seemingly contradictory decrees that affected different areas of social and public life as a whole. Between 395/1004 and 404/1013, al-Hakim issued a number of edicts, some of which he later revoked and re-issued, concerning doctrinal matters such as cursing the companions of the Prophet and prohibiting the performance of particular prayers and the celebration of the Epiphany, as well as more mundane matters such as the consumption of certain foods, and the playing of music along with the drinking and production of wine. Also, al-Hakim halted the manufacture of his clothes in Tinnis and Damietta, exiled all the singers and musicians, ordered that *zabīb* and honey (ingredients needed for wine production) be thrown into the Nile, and decreed that Christians and Jews should wear distinctive items of clothing and not ride horses.[24] Finally, al-Hakim ordered the destruction of some Christian churches and convents in Egypt and Sinai and, famously, he was deemed responsible for the destruction in 400/1009–10 of the Church of the Holy Sepulchre in Jerusalem.

Al-Hakim was not to be the only ruler to impose restrictions on women. In 414/1023, under his successor al-Zahir, with Sitt al-Mulk still acting as regent, women were specifically prohibited to go out in the evening in the alleys of al-Qarafa, and men as well as women were banned from gathering in areas such as Giza, Jazira and al-Qarafa, as well as singing publicly.[25] A few centuries later, under the Mamluks, the sultan Barsbay, in conjunction with an outbreak of plague, forbade women, but not if slaves, from going to the markets and decreed that women could go to the *ḥammām* only at night!

The appearance from the late tenth century of legal literature specifically dealing with women, whether Muslim or not, might point to a perceived need on the part of the rulers, or the jurists and scholars working under them, to regulate the private and public behaviour of women. The jurist Ibrahim b. al-Qasim al-Qayrawani (d. 425/1034), who had joined the Fatimid court at the time of al-Hakim, wrote the now lost *Kitāb al-Nisā'* (The Book of Women), and it is arguably to al-Hakim that is attributed the commissioning of epistles, some of which specifically dealing with women's conduct. The twelfth-century 'Abbasid Ibn al-Jawzi also wrote *Aḥkām al-nisā'*, a *ḥadīth* collection relating to women's conduct in ritual, and their public and private behaviour as wives, mothers and daughters. During the Mamluk period, the fourteenth-century Egyptian Maliki jurist Ibn al-Hajj, in his *Kitāb Madkhal al-shar' al-sharīf* (Introduction to the Noble Conduct), strongly opposed the presence of women in the marketplace. He lamented that women went out more often than men and recommended that, if they really need to go out, they should be totally covered and make themselves inconspicuous by walking along walls. He condemned women who dared to sunbathe, scantily dressed, on the banks of the Nile, and those who went on boats. Ibn al-Hajj advised that the husband should shop on behalf of the wife and, in particular, that women should avoid clothes and jewellery shops. Thus Ibn al-Hajj frowned upon female outings: on Mondays they would visit the tomb of Sayyid-na al-Husayn and then go shopping in the market for no reason; on Tuesdays they would party with friends; on Wednesdays they would visit the shrine of Sayyida Nafisa and stop at the market of Old Cairo with the excuse of having to satisfy their needs; and on Sundays they would go back to the old market. In keeping with well-established sentiments rooted in some *ḥadīth* literature, Ibn al-Hajj expressed indignation at women visiting cemeteries; he was also appalled by women who went en masse onto the streets and to markets on the occasion of Christian festivals, when they bought perfumes and jewellery.[26]

Al-Hakim's restrictions on mobility did not apply exclusively to women and were often enforced on men as well; moreover, they did not apply to all women and, in practice, only affected the urban population. Aristocratic, high-class and middle-class women would very rarely go out anyway, as this would not be befitting to their status. Their affairs were conducted by their husbands, their agents, their male and female servants, as well as by labourers and slaves who would, therefore, form the bulk of the crowd in city streets. Among lower-class women, certain categories were exempt from restrictions and licenses to circulate would be issued to widows, the washers of corpses, spinsters, paupers who needed to work to support themselves, women appearing in court and to women undertaking pilgrimages or other journeys.[27]

Besides the 'insanity' theory, other hypotheses have been put forward as to the reasons for al-Hakim's targeting of women in particular. His controversial measures have been linked to the caliph's personal inclination towards *zuhd* (asceticism) and to his attempt at restoring morality by translating into practice his vision of a stricter adherence to Islamic ethics.[28] Indeed, throughout his reign, al-Hakim eagerly enforced the *sharīʿa* upon his subjects, and measures such as the prohibition of wine production and its consumption, as well as the curbing of occasions for merriment and leisure, fit his policy. During his time, prostitution was rife in Cairo and Fustat, and it is not unlikely that al-Hakim's restrictions on women's mobility were partly imposed as an expedient to curb the practice of that profession; his prohibitions against holding festivals and engaging in leisurely gatherings might also have served as preventative measures against promiscuity. Al-Hakim's anti-women stance has also been linked to the uneasy relation he entertained with his powerful half-sister, Sitt al-Mulk, and other women of his household. While all the above factors might have contributed to al-Hakim's stance on women, they do not fully justify what appears to have been the imam-caliph's adoption of a systematic policy aimed at 'controlling' women in mainly three areas: visitation of cemeteries, participation in entertainment and frequentation of *ḥammāms* and markets. Participation in these activities was usually inter-related and promoted a potentially problematic occurrence: crowding. Of particular interest in this respect is al-Musabbihi's frequent reference to the mass participation of people at the funerals of a number of society ladies, such as the daughters of the *qāḍī* of Cairo, of those of Ibn al-Daqqaq al-Shahid and of Ibn al-Bakkar, as well as the wife of Abu 'l-Hasan al-Baghdadi.[29] Crowd behaviour impacted on public order, on public health and on circulation of money, that is, on domains that demanded careful monitoring within the context of a volatile economic, social and political climate such as the one during al-Hakim's reign.

During the first half of al-Hakim's rule, fierce famines, followed by epidemics, occurred with alarming regularity.[30] Medieval societies shared an understanding of the occurrence of famine and other natural disasters as being the consequence of a decline in faith and social mores. It was this view that underpinned the rationale for women's mobility. However, al-Hakim's reasons for restricting women's movement might lie elsewhere.[31] In his treatise on the prevention of illnesses occurring in Egypt, Ibn Ridwan provides a lucid analysis of domino-effect scenarios leading to famines and epidemics such as the ones he had witnessed during and after al-Hakim's reign. In illustrating these scenarios, Ibn Ridwan argues that, when pests affect plants, crops fail, prices rise and people are forced to change their eating habits. He adds that, as a large number of people increase their consumption of particular foods at one time, dyspepsia increases and illness occurs. This scenario would typically occur at festivals, when crowding and high consumption of food would converge. Ibn Ridwan also explains that epidemics may happen as a result of people's fear of the ruler, when they suffer prolonged sleeplessness due to worry about their safety. He argues that, under such pressures, people could become violent and if, in addition to that, they sense that famine is looming, they panic and hoard food. Almost certainly referring to the devastating combination of events coinciding with the revolt of Abu Rakwa in 395–7/1005–7, when some 30,000 men lost their lives, Ibn Ridwan cites the occurrence of a war causing such extensive loss of life that decaying corpses polluted the water and the air. He adds that, on that occasion, the Egyptians suffered greatly out of fear of the enemy combined with high prices and poor Nile performance. As a result, famine occurred with consequent high mortality.[32]

Though indirectly, Ibn Ridwan's analysis presents us with clues that may be useful in explaining al-Hakim's measures against women, whose mobility could have been perceived as a source of public hazard. The frequent reference in sources to streets or markets being crowded with more women than men points to the perception that ordinary women were clearly noticeable occupants of the capital's social and commercial landscape. Whether real or perceived, their overwhelming presence could have, at least in theory, consequences for public health; as the typical purchasers of food and household provisions, women in markets meant 'high demand'. By default, their presence could encourage speculative operations on the part of merchants, who would either inflate prices by limiting the availability of foodstuffs through hoarding, or exhaust their stock by engaging in price wars. Excessively high prices would in turn cause retail products to go unsold and, due to the climatic conditions of Egypt, unsold stock and hoarded foodstuffs would deteriorate fast.[33] On the other hand, extremely low prices would render merchants unable to acquire stock because the wholesaler (that is, the caliph) would be reluctant to make it available to the retailers when his return from its sale to them would be lower than the amount he had originally invested; inevitably, unsold wholesale stock would rot.[34] In either case, the outcome could be famine and epidemics.

Al-Hakim knew these scenarios well. In 397/1007, he denounced and paraded corrupt bakers who, following a massive devaluation of the *dīnār*, speculated on the sale of bread. In 399/1009, in response to the people's panic call for help, as famine loomed owing to the poor performance of the Nile, al-Hakim forced all those who had hoarded wheat to pile it in the streets and organised its rationing and fair sale, thus forcing the prices down.[35]

A statement by the thirteenth-century historian Bar Hebraeus adds to the view that al-Hakim's restrictions upon women's movement were motivated by his intention to control market forces. Bar Hebraeus stated that the merchants, who were affected by the lack of female presence in the markets due to the imam-caliph's measures, complained to al-Hakim, who replied that he was limiting female circulation to safeguard the economy of the country. To appease traders and allow women to obtain provisions, al-Hakim then ordered the merchants to sell their goods house-to-house by putting them in containers or baskets. The women could see the goods from behind a curtain or door, take what they needed and pay by placing the money in the baskets.[36]

Many of al-Hakim's restrictions appear to fit with a public health 'programme' that, in keeping with the medical knowledge available at the time, aimed at preventing or remedying the occurrence of famine and the spreading of disease. Though reprehensible, al-Hakim's draconian measures seem to have been effective, as, from 399/1009 to 415/1024, Egypt was virtually free from major famines and epidemics. Interestingly, al-Zahir (or Sitt al-Mulk on his behalf) had inaugurated his reign by restoring greater freedom of women's mobility. For instance, the palace slave-girls, escorted by the eunuchs, were known to undertake shopping trips to jewellery, money-exchange and carpet shops in Fustat. Ordinary women, too, would roam in the markets more freely and at times, one could say, carelessly if, in 415/1024 alone, at least two women were reported to have died in the streets after being run over by camels. But this renewed freedom of circulation was not continuous. In Rajab 414/1023, a *sijill* had been read in the markets re-introducing the restrictions of movement for women and men, which, significantly, coincided with an increasing difficulty in making bread in Cairo. Riots took place and fraud occurred, once more, with the sale at inflated prices of bread sold wet to increase its weight. To rescue the situation, a group of state officers made the wheat reserves available to the people and some bakers were fined and denounced. Restrictions were imposed on millers, who were only allowed to supply the bakers with daily rations, some shops were closed and some merchants arrested. However, by Dhu 'l-Hijja 415/1024, full-scale famine had erupted, and angry and hungry women and men had gone on a rampage, pillaging houses and attacking the police with stones.[37]

During al-Hakim's reign, the occurrence of famines and epidemics was entangled with the so-called 'silver famine', that is, a monetary crisis caused by severe fluctuations in the value of the silver *dirham*. Monetary crises were linked to the complex interplay of adverse causes, ranging from the unpredictability of the Nile, an excessive inflow of gold in the markets, instability in the international political and economic scene brought about by revolts in North Africa, Palestine and the Hijaz to the uneasy trade relations with Byzantium. Al-Maqrizi states that al-Hakim was the first to introduce the use of silver *dirhams* in Egypt for the purchase of everyday goods.[38] His statement is somewhat inaccurate, in that silver coinage already existed in Egypt under al-Hakim's predecessors, but al-Maqrizi appears to be accurate with regard to the use of the *dirham* as common currency during al-Hakim's reign. Thanks to the exploitation of gold mines in Nubia and Sudan, Fatimid Egypt was rich in gold but, lacking silver mines, had to rely on silver imports. This meant that, should the demand for silver *dirhams* escalate, either the treasury had to import more silver or the weight and purity of the *dirhams* in circulation had to be reduced, with inevitable devaluation. The monetary turmoil of the year 397/1006–7 well illustrates this scenario. In that year the Fatimid Treasury was forced to increase the minting of the *dirham*. The *dīnār–dirham* exchange ratio rose to 1:34 *dirhams* and prices dropped, with an unsettling effect on the populace. The demand for *dirhams* kept rising until the Treasury issued 20 crates full of 'new' *dirhams* to be distributed among the money-changers. A *sijill* was read about the introduction of this 'new' *dirham*, ruling that it was only possible to trade with it alone. Those in possession of 'old' ones had three days to return them to the Treasury. People rebelled because they would get only one new *dirham* in exchange for four old ones. Eventually the *dīnār–dirham* exchange was fixed at 1:18.[39] This monetary crisis was the outcome of the effects of natural calamity combined with high military spending sustained by the *dawla* to crush the revolt launched from

North Africa by Abu Rakwa. Similar monetary crises occurred in 394/1003 and in 395/1005, when the exchange of the *dīnār* was also frozen. For the year 402/1011, al-Maqrizi noted that there were many *dirhams* in circulation and, significantly, this remark appears in conjunction with information on the sanctioning of prohibitions.[40] In 403/1012, al-Hakim increased custom duties on all the goods arriving at ports and markets, such as fresh dates, soap, silk clothes and other commodities.[41]

Throughout his reign, al-Hakim attempted to secure economic stability in several ways. To control prices in times of shortage, he imposed rationing; in times of over-abundance, he curtailed the excessive offer of products by either forbidding their use and consumption or by having them destroyed. In 400/1010–11, in order to attract cash, al-Hakim tried to promote the Fatimid capital to the rank of holy city and to make it an obligatory stop for pilgrims by masterminding the successful 'transfer' of Ja'far al-Sadiq's relics from Madina to Cairo.[42] On several occasions, he resorted to a policy of confiscation targeted at high officials, Christians and the rich women of his household. All these measures, however, had only palliative effect on the excessive circulation of silver coinage – that is, the currency used by a large section of the population for most everyday transactions,[43] and particularly by women, who were the principal buyers of goods for daily use. It is possible that, by limiting typical forms of mass gathering and restricting the movement of women that went with them, al-Hakim sought to find one more way to 'pace' the circulation of the *dirham* in a way that the regime's economy could sustain. However, if limiting the circulation of women might well have resulted, at convenient times, in decreased circulation of money, the downside of this strategy was that products would remain unsold, unsold food would rot, severe shortages would occur, prices would rise and famine would erupt. Al-Hakim's shifting between the enforcement and the relaxation of measures is therefore a reflection of this arduous economic balancing act.

Al-Hakim's restrictions were not passively accepted by the people; indeed, they produced the effect of triggering the first clear manifestation of women's demand for freedom of movement. That al-Hakim had to resort to severe restrictive measures points to the fact that the norm for many women was to go outdoors unveiled, to drink wine and mix liberally with men, as indeed al-Musabbihi reported for the year 415/1024.[44] Women must have enjoyed a relaxed approach to life that they would not give up easily; but in 404/1013, women who did not comply with al-Hakim's orders were punished by beatings and imprisonment.[45] In 410/1019, in protest against al-Hakim, people stormed the shops and burned city areas while women 'went out shamelessly to the 'Atiq Mosque without any resistance'.[46] Women resorted to ruses to circumvent al-Hakim's prohibitions. According to Ibn al-Jawzi, in 405/1014, a woman who was very much in love with a man but was impeded by al-Hakim's decrees to see him, appealed to the chief judge Malik b. Sa'id al-Fariqi. She made him believe that she wanted to go to see her only brother, who was blind. The *qāḍī* agreed and allowed her to go out, escorted by two men, but when the woman's husband arrived home in the evening and found out from a neighbour what had happened, he went to complain to the *qāḍī* and to al-Hakim. The story goes that the caliph was so furious at having being fooled that he enforced even stricter rules on women. Meanwhile, the woman in question was burned and her lover beaten.[47] The anecdote is interesting in that it shows that women could, and did, petition against the caliphal decrees and that a 'procedure' was in place to handle such cases.

That women would hand petitions directly to the caliph must have been a common occurrence if, in at least two narrative contexts, popular discontent was conveyed through what turned out to be not a real person but a puppet in the shape of a woman. Al-Maqrizi reports that, in 410/1020, some inhabitants of Fustat made with palm leaves a puppet in the shape of a woman, covered it with a cloak and attached to its hand a sheet with a list of insults addressed to al-Hakim, cursing him for his prohibition against women's outings. When the caliph passed through that area, thinking that a woman was handing him a petition, he took the sheet. On reading the insults, the imam-caliph became enraged and ordered that the woman be fetched. When he discovered that it was just a puppet, his anger grew further and, in retaliation to the affront, he ordered Fustat to be put to the torch.[48] According to some sources, it was al-Hakim who instructed his black troops to burn Fustat, while others claim that the troops acted without his permission and that the imam-caliph ordered his soldiers to stop. Be that as it may, the troops were reported to have committed such 'shameful acts against the women folk of the town ... [that they] killed themselves for fear of disgrace'.[49]

3. Free and Bonding Agents: Free and Slave Women at Work

The facts of life of ordinary people, especially women, rarely attracted the attention of medieval chroniclers, whose works were mainly sponsored or commissioned by the court, and hence essentially concerned with its affairs. Therefore, while there are numerous direct as well as indirect references to working women in the service of the court, information about female work beyond the palace walls is less forthcoming, and, when found, it is at best incidental and often anecdotal or sensational in nature.[50] Despite the fragmentary character of references to working women, it can nevertheless be stated that throughout the Islamic world, whether in Baghdad or in Cairo, ordinary women were active in most working sectors, such as agriculture, midwifery, the food and textile industries, the social services, including welfare and support, prisons and tax collection, as well as more menial work. Many of the issues linked to the working conditions of women in medieval Islam are still conjectural; for example, questions about the amount of women's wages, the location of their work and of their 'professional' training are as yet not fully answered. As far as wages are concerned, one can safely assume that, on the whole, women earned much less than their male counterparts. This was certainly the case in other medieval societies, where, for example, women in the textile industry or as domestic servants were among the lowest-paid labourers.[51] On an informal basis, but still presumably paid, women would work by assisting others on a number of social services, such as acting as go-betweens, as marriage brokers or even as marriage counsellors! In Zirid Ifriqiya, for example, among ordinary people, a trustworthy woman (*amīna*) would act as conciliator for a couple having marital problems by going to live in the spouses' house, in order to observe them and guide them through this difficult period.[52]

In medieval sources, in contrast with the limited information on practical details about working women, references are found about the attitude towards them of some sections of society. Working women, especially those working outside the house, were held in contempt by many scholars, by some historians, by the religious authorities and, at times, by the rulers themselves. In reality any society, whether urban or rural, could not function without them. Even though there are references to women working for remuneration, the full extent of their participation in the working arena will probably never be known. This is because of the social stigma attached to the family, specifically to the husband or father, by having a woman contributing to the family income: that she worked for money indicated that the male members were not capable of maintaining or supporting their females. In theory, a Muslim woman could, according to *sharīʿa* law, ask for divorce if her husband failed to support her. Consequently, it goes without saying that working women were not something to write home about, even less to record in the history books. Even in the private correspondence of the Jewish merchants based in Fustat, it emerges that 'a wife earning money by her work was a disgrace and a loss of face for her husband'.[53] Judging from those professions practised by Jewish women, which are recorded in the Geniza documents, many Jewish husbands must have experienced such a 'loss of face'!

The most widespread female activity was spinning and weaving. Either as a pastime or out of necessity, both princesses and pauper women were involved in this pursuit. Even a Fatimid princess as wealthy as Rashida is known to have 'earned her living from spinning yarn', and the popularity of this pastime must have become very widespread in the Fatimid harems, if the vizier al-Afdal is reported to have supplied ladies and concubines of his harem with two boxes of golden needles.[54] As for ordinary women, literary and documentary sources supply evidence of a distinction between those women who were spinning for personal or family use and those who were spinning for wages.[55] Typical, but not exclusive, of the latter category would be the spinsters, the widows, the divorcees and the poor – that is, those women who would need to earn a living for themselves because of the lack of male financial support. Indeed, the law was adjusted to deal with such a reality. For example, a legal ruling was issued to decree whether or not spinning was permitted during the month of Ramadan, when, because of fasting, nothing was supposed to be put in the mouth, not even thread. In most cases lawyers recognised the need, especially for poor women, to carry on working and allowed them to do so when it could be demonstrated that their own livelihood depended on their work.[56] Whether spinning for personal use or for wages, women did so mainly in the privacy of the home. There is evidence that working for wages at home was a cause of concern for the authorities, especially in view of the workers' fiscal accountability.[57]

Two professions exclusively practised by women for financial remuneration were midwifery and nursing. Fully acknowledged in medical, legal, historical and *adab* literature, the services of the midwife (*qābila*) and the wetnurse (*dāya*) were considered essential services across all levels of society. Despite the existence of copious manuals detailing all aspects relating to the theory of these professions, it is unclear whether, in practice, midwives underwent 'formal' training, and if so, how the training was carried out. It is generally assumed that the midwife was a free woman; it also appears that, in post-Fatimid times, midwives might have worn some distinctive clothing similar to professional uniforms.[58] The practice of midwifery was fraught with legal implications, as the midwife could become the sole witness to occurrences such as the death of a mother at childbirth or a stillbirth. As for wetnurses, the conditions for hiring their services were regulated by *sharīʿa* law, and a number of legal sources even provide in detail the terms to be specified in their contract of hire. For example, in North Africa under the Zirids, wetnurses were contractually entitled to bedding and a full set of clothes and linen, in addition to good food and living conditions.[59]

A society where in theory – and, in several instances, in practice – gender separation was legally required, needed women to maintain, and work within, gender boundaries. Some documented female professions during the Fatimid age are linked to the practicalities involved in the running of services used exclusively by women. Hence, in the *ḥammāms* attended by women there would be female fee-collectors, bath attendants and hair-removers (*ṣāniʿa*), and in prisons with female inmates, women would work as wardens. Under the Zirids, women were jailed in a prison different from that of men and they would be under the surveillance of an *amīna*, a woman of trust who was either unmarried or married to a man of high social standing. Other gendered professions were related to lifetime rituals such as weddings and funerals: the bridal hair-dresser (*māshiṭa*), the female body-washer (*ghāsila*) of female corpses, and the wailing mourner (*nā'iḥa*).[60]

On several occasions, the Fatimid imam-caliphs formally condemned female mourners' expressions of grief, such as wailing, beating their chests or pulling their hair; however, their injunctions did not deter professional mourners from carrying on their work during and after the Fatimid era. At funerals, hired professional mourners dressed in plain clothes would eulogise the deceased, answer questions about the departed and above all perform wailing and lamentations. With the exception of a few known female mourners, women in this profession remained anonymous and were usually perceived as marginals in society. Among the famous professional mourners of the Fatimid age is a Khisrawan or Khusruwan, who presided over the funeral of the vizier al-ʻAdil b. al-Salar and to whom she dedicated a poem.[61] This profession could generate a good income if another Fatimid mourner, Sitt al-Riyad, owned a share of a house near Fustat, and if a slave-girl, who was a professional wailer, was bought at twice the price normally paid for a slave-girl.[62]

During the Fatimid period, women were also active in running small and large businesses, occasionally figuring in sources as employers of men, and as partners in trade. Some would sell and deal in 'cottage industry' products such as linseed and radish oil, wool, chickens, eggs and milk, and ready-made meals such as cooked beans and cakes.[63] Other women displayed entrepreneurial skills. In the Fatimid capital, for ordinary people to fetch drinking water was a complicated, but nonetheless essential, task. One woman who saw a gap in the market of water collection invested in some tools and turned water collecting into a profitable business. As Nasir-i Khusraw reports, a woman who owned 5,000 metal pitchers leased each one of them for one *dirham* a month and expected them to be returned to her in good condition at the end of the rental period.[64] On a more international scale, there is the instance of a woman who, intending to buy grain in Sicily to resell it in the market of al-Mahdiyya, sold her jewellery in Sicily in order to raise the funds for the transaction. She had a male commercial agent with whom she shared half of the profit.[65] There are also instances of female dealers or brokers (*dallāla*) – whether of products made by women, for female consumption or in general; they would typically visit the women in their own house and sell them goods, especially fabrics. Among the range of activities that women exercised in the market area, there was, at least in the last phase of the Fatimid period, that of 'policewoman'. Al-Maqrizi states that, since the days of al-Afdal, it was customary that every year a *jāriya* would close all the wine shops in the capital at the end of the month of Jumada II, warning against the purchase of wine.[66]

In literary as well as documentary sources, there are also references to women entertainers, such as singers and musicians, performing outside the palace at public and private functions, as well as in tavern-like places. It is known that, during the Fatimids, a man of some importance would have singers-cum-musicians at his personal service, for whom he would even provide the strings for their lutes![67] These singing-girls were also associated with less respectable forms of entertainment, as the 'Abbasid writer al-Jahiz had suggested when referring to the existence of singing-girls' houses (*manāzil al-qiyān*).[68] The ill-repute of these non-court singers was such that, in some cases, their very name was synonymous with prostitute.[69]

In the cities, prostitutes (*baghāyā, fawāḥish*) were active in busy market areas. Outside the cities, they would work near or at caravanserais[70] and at sea ports, where travellers would be their typical clients. Some conducted their business from home, while others frequented houses used as brothels, as inferred from the Fatimid chronicler al-Musabbihi's report that, in 415/1024, a chief of police of the capital beat and publicly reviled an effeminate (*mukhannath*) on the accusation that he acted as a pimp for five women in his house.[71] In Fatimid Cairo, a typical area populated with prostitutes would be the market of the Wheat Merchants, a bustling area full of shops and warehouses adjacent to al-Aqmar Mosque. Al-Maqrizi specifies that prostitutes wore a cloak and red leather shoes, which would make them recognisable, and that their working hours were extended to the night.[72] It appears that, during and after the Fatimid period, prostitutes' earnings were taxed and that, at times, these taxes would be collected by women. It was mainly male pimps and brokers, though, who would benefit financially from the prostitutes' work.[73] During the tenth and eleventh centuries, the most frequently reported form of punishment for the Cairo prostitutes and their pimps was public flogging. The punishment appears to have been harsher in cases in which Muslim women were involved with Christian and Jewish men, to the extent that the men could be condemned to death while the women could be flogged and subjected to public exposure.[74]

A large number of female palace workers, entertainers and concubines were slaves. In the Fatimid capital, slaves were sold and bought at the slave markets, such as the Khan Masrur located between Bab Zuhuma and the al-Azhar mosque.[75] The late tenth-century historian and traveller Ibn Hawqal listed slave-girls among the goods exported from the Fatimid empire to Baghdad. He specifies that mulatto female slaves were particularly sought after, and some would end up in the caliphal palace of Baghdad. Under al-Mustansir, in 470/1077, thousands of women of a rebellious Berber tribe were publicly sold as slaves in the markets of Cairo.[76] The price of female and male slaves seems to have been usually high and only the very and moderately rich could afford to buy them. Consequently, to own slaves was, to an extent, a status symbol. Cheaper prices were paid if the slave had defects, blemishes or dependants such as young children. According to some twelfth-century documents from the Cairo Geniza, the price of a female slave fluctuated around 20 *dīnārs*, the same price as an expensive book, when the average salary of a labourer was less than a *dīnār* per month! Once sold, slave-girls were brought to the houses of court officials, of doctors or merchants, and were presumably used as servants or nurses, even though the purpose for the transaction is not specified in the documents. As servants, they had much more freedom of movement than some of their mistresses, as they would go, unveiled, to the market to perform daily errands. Slave-girls were of various ethnic backgrounds, the most popular among the Geniza community being Sudanese-Nubians, followed by Europeans, and a few from India.

Some girls were born into slavery, some were minors accompanying their mothers while sold, and others were received as part of an inheritance or dowry.[77] There are records of slaves being manumitted at the master's or mistress's deathbed, or even during his/her lifetime, and, as a whole, it seems that a bond between the former proprietor and the freed slave continued to exist even after emancipation. It can be inferred by some legal sources that, unless manumission of a slave was conducted to the letter of the law, with all the necessary witnesses and required conditions, there were instances of heirs of the master over-riding a manumission decision.[78]

There are numerous references in the sources to slaves and even specific treatises providing guidelines for their purchase. The grim reality of selling and buying slaves was embellished with theoretical accounts of the qualities exhibited by this 'human merchandise' and the best way to make the most of them. In these accounts, slaves were therefore subdivided according to race and stereotype: Berber women were deemed good for housework, sex and child-bearing; black women were considered docile, robust and excellent wetnurses; Byzantine slave-girls could be entrusted with valuables; Persian women were reputed to be excellent child-minders; Arab girls had a reputation for being accomplished singers; finally, Indian and Armenian women were considered hard to manage, hence unsuited for slavery. The younger the slave, especially a girl, the more attractive in the eyes of the purchaser.[79]

A special and sought-after category of slaves included those with professional skills, which increased their market value. Ibn Butlan, the famous eleventh-century Christian Syrian physician, who might have composed his treatise on the purchase of slaves during his visit to Fatimid Cairo, identified a number of professions suitable for female slaves: cooks, nurses, singers and dancers. He stated that female cooks are better than male cooks because of their constancy in the job and their understanding of the secrets of high cuisine: good balance and good sauce-making. As for the female singer-slaves, Ibn Butlan says that *by nature* they have a better voice than their male counterparts. To illustrate the variety, specialisation and demand for female slave-musicians, Ibn Butlan categorises them into lutists, pipers and percussionists.[80]

Slaves were not just commodities, however, they were human beings, with specific rights that, at least in theory, were to be protected. Masters and mistresses were to treat them humanely and provide them with adequate food, drink and clothing. They were not to overwork them beyond their limits and, even though they were allowed to beat them, they could do so only to discipline them, not gratuitously. Masters were also to allow their slaves to keep their faith and to respect their religious practices, including praying times.[81] Slaves also had the right to ownership and to inheritance. From legal cases, we learn that skilled slaves also had the right to keep the wages earned from their profession, rather than passing them on to their master.[82] Nevertheless, even if Muslim, from a legal as well as a social point of view, slaves were treated and perceived of as a second-class group of people.

4. Women's Education and Educated Women

In Fatimid Egypt, there was no equivalent to the *madrasa*, a formally organised educational institution that, in other parts of the contemporary Islamic world, could provide informal but reliable teaching. The earliest *madrasas* had been operational since the first half of the eleventh century in Nishapur, but in Egypt it was only towards the end of the Fatimid rule that *madrasas* were established in Alexandria and Fustat. Instead, under the Fatimids, education intended as the imparting of knowledge by formal instruction was organised and provided for by the *da'wa* organisation through educational sessions, *majālis*, delivered to men as well as women, predominantly in the mosques or in the caliphal palace. From the time of the *dā'ī* Abu 'Abd Allah al-Shi'i onwards, by attending the *majālis*, women would be specifically instructed on matters such as personal conduct, how to perform ritual duties (*farā'iḍ*) in accordance with the Isma'ili *madhhab* and, particularly, how to adhere to purity laws. Women would also be informed about family-law related matters and initiated women would be further introduced to the core Isma'ili doctrinal tenets. In this respect, the instruction provided by the *dā'īs* could nowadays be seen more as a form of catechism than as an imparting of education and learning.

Individual imam-caliphs and viziers founded libraries and sponsored research centres, which attracted scholars from other parts of the Islamic world. However, these Fatimid centres of learning were not permanent establishments, as their functioning remained dependant upon the will and the policies of their founders. Although there is no reference to date of female scholars attending these Fatimid centres of learning, the contribution of eleventh century women to *ḥadīth* studies is nevertheless attested in Fatimid Cairo through the presence there of a number of prominent scholars known to have studied in Makka under the famous Karima al-Marwaziyya (d. 463/1070).[83]

Beyond the *da'wa* provisions and the academy-like centres, we need to look elsewhere to find ways in which ordinary people might have gained an education and sought knowledge. This requires us to enter into the realm of informal schooling, about which little information can be gathered from the extant sources. Not unlike in the rest of the medieval Islamic world, in the domains under Fatimid rule it was the mosque that provided the most basic form of schooling. There boys and girls, but also adults, would gather in the so-called *kuttāb* (broadly, elementary schools), usually a room in the mosque compound, where they would learn the Qur'an by heart under the supervision of teachers. Some, presumably, would also acquire literacy and numeracy skills. At a more advanced level, instruction on Qur'anic exegesis, inclusive of philological and theological studies, on *ḥadīth*s and on jurisprudence would also be imparted in mosques such as the famous 'Amr b. al-'As mosque in Fustat.

The very definition of education, learning and literacy within the context of a tenth- to twelefth-century Muslim society is in itself a complex issue, and one that lies beyond the scope of this chapter. It is not simply a matter of terminology, but requires a historically contextualised mentality on the part of the researcher. Would, for instance, an eleventh-century woman who did not know how to read or write, but who had memorised the whole of the Qur'an or significant portions of *ḥadīth*s, be deemed uneducated? Perhaps she would by the standards of a twenty-first-century observer; but for her own contemporaries, she was praised as an *'ālima*, a woman of learning.

Knowledge and learning (*'ilm*) were highly valued pursuits in any medieval Islamic society, as shown by frequent references in a variety of works to *ḥadīth*s on the authority of the Prophet Muhammad encouraging all Muslims to pursue knowledge. Some women became famous traditionists and others excelled in the pursuit of knowledge to the extent that medieval Islamic biographical dictionaries featured entries on a number of prominent learned women. Among them were concubines, including slaves, who mastered poetry and who received formal tuition by famous scholars,[84] but most were women from the *'ulamā'* families. Typically, these women would be the daughters, the wives and the mothers of judges, scribes, secretaries or scholars, and were described as being literate, well-educated and, occasionally, to have followed in their male relatives' footsteps.[85] Whether active learners or passive recipients of knowledge, the female members of a learned family were obviously well placed to benefit from the cultured environment they lived in. It is within the context of this cultural climate that we find recorded in the sources the names of women calligraphers, copyists and secretaries (*kātiba*),[86] such as the Zirid Qurra, who acted as intermediary for a court woman in the registration of her bequest of precious Qur'ans to the mosque of Qayrawan. Occasionally, women turned their calligraphical skills into a profitable family business, as shown by the following example from the Fatimid period. During the caliphate of al-Hafiz, the wife and daughter of the jurist and scholar Ibn al-Hati'a al-Fasi (d. 561/1165), who was a Qur'an reader in Cairo and Alexandria as well as being a *qāḍī*, were such highly skilled calligraphers that they could perfectly reproduce the *qāḍī*'s handwriting. Both women copied books on *fiqh*, *ḥadīth* and literature and, together with al-Fasi, they either leased them or sold them.[87] However, not all women were appreciative of being part of a cultured household, as shown by the case of the prominent wife of the well-known eleventh-century Fatimid intellectual and *amīr*, Mubashshir b. Fatik. According to an anecdote reported by the biographer Ibn Abi Usaybi'a, she resented so much her husband's commitment to his books, and the neglect she suffered as a result, that at his death she threw all the books of his extensive library into the house courtyard pool.[88]

With reference to education as the provision of literacy and numeracy skills, especially imparted to children, there were contrasting attitudes as far as the prominence that female literacy should be given. According to a prophetic *ḥadīth*, while merit is to be gained by providing an education for all children, to teach one's own daughters and to take their education further would gain their father nothing less than 'a shield and a veil to guard him from hellfire'.[89] It is perhaps with this intent that Ibn Ridwan adopted, as a form of meritorious act, an orphan girl during a period of famine and plague that affected Egypt in 445/1053. He is reported to have educated the girl while raising her in his own house. However, far from showing him her gratitude, the girl ran away with his gold and valuables worth 20,000 *dīnārs*. As for Ibn Ridwan, well known for his parsimony, he might have shielded himself from hellfire in the hereafter, but in his earthly life he was reported to have suffered the hell of insanity as a result of the loss of his material possessions!

Contrary to the prophetic advice on the merits to be gained from educating girls, there are doubtful reports ascribed to famous personalities, such as 'Umar b. al-Khattab, discouraging men from teaching women how to write, hence the maxim: a woman who is taught how to write is a 'viper who is given poison to drink',[90] which implies that literate women would be a danger to society. In keeping with such a resistance to teaching women literacy skills, in Zirid Ifriqiya, the early eleventh-century Maliki jurist al-Qabisi issued *fatwās* that, while encouraging fathers to give their daughters a general religious education, warned them against teaching girls how to write, fearing most their ability to write letters and to compose poetry.[91]

The full extent of literacy among women is impossible to assess, as most sources only provide a few and fragmentary references. Among the ruling elite, figures emerge such as the queen Arwa, who, in the words of the panegyrist

ʿUmara, showed textual interpretative skills, good knowledge of the Qur'an and displayed an overall good memory for events and stories. The correspondence addressed to her and that sent on her name may be another indication of her literacy and that of her female royal correspondents in Cairo. However, exchange of official correspondence alone is no proof that all parties involved were actually able to write or read; in fact, court women had their own private secretaries (*kātib*), who could have written under dictation, or could have been generally instructed on the contents of their missives.[92]

As far as ordinary women are concerned, there is almost no reference to them regarding their ability to write and read, except in the form of some sensationalist anecdotes, such as that of the handless woman from Tinnis who, in 532/1137, had an audience with the vizier al-Ma'mun and informed him that she could write and calculate with her feet. The vizier tested her and at this point the historian's comment is that she wrote in 'the best calligraphy that a woman could produce',[93] thus leading us to infer that for ordinary women to be able to write was not so uncommon. Even documentary sources such as the Geniza collection provide an overall fragmentary picture of female literacy among the Jewish merchant class. The letters sent by travelling husbands to their wives could be a partial indication of female ability to read, even though the recipients could have made use of relatives or professional readers. Among the Jews of Fustat, emphasis was placed on male literacy, especially on the ability to read the Torah, a skill that families would go to great expense to develop. There are, however, a few references to female education, too, such as a poignant account of the father who mourns the loss of his beloved daughter, to whom he had taught the Torah; or the concern of a dying mother for the education of her daughter, which she entrusts to her sister, despite the financial burden on the family that this would entail.[94]

All in all, during the Fatimid period, the extent of literacy among the populace appears to have been conditioned by social and financial status, as well as family background. This was particularly so for ordinary women. Upper-class women could be taught how to read and, at times, how to write by their own fathers, by relatives or by hired private tutors. However, as traditionists, as calligraphers or poetry reciters, women transmitted, repeated and memorised but hardly contributed original, analytical or interpretative insights to their fields of expertise.[95]

5. Appealing Women: Some Legal Rights and Wrongs

The Fatimid legal system drew inspiration, with some modifications, from the teachings and the instructions left by the early Shiʿi imams, thus making Ismaʿili law almost equivalent to Shiʿi Imami law, with a few exceptions. When the

Fatimids gained military and political control of Ifriqiya, and later on of Egypt, they kept the judicial system that was in place in those lands and confirmed in office those respected local judges who were willing to acknowledge the political authority of the new rulers. The Fatimids strove, from the early days of their rule, to convince the judges to enforce their interpretation of the law, especially in matters of family and ritual law. In Ifriqiya, following al-Mahdi's appointment of the Shi'i Muhammad al-Marwazi as *qāḍī* of Qayrawan in 296/909, the *qāḍī* ordered the other jurists to conform to the teachings of Ja'far al-Sadiq in matters of divorce and inheritance.[96] Upon the general al-Jawhar's arrival in Egypt in 359/969–70, the Maliki judge of Fustat, Abu Tahir al-Dhuhli (d. 368/978), went with other dignitaries to greet the general and to seek his protection, which the general granted, asking in return to adapt inheritance, divorce and ritual laws to Fatimid legal rulings.[97]

In time, the Fatimids expanded the areas under the *qāḍī*'s competence: no longer solely an administrative figure, the *qāḍī* acquired executive powers in judicial affairs, supervised preaching and prayers in mosques, the quality of coins and unclaimed inheritances, powers that he would enforce through deputies and a network system.[98] As the spheres of influence of the vizierate, the *da'wa* organisation and the judiciary would often overlap, the co-existence of these powerful offices as separate bodies was not without tension, with their respective heads often engaged in outsmarting each other to establish or defend the primacy of the body under their control. That the 'independence' of the judiciary in particular was seen as somewhat problematic is indicated by the fact that, at times, the post of chief *qāḍī* was either merged with that of the chief *dā'ī* or the vizier would assume the headship of the judiciary or, as in the case of al-Yazuri, the offices of vizier, chief *qāḍī* and chief *dā'ī* would be expleted by one person.

Ordinary men and women could have fairly direct access to the law by submitting legal queries and cases directly to the attention of the *qāḍī*, who held weekly sessions either in the mosque or, more rarely, at his house. A popular procedure for legal redress consisted of taking a case to the Court of Complaints (*majlis al-maẓālim*), through which some cases could even be brought in front of the caliph himself. Women did not shy from revealing in front of the judge the most intimate details of their marital life, especially when they were seeking divorce, which the judge nevertheless would grant only as a last resort. In practice, in marital disputes the judge would serve as a marriage counsellor. One such case was that of a woman who went to the judge of Fustat, Abu Tahir, complaining that she could no longer stand intimacy with her husband on account of him having a very hairy penis. The judge advised the husband to shave it with a depilatory cream and decreed that the wife could not reject him during the days he was shaven.[99] In trying to keep a couple together, a judge could resort to extreme measures, not always in the interest of both! Al-Musabbihi reports the case of a woman who appealed to the *qāḍī* Muhammad b. al-Nuʿman to enjoin her husband to give her the financial support she was entitled to. As the husband refused, the woman asked the judge to put him in jail, which he did. However, as the judge noticed that she was pretty and not at all sad about the imprisonment of her spouse, he requested that she join her husband in jail! She was far from pleased and in reply to her remonstrations the judge said: 'we jailed him because of your right and we now jail you because of his right'. When she was eventually released, the judge justified his decision by explaining that he feared that the woman would be lost by herself without her husband.[100]

Even powerful men were not exempt from having to appeal to the personal intervention of the caliph to resolve their family disputes. Such was, for instance, the case of the mighty al-Afdal, who, having been denied access to his youngest son by the boy's mother, sought al-Amir's intercession to defend his paternal rights. Al-Amir, who presumably acted as guarantor, personally took the boy to spend time with his father. The vizier is reported to have welcomed the boy, to have been kind to him and to have returned him safe and well to the mother, rather than, al-Maqrizi adds, having him killed as he had done with the boy's brothers.[101]

a. Marriage and Divorce

With reference to marital law, two of the issues where Ismaʿili and Imami law differ are that of temporary marriage and the need of a guardian for a bride. According to Fatimid legal theory, the general conditions for the validity of a marriage were: the presence of a guardian (*walī*) for the bride; two reliable witnesses; the consent of the bride, if mature (*bāligh*), and the stipulation of the dowry on the basis of ʿAli's tradition that 'there is no marriage without *mahr*'. Unlike Imami Shiʿi law, which did not require the consent of a guardian for the marriage of an adult woman, Fatimid marital law stipulated that every woman, irrespective of her age, should have the consent of a guardian. As guarantor, the guardian would typically be the woman's father, especially if the bride was a minor, or a close male relative. If no guardian could be found, the judge himself could act as one. If *bāligh*, a woman could appoint a guardian of her choice.

In practice, the presence of high judges, guardians and witnesses was still insufficient to avoid the legal pitfalls that could render a marriage null. The lack of assertiveness on the part of a *qāḍī*, the dubious reliability of the witnesses, a false declaration of age, a possible intrigue to damage a judge's reputation: all of these could contribute to a 'judicial scandal' that would need the personal intervention of the imam-caliph to be resolved. A case of this kind occurred in 375/985, when Ibn Killis, who, according to al-Musabbihi, was opposed to the al-Nuʿman family, agreed to the marriage between the son of Hasan b. Husayn al-Daqqaq and an orphan girl known as Bint al-Dibaji, with the authorisation of the *qāḍī* Muhammad b. al-Nuʿman. During the proceeds, however, one of the witnesses stood up and denounced the validity of the marriage by claiming that the bride was under age, to which Ibn al-Nuʿman replied that the girl had reassured him about her status as *bāligh*. The case was presented to al-ʿAziz and the girl brought to the palace, where it was established that she was indeed under age. As a result, the judge received an injunction to annul the marriage and to interdict the witnesses. The *qāḍī* obliged, advised the vizier to show no tolerance towards the witnesses and, as for the dowry money, he ordered that most of it was to be kept safe, while a quarter should be entrusted to the girl.[102] Beyond exposing a range of inadequacies at the highest level of the power apparatus, the importance of the report of this case rests in the fact that it ostensibly reveals the extent to which the most distinguished men of the regime would go to protect the marital and financial rights of a female individual in a vulnerable position, such as an under-age orphan girl. In reality, the case is more representative of the way in which court cases could become the battle-field on which the rivalries between the vizier and the judge could be played out at the expense of unaware pawns.

The modalities relating to the payment of the dowry to the bride demanded careful consideration given the fact that, particularly in the case of upper-class or court brides, a considerable amount of money would change hands. The groom would usually pay the dowry to the bride or to her family in two or more installments, one before the consummation of the marriage and the rest after-wards. The amount of the dowry, both in total and in installments, would be specified in the marriage contract. At times, the amount specified for later installments was higher than that paid at the signing of the contract, with the pretext that this method of payment would best guarantee the bride's financial security in case of divorce, or her husband's death. In case of widowhood, the outstanding dowry had to be paid to the wife before the inheritance could be shared. The dowry was intended to be the exclusive ownership of the bride, to the extent that the groom could not claim it back in case he asked for divorce. The father of a virgin bride who died before the marriage was consummated could even claim the payment of the dowry for himself. Likewise, a woman could claim her dowry from the father-in-law, if he was a guarantor for his son. Typically, the father or the groom-to-be would invest part of the dowry in the acquisition of jewellery on behalf of the bride, or would have jewellery especially made for her. Should the groom find himself unable to pay the dowry, the girl's father could make some allowances.

Notwithstanding its importance as one of the essential elements for the validity of marriage, both Sunni and Shiʿi law never fixed a minimum or maximum amount for the dowry. In Fatimid Egypt, the dowry for ordinary women would consist of gold coins and/or clothes, cooking utensils, precious materials and gems, for a value ranging from a few *dīnārs* to a few tens. A Jewish girl from a well-to-do family could be given as much as a hundred *dīnārs*. In 461/1069, while Cairo was gripped by famine and plague, in rural Egypt, south of al-Bahnasa, Diya, the daughter of a tent-maker, was given as a nuptial gift four Mustansiri gold *dīnārs*, one to be paid immediately and three after the fifth night from the date of the marriage document.[103]

Beyond general rules, *fiqh* theory was often adapted to meet local realities and to address differences in urban or rural contexts. In the case of a port city like al-Mahdiyya, where men would be out at sea for long periods of time, marriage contracts would include unusual clauses relating to the husband's period of absence from the matrimonial home and to his financial commitments towards his wife. In a marriage contract dated 515/1121, ʿAbd Allah al-Ra'is, groom of ʿA'isha bint ʿUthman b. Tayyib al-Ansari, agreed to her right to freedom from all matrimonial obligations if, in case of his absence from home for more than four consecutive months, he did not send her money and did not return to al-Mahdiyya. As it turned out, after the marriage was consummated, ʿAbd Allah left for Sicily, never to return or send money; thanks to her contractual terms, ʿA'isha was set free from her marital duties.[104]

In the context of a society where the number of non-Muslims was conspicuous, the law had to address the status and rights of spouses from different religions. The *sharīʿa* was clear enough about the validity of a marriage between a Muslim man and a *dhimmī* woman, who was not obliged to change her religion once married. The rights of a *dhimmī* wife vis-à-vis a Muslim co-wife were addressed by al-Qadi al-Nuʿman, who stipulated that both had to be treated by their husband in the same way to the minutest detail. A further practical issue arising from 'interfaith' marriages, that needed careful ruling, was to establish the religious identity and status of the progeny. In the Fatimid period, emblematic of the legal complexities affecting the reaching of a decision on such a matter, is a case involving the already mentioned *qāḍī*, Abu Tahir. A Christian woman who had converted to Islam, but whose husband had remained Christian, went to the *qāḍī* seeking his legal opinion about the religious status of her child. Abu Tahir decreed that the child was Christian on account of his father's religion. However, on hearing Abu Tahir's ruling that the child of a Muslim woman had been declared a Christian, the local people remonstrated, objecting that Shiʿi as well as Shafiʿi law would recognise the child to be a Muslim. At last, Abu Tahir gave in to pressure and proclaimed that the child was indeed a Muslim.[105]

One of the few differences between the Imami and the Ismaʿili legal systems is the abolition by the latter of the practice of temporary marriage (*mutʿa*). In use since before the time of the Prophet, Sunnis claim, on the basis of a few *ḥadīths*, that the Prophet had prohibited it and the caliph ʿUmar had confirmed the prohibition. Imami Shiʿis, however, on the basis of *ḥadīths* attributed to the imams Muhammad al-Baqir and Jaʿfar al-Sadiq, denounced its prohibition as an innovation, and kept it as a legal form of marriage, though somehow of an inferior status. By contrast, the Ismaʿili jurist al-Qadi al-Nuʿman, on the basis of some other *ḥadīths*, forbade *mutʿa* altogether, while also reporting that the imam-caliph al-Muʿizz rejected the practice.[106]

As far as divorce is concerned, Imami and Ismaʿili law went a further step forward than Sunni law in safeguarding the woman's interest through the abolition of *ṭalāq al-bidʿ*, the divorce formula that a husband could utter in a single declaration, a practice that Sunni jurisprudence deemed reprehensible but never abolished. For Ismaʿilis, as well as Imamis, the validity of a divorce depended on its formula being uttered by the husband *compos mentis* three times in separate occasions in front of two witnesses to a non-menstruating wife. Al-Qadi al-Nuʿman declared void a clause in the marriage contract granting the wife the right to ask for divorce at any time.[107] This ruling points to the fact that the inclusion of this clause must have occurred at times, as indeed is shown by the case of ʿA'isha from al-Mahdiyya.

b. Inheritance

In his *Daʿā'im*, by applying the broader Shiʿi principles of inheritance, al-Qadi al-Nuʿman stipulated the following degree of priority among the heirs: the descendants of the deceased, his ascendants and his conjoints. The group that is clearly absent from the immediate beneficiaries is that of the agnates, who would only be taken into consideration in the absence of any members from the three groups specified above. The principle of blood and family closeness was applied by al-Qadi al-Nuʿman irrespective of gender. Accordingly, if the deceased only had one daughter, she would get the full amount of inheritance because, as al-Nuʿman explains, she would be entitled to her Qur'anic share of half, plus an additional half, on account of being the closest blood relative. There are a number of instances during the Fatimid era of only daughters in receipt of the full amount of inheritance from either their father or their mother. Eleventh-century obituary records of Cairene notables contain some factual information on daughters as recipients of inheritance. In his entries for the year 415/1024 alone, al-Musabbihi refers to the immense inheritance, inclusive of real estates, passed in full by Ibna Abi ʿAbd Allah al-Husayn to her only daughter, Bint Abi Jaʿfar; to the bequest of 60,000 *dīnārs* by a wealthy man to his daughter and son; and to the fortune inherited by the daughter of a certain al-Adani al-Musulmani.[108]

That the practice at times did not live up to the expectations of legal theory is shown by the questionable intervention of the *qāḍī* in preventing daughters from receiving their legally sanctioned bequest. In the case of Bint Abi Ja'far, her inheritance was eventually impounded on dubious grounds, while in 419/1028 the *qāḍī* al-Fariqi was accused of plotting to disqualify an only daughter from receiving her inheritance after four of his witnesses pronounced her legally incompetent. The girl, however, appealed straight to the vizier, who ordered an investigation into the matter, which resulted in the witnesses' imprisonment and the *qāḍī*'s house-arrest for life.[109]

The early Shi'i imams, Muhammad al-Baqir and Ja'far al-Sadiq, had established that female heirs had no right to inherit land but only its corresponding value following liquidation or conversion into other types of goods. By contrast, al-Qadi al-Nu'man established that women could indeed inherit land. This ruling was rooted in the Shi'i interpretation of Fatima as intended heir of the Fadak orchard. The Qur'anic shares of inheritance for spouses are upheld, as is the principle that a male heir would receive twice as much as a female, which, Ja'far al-Sadiq argued, was justified on account of a woman not taking part in war, not being held liable to support family members and not having to pay blood money. With reference to a woman who had been divorced and whose former husband had died, al-Nu'man ruled that she could inherit from him on condition of her not re-marrying.[110]

c. Crime and Punishment

The majority of reported legal cases during the Fatimid period involving women fall within the field of family law, but there are also a few instances pertaining to criminal law. These are on the whole cases of adultery, rape and murder. As only very serious or high-profile cases of adultery were given a special mention in the chronicles of the time, it is thus far difficult to establish what the most common form of punishment for this crime might have been. The severity of the punishment was proportional to the perceived gravity of the case. The already mentioned woman who, during al-Hakim's time, fooled the *qāḍī* in order to get permission to meet with her lover was punished, according to Ibn al-Jawzi, by burning, a form of punishment which finds no justification either in *sharī'a* or, even less, in the Qur'an. By contrast, her lover was merely beaten. Another case was that of a man who, in 392/1001 in Egypt, had forced an 'Alid woman to commit fornication, a crime for which the *qāḍī* Muhammad b. al-Nu'man sentenced the man to death by stoning, which took place in the market of al-Dawwab, near the Ibn Tulun mosque. That this might in fact have been a case of rape can be inferred by the unusual omission of the mention of the woman's punishment or, indeed, of her fate.[111] Another case of rape, this time committed by a Christian man against a woman of high lineage who is reported to have been a descendant of the Prophet himself, resulted in a public lynching by the people of al-Mahdiyya.[112] Other cases of rape are reported as having occurred to Egyptian Jewish women while they were captives of Arab men, but, in this instance, there is no reference to any punishment.

As in every society, under the Fatimids women were both victims and perpetrators of murder. Chroniclers would record in some detail both the murder dynamics and the outcome of the ensuing police investigation. In the year 415/1024, on one occasion a man killed a woman who was his boss and robbed her of all that was in her house. A night patrol arrested him and sequestered the loot. When, the next day, the murdered woman was discovered, the criminal was beheaded and his body displayed on a rubbish heap in al-Qarafa. On another occasion, in the same year, a vulnerable woman known as al-Haqqaniyya, noted for her good reputation and piety, was suffocated. The woman had a servant who worked in the oven near her house; he, presumably, colluded with a gang that, having entered the premises, kept the oven going until she died of suffocation and took all her possessions. We are told that the gang and the servant were imprisoned to force them to confess but the final outcome of the investigation remains a mystery.[113] Murders perpetrated by women would be reported when the victim was a high-profile man, like in the case in Damascus of a woman who, in 487/1094, killed an esteemed scholar of the time, Abu Nasr al-Turaythithi al-Sufi. He had reprimanded the woman, described as mad for having exposed herself with her face uncovered by the mosque door. The scholar ordered her to cover herself and her face and, in return, she stabbed him in a frenzied attack.[114]

When the perpetrators of crime, whether men or women, were imprisoned, they faced a grim future. Not only were prisons dirty and smelly places, the prisoners were also expected to pay for their own sustenance, least they die of starvation. In addition to the social stigma of having relatives in jail, those who could not afford to pay for them had to resort to asking for money from relatives or from community leaders. Some letters from the Geniza collection testify to some women's efforts in pleading for financial support on behalf of their imprisoned husbands or sons.[115]

6. Healthy and Pure: Feminine Hygiene and Sexuality in Legal Theory and Medical Practice

Throughout most of the history of the dynasty, several Fatimid imam-caliphs and high dignitaries distinguished themselves as patrons of scientific learning by establishing rich libraries and commissioning the writing of scientific literature. Indeed, the presence at the Fatimid court of famed Jewish, Christian and

Muslim physicians is well documented.[116] Given the medical knowledge available at the time, and its means of transmission, the physicians of the Fatimid period perpetuated, with some adaptations and updates, the ancient Greek medical tradition in their approach to the diagnosis, prevention and treatment of diseases. Thus, in this respect, they were no different from their predecessors and their contemporaries in other parts of the Islamic world. However, health and welfare issues take a distinctive 'Fatimid' character when examined through the lens of a broader discourse addressing administrative, social, commercial, political, legal and ritual arrangements specific to the Fatimids that, at various levels, impinged on health matters, including women's health and welfare.

As the ability to procreate ultimately defined the social, economic and legal status of women in the medieval Islamic world, one can assume that women's health concerns revolved primarily around fertility-related matters. In support of this assumption is the fact that, when looking at the literature they produced, medieval physicians across the Muslim world addressed women's health issues essentially in sexual, gynaecological and obstetrical terms.

One of the most famous physicians of the early Fatimid period, and of medieval Islam as a whole, is the tenth-century Ifriqiyan Ibn al-Jazzar, active in Qayrawan at the time of the imam-caliph al-Mahdi and a pupil of al-Mahdi's Jewish court physician Ishaq b. Sulayman al-Isra'ili. Ibn al-Jazzar devotes a section of his most famous medical work, *Zād al-musāfir* or *Viaticum,* to women's diseases and their treatment.[117] The intended readership of his work was obviously not the general public, even less women, whose access to literature in general must have been limited. Instead, the *Viaticum* was intended as a guide for the use of other physicians and for those druggists, who, in real terms, represented – for both ordinary men and women – the likely first port of call for consultation on the treatment of most ailments.

In keeping with the then standards of his profession when dealing with women, Ibn al-Jazzar's focus is on menstrual-related problems, hysterical suffocation caused by either lack of sex or menstruation, tumours and ulcers in the uterus, conditions related to pregnancy and childbirth, abortion, infertility and contraception. For each of these conditions Ibn al-Jazzar indicates causes, symptoms and treatments, discussed broadly along Galenic lines adapted to the knowledge of his time, with the occasional detour into 'popular' wives' tale-like medicine. Through Ibn al-Jazzar's narrative, we gain glimpses of practices and attitudes to women's health prevalent at his time and in his region, especially given that, unlike most of his illustrious colleagues, Ibn al-Jazzar was not a court physician but ran a practice for ordinary people.

By and large, Ibn al-Jazzar's prescriptions ranged from plastering uteruses, keeping the legs tight together and dangling stones, to infusions, fumigation, decoctions, pessaries, electuaries, vaginal suppositories and pastilles. The ingredients he lists for the manufacture of medicaments spanned from fragrant oils such as rose and violet, honey and pomegranate juice, to powdered vitriol, dove or cat excrement and even human milk, which Ibn al-Jazzar deemed useful for the treatment of fevers and uterine ulcers.[118] Prescriptions were often complemented by dietary recommendations, mainly poultry and pulses, regular bathing and therapeutic massage. For the treatments of each disease Ibn al-Jazzar lists a variety of recipes, from the highly sophisticated and complex in composition as well as source to the rather basic; the prescription of expensive ingredients would also be customised for the rich, with cheaper but effective remedies to suit the poor.

The other physician of the early Fatimid period providing us with relevant information on women's health is the late tenth-century Ahmad b. Muhammad al-Baladi. Little is known of his life and career except that, shortly after 359/969, he arrived in Cairo probably from Mosul. In Egypt, he wrote the *Tadbīr al-ḥabālā wa-'l-aṭfāl*, a compendium on the cures to be administered to pregnant women and new-born babies, as well as on the diagnosis and cure of children's diseases, mainly based on sources from antiquity.[119] When dealing with the practicalities related to motherhood, through al-Baladi's work we gain an insight into health issues vis-à-vis the aristocratic and bourgeois social climate of his time. Indeed, his work may be invested with ideological value if we consider its commissioner: the famous vizier, Ibn Killis. As vizier, Ibn Killis was ultimately responsible for the effective management of all the political, administrative and economic sectors that ensured the continuity and prosperity of the dynasty he served. Ibn Killis's commissioning of the writing of the *Tadbīr* – in fact a health plan focused on progeny-related matters for the use of the court – acquires an ideological value where the scientific study of pregnancy, childbirth and childrearing may be seen as part of a political discourse.

In the medieval Islamic world, it was standard medical practice that consultations did not include a physical examination and would usually take place at the patient's home or in the doctor's surgery. Private court doctors, including Jewish physicians, took care of the female members of the royal family.[120] High-class women would consult their personal doctor, even on rather private matters. Ibn Ridwan, in criticising a number of famous doctors in Cairo, singled out a senior physician who, he claimed, deceived women by talking to them about what he deemed proper for them in matters of sexual intercourse.[121] Hospitals, hardly ever mentioned in relevant primary sources on the Fatimid period, might have been intended for the very poor and the incurables.[122] For ordinary women and men, medicaments would be manufactured by an in-house assistant to the physician or sold by 'pharmacists' or druggists. By contrast, eleventh-century Fatimid royal women would be supplied ingredients for treatments by the Treasury of Potions, while the Treasury of the Spices would allocate to them substances like camphor, musk, saffron, rose water and violet oil, which could also be used for the manufacture of medicaments.

To enhance their chances of becoming pregnant, women would resort to forms of popular medicine and healing such as astrology and magical practices, the recitation of incantations, the interpretation of dreams and the use of amulets (see Fig. 10). Moreover, to increase fertility, women would visit the shrines of saints, asking for their *baraka* (blessing) to help them conceive. Even the most important among the palace women were not indifferent to the benefits of *baraka* for healing purposes and general well-being, especially with reference to the power of the word resulting from the recitation or the writing of the Qur'an. On one occasion, the mother of the imam-caliph al-Hakim is reported to have administered her sick son with holy water from Zamzam mixed with ink used to write Qur'anic passages. In the Fatimid court of the twelfth century, on special religious festivals, palace women would have vessels of water placed in front of Qur'an reciters so that the water could be imbued with blessings.

In the first volume of his *A Mediterranean Society*, S. D. Goitein refers to the presence, among the Jewish community of Fustat during the Fatimid period, of female physicians, one female oculist and women expert in traditional medicine passed on within the family.[123] As religious, cultural and ethnic barriers did not affect the exercise of the medical profession, we can infer that these women were not exclusively serving the Jewish community to which the Geniza documents refer. In any event, the existence of a female doctor was the exception. By contrast, far more frequent is the reference in medieval Muslim sources to women working as carers and to the services provided by the midwife. Indeed, in Isma'ili sources, the most recurrent acknowledgement of women's role in the early *da'wa* is that of healers and carers.

The theory and practice of midwifery, intended as assistance to child delivery, occupies a large place in the medieval medical literature of the Islamic world. Beyond delivering babies, the service of a midwife would be required when the physical examination of a female patient and the application of medicaments for serious illnesses were needed. For example, in dealing with convulsions caused by lack of sex, Ibn al-Jazzar recommends that a midwife should rub gently with fragrant oils the orifice of the uterus of the patient. As for tumours in the uterus, the manual internal examination by a midwife would help establish their nature, and hence the appropriate treatment.[124] On the issue of female physical examination, Ibn Khaldun states that, as a general rule, it ought to be restricted to midwives only. However, the fifteenth-century scholar al-Suyuti reports the opinion of Ahmad b. Hanbal that the male physician may look at the 'forbidden parts' of a woman's body if his intervention is absolutely necessary. By and large, though, the male physician would be allowed to perform external treatments but not internal ones.[125] The prevailing opinion was

Fig. 10 Tenth-century bone 'doll' from Egypt, possibly an amulet (or a castanet used by dancing girls?).
LNS 48 I. Copyright © Dar al-Athar al-Islamiyyah, Kuwait National Museum. Photo: Muhammad Ali.

that male physicians should take active part in treating women only if it was impossible for a midwife to do so, as in the case of surgery. This is also the view that, at least in legal theory, was upheld by the Fatimids, as shown by a statement by al-Qadi al-Nuʿman based on a Jaʿfarite tradition.[126] It is unclear whether or not midwives were professionally or formally trained. However, the fact that Ibn al-Jazzar details techniques for the midwives on diagnosis of tumours and states 'we should tell the midwife'[127] how to administer certain types of treatment, indicates that some form of instruction from physician to midwife might have taken place.

Another essential healthcare service provided exclusively by women was that of wetnurse. Not only was there a relatively high percentage of mothers dying at childbirth, there were also legal provisions whereby, according to both Sunni and Shiʿi law, a mother was not obliged to breastfeed if she was unwilling or unable to do so. Consequently, either the death of the child's mother or her refusal to breastfeed would automatically make the husband or child's father bound to hire a wetnurse. Ibn al-Jazzar argued that the moral atmosphere in the house of the nurse was more important than any physical quality she might be endowed with. Thus, a nurse should be chosen from a family with similar traits to those of the nursling's family, as the milk was not simply regarded as a source of physical nourishment but also as an essential component for the moral and social sustenance of the child.[128] Besides these theoretical speculations, the majority of physicians in practice recommended to hire wetnurses on the basis of their health and the quality as well as quantity of their milk, irrespective of their status as free or slave women, or their ethnic and religious backgrounds.[129] In desperate circumstances, even royals would overlook a nurse's status or background; when in 381/991 Mansur, a son of the imam-caliph al-ʿAziz, became ill, the caliph was given a rural woman as a gift to breastfeed the boy who, after an initial recovery, nevertheless died.[130]

In his *Tadbīr*, al-Baladi dedicates a number of chapters to the wetnurse, his coverage of the topic effectively serving as a parents' guide on how to chose the right 'specimen'. Hence, he deals with the wetnurse's ideal age, her physical and moral qualities, her intellectual ability and the diet she should follow to ensure the good quality of her milk. Once hired, al-Baladi specifies the type of physical exercise and work that a wetnurse could be asked to perform in order to ensure her fitness, which included practicing ball games and abstaining from sex. In the event that she did not abstain and fell pregnant, al-Baladi recommends her dismissal. One chapter is entirely dedicated to the aid that one ought to provide the wetnurse with, specifically a servant to help her in her chores.[131] This recommendation points to the fact that the type of wetnurse al-Baladi had in mind did not come cheap, thus confirming the wealthy status of al-Baladi's intended readership.

Outside the court environment, the costs involved in the hiring of a wet- or dry-nurse point to the fact that her service could be afforded mainly by wealthy bourgeois families. References to the work of nurses among the populace during the Fatimid period are far too rare for us to form a picture of how nursing worked in practice. It is only when reporting unusual or sensational events that sources mention common nurses working for common people, one instance being al-Maqrizi, who records an event occurring in Cairo in 552/1157 when, from under the rubble of a collapsed house, a nurse managed to free the baby she was caring for out of the debris with the help of her own son. The baby grew up and lived to an old age![132]

a. Contraception

By detailing products that women should avoid to prevent miscarriages and combat infertility, Ibn al-Jazzar gives away at the same time a comprehensive list of contraceptives and abortifacients for the use of women. Among the most effective ingredients he recommended for the manufacturing of contraceptives was the use of tar, either smeared on male genitalia, mixed with powdered seeds of leek and garden cress, or blended with scammony and pulp of colocynth and placed in the vagina as a suppository. He also recommends suppositories of blossom of cabbage, mint pessaries inserted in the vagina before intercourse, juice of mint smeared on the penis, and alum placed in the woman's uterus. Pessaries of pepper inserted in the vagina after sex would work as a day-after pill. Effective abortifacients would be pessaries of cyclamen or bitter lupine mixed with myrrh and honey; Chinese cinnamon taken orally or as suppositories mixed with myrrh; fumigation with cardamom; and plastering the navel with the juice of cyclamen.[133]

The blasé attitude that Ibn al-Jazzar and others display in dealing implicitly with contraception reflects the lack of stigma attached to the use of contraceptives and abortifacients in the medieval Islamic world, as recourse to both was regulated by Islamic law. Indeed, medieval Sunni and Shiʿi jurists consistently approved of contraception by *coitus interruptus* (and by analogy, other forms of contraception) with a free woman provided that she consented, given her rights to have children and to sexual fulfilment. In particular, Fatimid law favoured the stipulation in the marriage contract of a free woman's consent to the use of *coitus interruptus*. As far as a slave-woman was concerned, however, Fatimid law sanctioned that, since the master had property rights over his slaves and their offspring, his property prerogative took precedent over their marital rights to the extent that, at least in theory, the practice of *coitus interruptus* was only permitted with the master's consent.[134] Since the requirement to ask anyone's permission for the practice of *coitus interruptus* was either based on property or marital rights, all jurists agreed that a man could practice it unconditionally with his own slave or concubine. Nevertheless, Fatimid law decreed a period of restraint from sex with a slave-girl before and after her sale, to ensure lack of confusion over a possible paternity. As for the recourse to contraception on the part of the woman, according to Twelver Shiʿi jurists (and probably Fatimids as well) she was not obliged to ask her husband's permission – although that was advisable – since, in order to legislate in favour or against it, there were no precedents to refer to.

b. Purity Laws and Personal Hygiene

As a large number of Fatimid laws on female ritual purity revolved around sexual and blood-related pollution, the adherence to religious law had in turn effects on women's personal hygiene. In keeping with the *sharīʿa*, Fatimid law made ritual bathing obligatory for women after sex, menstruation, wet dreams, childbirth, conversion, regaining sanity, falling in filth and washing corpses. On the imams' authority, al-Qadi al-Nuʿman sanctioned that a woman in a state of pollution should not read the Qur'an and that, when taking a purification bath, she should untwist her hair. On the basis of the same authority, as a precaution against bleeding and to verify her impurity-free status, a woman should insert a piece of cloth or a cotton pad in her private parts. Different rules applied for non-menstrual and non-puerperial bleeding. As for a free non-Muslim woman who was married to a Muslim man, Fatimid law exempted her from bathing after sex but kept it mandatory after her period.[135]

The fact that, on the imams' authority, Fatimid law defined sex also as the 'meeting of two circumcised parts', where by 'two circumcised' the early imams meant the penis and vulva, makes us infer that, by Fatimid law, women were expected to be circumcised. On the matter of female circumcision, al-Qadi al-Nuʿman thus reported a tradition ascribed to ʿAli b. Abi Talib: 'O women, when you circumcise your daughters, leave part [of the labia or clitoris]. For this will be chaster for their character, and it will make them more beloved by their husbands.'[136] Finally, not unlike Islamic law in general, Fatimid law permitted love play with a ritually impure or menstruating woman, provided that she wore an undergarment below the navel down to the knee.

Beside the theory, it is difficult to ascertain the extent to which such religious prescriptions translated into practice. Evidence from the sources pointing to women regularly visiting the *ḥammāms* makes us infer that, ostensibly, women did adhere to the ritual bathing rules as legally prescribed. We suggest that such a diligent recourse to ritual purification was motivated by the fact that, besides visiting cemeteries, family and markets, the *ḥammām* offered women yet another good chance to go out and socialise. *Ḥammāms* were indeed very popular throughout Fatimid Egypt. In Cairo, baths had first been built by the imam-caliph al-'Aziz, and by the eleventh-century their provision in Fustat was so extensive as to prompt Ibn Ridwan to comment that their large hearths produced so much steam and smoke as to affect the quality of the air.[137] That women might have been perceived as 'abusing' the freedom of frequenting the public baths is reflected in the set of restrictions imposed by al-Hakim curtailing women's freedom of movement.

Related to the issue of ritual purity and personal hygiene were the burial regulations set by Fatimid law. On the imams' authority, al-Qadi al-Nu'man states that a corpse should be bathed three times: first with potash mixed with water, then with aromatic water perfumed with sweet smelling rush and camphor, and finally with pure water. On the basis of the precedent of 'Ali with Fatima, a husband could wash his wife; a wife could also wash her husband, although in both cases discretion ought to be observed in washing or looking at the private parts of the deceased. Men as well as women would be embalmed in the same way: after washing, the corpse should be wiped with a cloth and camphor and either balm or musk placed on the spots of prayer prostration. For burial, a woman's head should be donned with a head-covering (*khimār*).[138] As shown by archeological evidence, the head of the deceased was indeed wrapped in *ṭirāz* embroided with blessings and the name of the imam-caliph of the time.

The overall picture that we draw from all the above is that, in Fatimid times, legal and medical literature predominantly addressed the theory rather than the practice of health concerns related to womanhood. Gender boundaries and taboos might have influenced the lack of references to specific medical case studies involving 'real' women with 'real' afflictions. We have to step out of strictly medical and legal literature to find anecdotes relating to some extraordinary medical conditions that afflicted identifiable women during the Fatimid period. Among these oddities, al-Maqrizi cites the case in Tinnis of a man who repudiated his wife after the first wedding night, having discovered that the woman was a hermaphrodite. Incidentally, according to Fatimid law, to decide on the sex of a hermaphrodite was not the prerogative of physicians, but of the imam himself, who would deliberate on the matter through a form of divination involving the use of arrows.[139]

Another unusual occurrence is recorded for the year 397/1006–7, again in Tinnis, where a young woman gave birth to a baby girl with two heads; the baby was shown to the imam-caliph al-'Aziz, and died after a few months.[140] Also from Tinnis was the handless woman who demonstrated her calligraphic skills at the palace. Nasir-i Khusraw reports in his *Safar nameh* that, in Tinnis, women were affected by a disease, similar to epilepsy, that would make them faint after screaming two or three times. This is possibly the condition known as *al-fawāq al-tinnīsī*, or the 'Tinnis convulsion'. Nasir-i Khusraw observed that he had heard in Khorasan of an island, which he appears to identify with Tinnis, where women were affected by a condition that would make them meow like cats.[141] Medieval observers indeed looked at the overall quality of life of the people of Fatimid Tinnis with some concern. According to Ibn Ridwan, the predominant humidity of the city caused 'the effeminate character of the people',[142] while Nasir-i Khusraw claimed that the climate was very hot and diseases were frequent. The physician Abu 'l-Sari lamented that the people of Tinnis did not engage in exercise, and Ibn Butlan, having visited Egypt, expressed his concerns about the Tinnis inhabitants' diet, which consisted exclusively of cheese, fish and cow's milk. Although we must be open to the possibility that these observations might be ultimately conditioned by stereotypes attached to the predominantly Christian population of that city, it was a fact that Tinnis, because of its geographical location, suffered major problems with regards to the availability of good quality water. Assuming that women were largely employed as labourers in Tinnis's famed textile production, an industry dependent upon water supply for its functioning, one wonders if the combination of constant contact with polluted water, poor diet and poor working conditions might have indeed made them more susceptible to disease than other women at the time.

All in all, because of the chroniclers' almost exclusive interest in the affairs of the elite, we can only aim at a fragmentary and selective portrayal of the daily affairs of the ordinary people during the Fatimid era. However, a more homogeneous overview can be attained when resorting to, comparing and carefully interpreting as many and as varied sources as are available. For example, theoretical legal literature of the Fatimid time, where glimpses of real cases can only be inferred, is supplemented by documentary sources of the same period referring to real-life legal cases. Similarly, treatises and manuals on professions have been used in conjunction with documentary and literary sources that include references to working women or the prevalent attitudes towards them. When used together, these varied sources highlight the existence of a gap between the theory and the practice, but also some overlapping between the two. The theory of medical treatises is supplemented by references to people's resort to popular remedies; the legal theory of family law is tested against documented cases involving real people in real locations; and, finally, the authoritative nature of caliphal decrees is questioned by narratives about the tricks played to circumvent them.

But to what extent was the daily life of these ordinary women influenced or shaped by the worldview that the Fatimid scholars were elaborating and attempting to endorse through legal rulings, teaching sessions and other means? Although the vast majority of people under Fatimid rule did not embrace Isma'ilism, the Isma'ili reformulation of Islamic law, through its implementation in Fatimid domains, particularly in Egypt, touched people's lives at various levels and to different degrees. Women's conduct and rights became affected by Isma'ili family and purity laws, as well as by Fatimid caliphal decrees on the regulation of their free movement. Their working lives and their instruction depended mainly on the provisions offered by Fatimid institutions or individuals linked to them.

For over two centuries women and men, Muslims and *dhimmīs*, free and bound, wealthy and poor were the audience and the participants of public events, teaching sessions and festivals that celebrated the role of the Fatimid imam-caliph. They were the occupants of a landscape, be it rural or urban, marked by buildings erected to commemorate the achievements of the Fatimid imam-caliphs and their viziers. Ordinary people shopped with currency lauding the virtues of the imam-caliphs and their 'Alid ancestry, heard *khuṭbas* blessing the Fatimid imam-caliphs; those who could afford it wore and displayed the expensive fabrics from the famed Fatimid textile factories, while those who could not followed the fashion by wearing imitation *ṭirāz*. The rich adorned themselves and their houses with exquisite artefacts crafted in a distinctive Fatimid style, while the poor could be the recipients of the benevolence of the caliphal family and high dignitaries. Their food was plenty when the Fatimid policies worked and was lacking when they did not.

However, during the last decades of the Fatimid rule in Egypt, the Isma'ili ethos, promoted by the dynasty, was losing momentum, the implementation of Isma'ili law and rituals becoming almost irrelevant in the hands of non-Isma'ili viziers. When the dynasty of the descendants of Fatima eventually came to an end, ordinary women and men found themselves living under new foreign rulers, heard a more conventional *khuṭba*, shopped with new coins and, on the whole, faced new upheavals and joys, but, this time, under the flag of Sunni Islam.

Notes

1 Nāṣir-i Khusraw, *Sefer nameh: Relation du Voyage de Nassiri Khosrau*, ed. and French trans. Schefer, C., Amsterdam: Philo Press, 1970, pp. 145–56.

2 [Ibn Riḍwān, 'Alī, *Daf' maḍār al-abdān*] trans. Dols, M. W., *Medieval Islamic Medicine. Ibn Riḍwān's treatise 'On the Prevention of Bodily Ills in Egypt'*, ed. of Ar. text by Gamal, 'A. G., Berkley and London: University of California Press, 1984, pp. 105–9.

3 al-Maqrīzī, Taqī al-Dīn, *al-Mawā'iẓ wa-'l-i'tibār fī dhikr al-khiṭaṭ wa-'l-āthār*, Beirut: Dār al-ṣādir, n.d., offset of Būlāq, 1324 edn, vol. 2, p. 319, on the vizier al-Baṭā'iḥī ordering in 516/1122 the building of a mill.

4 For references to the owners of the houses of the *munqaṭi'īn* and on the houses of the *munqaṭi'āt*, which were part of the *waqf* compound of al-Ḥāfiẓ, see al-Maqrīzī, *Khiṭaṭ*, vol. 2, pp. 445, 449. See also the description of the events on the occasion of the night of half Sha'bān held in the *jawsaq al-Mādarānī*, in al-Maqrīzī, *Khiṭaṭ*, vol. 2, p. 453. On more primary sources, see Taylor, C. S., *In the Vicinity of the Righteous: Ziyara and the Veneration of Muslim Saints in Late Medieval Egypt*, Leiden: E. J. Brill, 1999, p. 35, n. 48.

5 On al-Musabbiḥī and Ibn Zawlāq, see Lev, Y., 'Aspects of Egyptian society', in Vermeulen, U. and van Steenbergen, J. (eds), *ESFAME*, Leuven: Peeters, 2001, pp. 9–17.

6 al-Qāḍī al-Nu'mān, *Da'ā'im al-Islām fi dhikr al-ḥalāl*, trans. Fyzee, A. A. A., *The Pillars of Islam: Vol. 1, Acts of Devotion and Religious Observances*, revised and annotated by Poonawala, I. K. H., New Delhi and Oxford: OUP, 2002, p. 145.

7 Kraemer, J., 'A Jewish Cult of the Saints in Fāṭimid Egypt' in Barrucand, M. (ed.), *L'Égypte Fatimide: son art et son histoire*, Paris: Presses de l'Université de Paris-Sorbonne, 1999, p. 584.

8 For the case of a Jewish woman who had a liaison with a Christian doctor and whose fellow-Jews thought she was a Muslim, see Goitein, S. D., *A Mediterranean Society*, Berkeley: University of California Press, 5 vols, 1967–88, vol. 2, p. 286. Naturally, this could also mean that men rather than women were to wear a distinguishable apparel. In Zīrīd Ifrīqiyā, the jurist al-Lakhmī ruled that there was no need for Jewish women to wear distinctive clothes contrary to what was required of men: see Idris, H. R., *La Berbérie Orientale sous les Zīrīdes*, Paris: A. Maisonneuve, 1962, vol. 2, p. 767.

9 See Lev, Y., 'Aspects', pp. 12, 22–3. A possible reason for the Fāṭimid imam-caliph and high officials such as viziers to attend these festivals, especially during difficult inter-communal strife, was to prevent harassment and troubles between the communities. Before the Fāṭimids, the Ikhshīdid leaders also attended the festival of the Epiphany.

10 al-Maqrīzī, Taqī al-Dīn, *Itti'āẓ al-ḥunafā' bi-akhbār al-a'imma al-Fāṭimiyyīn al-khulafā'*, ed. al-Shayyāl, J. and Ḥilmī, M., Cairo: Lajnat iḥyā' al-turāth al-islāmī, 1387–93/1967–73, vol. 2, p. 245.

11 Mansouri, M.-T., 'Juifs et Chrétiens dans le Maghreb fatimide (909–969)', in Barrucand, M., *L'Égypte Fatimide*, pp. 606–8.

12 See the case, among others, of three eleventh century Christian ladies selling their share of a property to a Jew, in Goitein, S. D., MS, 2, p. 292. For interactions of Jews, Christians and Muslims in the marketplace, the role of the *muḥtasib* in regulating or supervising them, and occurrences of inter-faith resistance and even 'strikes' to counteract the regulations, see Weigert, G., 'A Note on the Muḥtasib and Ahl al-Dhimma', *Der Islam*, 75 (1998), pp. 335–7.

13 Goitein, S. D., *MS*, vol. 2, pp. 301, 305.

14 Serjeant, R. B., 'Material for a history of Islamic textiles up to the Mongol conquest', *ArI*, 13–14 (1948), p. 91.

15 The linguistic situation varied for urban and rural Copts and Jews, see Sanders, P., 'The Fatimid state, 969–1171', in Daly, M. W. (ed.), *The Cambridge History of Egypt*, vol. 1: Islamic Egypt, 640–1517, ed. Petry, C. F., Cambridge: CUP, 1998, pp. 169–70. For an analysis of the Arabisation process and linguistic situtation of the Copts during the tenth to thirteenth centuries, see Khalil, S., 'Arabic sources for early Egyptian Christianity', in Pearson, B. A, *The Roots of Egyptian Christianity*, Philadelphia: Fortress, 1986, pp. 82–97.

16 The Armenian Abū Ṣāliḥ reports that Muslims opposed the restoration of the church of Abū Ṣayfayn outside Fusṭāṭ, for they had turned it to a sugar warehouse: cited by Lane-Poole, S., *A History of Egypt in the Middle Ages*, London: Methuen, 1925, vol. 6, p. 119. Perhaps it is within this context of popular resentment that al-'Azīz at times forbade the celebrations of some Christian festivals.

17 The extent of the Armenians' conversion to Islam is unclear and the suspicion arises that Arab-Muslim sources might have played down the number of non-Muslim Armenians, see Lev, Y., *State and society in Fāṭimid Egypt*, Leiden: E. J. Brill, 1991, pp. 95–6. For a detailed analysis of the history of the Armenians under the Fāṭimids, see Dadoyan, S. B., *The Fatimid Armenians. Cultural and Political Interaction in the Near East*, Leiden: E. J. Brill, 1997.

18 See the example of a Jewish woman who had been raped while imprisoned by Arabs and agreed to share her new husband with other co-wives, in Reif, S. C., *A Jewish Archive from Old*

Cairo, Richmond: Curzon, 2000, p. 185.

19 For spinning as one of the wife's duties, and embroidering, see Goitein, S. D., *MS*, vol. 3, pp. 132, 342; for the *mu'allima*, see vol. 2, p. 185, and vol. 1, p. 128; for body-washers, see vol. 1, p. 129.

20 For al-Wuhsha's story, see Goitein, S. D., MS, vol. 3, pp. 347–52.

21 Nāṣir-i Khusraw, *Sefer nameh*, p. 127.

22 Goitein, S. D., 'Urban housing in Fatimid and Ayyubid times (as illustrated by the Cairo Geniza documents)', *SI*, 47 (1978), pp. 18, 22–3.

23 Ibn Riḍwān, *Daf'*, pp. 131–6.

24 For al-Ḥākim's restrictive measures, see al-Maqrīzī, *Itti'āẓ*, vol. 2, pp. 38, 53, 76, 87, 90–1, 95–6, al-Anṭākī, Yaḥyā b. Sa'īd, *Ta'rīkh*, partial ed. and French trans. Kratchkovsky, I. and Vasiliev, A., 'Histoire de Yahya-ibn Sa'īd d'Antioche', *Patrologia Orientalis*, 23 (1932), fasc. 2, pp. 469–516; Ibn Ḥammād, Abū 'Abd Allāh, *Akhbār mulūk banī 'Ubayd*, ed. and French trans. Vonderheyden, M., *Histoire des Rois 'Obaïdites (Les Califes Fatimides)*, Algiers: J. Carbonel; Paris: P. Geuthner, 1927, pp. 52–4 (Ar.), 80–2 (Fr.).

25 al-Musabbiḥī, Muḥammad b. 'Ubayd Allāh, *Akhbār Miṣr*, vol. 1, ed. Sayyid, A. F. and Bianquis, T., Cairo: IFAO, 1978, vol. 1, pp. 14–15.

26 Ibn al-Ḥajj as in Raymond, A. and Wiet, G., *Les marchés du Caire: traduction annotée du texte de Maqrizi*, Cairo: IFAO, 1979, pp. 79–80. On Ibn al-Ḥajj's sections dealing with women, see H. Lutfi's study in Keddie, N. R. and Baron, B. (eds), *Women in Middle Eastern History*, New Haven and London: Yale University Press, 1991.

27 'Abd al-Karīm Aḥmad, Nurīmān, *al-Mar'a fī Miṣr fī'l-'aṣr al-Fāṭimī*, Cairo: al-Hay'a al-miṣriyya al-'āmma li-'l-kitāb, 1993, p. 88.

28 'Abd al-Karīm Aḥmad, N., *al-Mar'a*, p. 84.

29 al-Musabbiḥī, *Akhbār Miṣr*, vol. 1, pp. 94, 102, 104 and 106.

30 For example, in 387/997, in 395/1005, in 397/1007, in 398/1008 and in 399/1009, according to al-Maqrīzī, Taqī al-Dīn, *Ighāthat al-umma fī kashf al-ghumma*, French trans. Wiet, G., 'Le Traité des famines de Maqrīzī', *JESHO*, 5 (1962), pp.15–17.

31 For example, in time of epidemics under the reign of al-Mustanṣir, women were witch-hunted as infecting agents.

32 Ibn Riḍwān, *Daf'*, pp. 113–14.

33 On food deteriotation in Fāṭimid Egypt, see Ibn Riḍwān, *Daf'*, p. 90.

34 al-Maqrīzī reports such a scenario for the year 444/1052, under al-Mustanṣir, in his *Ighātha*, pp. 20–1.

35 al-Maqrīzī, *Ighātha*, pp. 15–17.

36 From Bar Hebraeus, *Ta'rīkh mukhtaṣar al-duwal*, as in 'Abd al-Karīm Aḥmad, *al-Mar'a*, pp. 90–1. See also Ibn al-Athīr, 'Izz al-Dīn, *al-Kāmil fī'l-ta'rīkh*, Beirut: Dār al-kitāb al-'arabī, 1967, vol. 7, p. 305.

37 al-Musabbiḥī, *Akhbār Miṣr*, vol. 1, pp. 15–16, 18, 88–9, 91.

38 al-Maqrīzī, *Ighātha*, pp. 63–64.

39 al-Musabbiḥī, Muhammad b. 'Ubayd Allāh, *Nuṣūṣ ḍā'i'a min akhbār Miṣr*, ed. Sayyid, A. F. Cairo: IFAO, n.d. [1981], p. 24. For a preliminary analysis of the exchange rate between gold and silver money emerging from the Geniza records, see Goitein, S. D., 'The Exchange Rate of Gold and Silver money in Fatimid and Ayyubid times: A Preliminary Study of the relevant Geniza material', *JESHO*, 8 (1965), pp. 1–46, where the writer specifies that there were full- and low-value silver coins and concludes that, despite the frequent fluctuations, the average gold/silver money exchange rate throughout the Fāṭimid period was between 1/35 and 1/40.

40 al-Maqrīzī, *Itti'āẓ*, vol. 2, p. 91.

41 Ibn Ḥammād, *Histoire*, pp. 53–4 (Ar.), 81–2 (Fr.).

42 Rāghib, Y., 'Une épisode obscur d'histoire Fatimide', *SI*, 48 (1978), p. 129.

43 Goitein, S. D., 'The Exchange', pp. 43–4, argues that, even though this is a fair assumption, the Geniza documents show that most transaction records were in *dīnārs*.

44 al-Musabbiḥī, *Akhbār Miṣr*, vol. 1, p. 21.

45 al-Maqrīzī, *Itti'āẓ*, vol. 2, p. 103.

46 Ibn al-Dawādārī, Abū Bakr b. 'Abd Allāh, *Kanz al-durar wa-jāmi' al-ghurar: al-durra al-muḍīya fī akhbār al-dawla al-Fāṭimiyya*, al-juz' al-sādis, ed. al-Munajjid, Ṣ., Cairo: O. Harrassowitz, 1961, vol. 6, p. 298.

47 As reported in Ibn Kathīr, Abu 'l-Fidā, *al-Bidāya wa-'l-nihāya*, Beirut, Dār al-turāth al-'arabī, 2nd edn, 1977, vol. 11, p. 353.

48 The event is reported to have taken palace in the tents' market: see Raymond, A., *Les marchés*, p. 187. Interestingly, before al-Maqrīzī, the incident of the dummy had been reported by Juvaynī, 'Aṭā Malik, *Ta'rīkh-i jahān-gushā*, trans. Boyle, J. A., *The History of the World-Conqueror*, Manchester: Manchester University Press, 1997, vol. 2, p. 655; and Ibn al-Athīr, *al-Kāmil*, vol. 7, p.305. On the use of a puppet in the shape of a woman during al-'Azīz's reign to complain of his appointment of Christian and Jewish high officials, see Sayyid, A. F., *La capitale de l'Égypte jusqu' à l'époque Fatimide*, Beirut/Stuttgart: F. Steiner, 1998, p. 135.

49 Juvaynī, *History*, vol. 2, p. 655.

50 By and large, medieval Islamic treatises on professions only directly mention three working activities for women – the midwife, the hairdresser and the prostitute – as does the tenth-century Iraqi al-Qāsimī against some 200 male professions, in Fahd, T., 'Les corps de métiers au IV/Xe siècle a Bagdād', *JESHO*, 8 (1965), pp. 186–212.

51 See the example of thirteenth-century Genoa, a city renowned for its shipping and textile industries, in Epstein, S. A., 'Labour in thirteenth-century Genoa', *MHR*, 3 (1988),1, p. 120.

52 Idris, H. R., *La Berbérie*, vol. 2, p. 587.

53 Goitein, S. D., *MS*, vol. 5, p. 257.

54 See al-Safadī Ṣalāḥ al-Dīn, *Kitāb al-Wafī bi-'l-wafāyāt*, Wiesbaden: F. Steiner, 1981–, vol. 16, pp. 92–3.

55 On poor women spinning for others under the Zīrīds, see Idris, H. R., *La Berbérie*, vol. 2, p. 635.

56 Shatzmiller, M., 'Women and wage labour in the medieval Islamic West: legal issues in an economic context', *JESHO*, 40 (1997) p. 194.

57 Goitein, S. D., *MS*, vol. 2, pp. 66–7; for women working from home, see Shatzmiller, M., *Labour in the Medieval Islamic World*, Leiden: E. J. Brill, 1994, p. 358–9.

58 Guthrie, S., *Arab Social Life in the Middle Ages: An Illustrated History*, London: Saqi Books, 1995, p. 160.

59 Shatzmiller, M., 'Women and wage labour', pp. 182–8. With reference to the Zīrīds, see Idris, H. R., *La Berbérie*, vol. 2, p. 599.

60 Goitein, S. D., *MS*, vol. 1, p. 127; vol. 5, p. 43 and pp. 97–100. See also references in Shatzmiller, M., *Labour*, pp. 355–6; and in Idris, H. R., *La Berbérie*, vol. 2, p. 527.

61 For the emotional appeal of the lament on the death of the vizier al-'Ādil composed by Khisrawān, see Smoor, P., 'Murder in the Palace: Poetical Reflections', *AI*, 37 (2003), pp. 400–1.

62 'Abd al-Karīm Aḥmad, *al-Mar'a*, p. 79. As for the pay of a wailing slave-girl, it is recorded that, in the year 551/1156, she was paid over forty *dīnārs*, Goitein, S. D., *MS*, vol. 1, p. 139.

63 For women selling milk in Zīrīd Ifrīqiyā, see Golovin, L., *Le Magrib central a l'époque des Zirides*, Paris: Arts et Metiers Graphiques, 1957, p. 179; on Egyptian women, see Shatzmiller, M., *Labour*, p. 349; on Jewish women selling cooked beans and cakes, see Goitein, S. D., *MS*, vol. 1, p. 129.

64 Nāṣir-i Khusraw, *Sefer nameh*, p. 152.

65 Based on an early twelfth-century *fatwā* by al-Mazarī, see Idris, H. R., *La Berbérie*, vol. 2, p. 667; and Shatzmiller, M., *Labour*, p. 349.

66 al-Maqrīzī, *Itti'āẓ*, vol. 3, p. 82.
67 al-Maqrīzī, Taqī al-Dīn, *Kitāb al-Muqaffā al-kabīr*, ed. al-Ya'lāwī, M., Beirut: Dār al-gharb al-islāmī, 1991, vol. 1, p. 504.
68 See *The epistle on singing-girls of Jāhiẓ*, trans. Beeston, A. F. L., Warminster: Aris & Phillips, 1980, p. 26. The image of singing girls and the taverns where they were performing might have been a literary topos, following from the Umayyad poets' laudes of girls singing to their masters and guests, reclining on cushions and inhaling perfumes and spices: see Hitti, P., *History of the Arabs*, London: Macmillan, 1970, p. 237.
69 See al-Maqrīzī's mention of 'taxes of the singing girls', which he later explains were taxes collected from prostitutes: al-Maqrīzī, *Khiṭaṭ*, vol. 1, p. 89.
70 Goitein, S. D., *MS*, vol. 1, p. 350.
71 al-Musabbiḥī, *Akhbār Miṣr*, vol. 1, p. 68.
72 al-Maqrīzī, *Khiṭaṭ*, vol. 2, p. 96.
73 See Shatzmiller, M., *Labour*, p. 356; for prostitution under the Mamlūks, see 'Abd ar-Rāziq, Aḥmad, *Le femme au temps des Mamlouks en Égypte*, Caire: IFAO, 1973, pp. 45–8, 79–80.
74 al-Musabbiḥī, *Akhbār Miṣr*, vol. 1, pp. 50 and 98. See also Lev, Y., 'The Suppression of Crime, the Supervision of Markets, and Urban Society in the Egyptian Capital during the Tenth and Eleventh Centuries', *MHR*, 3 (1988), 2, p. 83.
75 al-Maqrīzī, *Khiṭaṭ*, vol. 2, p. 92: the area was so-named after a slave serving at the Fāṭimid court; see Raymond, A., *Les marchés*, pp. 133–4.
76 Halm, H., *The Empire of the Mahdi. The Rise of the Fatimids*, trans. M. Bonner, Leiden: E. J. Brill, 1996, p. 361; and Brunschvig, R., "Abd', *EI2nd*, vol. 1, p. 32.
77 Goitein, S. D., *MS*, vol. 1, pp. 130–47.
78 Grohmann, A., *From the World of Arabic Papyri*, Cairo: al-Ma'ārif Press, 1952, pp. 189–91, refers to an early eleventh-century manumission deed of a Copt slave-girl by her mistress; the girl's mother had also been a slave working for the same mistress.
79 For stereotypes on slave-girls see the twelfth-century Spanish Ibn 'Abdūn in Brunschvig, R., "Abd', *EI2nd*, vol. 1, p. 32; for a description of the ideal slave-girl according to a North African slave merchant, see Idris, H. R., *La Berbérie*, vol. 2, pp. 684–5, where it is also indicated that during the Zīrīds the main purveyors of European 'Rūm' slaves were corsairs.
80 Ibn Buṭlān, *Risāla fi shirā' al-raqīq wa-taqlīb al-'abīd*, Cairo: Maṭba'a lajnat al-ta'līf wa-'l-tarjama wa-'l-nashr, 1954, pp. 386–8.
81 On slaves and masters' rights under the Fāṭimids, see [al-Malījī, Abu'l-Qāsim], *al-Majālis al-Mustanṣiriyya*, ed. Muḥammad Kāmil Ḥusayn, Cairo: Dār al-fikr al-'arabī, [1947] , pp. 101–2.
82 Shatzmiller, M., 'Women and wage labour', pp. 192–3; the legal case referred to is about a slave-girl who sang at weddings in tenth-century Qayrawān.
83 al-Maqrīzī, *al-Muqaffā*, vol. 1, p. 300; vol. 3, p. 760; vol. 5, pp. 427–591.
84 On educated concubines, some Byzantine, at the 'Abbāsid court, see Ibn al-Sa'i', 'Alī, *Nisā' al-khulafā': jihāt al-a'immat al-khulafā' min al-ḥarā'ir wa-'l-imā'*, Cairo: Dār al-ma'ārif bi-Miṣr, n.d. [1960?], ed. Musṭafā Jawād; in particular, p. 82, where Qurra, al-Mu'taṣim's concubine, is portrayed as both *jāriya* and *adība*. Another educated concubine is al-Mu'tamid's mother, called Munya al-Kātiba, who had been tutored by the tenth-century grammarian al-Washshā', see al-Safadī, *al-Wafi*, vol. 2, no. 290, pp. 32–3.
85 On the erudition of Sutayta, Bint al-Muhamalī (d. 377/ 987), the daughter of a *qāḍī* and mother of a *qāḍī*, who was well versed in the Arabic language, studied *fiqh*, learnt the *farā'iḍ* and was known as a *ḥadīth* transmitter, see al-Safadī, *al-Wafi*, vol. 9, no. 4317, p. 387.
86 On Bint Yaqtīn, a well-known twelfth-century *kātiba* from Baghdad, see al-Safadī, *al-Wafi*, vol. 14, n. 164, p. 128. Other poetesses and calligraphers much admired by al-Safadī were the Baghdadi Shuhda Bint al-Ibārī, well connected at court and visited by literati attending her

house, and the eleventh-century Andalusian poetess and calligrapher, 'Ā'isha al-Qurṭubiyya (see above Chapter 3).

87 al-Maqrīzī, *al-Muqaffā*,, vol. 1, p. 511.

88 Ibn Abī Usaybī'a, Muwaffaq, *'Uyūn al-anbā' fi ṭabaqāt al-aṭibbā'*, Beirut: Dār al-thaqāfa, 1981, part 3, p. 163.

89 Ibn al-Jawzī, Abu'l-Faraj, *Aḥkām al-nisā'*, Beirut: Dār al-kutub al-'ilmiyya, 1985, pp. 93–4

90 al-Qalqashandī, Shihāb al-Dīn, *Subḥ al-a'shā fi ṣinā'at al-inshā'*, photostatic copy of the Āmiriyya edition, Cairo, n.d. [1963], vol. 1, p. 64, referring to unnamed wise men whose opinion is reported in the maxim.

91 Idris, H. R., *La Berbérie*, vol. 2, pp. 773–4.

92 In addition to the private secretaries of Fāṭimid women, see, on queen Asmā''s poet, who then became her secretary, Shakir, M., *Sīrat al-Malik al-Mukarram: an edition and a study*, PhD thesis, SOAS, London: University of London, 1999, vol. 1, p. 175.

93 Ibn Muyassar, *Akhbār Miṣr*, p. 83.

94 Reif, S. C., *A Jewish Archive from Old Cairo*, Richmond: Curzon, 2000, pp. 227–8.

95 Berkey, J., *The Transmission of Knowledge in Medieval Cairo*, Princeton: Princeton University Press, 1992, pp. 180–1.

96 Ibn 'Idhārī al-Marrākushī, Aḥmad, *Kitāb al-Bayān al-mughrib, Histoire de l'Afrique et de l'Espagne intitulée al-Bayano'l-Mogrib*, vol. 2, French trans. Fagnan, E. R., Algiers: Imprimerie Orientale P. Fontana, 1901, vol. 1, p. 221.

97 Ibn Ḥajar al-'Asqalānī, *Raf' al-iṣr*, ed. Guest, R., in appendix to al-Kindī, *Kitāb al-umarā' (al-wulāt): The Governors and Judges of Egypt*, Leiden: E. J. Brill/London: Luzac, 1912, p. 584.

98 On the office of *qāḍī*, see Lev, Y., 'The Cadi and the Urban Society: the Case Study of Medieval Egypt, 9–12th centuries' in Lev, Y. (ed.), *Town and Material Culture in the Medieval Middle East*, Leiden: E. J. Brill, 2002, pp. 89–102.

99 Ibn Ḥajar al-'Asqalānī, *Raf' al-iṣr*, p. 584.

100 al-Musabbiḥī, *Nuṣūṣ*, p. 33

101 al-Maqrīzī, *al-Muqaffā*, vol. 1, p. 394.

102 al-Musabbiḥī, *Nuṣūṣ*, p. 33.

103 Grohmann, A., *From the World*, pp. 197–9.

104 Idris, H. R., *La Berbérie*, vol. 2, pp. 668.

105 Ibn Ḥajar al-'Asqalānī, *Raf' al-iṣr*, p. 586.

106 al-Qāḍī al-Nu'mān, *Kitāb al-Majālis wa-'l-musāyarāt*, ed. al-Faqī, Ḥ. et al., Tunis: al-Maṭba'a al-rasmiyya li-'l-jumhūriyya al-tūnsiyya, 1978, p. 65.

107 Fyzee, A. A. A., *Compendium of Fatimid Law*, Simla: Indian Institute of Advanced Study, 1969, pp. 20, 43–4.

108 al-Musabbiḥī, *Akhbār Miṣr*, pp. 92–3, 104.

109 See Lev, Y., 'The Cadi', p. 100.

110 Fyzee, A. A. A., *Compendium*, p. 49. For a detailed account of the legal rulings about women's inheritance shares during the late Fāṭimid period, see Cooper, R. S., *Ibn Māmmatī's Rules for the Ministries: Translation with Commentary of the Qawānīn al-Dawāwīn*, PhD thesis, Berkeley: University of California, 1973, p. 272.

111 al-Musabbiḥī, *Nuṣūṣ*, p. 34.

112 Idris, H. R., *La Berbérie*, vol. 1, p. 86.

113 al-Musabbiḥī, *Akhbār Miṣr*, vol. 1, pp. 97, 101.

114 al-Maqrīzī, *al-Muqaffā*, vol. 1, p. 646.

115 Goitein, S. D., *MS*, vol. 2, pp. 372–3.

116 Ibn Abī Usaybī'a, *'Uyūn*, part 3, p. 147 ff. Also Goitein, S. D., *MS*, vol. 2, pp. 244 and 352.

117 See Bos, G., 'Ibn al-Jazzār on women's diseases and their treatment', *MH*, 37 (1993), 3, pp.

296–312; and Bos, G., *Ibn al-Jazzār on Sexual Diseases and Their Treatment*, London and New York: Kegan Paul, 1997.

118 Bos, G., *Ibn al-Jazzār on Sexual*, p. 282; and Bos, G., *Ibn al-Jazzār on Fevers*, London and New York: Kegan Paul International, 2000, p. 119.

119 al-Baladī, Aḥmad, *Tadbīr al-ḥabālā wa-'l-aṭfāl wa-'l-ṣibyān wa-ḥifẓ ṣiḥḥati-him wa-mudawat al-amrāḍ al-'āriḍa la-hum*, ed. Maḥmūd al-Ḥajj Qāsim Muḥammad, Baghdad: 1987.

120 al-Maqrīzī, *Khiṭaṭ*, vol. 1, p. 420. On a Jewish doctor in attendance to a Fāṭimid royal lady around 554/1159, see Goitein, S. D., *MS*, vol. 2, p. 352.

121 Ibn Riḍwān, *Daf'*, p. 124.

122 In the Geniza documents there are records of one hospital in Fāṭimid times, presumably the only one, in Fusṭāṭ, see Goitein, S. D., MS, vol. 2, p. 251.

123 Goitein, S. D., MS, vol. 1, pp. 127–8.

124 Bos, G., *Ibn al-Jazzār on Sexual*, pp. 275, 277.

125 Bos, G., 'Ibn al-Jazzār on women's', p. 305.

126 al-Qāḍī al-Nu'mān, *Da'ā'im al-Islām fī dhikr al-ḥalal*, ed. Fyzee, A. A. A., Cairo: Dār al-Ma'ārif, 1959–61, vol. 2, p. 142.

127 Bos, G., *Ibn al-Jazzār on Sexual*, p. 275.

128 Giladi, A., *Infants, Parents and Wet Nurses*, Leiden: E. J. Brill, 1999, p. 51.

129 For slave wetnurses, see Ibn Buṭlān, *Risāla fī shirā'*, p. 387, where black slaves are indicated as the best wetnurses. Jewish wetnurses were employed in Muslim households and, famously, the Zīrīd al-Mu'izz b. Badīs's nurse was originally a Christian.

130 al-Maqrīzī, *Itti'āẓ*, vol. 1, p. 272.

131 Dagorn, R., 'Al-Baladi: un medicin obstetricien et pediatre à l'époque des prèmiers Fatimides du Caire', *MIDEO*, 9 (1967) p. 99.

132 al-Maqrīzī, *Itti'āẓ*, vol. 3, p. 232.

133 Bos, G., *Ibn al-Jazzār on Sexual*, pp. 290–3.

134 al-Qāḍī al-Nu'mān, *Da'ā'im*, vol. 2, p. 210.

135 al-Qāḍī al-Nu'mān, *Da'ā'im* (trans. Fyzee), pp. 160–1, 143–4.

136 al-Qāḍī al-Nu'mān, *Da'ā'im* (trans. Fyzee), p. 154. On the lawfulness of loveplay, see p. 158.

137 Ibn Riḍwān, *Daf'*, p. 106.

138 al-Qāḍī al-Nu'mān, *Da'ā'im* (trans. Fyzee), pp. 283, 286, 288.

139 Lo Jacono, C., 'Su un caso di *istiqsām* nel *fiqh* imamita e ismailita-fatimide: il ricorso alla Qur'ah nelle *Farā'iḍ*', in *La Bisaccia dello Sheikh, Omaggio ad Alessandro Bausani, Islamista, nel sessantesimo compleanno, Quaderni del Seminari di Iranistica, Uralo-altaistica e Caucasologia*, 19 (1981), pp. 221–4.

140 al-Maqrīzī, *Khiṭaṭ*, French trans. Bouriant, M. U., *Description topographique et historique de l'Égypte*, Paris and Cairo: Mission Archeologique Française du Caire, 1895, part 2, p. 516.

141 Nāṣir-i Khusraw, *Sefer nameh*, p. 114.

142 Ibn Riḍwān, *Daf'*, p. 115.

CONCLUSIONS

The primary aim of this research project was to fill a vacuum in the field of studies on women belonging to and living under medieval Islamic dynasties by comprehensively covering women under the Fatimids. After all, this was and still remains the only Islamic dynasty to be named after a woman. Moreover, to this dynasty were linked those women who, on account of the power they commanded, were to become among the most famous female personalities of the medieval Islamic world: Sitt al-Mulk, the Sulayhid queens of the Yemen and the mother of the imam-caliph al-Mustansir. The recurring lament by contemporary scholars of the limited availability of primary material for the study of women in the medieval Islamic world in general did not deter us from pursuing our plan. We soon realised that information, far from being minimal, was in fact plentiful to those looking for it, interspersed, as it is, within historical, doctrinal, literary and other narratives. After several years of research, we hope we have achieved our primary aim: to throw some light on the erstwhile silent and shadowy figures of women under the Fatimids and give them a presence in the history of women in medieval and pre-modern dynasties.

To be pioneers always involves risks, among which is that of being superseded by the addition of new data, by alternative interpretations of the data provided, and by the in-depth analysis of those areas of investigation that, in a study of this type, could only be touched upon. Indeed, there are several areas that deserve further inquiry: the doctrinal and esoteric imagery of the feminine in Fatimid literature, the role of women in commerce and trade following the ongoing discovery of new documentary material, the impact of Isma'ili jurisprudence upon women's lives in the Fatimid era, the social and legal status of children and the women who cared for them. Nevertheless, we have taken this risk, so as to make a contribution not only to pave the way for a more rounded evaluation of the Fatimids and their impact on medieval history, but also to enrich, with new data and perspectives, the broader fields of Islamic and medieval studies.

To take the Fatimid period as a framework for a study of women in medieval Islam has had its advantages. Stretching, as it does, over a period of two and half centuries, the Fatimid era is fairly well defined in its beginnings and in its demise. It is neither too long a period, so as to risk falling into over-generalisations, nor too short, so as to prevent the identification of an internal periodisation. In the instance of female architectural patronage, such periodisation has proved fruitful in enabling us to detect a shift in the dynastic uses of patronage as well as in the status of women patrons. In the case of the *da'wa*, a periodised assessment of its activities has allowed us to identify changing degrees and levels of female participation. Geographically, the territories within the Fatimid *dawla* are clearly circumscribed: first Ifriqiya and later Egypt, while of the territories outside the *dawla*, the Sulayhid Yemen represents in this context the most clear example of a spatially and temporally defined dominion ruled by a consistently loyal vassal dynasty. Finally, as the first major foreign Shi'i dynasty ruling over predominantly Sunni territories, the Fatimids, more than others, attracted the attention and curiosity of contemporary and subsequent chroniclers who, besides their politics and warfare, reported on their missionary activities, their 'heterodox' celebrations, rituals and court life, all of which included, even if just by default, an unusually rich and varied set of information about women.

There are two main guiding threads woven into the fabric of this work. The first is the recurring references to the interplay between the ethnically, religiously and culturally diverse subjects, allies and supporters of the Fatimids. Being culturally and doctrinally 'foreigners' themselves in the regions they ruled, the imam-caliphs encouraged, and to some extent relied upon, such diversity when, for instance, appointing Berbers and Turks, Christians and Jews as their viziers, secretaries and military commanders. This diversity was in turn reflected in the composition of the harem and in the background of most of the imam-caliphs' spouses and concubines, thus representing an important factor in the emergence of a 'natural' collusion (or collision) between the harem and those in charge of the management and the defence of the *dawla*. In times of heightened tension between the different power bases, women emerge as holders of positions of considerable influence and power, such as the 'Ifriqiyan' Sitt al-Mulk or the 'Sudani' Rasad. As with other dynasties, what made these and other women under the Fatimids influential and powerful were their links to powerful men. However, what appears to be a strong feature of the Fatimid period is that, by and large, these powerful women either represented the interests of one faction against another, or they were manipulated as figureheads by those powerful men engaged in rivalries, such as those between the *mashāriqa* and the *maghāriba*, the caliphs and the viziers, the viziers and the *qāḍīs*, as well as between the competing claimants to the caliphate.

The second guiding thread is represented by the evidence of an interconnectedness between Fatimids, women and trade. Trade had been of paramount importance to the Fatimids throughout their history: from the period leading to the establishment of the dynasty and its success in Ifriqiya and Egypt, to the dynasty's hold of the Yemen, its alternating fortunes in Syria, and down to the time of the dynasty's demise. Women have played a significant role in securing the Fatimids' success in both trade and propaganda. During the early missionary activities, when Isma'ili missionary-cum-merchants were selling their goods in the local marketplaces, in the cemeteries or door-to-door, women were both the purchasers of their goods and their informants on local news. With the establishment of the dynasty in Cairo, the role of women as consumers comes again to the fore, particularly in connection with al-Hakim's issuing of decrees restricting women's movements. As beneficiaries or investors of the wealth and riches that were also accumulated as a result of successful local and international commerce, royal women served as 'deposit banks' or, in times of conflict, as financiers and supporters of the army or as moneylenders to rescue the economy of the *dawla*. Mission, trade and women came together once more when al-Mustansir entrusted queen Arwa with a double role: to represent the Fatimid sovereignty in the Yemen and to spread the mission to India; in other words, to secure the Yemen as a trading base for the Indian route.

Research has shown that, with reference to the possibilities women had, or were given, to show their status and to push the boundaries of their traditional roles, the Fatimids emerge as forerunners in many ways. First, under the Fatimids, both royal and ordinary women were the recipients of regular doctrinal instructions specifically designed for them; it would take several centuries before women in the Islamic world would receive tailor-made education formally delivered by the state. Second, during the Fatimids, court women marked their status and influence by way of grand-scale architectural patronage for the use of propaganda. These women's choice of the type of buildings to sponsor, and of location, could be viewed as a further reflection of the dynasty's attention to the interplay between the diverse religious and ethnic groups among their subjects. Third, prominent women of the Fatimid caliphal family emerge as having been actively engaged in diplomatic relations not merely as hostesses during diplomatic visits, but also as signatories of official correspondence exchanged between the powerful men and women of the time. Fourth, the Fatimids were forerunners in the practice of frequently appointing as heirs children born of concubines rather than those born of wives. This practice was to become standard a few centuries later among the Ottoman sultans. Finally, it appears that political and dynastic motivations lay behind the Fatimid imam-caliphs' enforcement of 'political' spinsterhood on their daughters, a policy that was to be replicated by subsequent Muslim dynasties. However, what makes the Fatimids unique among Muslim dynasties is the fact that, in the case of queen Arwa, an imam-caliph formally endorsed a woman as holder of both temporal and religious authority. From being appointed as supervisor of the *da'wa* in the Yemen, Arwa's status has been reinterpreted in Tayyibi Isma'ilism as occupying the position of *ḥujja* – that is, the spiritual rank second only to that of the imam.

This book opened with the description of a religious ceremony held in the National Stadium of Karachi in 1958, which celebrated the appointment of the new imam of the Isma'ilis. A woman, the mother of the imam, figured prominently in the elaborate protocol, which was designed to mark the event. Under the Fatimids, royal mothers endorsed and supported the succession to the imamate of their own sons, they exercised their power as regents, as queen mothers they influenced the court and beyond, and they erected buildings to perpetuate their son's and their own names. Then, the Fatimid imam-caliph was a spiritual and temporal leader; today, the Isma'ili imam, although no longer the ruler of an empire, is nevertheless the spiritual leader of a prosperous multi-ethnic community with no boundaries, living, as it does, in every continent of the world.

APPENDICES

Appendix 1
The Fatimid Imam-Caliphs and Their Mothers

1. Abu Muhammad ʿAbd Allah **al-Mahdi** bi-'llah (d. 322/934) + *daughter of Abu 'l-Shalaʿlaʿ*

2. Abu 'l-Qasim Muhammad **al-Qa'im** bi-Amr Allah (d. 334/946) + *Karima*

3. Abu Tahir Ismaʿil **al-Mansur** bi-'llah (d. 341/953) + *Durrzadeh (d. 364/974)*

4. Abu Tamim Maʿad **al-Muʿizz** li-Din Allah (d. 365/975) + <u>*Durzan "Taghrid"*</u> *(d. 385/995)*

5. Abu Mansur Nizar **al-ʿAziz** bi-'llah (d. 386/996) + ?

6. Abu ʿAli al-Mansur **al-Hakim** bi-Amr Allah (d. 411/1021) + <u>*Amina "Ruqayya"*</u>

7. Abu 'l-Hasan ʿAli **al-Zahir** li-Iʿzaz Din Allah (d. 427/1036) + <u>*Rasad*</u>

8. Abu Tamim Maʿadd **al-Mustansir** bi-'llah (d. 487/1094) + *unnamed Byzantine* + *unnamed 'jiha ʿazima'*

Abu 'l-Qasim Muhammad

9. **al-Mustaʿli** bi-'llah + ? (d. 495/1101)

9i. **Nizar** + ? (d. 488/1095)

10. **al-Amir** + ? (d. 524/1130)

(Nizari imams continue to this day as Shiʿa Imami Ismaʿilis/Khojas)

11. **al-Hafiz** + *"Sitt al-Wafa'"* (d. 544/1149)

11i. **al-Tayyib**

(Hidden Tayyibi imams Sulaymani and Da'udi Bohras continue to this day)

12. **al-Zafir** + *Ihsan "Zayn al-Kamal"* (d. 549/1154)

Yusuf + *"Sitt al-Muna"*

13. **al-Fa'iz** (d. 555/1160)

14. **al-ʿAdid** (d. 567/1171)

Da'ud (d. 604/1207)

<u>*Name* = consensus among sources, name attested</u>
"…" = title, epithet

Appendix 2
Glossary

ʿAbbāsids: dynasty of caliphs (132/749–656/1258), descendants from the uncle of the Prophet Muḥammad, al-ʿAbbās b. ʿAbd al-Muṭṭalib.

Aghlabids: dynasty (184/800–296/909) that ruled part of North Africa prior to the advent of the Fāṭimids.

Ahl al-Bayt: lit. the people of the house; the Prophet's household, typically including in Shīʿī context: Muḥammad, ʿAlī, Fāṭima, al-Ḥasan, al-Ḥusayn and their progeny.

ahl al-dhimma: see *dhimmī* (q.v.).

ʿAlīds: the descendants of ʿAlī b. Abī Ṭālib, cousin and husband of Fāṭima, the Prophet's daughter. ʿAlī became the fourth caliph following Muḥammad's death and first Shīʿī imam.

ʿālima: learned woman, particularly in religious sciences.

ʿāmma: the common, ordinary people; but also *ʿāmm* in the sense of 'public' as opposed to 'private', *khāṣṣa* (q.v.).

ʿāshūrā': Shīʿī day of atonement on 10 Muḥarram, commemorating the martyrdom of the imam al-Ḥusayn.

awliyā': lit. 'friends', usually referring to the Ismāʿīlī devotees.

Ayyūbids: dynasty that ruled Egypt immediately after the demise of the Fāṭimids until 660/1260.

bāb: lit. gate, door; the highest rank after the imam in Fāṭimid Ismāʿīlī *daʿwa* hierarchy, often equivalent to *dāʿī al-duʿāt* (q.v.).

bāligh: legal term to indicate maturity and legal competence.

bāṭin: esoteric meaning behind the exoteric wording of sacred texts and religious laws. Bāṭinis or Bāṭiniyya are those people, mostly Shīʿī, who uphold this belief.

batūl: pure, virgin. An adjective particularly used for Fāṭima, the Prophet's daughter, and for Mary, the mother of Jesus.

bayt al-māl: the Treasury in an Islamic state.

dāʿī: lit. summoner, religious propagandist or missionary. In Ismāʿīlī context, a high ranking person in the *daʿwa* (q.v.) hierarchy trained and authorised to spread Ismāʿīlīsm by winning converts and to act as the imam's representative. The chief *dāʿī* was called *dāʿī al-duʿāt*.

dāʿī muṭlaq: lit. absolute *dāʿī*, the highest rank in the *daʿwa* hierarchy of the Mustaʿlī-Ṭayyibī branch of Ismāʿīlīsm and its Dāʾūdī Bohra and Sulaymānī offshoots, with absolute power over the affairs of his community.

dār al-hijra: lit. the Abode of Migration, allegedly founded by Ḥamdān Qarmaṭ as an operational base for anti-ʿAbbāsid activities.

dār al-ʿilm: lit. the Abode of Knowledge, a meeting place for scholars founded under al-Ḥākim.

daʿwa: mission or propaganda. In Ismāʿīlī context, invitation to uphold the right of an individual or a family to the imamate; also the entire hierarchy of ranks within the religious organisation. The Ismāʿīlīs used the term as synonymous with their movement, often indicated also as *al-daʿwa al-hādīya*, 'the rightly-guiding mission'.

dawla: the dynasty, the Fāṭimid regime; loosely, 'the Fāṭimid state'.

dhimmī: a member of the *ahl al-kitāb*, the 'People of the Book', that is, non-Muslims, mainly Jews or Christians, who, upon acknowledging the temporal authority of the Muslim ruler and paying the due taxes, are legally protected and entitled to keep their own religion.

dīnār: gold monetary unit widely used across the medieval Islamic world. The value of the *dīnār* varied from region to region, from period to period, and depended, among other factors, on the purity of the gold and the refinement of the mint. Fāṭimid *dīnārs* were highly praised for their quality.

dirham: silver monetary unit, less valuable than *dīnār*.

dīwān: 1) office, department, here often referring to the office administering the finances and general affairs of a prominent court person; government department; 2) collection of poems.

faqīh (pl. *fuqahā'*): jurist or specialist in Islamic jurisprudence, *fiqh*.

Fāṭimids: the Ismāʿīlī dynasty of imam-caliphs (297/909–567/1171) claiming descent from Fāṭima, the daughter of the Prophet Muḥammad, and ʿAlī b. Abī Ṭālib.

fatwā: a legal opinion uttered by an authoritative legal Muslim scholar, such as a *muftī*.

fiqh: religious jurisprudence, explanation and application of the *sharīʿa*.

fitna: division or dissent within a society. Shīʿī scholars refer to ʿĀ'isha, the favourite wife of the Prophet, as causing the first *fitna* of Islam by opposing ʿAlī's choice as caliph.

G*hadīr*: the Shīʿī festival celebrating the Prophet's appointment of ʿAlī as his successor at Ghadīr Khumm.

ghayba: occultation or concealment, the condition of anyone believed to have been absconded by God from human vision and whose life is miraculously prolonged while in occultation until his reappearance at a pre-ordained time before the Day of Resurrection, *qiyāma*. A number of Shīʿī groups believed in the *ghayba* of one imam or another, thus awaiting his return at the end of time as *mahdī* (q.v.).

ḥadīth: report or tradition relating the doing and saying of the Prophet Muḥammad; collectively the second major source of Islamic law. For the Shīʿīs, it refers also to a report of an action or statement by one of their imams.

Ḥāfiẓiyya: the supporters of Abu'l-Qāsim al-Ḥāfiẓ (d. 544/1140), who became the eleventh Fāṭimid caliph and was a cousin of the former Fāṭimid caliph al-Āmir.

ḥājib: a palace chamberlain or master of ceremonies.

ḥajj: annual pilgrimage to Makka that every Muslim must perform at least once in his or her lifetime. It takes place in the month of *Dhu'l-Ḥijja*, the last month of the Islamic calendar.

ḥammām: public bath, visited for ritual, medical and social purposes.

ḥaqā'iq: eternal, unchanging truths contained in the *bāṭin* (q.v.).

ḥarīm/harem: lit. a sacred or inviolable place; 1) the living quarter of the palace reserved to women, to which access is limited to very few selected individuals; 2) its female and eunuch residents.

ḥaẓīya: see *jāriya* (q.v.).

ḥujja: lit. proof or the presentation of proof. In Shīʿī context, it refers to a person – typically an imam after Muḥammad's death – who at any given time served as 'proof' among humankind of God's will. In pre-Fāṭimid Ismāʿīlīsm, *ḥujja* also referred to a dignitary in the religious hierarchy who would act as intercessor between the adherent and the imam in *ghayba*. In Fāṭimid Ismāʿīlīsm, the *ḥujja* also indicated a high-rank person in charge of a particular *daʿwa* region or 'island', *jazīra*.

ʿīd: festival, in addition to the traditional Muslim festivals of *ʿīd al-fiṭr* (the breaking of the fast at the end of Ramadan) and *ʿīd al-aḍḥā* (the festival of sacrifice, during the *ḥajj* month), the Fāṭimids commemorated the Shīʿī festivals of *ʿāshūrāʾ* and *Ghadīr* (q.v.) and introduced the *mawlids* (q.v.). Other festivals included the Christian festival of the Epiphany and civil festivals.

Ifrīqiyā: part of North Africa, broadly corresponding to today's Tunisia.

Ikhshīdids: pro-ʿAbbāsid dynasty (323/935–358/969) that ruled Egypt prior to the arrival of the Fāṭimids.

imām: prayer leader. In Shīʿī context, he is the person recognised as the spiritual and secular head of the Muslim community after the Prophet. ʿAlī b. Abī Ṭālib and some of his descendants are considered to be such leaders, imams, as legitimate successors to Muḥammad. The imams are regarded as infallible, sinless, divinely appointed, divinely guided in their special spiritual functions and as the ultimate repositories of all esoteric knowledge. The office of the imam is termed imamate, *imāma*.

iqṭāʿ / *iqṭāʿāt*: lit. a portion, assignment, allocation; an administrative (usually land) grant from which the beneficiary would gain a constant revenue.

Jaʿfarite: referring to teachings and traditions going back to the Shīʿī imam (q.v.) Jaʿfar al-Ṣādiq.

Jāmiʿa: congregational mosque.

jāriya: usually concubine, but also slave-girl and lady's maid when at the service of Fāṭimid royal women. Occasionally used with similar meaning are *ḥaẓīya* and *sarārī* (pl. of *surrīya*).

jazīra (pl. *jazāʾir*): lit. island; here a particular *daʿwa* (q.v.) region. According to Fāṭimid Ismāʿīlī cosmology, the world was divided into twelve regions to be penetrated by the *daʿwa* and to be placed under the leadership of a *ḥujja* (q.v.).

jiha: lit. side; here a consort of the imam-caliph. As *al-jiha al-ʿālīya*, lit. the high side; the title usually designates acknowledgement of one or more royal consorts as being the most important.

jizya: a personal tax to be paid by all *dhimmīs* (q.v.).

khādim: lit. servant, a term used to refer to a eunuch; the other, more common term is *ustādh*.

Khalīj: the canal from the Nile, on the west side of Fāṭimid Cairo.

khāṣṣa: the elite, the privileged people as opposed to the *ʿāmma* (q.v.); but also *khāṣṣ* in the sense of 'private' as opposed to 'public', *ʿāmm* (q.v.).

khatima: the celebration for the completion of the recitation of the whole Qur'an at the end of Ramaḍān.

khilaʿ: robe of honour bestowed in the name of the Fāṭimid imam-caliph upon *mawālī* (q.v.) supporters of the Fāṭimid dynasty as well as worthy individuals, whether Muslims or non-Muslims.

khizānat al-khaṣṣ: the imam-caliph's Private Treasury.

khizānat al-kiswa: Treasury of Fabrics and Clothes.

Khoja: loosely, an Indian Nizārī Ismāʿīlī or a Nizārī of Indian origin.

khuṭba: sermon delivered during the Friday midday public prayer in a mosque, usually inclusive of blessings upon the caliph (and his family) or the ruler.
Fāṭima's *khuṭba*: the Speech she gave after the Prophet's death, claiming her inheritance from her father of the Fadak orchard.

laqab: nickname, honorific title.

madhhab: a system of belief within Islam or a school of religious law.

madrasa: religious college or school, often attached to the mosque.

mahr: dowry or gift promised by the prospective husband and stipulated in a marriage contract.

maghāriba (sing. *maghribī*): faction of administrative and army high dignitaries serving the Fāṭimids, of North African, particularly Kutama Berber, extraction.

mashāriqa (sing. *mashriqī*): faction of administrative and army high dignitaries serving the Fāṭimids, of Eastern, particularly Turkish, extraction.

mahdī: the 'rightly guided one' who will reappear at the end of time to restore religion and justice. Applied to various individuals across Islamic history; in broad Shīʿī context, the term denoted a member of the Prophet's family who, after a period of *ghayba* (q.v.), would eventually return in full glory.

majlis (pl. *majālis*): session; here usually indicated as *majālis al-ḥikma*, sessions of 'wisdom', which the *dāʿī* (q.v.) would hold to deliver sermons to male and female Ismāʿīlī initiates.

malika (m. *malik*): sovereign, queen.

mawlā (pl. *mawālī*): master, 'client' of an Arab tribe or group or dynasty. Also a convert to Islam, a freed slave.

mawlid: birthday, festival; in Fāṭimid times, the *mawlid* of Muḥammad, Fāṭima, ʿAlī, al-Hasan and al-Ḥusayn as well as the living Fāṭimid imam became official holidays. The *mawlid* of the Prophet, inaugurated as a festival by the Fāṭimids, is celebrated to this day, despite some Sunnī purist scholars' opposition to the practice.

miḥrāb: mosque prayer niche, indicating the direction of prayer towards Makka.

minbar: pulpit in a mosque from where the *khuṭba* (q.v.) is delivered.

Miṣr: term used to indicate 1) the two urban areas of Fusṭāṭ and al-Qaṭā'iʿ, being distinct from al-Qāhira, further north, the Fāṭmid capital; 2) Egypt.

muḥtasib: market supervisor, also controlling proper behaviour in public.

munqaṭiʿa: female member of staff working at the Fāṭimid court not resident at the palace, as opposed to the *muqīma* (q.v.), a resident one.

muqīma: see *munqaṭiʿa* (q.v.).

mutʿa: the temporary marriage allowed in Shīʿī law but illegal for the Sunnī and Ismāʿīlī interpretation of the *sharīʿa*.

naṣṣ: the explicit designation by an imam of his successor.

Nizārīs: those Ismāʿīlīs who upheld the succession rights of Nizār, the eldest son of the imam-caliph al-Mustanṣir, against those of his half-brother al-Mustaʿlī. The Nizārīs believed in the continuation of the imamate in the line of descendants of Nizār b. al-Mustanṣir.

qāḍī (pl. *quḍāt*): judge administering the *sharīʿa*; *qāḍī al-quḍāt* denotes the chief judge. In Fāṭimid Ismāʿīlīsm, the positions of *dāʿī al-duʿāt* (q.v.) and *qāḍī al-quḍāt* were often held by one person.

qā'im: the resurrector; the eschatological *mahdī* (q.v.). In the Fāṭimid period, the name al-Mahdī was reserved for the first Fāṭimid imam-caliph, while *qā'im*, besides being the dynastic name of al-Mahdī's son and successor, was used to indicate the eschatological imam awaited for the future. In a Nizārī (q.v.) context, the denominations 'imam-*qā'im*' and '*qā'im al-qiyāma*' were applied to the Nizārī imams of the so-called *qiyāma* period in Alamūt.

qaṣīda: lengthy poetical composition, usually a eulogy or a panegyric.

qaṣr: fortified building and complex, castle.
raṭl: weight unit/measure: 1 *raṭl* = 0.57 kg.
ṣalāt: ritual obligatory prayer for Muslims.
satr: concealment, referring to the period when the imams were concealed from the eyes of their followers, or to the utter concealment of the *ḥaqā'iq* (q.v.).
sayyida: lady. Here title used to indicate seniority of age or rank, or indeed both, of Fāṭimid royal women. As *al-sayyida al-malika* (lit. 'lady queen, sovereign'), this title usually applied to the most influential among the wives and concubines of the imam-caliph, specifically the mother of the designated heir, the queen mother, or even one of the elderly female members in his family.
shaykh: lit. an elder, honorific term used for a scholar, or for a tribal leader.
al-shidda al-Mustanṣiriyya: denoting the most serious economic, political and civil collapse that, together with famine, devastated Egypt during the reign of al-Mustanṣir.
sijill: scroll, register; here formal, official letter.
sitt al-mulk: lit. the lady of sovereignty, this title was typically reserved for the female offspring of the Fāṭimid imam-caliphs. Famous is the case of al-'Azīz's daughter, who came to be known by it. In time, the title came to be also bestowed on the daughters of viziers. The title appears also in variants like *sitt al-malik*.
taqīya: precautionary religious dissimulation to escape persecution or danger.
ta'wīl: the inner or esoteric meaning of a text or a ritual; the method of educing the *bāṭin* (q.v.) from the *ẓāhir* (q.v).
Ṭayyibiyya: those who upheld the succession rights of al-Ṭayyib, the infant son of the Fāṭimid caliph al-Āmir against the Ḥāfiẓiyya (q.v.), the supporters of al-Āmir's cousin al-Ḥāfiẓ.
ta'ziya: Shī'ī 'passion' play, staged especially during the month of Muḥarram.
ṭirāz: a type of linen embroidered with gold or silver threads featuring bands inscribed with the imam-caliph's name.
'ulamā': learned individuals, scholars in Islamic religious sciences; the religious class.
umm al-walad: lit. the son's mother; term commonly used to refer to a concubine, whether free or slave, who would acquire rights upon giving birth to her master's child.
ustādh: see *khādim* (q.v.).
waqf: a charitable foundation, family or public charity endowment; voluntary alienation of property by its owner and dedication of its usufruct ostensibly to charitable aims (public buildings, education, relief for poor, for widows, and so on).
walī: guardian, governor, defender; also a title used for the imams.
walī al-'ahd: heir designate, designated successor.
waṣī: legatee, executor of a will, also the successor to a prophet.
wāsiṭ/wāsiṭa: the highest (after the vizier) administrator/broker between the people and the caliph. In some cases the same person held the office of both vizier and *wāsiṭ*.
wazīr (vizier): chief minister, high officer in the state apparatus. The office of the vizier was the vizirate, *wizāra*.
zakāt: alms-giving, one of the five religious obligations of a Muslim man or woman.
ẓāhir: the outer, exoteric meaning of sacred texts and religious laws; counterbalancing the *bāṭin* (q.v.).
Zīrīds: vassal dynasty of the Fāṭimids in Ifrīqiyā.
ziyāra: visitation of tombs and shrines.

BIBLIOGRAPHY

Primary Sources

al-Anṭākī, Yaḥyā b. Sa'īd, *Ta'rīkh*, partial ed. and French trans. Kratchkovsky, I. and Vasiliev, A., 'Histoire de Yahya-ibn Sa'īd d'Antioche', *Patrologia Orientalis*, 23 (1932), pp. 347–520.

[al-Antākī, Yaḥyā b. Sa'īd], *Yahya al-Antaki: Cronache dell'Egitto fatimide e dell'impero bizantino (937–1033)*, ed. and Ital. trans. Pirone, B., Milano: Jaca Book, 1998.

al-Baladī, Aḥmad, *Tadbīr al-ḥabālā wa-'l-aṭfāl wa-'l-ṣibyān wa-ḥifẓ ṣiḥḥati-him wa-mudawat al-amrāḍ al-'āriḍa la-hum*, ed. Maḥmūd al-Ḥajj Qāsim Muḥammad, Baghdad: 1987.

Comnena, A., *The Alexiad of Anna Comnena*, trans. Sewter, E. R. A., Harmondsworth: Penguin Classics, 1969.

al-Ḥāmidī, Ibrāhīm, *Kitāb Kanz al-walad*, ed. Ghālib, M., Wiesbaden: F. Steiner, 1391/1971.

Ibn Abī Usaybī'a, Muwaffaq, *'Uyūn al-anbā' fī ṭabaqāt al-aṭibbā'*, Beirut: Dār al-thaqāfa, 1981.

Ibn al-Athīr, 'Izz al-Dīn, *al-Kāmil fi'l-ta'rīkh*, Beirut: Dār al-kitāb al-'arabī, 1967.

Ibn al-Athīr, 'Izz al-Dīn, *al-Kāmil fi'l-ta'rīkh*, ed. Torneberg, C., Leiden: 1851–76.

Ibn Buṭlān, *Risāla fī shirā' al-raqīq wa-taqlīb al-'abīd*, Cairo: Maṭba'a lajnat al-ta'līf wa-'l-tarjama wa-'l-nashr, 1954.

Ibn al-Dawādārī, Abū Bakr b. 'Abd Allāh, *Kanz al-durar wa-jāmi' al-ghurar: al-durra al-muḍiya fī akhbār al-dawla al-Fāṭimiyya*, ed. al-Munajjid, Ṣ., Cairo: O. Harrassowitz, 1961.

Ibn Duqmāq, Ibrāhīm b. Muḥammad, *Kitāb al-Intiṣār li-wāsiṭat 'aqd al-amṣār*, ed. Vollers, Beirut: al-Maktab al-tijārī, 1893.

Ibn Ḥajar al-'Asqalānī, *Raf' al-iṣr*, ed. Guest, R., in appendix to al-Kindī, *Kitāb al-umarā' (al-wulāt): The Governors and Judges of Egypt*, Leiden: E. J. Brill/London: Luzac, 1912.

Ibn Ḥammād, Abū 'Abd Allāh, *Akhbār mulūk banī 'Ubayd*, ed. and French trans. Vonderheyden, M., *Histoire des Rois 'Obaïdites (Les Califes Fatimides)*, Algiers: J. Carbonel; Paris: P. Geuthner, 1927.

Ibn Hāni', al-Andalusī, *Dīwān*, ed. Zāhid 'Alī, *Tabyīn al-ma'ānī fī sharḥ dīwān Ibn Hāni'*, Cairo: Maṭba'at al-ma'ārif, 1352/1933.

Ibn al-Haytham, Abū 'Abd Allāh, *Kitāb al-Munāẓarāt*, trans. Madelung, W. and Walker, P. E. in *The Advent of the Fatimids: A Contemporary Shi'i Witness*, London: I. B. Tauris, 2000.

Ibn 'Idhārī al-Marrākushī, Aḥmad, *Kitāb al-Bayān al-mughrib*, ed. Colin, G. S. and Levi-Provencal, É., Leiden: E. J. Brill, 1948.

Ibn 'Idhārī al-Marrākushī, Aḥmad, *Kitāb al-Bayān al-mughrib*, *Histoire de l'Afrique et de l'Espagne intitulée al-Bayano'l-Mogrib*, vol. 2, French trans. Fagnan, E. R., Algiers: Imprimerie Orientale P. Fontana, 1901.

Ibn Kathīr, Abu'l-Fidā', *al-Bidāya wa-'l-nihāya*, Beirut, Dār iḥyā' al-turāth al-'arabī, 2nd edn, 1977.

Ibn Khaldūn, 'Abd al-Raḥmān, *Kitāb al-'Ibar*, Beirut: Dār al-'ilm li-'l-jāmi', n.d. and Beirut edn 1958.

Ibn Khallikān, Aḥmad, *Kitāb Wafayāt al-a'yān*, trans. MacGuckin De Slane, W., *Biographical Dictionary*, Paris: 1842–71, repr. Beirut: Librairie du Liban, 1970, 2 vols.

Ibn Khallikān, Aḥmad, *Kitāb Wafayāt al-a'yān*, ed. Iḥsān 'Abbās, Beirut: Dār al-thaqāfa, n.d. [1968].

Ibn al-Ma'mūn al-Baṭā'iḥī, Jamāl al-Dīn, *Nuṣūṣ min akhbār Miṣr*, ed. Sayyid, A. F., Cairo: IFAO, 1983.

Ibn Muyassar, Tāj al-Dīn, *Akhbār Miṣr*, ed. Massé, H., as *Annales d'Égypte*, Cairo: IFAO, 1919.

Ibn Muyassar, Tāj al-Dīn, *al-Muntaqā min akhbār Miṣr*, ed. Sayyid, A. F., Cairo: IFAO, 1981.

Ibn al-Qalānisī, Ḥamza b. Asad, *Dhayl Ta'rīkh Dimashq*, ed. Amedroz, H. F., Beirut: Catholic Press of Beirut, 1908.

Ibn al-Qalānisī, Ḥamza b. Asad, *Ta'rīkh Dimashq*, ed. Zakār, S., Damascus: Dār Ḥassān, 1983.

Ibn Riḍwān, 'Alī, *Daf' maḍār al-abdān*, trans. Dols, M. W., *Medieval Islamic Medicine. Ibn Riḍwān's treatise 'On the Prevention of Bodily Ills in Egypt'*, ed. of Ar. text by Gamal, 'A. G., Berkley and London: University of California Press, 1984.

Ibn Sa'īd, 'Alī b. Mūsā, *al-Nujūm al-ẓāhira fī ḥulā ḥadhrat al-Qāhira*, ed. Ḥusayn Naṣṣār, Cairo: Dār al-Kutub al-Miṣriyya, 1970.

Ibn al-Ṣayrafī, Abu'l-Qāsim, *al-Ishāra ilā man nāla al-wizāra*, BIFAO, 25 (1925), pp. 49–112; and 26 (1926); pp. 49–70.

Ibn Taghrībirdī, Jamāl al-Dīn Abu'l-Maḥāsin, *al-Nujūm al-ẓāhira fī mulūk Miṣr wa-'l-Qāhira*, Cairo: Dār al-Kutub al-Miṣriyya, 1353–53/1933–35.

Ibn Taghrībirdī, Jamāl al-Dīn Abu'l-Maḥāsin, *al-Nujūm al-ẓāhira fī mulūk Miṣr wa-'l-Qāhira*, Cairo, 1383–90/1963–70.

Ibn al-Ṭuwayr, al-Murtaḍā, *Nuzhat al-muqlatayn fī akhbār al-dawlatayn*, ed. Sayyid, A. F., Stuttgart and Beirut: F. Steiner, 1992.

Ibn al-Walīd, al-Ḥusayn b. 'Alī, *Risālat al-Mabda' wa-'l-ma'ād*, ed. and French trans. Corbin, H., *Trilogie Ismaélienne*, Paris and Tehran: Paris University Press and Kayam, 1961.

Ibn Ẓāfir, Jamāl al-Dīn, *Akhbār al-duwal al-munqaṭi'a*, ed. Ferré, A., Cairo: IFAO, 1972.

Ibn Ẓahīra, Ibrāhīm, *al-Faḍā'il al-bāhira fī maḥāsin Miṣr wa-'l-Qāhira*, al-Saqā, M. and al-Muhandis, K. (eds), Cairo: Dār al-Kutub al-Miṣriyya, 1969.

Ibn al-Zubayr, *Kitāb al-Dhakhā'ir wa-'l-tuḥaf*, ed. Muḥammad Ḥamīd Allāh, Kuwait: Kuwait Government Press, 1959.

Ibn al-Zubayr, *Kitāb al-Dhakhā'ir, Kitāb al-Hadāyā wa-'l-tuḥaf*, ed. and trans. al-Hijjāwī al-Qaddūmī, G., *Book of Gifts and Rarities*, Cambridge, MA: Harvard University Press, 1996.

Idrīs 'Imād al-Dīn, *'Uyūn al-akhbār wa-funūn al-athār*, ed. Ghālib, M., vols 4–6, Beirut: Dār al-Andalus, 1973–8.

Idrīs 'Imād al-Dīn, *'Uyūn al-akhbār*, vol. 7, ed. and trans. Sayyid, A. F., *The Fatimids and their Successors in Yaman*, London: I. B. Tauris, 2002.

Ja'far b. Manṣūr al-Yaman, *Kitāb al-'Ālim wa-'l-ghulām*, ed. and trans. Morris, J. W., *The Master and the Disciple: An Early Islamic Spiritual Dialogue*, London: I. B. Tauris, 2001.

Ja'far b. Manṣūr al-Yaman, *Kitabu'l-Kashf*, ed. Strothmann, R., London: OUP, 1952.

Ja'far b. Manṣūr al-Yaman, *Kitāb al-Kashf*, ed. Ghālib, M., Beirut: Dār al-Andalus, 1984.

al-Janadī, Bahā' al-Dīn, *Kitāb al-Sulūk fī ṭabaqāt al-'ulamā' wa-'l-mulūk*, ed. and trans. Kay, H. C., in his *Yaman, its Early Medieval History*, London: E. Arnold, 1892: Arabic text pp. 139–52, trans. pp. 191–212.

Juvaynī, 'Aṭā Malik, *Ta'rīkh-i jahān-gushā*, trans. Boyle, J. A., *The History of the World-Conqueror*, Manchester: Manchester University Press, 1958.

Jūzjānī, 'Uthmān, *Ṭabaqāt-i Nāṣirī*, ed. Ḥabībī, 'A. H., Kabul: The Historical Society of Afghanistan, 1342–3/1963–4.

al-Kulaynī, Muḥammad b. Ya'qūb, *al-Uṣul min al-kāfī*, ed. al-Ghaffārī, 'A. A., Tehran: Dār al-kutub al-islāmiyya, 1973.

[al-Malījī, Abu'l-Qāsim], *al-Majālis al-Mustanṣiriyya*, ed. Muḥammad Kāmil Ḥusayn, Cairo: Dār al-fikr al-'arabī [1947].

al-Maqrīzī, Taqī al-Dīn, *Ighāthat al-umma fī kashf al-ghumma*, French trans. Wiet, G., 'Le Traité des famines de Maqrīzī', *JESHO*, 5 (1962), pp. 1–90.

al-Maqrīzī, Taqī al-Dīn, *Itti'āẓ al-ḥunafā' bi-akhbār al-a'imma al-Fāṭimiyyīn al-khulafā'*, ed. al-Shayyāl, J. and Ḥilmī, M., Cairo: Lajnat iḥyā' al-turāth al-islāmī, 1387–93/1967–1973, 3 vols.

al-Maqrīzī, Taqī al-Dīn, *al-Mawā'iẓ wa-'l-i'tibār bi-dhikr al-khiṭaṭ wa-'l-āthār*, ed. al-Sharqāwī, Beirut: Maktabat madbūla, 1998.

al-Maqrīzī, Taqī al-Dīn, *al-Mawā'iẓ wa-'l-i'tibār fī dhikr al-khiṭaṭ wa-'l-āthār*, Beirut: Dār al-ṣādir, n.d., offset of Būlāq 1324 edn.

al-Maqrīzī, Taqī al-Dīn, *Khiṭaṭ*, French trans. Bouriant, M. U., *Description topographique et historique de l'Égypte*, Paris and Cairo: Mission Archéologique Française du Caire and E. Leroux, 1895.

al-Maqrīzī, Taqī al-Dīn, *Kitāb al-Muqaffā (tarājim maghribiyya wa-mashriqiyya min fatra al-'ubaydiyya)*, ed. al-Ya'lāwī, M., Beirut: Dār al-gharb al-islāmī, 1987 (abridged edn).

al-Maqrīzī, Taqī al-Dīn, *Kitāb al-Muqaffā al-kabīr*, ed. al-Ya'lāwī, M., Beirut: Dār al-gharb al-islāmī, 7 vols, 1991.

al-Mu'ayyad fi'l-Dīn al-Shīrāzī, *Sīrat al-Mu'ayyad fi'l-Dīn dā'ī al-du'āt*, ed. Kāmil Ḥusayn, M., Cairo: Dār al-kātib al-miṣrī, 1949.

al-Musabbiḥī, Muḥammad b. 'Ubayd Allāh, *Akhbār Miṣr*, vol. 1, ed. Sayyid, A. F. and Bianquis, T., Cairo: IFAO, 1978.

al-Musabbiḥī, Muḥammad b. 'Ubayd Allāh, *Akhbār Miṣr*, vol. 2, ed. Ḥusayn Naṣṣār, Cairo: IFAO, 1984.

al-Musabbiḥī, Muḥammad b. 'Ubayd Allāh, *Nuṣūṣ ḍā'i'a min akhbār* Miṣr, ed. Sayyid, A. F. Cairo: IFAO, n.d. [1981].

al-Mustanṣir bi-'llāh, Abū Tamīm Ma'add, *al-Sijillāt al-Mustanṣiriyya*, ed. 'Abd al-Mun'im Mājid, Cairo: Dār al-fikr al-'arabī, 1954.

Nāṣir-i Khusraw, *Sefer nameh: Relation du Voyage de Nassiri Khosrau*, ed. and French trans. Schefer, C., Amsterdam: Philo Press, 1970.

Nāṣir-i Khusraw, *Book of travels (safarnama)*, trans. Thackston Jr, W. M., New York: The Persian Heritage Foundation, 1986.

al-Nīsābūrī, Aḥmad, *Istitār al-imām wa-tafarruq al-du'āt*, ed. and trans. Ivanow, W., *Ismaili Tradition Concerning the Rise of the Fatimids (Rise)*, London: OUP, 1942, pp. 157–83.

al-Nīsābūrī, Aḥmad, *al-Risāla al-Mūjiza al-kāfiya fī shurūṭ al-da'wa al-hādiya*, facsimile ed. in Klemm, V., *Die Mission des fāṭimidischen Agenten al-Mu'ayyad fī d-Dīn in Šīrāz*, Frankfurt: P. Lang, 1989.

Niẓām al-Mulk, Abū 'Alī Ḥasan, *The Book of Government or Rules for Kings*, trans. Darke, H., London, Henley and Boston: Routledge & Kegan Paul, 1978, 2nd edn.

al-Nuwayirī, Shihāb al-Dīn, *Nihāyat al-arab fī funūn al-adab*, ed. al-Ḥusaynī, M., Cairo: al-Maktaba al-'arabiyya, 1984.

Psellus, M., *Chronographia*, trans., Sewter, E. R. A., *Fourteen Byzantine rulers*, Harmondsworth: Penguin, 1966.

al-Qāḍī al-Nu'mān, Abū Ḥanīfa, *Da'ā'im al-Islām fī dhikr al-ḥalāl*, trans. Fyzee, A. A. A., *The Pillars of Islam: Vol. 1, Acts of Devotion and Religious Observances*, revised and annotated by Poonawala, I. K. H., New Delhi and Oxford: OUP, 2002.

al-Qāḍī al-Nu'mān, Abū Ḥanīfa, *Da'ā'im al-Islām fī dhikr al-ḥalāl*, ed. Fyzee, A. A. A., Cairo: Dār al-Ma'ārif, 1959–61, 2 vols.

al-Qāḍī al-Nu'mān, Abū Ḥanīfa, *Kitāb Iftitāḥ al-da'wa*, ed. Dachraoui, F., Tunis: al-Sharika al-Tūnisiyya li-'l-tawzī', 1975.

al-Qāḍī al-Nu'mān, Abū Ḥanīfa, *Kitāb al-Majālis wa-'l-musāyarāt*, ed. al-Faqī, Ḥ. et al., Tunis: al-Maṭba'a al-rasmiyya li-'l-jumhūriyya al-tūnisiyya, 1978.

al-Qāḍī al-Nu'mān, Abū Ḥanīfa, *Sharḥ al-akhbār fī faḍā'il al-a'imma al-aṭhār*, ed. al-Jalālī, M. H., Qum: Mu'assasat al-nashr al-islāmī, n.d., 1409–12/1988–92, 3 vols.

al-Qalqashandī, Shihāb al-Dīn, *Subḥ al-a'shā fī ṣinā'at al-inshā'*, ed. Ibrāhīm, Cairo: Dār al-Kutub al-Miṣriyya, 1331–8/1913–20.

al-Qalqashandī, Shihāb al-Dīn, *Subḥ al-a'shā fī ṣinā'at al-inshā'*, photostatic copy of the Āmiriyya edition, Cairo, n.d. [1963].

Rashīd al-Dīn, Faḍl Allāh, *Jāmi' al-tawārīkh: qismat-i Ismā'īlīyān va-Fāṭimiyān va-Nizāriyān va-dā'īyān va-rafīqān*, ed. Dānishpazūh, M. T., Tehran: Bungāh-i tarjama va-nashr-i kitāb, 1338/1959, repr. 1977.

al-Ṣabī', Abu 'l-Ḥusayn Hilāl, *Rusūm dār al-Khilāfa*, Baghdad: maṭba'at al-'ānī, 1383/1964.

al-Ṣabī', Hilāl, *Rusum dar al-Khilafah: the rules and regulations of the 'Abbasid court*, trans. Salem, E. A., Beirut: Lebanese Commission for the Translation of Great Works, 1977.

al-Safadī, Ṣalāḥ al-Dīn, *Kitāb al-Wafī bi-'l-wafāyāt*, Wiesbaden: F. Steiner, 1981–.

Sharī 'atī, 'A., *Fāṭimah Fāṭimah ast*, trans. Bakhtiar, L., *Fatima is Fatima*, Tehran: Sharī'atī Foundation, 1981.

al-Ṭabarī, Abū Ja'far, *The History of al-Ṭabarī (Ta'rīkh al-rusul wa-'l-muluk). Vol. 38: The Return of the Caliphate to Baghdad*, trans. Rosenthal, F., Albany: SUNY Press, 1985.

'Umāra, Najm al-Dīn, *Ta'rīkh al-Yaman*, ed. and trans. Kay, H. C., *Yaman: its early medieval history*, London: E. Arnold, 1892.

'Umāra, Najm al-Dīn, *Ta'rīkh al-Yaman*, ed. Muḥammad b. 'Alī al-Akwa', Beirut: Maṭba'at al-sa'āda, 1976, 2nd edn.

William of Tyre, *A History of Deeds Done Beyond the Sea*, ed. and trans. Babcock, E. A. and Krey, A. C., New York: Octagon Books, 1976, 2 vols.

al-Yamānī, Muḥammad b. Muḥammad, *Sīrat al-ḥājib Ja'far*, ed. and trans. Ivanow, W., *Rise*, pp. 184–223.

Anonymous Works

al-Hidāya al-Āmiriyya fī abṭāl da'wat al-Nizāriyya, ed. Fyzee, A. A. A., London: OUP, 1938.

Sīrat al-ustādh Jawdhar, ed. Ḥusayn, M. K., and Sha'īra, M. 'A. H., Cairo: Dār al-fikr al-'arabī, 1954.

Manuscripts

'Abdān, *Kitāb al-Rusūm wa-'l-izdiwāj wa-'l-tartīb* in Cortese, D., *Arabic Ismaili Manuscripts, The Zāhid 'Alī Collection in the Library of the Institute of Ismaili Studies*, London: I. B. Tauris, 2003.

Anon., *Muqābalat al-adwār wa-mukāshafat al-asrār*, in Cortese, D., *Arabic Ismaili Manuscripts, The Zāhid 'Alī Collection in the Library of the Institute of Ismaili Studies*, London: I. B. Tauris, 2003, no. 108.

Idrīs 'Imād al-Dīn, *Risalat al-Bayān li-mā wajab min ma'rifat al-ṣalāt*, in Cortese, D., *Arabic Ismaili Manuscripts, The Zāhid 'Alī Collection in the Library of the Institute of Ismaili Studies*, London: I. B. Tauris, 2003, no. 132.

'Ahd nāmah (*Khuṭbat 'ahd al-nisā'* ff.17v–31r), in Cortese, D., *Ismaili and Other Arabic Manuscripts*, London: I. B. Tauris, 2000, no. 140/881.

Secondary Sources

'Abd al-Karīm Aḥmad, Nurīmān, *al-Mar'a fī Miṣr fī'l-'aṣr al-Fāṭimī*, Cairo: al-Hay'a al-miṣriyya al-'āmma li-'l-kitāb, 1993.

'Abd al-Rāziq, Aḥmad, *Le femme au temps des Mamlouks en Égypte*, Caire: IFAO, Textes Arabes et Études Islamique, 5, 1973.

Angold, M., *The Byzantine Empire (1025–1204): a political history*, London and New York: Longman, 1997, 2nd edn.

al-'Aqqād, 'A. , *Fāṭima al-zahrā' wa-'l-Fāṭimiyyūn*, n.p.: Dār al-hilāl, n.d.

Asani, A. S., 'Bridal Symbolism in Ismā'īlī Mystical Literature of Indo-Pakistan', in Herrera, R. A. (ed.), *Mystics of the Book: Themes, Topics and Typologies*, New York: Peter Lang, 1993, pp. 389–404.

Assaad, S. A., *The Reign of al-Hakim bi Amr Allah (386/996–411/1021): A Political Study*, Beirut: The Arab Institute for Research and Publishing, 1974.

Bariani, L., 'Parentela e potere: uso ed abuso. Indagine sulle "madri" del califfo al-Ḥākim bi-Amr Allāh al-Fāṭimī', *Al-Qanṭara: revista de estudios Árabes*, 16, 2 (1995), pp. 357–67.

Barrucand, M. (ed.), *L'Égypte Fatimide: son art et son histoire*, Paris: Presses de l'Université de Paris-Sorbonne, 1999.

Behrens-Abouseif, D., 'The façade of the Aqmar mosque in the context of Fatimid ceremonial', *Muqarnas*, 9 (1992), pp. 29–38.

Berkey, J., *The Transmission of Knowledge in Medieval Cairo*, Princeton: Princeton University Press, 1992.

Bierman, I. A., *Writing Signs: the Fatimid Public Text*, Berkeley: University of California Press, 1998.

Bloom, J. M., 'The Mosque of al-Ḥākim in Cairo', *Muqarnas*, 1 (1983), pp. 15–36.

Bloom, J. M., 'The Mosque of the Qarāfa in Cairo', *Muqarnas*, 4 (1987), pp. 7–20.

Bloom, J. M., 'The Introduction of the *Muqarnas* into Egypt', *Muqarnas*, 5 (1988), pp. 21–8.

Bos, G., 'Ibn al-Jazzār on women's diseases and their treatment', *MH*, 37 (1993), 3, pp. 296–312.

Bos, G., *Ibn al-Jazzār on Sexual Diseases and Their Treatment*, London and New York: Kegan Paul, 1997.

Brett, M., *The Rise of the Fatimids: the World of the Mediterranean & the Middle East in the Tenth Century* CE, Leiden: E. J. Brill, 2001.

Casanova, P., 'Un nouveau manuscript de la secte des Assassins', *JA*, 19 (1922), pp. 126–35.

Cohen, M., 'In the court of Ya'qub ibn Killis: a fragment from the Cairo Genizah', *JQR*, 80 (1990), 3–4, pp. 283–314.

Corbin, H., *Trilogie Ismaélienne*, Paris and Tehran: Paris University Press and Kayan, 1961.

Cortese, D., *Arabic Ismaili Manuscripts, The Zāhid 'Alī Collection in the Library of the Institute of Ismaili Studies*, London: I. B. Tauris, 2003.

Cortese, D., *Ismaili and Other Arabic Manuscripts*, London: I. B. Tauris, 2000.

Creswell, K. A. C., *The Muslim Architecture of Egypt, vol. 1: Ikhshīds and Fāṭimids* AD *939–1171*, Oxford; Clarendon Press, 1952; repr. New York: Hacker, 1978.

Dadoyan, S. B., *The Fatimid Armenians. Cultural and Political Interaction in the Near East*, Leiden: Brill, 1997.

Daftary, F., *Ismaili Literature: A Bibliography of sources and studies*, London/New York: I. B. Tauris, 2004.

Daftary, F., *The Ismā'īlīs: Their History and Doctrines*, Cambridge: CUP, 1990.

Daftary, F., 'Sayyida Ḥurra: The Ismā'īlī Ṣulayḥid Queen of Yemen', in Hambly, G. R. G. (ed.), *Women in the Medieval Islamic World: Power, Patronage and Piety*, New York: St Martin's Press, 1998, pp. 117–30.

Dagorn, R., 'Al-Baladi: un medicin obstetricien et pediatre a l'epoque des prèmiers Fatimides du Caire', *MIDEO*, 9 (1967), pp. 73–118.

Daum, W. (ed.), *Yemen: 3000 years of art and civilization in Arabia felix*, Innsbruck: Pinguin/Frankfurt: Umschau, 1988.

Ehrenkreutz, A. S. R. and Heck, G. W., 'Additional Evidence of the Fāṭimid Use of Dīnārs for Propaganda Purposes' in Sharon, M. (ed.), *Studies in Islamic History and Civilization in Honour of Professor David Ayalon*, Jerusalem, Cana and Leiden: E. J. Brill, 1986, pp. 145–51.

Ettinghausen, A. S. R., 'Early realism in Islamic art', *Studi orientalistici in onore di Giorgio Levi Della Vida*, vol. 1, Rome: Istituto per l'Oriente, 1956, pp. 250–73.

Fairchild Ruggles, D. (ed.), *Women, Patronage and Self-representation in Islamic Societies*, Albany: SUNY, 2000.

Fierro, M. I., 'On *al-Fāṭimī* and *al-Fāṭimiyyūn*', *JSAI*, 20 (1996) pp. 130–61.

Finster, B., 'An outline of the history of Islamic religious architecture in Yemen', *Muqarnas*, 9 (1992), pp. 124–47.

Frantz-Murphy, G., 'A new interpretation of the economic history of Medieval Egypt: the role of the textile industry 254–567/868–1171', *JESHO*, 24 (1981), 3, pp. 274–97.

Fyzee, A. A. A., *Compendium of Fatimid Law*, Simla: Indian Institute of Advanced Study, 1969.

Giladi, A., *Infants, Parents and Wet Nurses*, Leiden: E. J. Brill, 1999.

Goeje, M. J. de, *Mémoire sur les Carmathes du Bahraïn et les Fatimides*, Leiden: E. J. Brill, 1886, 2nd edn.

Goitein, S. D., 'The Exchange Rate of Gold and Silver money in Fāṭimid and Ayyūbid Times: A Preliminary Study of the Relevant Geniza Material', *JESHO*, 8 (1965), pp. 1–46.

Goitein, S. D., *A Mediterranean Society*, Berkeley: University of California Press, 1967–88, 5 vols.

Goitein, S. D., 'Urban housing in Fāṭimid and Ayyūbid times (as illustrated by the Cairo Geniza documents)', *SI*, 47 (1978), pp. 5–23.

Golovin, L., *Essai sur l'architecture religieuse musulmane*, vol. 4: L'art Hispano-Musulman, Paris: Klincksieck, 1979.

Golovin, L., *Le Magrib central a l'époque des Zirides*, Paris: Arts et Metiers Graphiques, 1957.

Grohmann, A., *From the World of Arabic Papyri*, Cairo: al-Ma'arif Press, 1952.

Halm, H., 'Le destin de la princesse Sitt al-Mulk', in Barrucand, M., *L'Égypt Fatimide*, pp. 69–72.

Halm, H., *The Empire of the Mahdi. The Rise of the Fatimids*, trans. Bonner, M., Leiden: E. J. Brill, 1996.

Halm, H., *The Fatimids and their Traditions of Learning*, London: I. B. Tauris, 1997.

Halm, H., 'The Isma'ili Oath of Allegiance (*'ahd*) and the "Sessions of Wisdom" (*Majālis al-ḥikma*) in Fatimid Times', in Daftary, F. (ed.), *Medieval Isma'ili History and Thought*, Cambridge: CUP, 1996, pp. 91–115.

Halm, H., *Die Kalifen von Kairo*, Munchen: C. H. Beck, 2003.

Halm, H., 'Sitt al-Mulk', *EI2nd*, vol. 9, pp. 685–6.

Hamdani, A., 'The Dā'ī Ḥātim Ibn Ibrāhīm al-Ḥāmidī (d. 596H./1199AD) and his Book *Tuḥfat al-qulūb*', *Oriens*, 23–4 (1974), pp. 258–300.

al-Hamdānī, Ḥ. F., 'The Life and Times of Queen Saiyidah Arwā the Ṣulaiḥid of the Yemen', *JRCAS*, 18 (1931), pp. 505–17.

Heijer, J. den, 'Considérations sur les communautés chrétiennes en Égypte Fatimide: l'État et l'Église sous le vizirat de Badr al-Jamālī (1074–1094)', in Barrucand, M., *L'Égypte Fatimide*, pp. 569–78.

Hodgson, M. G. S., *The Order of Assassins, the Struggle of the Early Nizārī Ismā'īlīs Against the Islamic World*, The Hague: Mouton, 1955.

Idris, H. R., *La Berbérie orientale sous les Zīrides*, Paris: A. Maisonneuve, 1962, 2 vols.

al-Imad, L., 'Women and Religion in the Fatimid Caliphate: The Case of al-Sayyidah al-Hurrah, Queen of Yemen' in Mazzaoui, M. M. and Moreen, V. B. (eds), *Intellectual Studies on Islam: Essays Written in Honor of Martin B. Dickson*, Salt Lake City: University of Utah Press, 1990, pp. 137–44.

Ivanow, W., *Ismaili Tradition Concerning the Rise of the Fatimids*, London: OUP, 1942.

Ivanow, W., 'The Organization of the Fatimid Propaganda', *JBBRAS*, NS, 15 (1939), pp. 1–35.

Jayyusi, S. K. (ed.), *The Legacy of Muslim Spain*, Leiden: E. J. Brill, 1994.

Kazan, W., *The Coinage of Islam: Collection of William Kazan*, Beirut: Bank of Beirut, 1404/1983.

Lane-Poole, S. A., *A History of Egypt in the Middle Ages*, London: Methuen, 1925.

Lassner, J., *Demonizing the Queen of Sheba*, Chicago and London: University of Chicago Press, 1993.

Lev, Y., 'Aspects of Egyptian society', in Vermeulen, U. and van Steenbergen, J. (eds), *Egypt and Syria in the Fāṭimid, Ayyūbid and Mamluk Eras*, Leuven: Peeters, 2001, pp. 1–31.

Lev, Y., 'The Fāṭimid Imposition of Ismāʿīlism on Egypt (358–86/969–96)', *ZDMG*, 138 (1988), 2, pp. 313–25.

Lev, Y., 'The Fatimid Princess Sitt al-Mulk', *JSS*, 32 (1987), pp. 319–28.

Lev, Y., 'The Faṭimid vizier Yaʿqub ibn Killis and the Beginning of the Faṭimid Administration in Egypt', *Der Islam*, 58 (1981), pp. 237–49.

Lev, Y., *State and Society in Fāṭimid Egypt*, Leiden: E. J. Brill, 1991.

Lev, Y., 'Tinnīs: an industrial medieval town', in Barrucand, M. (ed.), *L'Égypte Fatimide*, 1999, pp. 83–96.

Levy, R., *The Social Structure of Islam*, Cambridge: CUP, 1957.

Mājid, ʿAbd al-Munʿim, *al-Ḥākim bi-Amr Allāh*, Cairo: Maktabat al-Anjlū al-Miṣriyya, 1959.

Mernissi, F., *The Forgotten Queens of Islam*, London: Polity, 1993.

Musallam, B. F., *Sex and Society in Islam*, Cambridge: CUP, 1983, repr. 1989.

Peirce, L. P., *The Imperial Harem: Women and Sovereignty in the Ottoman Empire*, New York, Oxford: OUP, 1993.

Petry, C., 'A paradox of patronage during the later Mamluk period', *MW*, 73 (1983), pp. 182–207.

Poonawala, I. K., *Biobibliography of Ismāʿīlī Literature*, Malibu: Undena Publications, 1977.

Poonawala, I. K. (ed.), *al-Sulṭān al-Khaṭṭāb: ḥayātu-hu wa-shiʿru-hu*, Beirut: Dār al-gharb al-islāmī, 1999.

al-Qaddūmī, G. al-Hijjāwī, *Book of gifts and rarities: Kitāb al-Hadāyā wa-'l-Tuḥaf*, trans. and annotations, Cambridge, MA: Harvard University Press, 1996.

Rabie, H., *The Financial System of Egypt*, London: OUP, 1972.

Rāghib, Y., 'Deux monuments Fatimides au pied du Muqaṭṭam', *REI*, 46 (1978), pp. 91–155.

Rāghib, Y., 'Le mausolée de Yūnus al-Saʿdī est-il celui de Badr al-Gamālī?', *Arabica*, 20 (1973) pp. 305–7.

Rāghib, Y., 'Les mausolées Fatimides du quartier d'al-Mašāhid', *AI*, 17 (1981), pp. 1–30.

Rāghib, Y., 'Al-Sayyida Nafīsa, sa légende, son culte et son cimetière', *SI*, 44 (1976), pp. 61–86; 45 (1977), pp. 27–55.

Rāghib, Y., 'Sur deux mouments funéraires du cimitière d'al-Qarāfa al-Kubrā au Caire', *AI*, 12 (1974), pp. 67–83.

Rāghib, Y., 'Une épisode obscur d'histoire Fatimide', *SI*, 48 (1978), pp. 125–32.

Raymond, A. and Wiet, G., *Les marchés du Caire: traduction annotée du texte de Maqrizi*, Cairo: IFAO, 1979.

Reif, S. C., *A Jewish archive from Old Cairo*, Richmond: Curzon, 2000.

Roded, R., *Women in Islamic Biographical Collections*, Boulder and London: Lynne Rienner, 1994.

Roy, B. and Poinssot, P., *Inscriptions Arabes de Kairouan*, Paris: C. Klincksieck, 1950.

Sanders, P., 'Claiming the past: Ghadīr Khumm and the rise of Ḥāfiẓī historiography in late Fāṭimid Egypt', *SI*, 75 (1992), pp. 81–104.

Sanders, P., *Ritual, Politics, and the City in Fatimid Cairo*, Albany: SUNY Press, 1994.

Sayyid, A. F., *La capitale de l'Égypte jusqu'à l'époque Fatimide*, Beirut/Stuttgart: F. Steiner, 1998.

Sayyid, A. F., *al-Dawla al-Fāṭimiyya fī Miṣr: tafsīr jadīd*, Cairo: al-Dār al-Miṣriyya al-Lubnāniyya, 1992 (2nd edn, 2000).

Serjeant, R. B., 'Material for a history of Islamic textiles up to the Mongol conquest', *ArI*, 13–14 (1948), pp. 77–117.

Shatzmiller, M., *Labour in the Medieval Islamic World*, Leiden: E. J. Brill, 1994.

Shatzmiller, M., 'Women and wage labour in the medieval Islamic West: legal issues in an economic context', *JESHO*, 40 (1997), pp. 174–206.

Smoor, P., 'Fatimid poets and the "*takhallus*" that bridges the nights of time to the imam of time", *Der Islam*, 68 (1991), pp. 232–62.

Smoor, P., '"The Master of the Century": Fāṭimid Poets in Cairo', in Vermeulen, U. and De Smet, D. (eds), *ESFAME*, Leuven: Peeters, 1995, pp. 139–62.

Smoor, P. 'Murder in the palace: Poetical Reflections', *AI*, 37 (2003), pp. 383–442.

Smoor, P., ''Umāra's elegies and the lamp of loyalty', *AI*, 34 (2000), pp. 467–564.

Smoor, P., ''Umāra's odes describing the imām', *AI*, 35 (2001), pp. 549–626.

Sourdel, D., *Le Vizirat 'Abbāside de 749 à 939*, vol. 2, Damascus: Institut Français de Damas, 1960.

Stern, S. M., *Fatimid Decrees, Original Documents from the Fatimid Chancery*, London: Faber & Faber, 1964.

Stern, S. M., 'The Succession to the Fatimid Imam al-Āmir, the Claims of the Later Fatimids to the Imamate, and the Rise of Ṭayyibī Ismā'īlīsm', *Oriens*, 4 (1951), part 2, pp. 93–255.

Taylor, C. S., *In the Vicinity of the Righteous: Ziyara and the Veneration of Muslim Saints in Late Medieval Egypt*, Leiden: E. J. Brill, 1999.

Taylor, C. S., 'Reevaluating the Shi'i role in the Development of Monumental Islamic Funerary Architecture: The Case of Egypt', *Muqarnas*, 9 (1992), pp. 1–10.

Thys-Senocak, L., 'The Yeni Valide Mosque Complex at Eminönü', *Muqarnas*, 15 (1998), pp. 52–71.

Vatikiotis, P., *The Fatimid Theory of State*, Lahore: Orientalia Publishers, 1957.

Weigert, G., 'A Note on the Muḥtasib and Ahl al-Dhimma', *Der Islam*, 75 (1998), pp. 331–7.

Wenzel, M., *Ornament and Amulet, Rings of the Islamic Lands. The Nasser D. Khalili Collection of Islamic Art*, vol. 14, London and Oxford: Azimuth Editions and OUP, 1993.

Wiet, G., 'Une nouvelle inscription Fatimide au Caire', *JA*, 249 (1961), pp. 13–20.
Wiet, G., 'Le Traité des famines de Maqrīzī', *JESHO*, 5 (1962), pp. 1–90.
Williams, C., 'The cult of 'Alid Saints in the Fatimid Monuments of Cairo – part I: the Mosque of al-Aqmar', *Muqarnas*, 1 (1983), pp. 37–52.
Williams, C., 'The cult of 'Alid Saints in the Fatimid Monuments of Cairo – part II: the Mausolea', *Muqarnas*, 3 (1985), pp. 39–60.
al-Ya'lāwī, M., *Ibn Hāni' al-Maghribī al-Andalusī: shā'ir al-dawla al-Fāṭimiyya*, Beirut: Dār al-gharb al-islāmī, 1985.
Yalaoui, M., *Un poète chiite d'occident au IVème/Xème siècle: Ibn Hāni' al-Andalusī*, Tunis: Publications de l'Université de Tunis, 1976.
Zāhid, 'Alī, *Tabyīn al-ma'ānī fī sharḥ dīwān Ibn Hāni'*, Cairo: Maṭba'at al ma'ārif, 1352/ 1933.

Unpublished material

Bierman, I. A., *Arts and politics: the impact of Fatimid uses of ṭirāz fabrics*, PhD thesis, Chicago: University of Chicago, 1980.
Bloom, J. M., *Meaning in early Fatimid architecture: Islamic art in North Africa and Egypt in the fourth century AH/10c. AD*, PhD thesis, Cambridge, MA: Harvard University, 1980.
Cooper, R. S., *Ibn Māmmatī's Rules for the Ministries: Translation with Commentary of the Qawānīn al-Dawāwīn*, PhD thesis, Berkeley: University of California, 1973.
Frantz, G. M., *Saving and Investment in Medieval Egypt*, PhD thesis, University of Michigan, 1978.
Hamdani, A. H., *The Sira of al-Mu'ayyad*, PhD thesis, London: University of London: 1950.
Khemir, S., *The Palace of Sitt al-Mulk and Fāṭimid Imagery*, PhD thesis, SOAS, London: University of London, 1990, 2 vols.
Lowe, J. D., *Monetary Development in Fatimid Egypt and Syria*, MA thesis, University of Arizona, 1985.
Sanders, P., *The Court Ceremonial of the Fatimid Caliphate in Egypt*, PhD thesis, Princeton: Princeton University, 1984.
Shakir, M., *Sīrat al-Malik al-Mukarram: an edition and a study*, PhD thesis, SOAS, London: University of London, 1999.
Soufi, D. L., *The Image of Fatima in Classical Muslim Thought*, PhD thesis, Princeton: Princeton University, 1997.
Stillman, Y. K., *Female Attire of Medieval Egypt According to the Trousseau Lists and Cognate Material from the Cairo Geniza*, PhD thesis, Philadelphia: University of Pennsylvania, 1972.

INDEX